T0330289

Economic Development in China, India and East Asia

Economic Development in China, India and East Asia

Managing Change in the Twenty First Century

Kartik Roy

Professor, Auckland Institute of Studies, New Zealand

Hans Blomqvist

formerly of the Hanken School of Economics, Finland

Cal Clark

Professor, Auburn University, USA

Edward Elgar

Cheltenham, UK • Northampton, MA, USA

Published by
Edward Elgar Publishing Limited
The Lypiatts
15 Lansdown Road
Cheltenham
Glos GL50 2JA
UK

Edward Elgar Publishing, Inc.
William Pratt House
9 Dewey Court
Northampton
Massachusetts 01060
USA

A catalogue record for this book
is available from the British Library

Library of Congress Control Number: 2012938050

MIX
Paper from
responsible sources
FSC
www.fsc.org   FSC® C018575

ISBN 978 1 84720 751 7

Printed and bound by MPG Books Group, UK

Contents

Preface

This book presents an analysis and interpretation of industrialization and development in Asia; in particular, India, China, Japan, Malaysia, Singapore, South Korea and Taiwan. These countries have been widely seen as economic success stories during the post-war era. Japan's 'economic miracle' commenced in the 1950s as it quickly regained its place among the developed nations after the devastation of World War II and challenged the United States for global economic leadership in the 1980s, although it has generally stagnated since its economic bubble burst in 1989. During the 1960s, Singapore, South Korea and Taiwan commenced rapid industrialization drives; China and Malaysia followed suit in the 1980s; and India has made considerable progress over the last two decades.

An analysis of the Asian experience, therefore, should be quite instructive for understanding the dynamics of development in the contemporary world. Certainly, these Asian countries challenge the orthodoxy of laissez-faire economics. While all except India have pursued export-led growth, all seven including India have had states that intervened aggressively in their economies. More broadly, this points to the importance of examining the 'institutions' that shape economic success. Why was statism successful in China and the East Asian capitalist nations, while it inhibited economic growth in India? Thus, we develop an institutionalist model based on the governance regime, religion, culture and geography, and then apply it to explain the disparate economic strategies and outcomes among the Asian countries.

Another central finding of the book is the need for balance among political and economic institutions. In particular, while economic openness and political openness are often considered compatible and mutually reinforcing because both are manifestations of individual freedom, even a cursory glance at the Asian experience demonstrates that this is far too simplistic. India achieved almost complete political openness and a high degree of democracy at independence, but this created strong obstacles to the economic reforms necessary to create economic openness and promote development. In stark contrast, China, South Korea and Taiwan aggressively promoted economic openness under strongly authoritarian regimes, while Singapore and Malaysia did so under softer semi-authoritarian regimes. Yet, before concluding that political openness hurts economic performance, it must also be noted that democratic

Japan achieved an economic miracle, that South Korea and Taiwan had very successful democratic transitions, and that, indeed, political openness is almost required to achieve human fulfilment and development.

We wish to express our great gratitude to our editor, Alexandra O'Connell, for her encouragement, support and help during this project.

1. Evolution of the developmental state

The 1980s witnessed the growth of a consensus among many development agencies and Western governments that development was best promoted by laissez-faire policies and limited government. This reflected the growing economic problems both in the communist command economies and in the many developing nations that had tried to promote import substitution industrialization. This was ironic, however, because at the same time there was growing recognition of the rapid development that was occurring in many Asian countries with highly interventionist governments (Clark and Roy, 1997; World Bank, 1993). Consequently, an important branch of political economy began to emphasize the 'developmental state' (Evans et al., 1985; Johnson, 1982).

This book, thus, analyses the role of the state in Asia during the post-war era. The first two chapters develop the theoretical framework that will structure our analysis. This chapter provides an overview of the evolution of the developmental state, and Chapter 2 discusses the institutional factors that shape the nature and performance of state economic activities.

The controversy of the role of the state in development has certainly not abated over the past several decades. Chapter 3 looks at the specific institutional foundations of the Asian states included in our analysis. The next three chapters then provide summaries of the socio-economic performances of the developmental states under consideration here: Chapter 4 on trade, technology and industrialization; Chapter 5 on growth and income distribution; and Chapter 6 on poverty and human development. Based on these descriptive materials, Chapter 7 analyses how the Asian states have managed development during the post-war period; and Chapter 8 considers whether authoritarianism or democracy is better for development. Finally, Chapter 9 presents the major conclusions from this study.

THE PERCEIVED ROLE OF THE STATE IN THE ECONOMY: A BRIEF OVERVIEW

Governance of one kind or another is virtually as old as mankind. Even in prehistoric times in 'hunter and gatherer' tribes, an informal system of state governance existed to distribute gains or returns from economic activities, to settle disputes if and when they occurred among members, and to organize the protection of members from attacks by members of other tribes. As the number of members of the tribe increased, the selection of a formal head became a necessity. Even for a state in a rudimentary form to exist, individuals and groups had to cede authority in key areas such as defense to a public agency, a head or a council of elders. This agency had to possess coercive power over all other organizational forms within designated territory (Clark and Roy, 1997). States have subsequently taken different shapes and sizes depending on a mix of factors including culture, natural endowments, opportunities for trade and the distribution of power.

East and South Asia have examples of sophisticated states very early. In particular, three regions stand out: those that became China and India, and Mesopotamia (present Iraq). These areas have been characterized by very advanced state formations even later, such as imperial China, the Moghul Empire in India, the caliphate of Baghdad, etc. Since the eighteenth century, major European states through conquest and colonization incorporated most of the world, including large parts of Asia, into their own mutually exclusive territories with the primary objective of increasing the mother countries' wealth. Towards these territories the colonial state was predatory, with little regard for the welfare of its subjects. However, in pursuance of the same goal of increasing the mother countries' wealth by trade, the colonial masters had to provide basic public goods such as roads, communications, port facilities, schools, hospitals, etc. They also imposed key institutions, such as the protection of human lives and of private property, which made productive activities possible. Sometimes they only replaced indigenous institutions with their own, however, which was sometimes rather counterproductive from the colony's point of view.

In classical writings like Kautiliya's *Arthasashtra*, Ibn Khaldoun's *The Muquadimah*, Niccolò Machiavelli's *The Prince*, as well as in Confucius's *Analects*, the main thrust of discussion was the mutual rights and obligations of states and their citizens. Thomas Hobbes saw the relationship between the state and the citizens as a 'social contract'. His book *Leviathan* (1968, first published in 1651) emphasized the primary role of the state as being the protector of human lives and private property, as well as the defender of the country's freedom. John Locke (1690) in his *Two Treaties of Government* also emphasized the need for the state to give recognition to and protect private property so that private sector individuals and enterprises could carry on their productive economic activities. But neither Hobbes nor Locke spoke in favour of an interventionist state in the economic realm. The prevailing doctrine at the time, 'mercantilism', however, was more favourably inclined towards the interventionist state. In fact, the mercantilists did not shy from government interventions, e.g. subsidies, concessions, monopolies and other early forms of industrial policy, if they were regarded as conducive to economic growth. Adam Smith represented a crucial break with this line of thought, arguing that mercantilism was a result of the selfish interest of merchants and industrialists, and against the interest of the people in general.

In the early eighteenth century, in response to the question of Louis XIV's chief minister to a French manufacturer regarding what the state could do to help him, the reply to the chief minister, '*laissez-nous faire*', became the buzz-word for the newly perceived role of the state in economic development (van den Berg, 2001). Adam Smith ([1776] 1976) became the most eloquent proponent of this view. Although he has been criticized for prescribing a simplistic laissez-faire policy for the state and for accepting that the market was the best instrument for realizing economic growth and for improving the welfare of the citizens in a country, Smith did address the need for providing public goods and establishing institutions necessary for markets to function efficiently. A Smithian state was supposed to perform the following three tasks:

1. protection of the society from the violence and invasion of other independent societies;
2. protection of every member of the society from the injustice and oppression of every other member of it; and
3. provision of certain public works and certain public institutions, which can never be for the interest of any individual or small number of individuals to provide and maintain. These are public goods, which are both non-rival and non-excludable.

Apart from the provision of certain basic public goods, what else should a state arguably do? There is no objectively correct answer to that question, and the discussion is still continuing. Smith himself did recognize the need for the state to provide an institutional framework for the markets to function properly.

During the nineteenth and early twentieth centuries, the expert opinion in the Anglo-Saxon countries leaned towards a small non-interventionist state, while a more intrusive state was regarded as ideal in other countries, such as Continental Europe and Japan. After World War II, the prevailing view as to the proper role of the state has altered between laissez-faire and interventionism like the swings of a pendulum (Blomqvist, 2002, 2007). To a great extent, the ideological standpoint of those who discuss the matter seems to affect their views. One thing which is certain, though, is that the expanded role of the state does not include wanton destruction of state and private property and human lives, nor the establishment of a reign of terror, nor channelling private and public property into the pockets of a small government elite and its cronies. Such a state may be interventionist, but it cannot be called developmental. The crucial matter from a development point of view is not the degree but the kind of state intervention (cf. Blomqvist, 2002).

The role of the state in identifying and remedying so-called market failures gained prominence from the late nineteenth century with the emergence of welfare economics and is now generally recognized (Backhouse, 1985; see also Balassa, 1991; World Bank, 1993, 1997). The term 'market failure' refers to situations where free, unregulated markets are unable to achieve the optimal allocation of resources from society's point of view. The reasons for this are various, such as monopoly power, incomplete or missing markets and asymmetric information, as well as macro-economic imbalances. All these deficiencies, at least theoretically, justify government intervention in the economy. However, matters unrelated to efficiency, like equity and national goal considerations, also provide a reason to intervene for an activist government. Moreover, some writers believe in achieving superior development through 'governing the market' (Wade, 1990). These issues are examined briefly below.

Monopoly Power

The justification of state intervention in a monopolist's industry revolves around the need for the recovery of the deadweight loss created through the pricing behaviour of a monopolist and its transfer to the society. In the absence of any regulation, a monopolist's optimal output will be reached at the intersection of its marginal revenue (MR) and marginal cost (MC) curves. Its monopoly power will allow it to raise its price above the marginal cost, and the monopolist will make excess profit and the society will incur a deadweight loss. Economists advocate that a government regulatory commission should either force the monopoly to split up or to bring the price down to make it equal to its long-run marginal cost (LMC) curve. Then the output level will increase to the point where the $P = MR = LMC = AR$ condition is fulfilled. The deadweight loss will disappear and consumers will regain their lost consumer surplus. This is shown in Figure 1.1.

It can be seen from the figure that the optimal output from the firm's point of view is OQ_1. The firm's unregulated price is OP_1 and its profit is P_1EGS. The consumer surplus is P_1DE and the deadweight loss to the society is the triangle GEF. Now if the regulatory commission mandates a price of OP_2, then in its own interest the monopolist will increase its output to OQ_2 as at this output, the condition $P = MR = LMC = AR$ is fulfilled. The deadweight loss disappears.

Discrepancies Between Private and Social Costs and Benefits

In several cases the market is unable to induce a private firm to produce the optimal quantity of a particular product and to determine an optimal price for

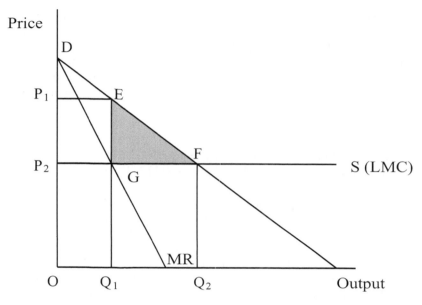

Figure 1.1   Monopoly pricing behaviour

a product. This is when a discrepancy arises between social and private returns or costs resulting from the production of a good. In the case of large, interdependent projects for which the optimum scale depends on simultaneous investment in upstream and downstream industries, a particular investment may not come forth because the investor may not be able to capture the full benefit. When investment in interdependent projects continues to rise, the indivisible returns also become larger. This indivisibility means that returns accrue to the individual private investor as well as to the non-investor, i.e. the society at large. This creates the problem of 'appropriability'. This problem also arises in cases where the investment in a new project, although not an interdependent one, involves considerable sunk cost for which the investor does not get any return. If the investor has also to invest in infrastructure, for example, the return also accrues to the society and to other investors. Hence, private initiative is likely to be weak or absent in this case.

The problem of appropriability also arises where an investor in a project wants to attract foreign capital involving sale of knowledge (technology, blueprints, etc.) for which an appropriate price is difficult to arrive at through private negotiations. This leads us to strategic negotiations. In negotiations with other economies and foreign companies, governments can alter the nature of the market environment by intervention. The outcome of any bargaining problem depends on the strength of the competition on both sides. By coordinating the actions of buyers of technology and trying to increase competition among sellers, government can appropriate more of the surplus associated with the transfer of technology than could otherwise be obtained.

Externalities occur where the benefits or costs of actions of one economic agent accrue to other economic agents as well. In the former case there is a positive externality and in the latter case, there is a negative externality. We cite here three famous examples:

1. 'The lighthouse' (Coase, 1974);
2. 'The fable of the bees' (Steven and Cheong, 1973); and
3. 'The hydroelectric dam' (Perkins, Radelet and Lindauer, 2006).

A private shipping company would not – according to the reasoning of many economists – construct a lighthouse because it would not be able to prevent other shipping companies from receiving the services of the lighthouse while paying nothing for its construction. According to this argument, there are thus external, positive effects that cannot be appropriated by the operator of the installation. Ronald Coase (1974), however, having investigated how the British lighthouse system actually worked, argued that a lighthouse can be built and operated by private sector companies!

A beekeeper benefits from the honey that their bees produce but not from the pollination of the neighbour's fruit trees. Since the beekeeper does not capture all benefits from keeping bees, they may not produce an optimal quantity from the society's point of view.

A hydroelectric dam constructed in the headwaters of a river to irrigate agricultural lands on both sides of the river's headwater also benefits farmers living alongside downstream waters as the dam prevents flooding of lands. In all similar cases where an investment by a private producer generates a positive externality, the state needs to intervene in the market in order to achieve an optimal result.

Pecuniary External Economies

Pecuniary external economies arise if, due to the increase in the size of a competitive industry, the long-run supply curve embodying so-called Marshallian real externalities (external economies of scale) slopes downwards. Here gains in productivity result from economies of scope in using specialized equipment and specialized skills. Industrial clusters thus provide a value over and above that of what the sum of single firms can achieve. If the economies of scope are small, then the current production process may not convey enough information about the prospect of lowering the cost of production through a larger cluster. In that case the state may contribute by encouraging and supporting the formation of such clusters. Therefore many economists suggest that the state has to intervene directly in the industrial production sector by providing protection to infant industries. This is one of the main reasons invoked for so-called import-substituting industrialization.

Furthermore, externalities can arise from the interaction between suppliers and buyers about the design or the production of a good, if such interaction makes the product better or cheaper than what is currently available internationally. In this case, the source of beneficial externality is not the international supplier of technology but internal input and knowledge (cf. World Bank, 1993).

Learning-Based Economies

When firms gain knowledge of production processes from other firms without incurring costs, real externalities are present. Due to the problem of appropriability in the transfer of knowledge, firms may spend less time on acquiring production knowledge than is socially optimal. But externalities due to learning may be conferred on other firms by the first entrant into a sector by demonstrating that the production in the sector is physically and economically feasible and by the leakage of information on technology and marketing. Then a newcomer to the industry may be able to undercut the pioneer because it does not have to invest in R&D. Hence due to these market failures, the private sector may not be willing to undertake any investment in order to establish new industries. This is why innovation is supported by most states through granting of patents, intellectual property rights (IPR), etc.

Incomplete Markets, Asymmetric Information and Intertemporal Transactions

Markets are not complete when they fail to provide a good or service even though the cost would be less than what individuals are willing to pay. In other cases, consumers may not be willing to pay what the good or service is worth to them because of imperfect information. They may have problems valuing services such as primary education and healthcare. On the other hand, when a supplier knows more about a product than consumers, then the asymmetry of information can lead to excessive supplier-induced demand for a service, such as health insurance. Excessive demand leads to increasing marginal costs for the service provider, which also raises the insurance premium for those who are likely to require more healthcare. These are also the people who are more likely to be turned down by the insurer. Furthermore, those who have insurance become less inclined to take preventive care and have greater incentive to make the event happen for claiming insurance. This is the so-called 'moral hazard' problem. Hence, when there is a third party to take care of healthcare costs, both doctors and patients make greater use of healthcare services. The state has tried to deal with this problem by providing sufficient information and keeping costs down through regulating private health insurance and through providing public health insurance as well as healthcare services.

When markets do not have adequate information for the intertemporal allocation of resources, the state can, as the third party, force the two parties to reveal more information than they would do voluntarily. To eliminate the moral hazard problem in intertemporal transactions the state can also force the two parties to sign a contract to recover damages when contracts are not met. Purchase contracts, which are long-term multilateral agreements, stipulate a minimum price at which importing nations agree to purchase a specified quantity of a commodity and a maximum price at which exporting countries agree to sell specified quantities of the commodity over a certain period of time. Here the state can be involved to force both parties to sign a contract to recover damages when contracts are not met.

Macro-economic Imbalances

Macro-economic imbalances occur in every economy. Recognizing this and suggesting remedies was, of course, the great contribution of J.M. Keynes to economics (Keynes, 1936). Wages tend to adjust slowly to changing demand and supply conditions. The markets for credit and foreign exchange also do not necessarily adjust rapidly to balance supply and demand, especially in developing countries. Due to imperfect information and coordination problems, wrong expectations may contribute to shortages and surpluses in many sectors of an economy. Hence, the state may have to intervene in monetary and fiscal policy management, exchange rate adjustment and income determination.

Pursuing National Goals

The state can also intervene in the economy if the society imposes on its leaders a national goal that even a well-functioning market cannot satisfy. For example, a policy favouring the poor majority over Hagen's (1962) dynamic and entrepreneurial minorities may not lead to optimal results in terms of resource allocation and economic growth, but can help the poor through targeted income distribution to catch up with the economically better-off minority. Almost every state aims, officially, at reducing income differences among its citizens, although this may sometimes be political rhetoric. This official goal of levelling income differences is a major factor affecting the design of tax systems and government transfers. However, in a democracy, where leaders are elected, their primary objective is to stay in power; hence in the name of poverty alleviation they deliberately pursue policies that may in the end help neither the poor nor the well-off minority in order to maximize votes.

Authoritarian regimes represent a more diverse picture. The socialist experiment, drawing its inspiration from the writings of Karl Marx in the nineteenth century and reaching its extreme form under Stalin in the Soviet Union, aimed officially at abolishing inequality and exploitation through eliminating markets altogether. As we know now, the result was a disaster, as the system was not only extremely inefficient, but also failed to promote equality. Instead it protected the interests of a small elite while the ordinary citizen remained poor and powerless. This has been the case with many other authoritarian states as well, although some have been quite successful at promoting development and improving the life of the poor. Several East Asian countries, such as South Korea and Taiwan, belong to this category.

Some social customs and religious teachings that encourage people to be industrious, respectful and obedient to their superiors, and be thrifty, honest, truthful and so on, provide positive incentives for socially optimal behaviour. But there are also many customs that support the maintenance of the status quo and make any change for the betterment of the economy difficult. Thus, they need to be broken down by state intervention. Sometimes this is possible only after a major upheaval, such as a war, which can destroy old institutions very effectively and prepare the ground for new ones that are more conducive to economic development. The major losers in World War II, Germany and Japan, turned out to be the winners in terms of economic development during the post-war period. China embarked on a path of rapid growth after a period of dogmatic rule and social upheaval. Also, Singapore and Taiwan have been very successful in this area, possibly because of their need to mobilize whatever resources they had against immediate threats to their survival. The success of nations in the modern era is thus closely tied to the breakdown of institutional barriers to productive activity in both the public and private sectors (Olson, 1982).

THE DEVELOPMENTAL STATE

All existing states intervene, more or less, in the markets for the reasons discussed above. However, this does not automatically make them 'developmental' as the reasons for intervention may be less than altruistic. The term 'developmental' is, unfortunately, not exact; different writers may mean different things when they use it. A state that, in effect, functions as a special interest aiming at enriching the political elite can hardly be regarded as a developmental state, despite the fact that it may be highly interventionist. Even a benevolent state that purportedly steps in to provide public goods, stabilize economic activity, reduce income differences, etc., cannot automatically be classified as 'developmental'. Even if the state institutions may have been set up in order to promote development, this may not happen. Instead they may become effective instruments for rent seeking and predation.

The success of state-led development depends on a strong, relatively autonomous state that is able to keep the private sector in check and does not need to defer to special interests. However, the state itself must be disciplined. If economic development benefits the state, or rather those who act in the name of the state as well as the private sector, the state is likely to favour development. But if the prospects for development are weak or if the political elite cannot count on staying in office long enough to benefit from development, the prospects for developmental policies are poor.

Hence, a developmental state is strong and stable and provides efficient and predictable institutions. Moreover, many authors also regard, for instance, a strongly interventionist industrial policy and suppressed credit markets as typical characteristics of a developmental state. We will not apply a strong version of the concept in this book. Any state that is inclined towards economic development and intervenes in the markets in order to achieve this goal is counted as developmental. Many East and South Asian states fulfil that requirement.

The Expanding Role of the State: Early Developed Countries

Although some states in Europe and North America mainly followed the laissez-faire model in the nineteenth century, state intervention did play a vital, catalytic role in the development and growth of markets in the early developed countries. Even in the United States, where state involvement in the economy was more limited than in Europe and Japan, the government was instrumental in constructing infrastructure (e.g. the first telegraph line) which spurred development of the telecommunications industry, and in agricultural research and extension, which stimulated productivity gains (World Bank, 1997). With the exception of Britain, Europe was, by and large, much more interventionist. The industrialization process of Germany, for example, took place behind high protective trade barriers. This was the case in Japan as well.

The state's role in the distribution of income was quite limited before World War II. The first sign of the emergence of a modern welfare state was seen towards the end of the nineteenth century in Germany where the Chancellor Otto von Bismarck introduced the first nationwide system of social insurance. After World War I, the first turning point in the state's perceived role in economic development was the Russian revolution in 1917, which led to the abolition of almost all private property as well as the market system itself and placed the state in control through the comprehensive central planning of all economic activities. The second one was the Great Depression of the 1930s, which caused in the non-communist world such massive economic devastation that the states were forced to undertake countercyclical economic policies to push the economy back on to the path of economic recovery and to restore economic growth. To begin with, they did so with little theoretical underpinnings. These were not in place before 1936 when Keynes's *General Theory* was published. However, the direct impact of Keynesianism was not great before the war.

The third defining development, which unfolded after World War II, was the restructuring of institutions, especially in countries devastated by the war. The lure of communism was then perceived as a serious threat in Western Europe and measures had to be taken to reduce the attraction of communist parties, some of which were large and powerful. One consequence was a gradual introduction of social insurance, subsidized healthcare, etc. in the industrial economies, which forced the policy debate to focus on a more activist role for the state in economic development. The prevailing economic doctrine of the day, Keynesianism, provided an intellectual foundation for a more activist state, particularly in terms of countercyclical policy.

In the post-World War II period, leading up to 1973 when the Organization fo the Petroleum Exporting Countries (OPEC) increased the price of a barrel of oil by 400 per cent from $US2 to $US10 per barrel, the role of the developmental state in industrial countries centred on the following three issues:

1. the need for the state to provide welfare benefits to those suffering from the loss of income and deprivation – a direct socio-economic outcome of war;
2. the desirability of a mixed economy consisting of public and private sectors requiring nationalization of a number of strategic industries to enable such an economy to operate smoothly; and
3. the need for a coordinated macro-economic policy aiming to reach such goals as full employment, price stability and balance of payment equilibrium, which could not be achieved by the market alone.

By 1950, the tasks performed by state institutions had expanded from the provision of infrastructure and utilities to a more extensive support to expansion of education, healthcare, unemployment benefits, etc. Between 1960 and 1995, while the total size of OECD governments' budget doubled, much of the increase in expenditures was directed to public transfers and subsidies rather than to traditional public goods (IMF, 1965 to 1995) due, among other things, to demographics which reinstated larger funding for pensions and healthcare for the aging population.

Developing Countries

As the former colonies of the European countries began to gain independence from their colonial masters after World War II, the role of the newly emerging states began to expand for a number of reasons. The most pressing problems that many of these states (with the possible exception of some of the oil-rich countries) had to face were pervasive poverty, unemployment, unequal income distribution and low domestic savings. The collapse of international trade in the 1930s, leading to falling commodity export prices, made it difficult for the leaders and bureaucrats of the newly independent states to make long-term plans for development on the basis of export growth. Export-led growth was inconceivable to technocrats and politicians in many developing countries, as they had witnessed the falling raw materials prices and shrinking world trade in the 1930s. Furthermore, trade expansion continued to look bleak well into the mid-1950s, while Europe was rebuilding and its currencies were still not fully convertible. The doctrine of 'export pessimism' took root, implying that the demand for raw materials was bound to increase slowly because of low income elasticity of demand (see Blomqvist and Lundahl, 2002).

Therefore, being confronted with foreign exchange constraints, many of these emerging states shifted their economic focus to domestic markets. In some countries a fledgling manufacturing industry had already been established during the war, when manufactures could not be imported from the developed economies. Economic nationalism, embodied in state control of the major sectors of the economy and led by import substituting industrialization (ISI) policy, gained widespread popularity among political leaders (Shapiro and Taylor, 1992) as they were determined not to remain under the economic colonialization of Western powers, having just escaped political colonialization.

The confidence in the market system was rather low worldwide after the war. The Great Depression of the 1930s already signalled the failure of capitalism and market-led development. The teachings of Keynes, as mentioned above, also supported the idea of the proactive state. The rise of the Soviet Union under comprehensive centralized planning further inspired leaders of political coalitions to expand their state's control over the economy, following the Soviet model by mobilizing resources and people, and directing them towards rapid growth and the elimination of social injustice. The main elements of the new strategy, under which the state was accorded a central role in overcoming market failures, consisted of centralized planning, corrective intervention in resource allocation, a heavy state hand in infant-industry development, the promotion of state enterprises and help for the emerging indigenous private sector businesses. By the end of the 1960s the expanded state had become involved in almost every aspect of the economy, administering prices, exercising control over the production, distribution and consumption of goods and services, regulating the labour market as well as the foreign exchange and financial markets. India in the 1960s and 1970s and Tanzania in the 1970s and 1980s are the perfect examples of an all-encompassing and overbearing state. Few developing countries – not even those that officially declared themselves socialist – adopted a fully-fledged planned economy, however. One reason for this was no doubt the lack of needed technocratic and administrative capacity rather than a lack of political will.

Import substitution cum state planning as an industrialization policy turned out to be a failure for several reasons (Krueger, 1997). The infant industries tended never to grow up and become internationally competitive. It was also hard to 'pick winners'; promoting too advanced industries too early will deprive the rest of the economy of skilled labour, capital, etc. Import substitution also works against exports, as resources are drawn from export industries and relative prices turn against export industries. Because of overvalued exchange rates, the industries actually created were often far too capital-intensive because of artificially cheap imported real capital. Their effect on employment was therefore not what it could have been; and the benefits to the poor, who are the ones who benefit most from employment opportunities, were small. Protection also creates vested interests, as well as coalitions between trade unions and capitalists who are unwilling to dismantle protection when the industry matures. Thus, many countries got stuck in an uncompetitive industrial structure.

As the price of crude oil continued to rise rapidly after 1973, the oil-exporting countries began to deposit a large part of their export income in European and American banks which then was channelled to non-oil exporting countries as loans with high interest rates to carry forward their planned development programmes. The unimpressive result of import substitution combined with a sharp rise in amortization payments due to the high interest rates on these 'petrodollar' funded loans began to widen the balance of payment deficits of a large number of developing countries which were eventually hit by a debt crisis in the 1980s. Meanwhile oil-exporting countries ran into difficulties, too. Indonesia, Nigeria and Mexico, just to mention a few, which had greatly expanded state-sponsored activities in the 1970s and early 1980s in the expectation that the high oil price would remain steady, found oil prices falling sharply after the mid-1980s, thereby suddenly exposing the cost of this development strategy.

On 8 December 1991, the Soviet Union ceased to exist. Although the Soviet system had not been able to act as an attractive developmental model for some time, as its weaknesses began to show in the 1960s and 1970s, this event symbolically sounded the death knell of a developmental era (World Bank, 1997); and the old-style developmental state seemed glaringly inadequate. Many states were forced to try to reduce their level of involvement in the economy by gradually lessening their control over production, prices, finance, exchange rates, trade and so on, and by allowing market forces to play a more prominent role.

While import substitution was the dominating strategy well into the 1980s, a number of small and mid-sized Asian countries pursued a much different strategy, which has subsequently been followed by many other countries. The idea was to export to the world market concentrating on products where the country had a comparative advantage. With the exception of Hong Kong, the East Asian 'tigers' were not good examples of a non-interventionist state, however, even if some early observers misinterpreted the situation (e.g. Balassa, 1981; Burenstam Linder, 1986). In fact, they intervened heavily in both goods and factor markets, for instance, through tariff exemptions for imported inputs and subsidized credit as well as through establishing public sector enterprises (PSEs) in strategic industries. Some provided extensive tax incentives in 'pioneering' industries, which in practice worked as a strong incentive for foreign direct investment (FDI).

However, the results were not always impressive. Distorting markets in favour of exports is not necessarily a priori a better idea than favouring industries producing for the domestic market. Korea's emphasis on the heavy and chemical industries in the late 1970s, for example, was an expensive mistake (Haggard, 1994). Nevertheless, the countries that applied an export-oriented development strategy were immensely more successful than those that had gone for import substitution. One of the reasons for that may be these countries' ability to reverse unsuccessful policies quickly, which in turn they could do because they had not built up powerful lobby groups behind protective barriers.

India and China

Until just a few decades ago, both India and China sported planned economies, although of quite different types. China had no private ownership while the private sector in India was big, although heavily regulated. India was a federal, democratic state, while China was highly centralized and authoritarian. While some smaller states in Asia have been successful in reducing their direct involvement in the economy, many larger states such as India and China have been slower. China has been more successful in dismantling its PSEs than India, which has failed to divest any of its loss-making PSEs. Consequently the bloated bureaucracy and the vast unproductive labour force in Indian PSEs continue to receive salaries, wages and all other perks associated with public sector employment (Chai and Roy, 2006). The labour force in the organized public and private sector enterprises and in government departments in India is mostly under the control of highly militant unions affiliated with communist parties; and this has made changes very difficult.

Towards the end of the 1980s, subsidies, public transfers and interest payment on public debt accounted for more than 100 per cent of the central government's budgetary deficit (Roy, 1992). If subsidies and public transfers to provincial governments could have been drastically cut down, the central government would have been able to maintain a balanced budget. The drag on the government's budgetary resources to finance PSEs and government departments would not have posed a serious problem for the state either, if the Indian economy had been able to grow at a rate closer to that of the Chinese economy. Furthermore, due to widespread tax evasion, the contribution of the personal income tax and business profit tax to the budgetary revenue was minimal (IMF, 1965 to 1995; GOI, 1970 to 1995). If the economy had grown at a rate similar to that of China, many jobs would have been created in newly established enterprises and organizations in the private sector, and the labour force made redundant due to the dismantling or privatization of loss-making PSEs could have been absorbed in these jobs. However, the issues of reducing subsidies and privatizing PSEs came into prominence in the 1990s when India began to open up its economy to market forces and competition. India has been a member of the World Trade Organization (WTO) since 1995. Unfortunately, during this same period, although the growth rate of the economy increased significantly, no national Indian government enjoyed an absolute majority in the lower house of the federal parliament. As a result, no law relating to economic reform could be passed by coalition governments consisting of a number of political parties, including the two communist parties whose leaders were against any economic reform and role for the free market.

In its attempt to reduce the size of its budget deficit, the central government reduced some expenditures on healthcare, the public distribution of some basic necessities to the poor, education and public works. In education and healthcare, these cuts took place mostly in infrastructure, while the salaries of the existing staff in educational institutions and of public sector employees (under organized unions) were raised considerably. The reductions in all these areas affected mostly students and poor families. Less money for improvements of roads and other key infrastructure has adversely affected India's growth as well. But the government has at least been able to increase revenue from personal income taxes and business profit taxes in recent years (GOI, 1970 to 1995), mainly by improving the tax collection mechanism. On the other hand, the central government's attempt to increase revenue from indirect taxes by introducing a value added tax (VAT) virtually failed because a large number of items were excluded from the preview of VAT and because many provincial governments, under pressure from different lobby groups, refused to implement this tax.

Although the autocratic state of China is still governed by the communist party, the party leaders began to open up the closed economy and to allow market forces and entrepreneurial dynamism to play their role in the late 1970s. Although, due to the dismantling of a large number of unproductive PSEs, millions of workers became redundant, they were largely absorbed in alternative employment in transport, construction, and other low-skilled areas in the manufacturing and service sector industries created in special economic zones (SEZ) along the eastern coastline of China. There are still many PSEs in China, but these are being forced to modernize by the state. Making and implementing decisions to reform the economy has been easy in China because of the autocratic regime, one-party rule, centralized administration, and the desire of the ruling elites to modernize the old-style developmental state. For the same reasons, no powerful vested interests have been there to resist reforms. However, since the PSEs used to take care of many basic needs of their employees, such as housing and healthcare, the dismantling of these enterprises has caused social standards to deteriorate for many people (Clark and Roy, 1997).

Although many deficiencies of the old-style developmental state still remain, the explosive growth generated by the free market forces has consistently raised the government's budgetary revenue (GOC, various years). Although the state has retained its control over many activities in the economy, it has removed restrictions on several vital areas such as the labour market and capital inflows and has not allowed union power to interfere in the operation of enterprises. China became a member of the WTO in 2001, which will add pressure towards further opening the economy.

DEVELOPMENTAL STATE OR RENT SEEKING STATE: THE GREAT DEBATE

Development economics as a separate field of study gained prominence as European governments began to systematically apply Keynesian interventionist state philosophy in formulation and implementation of reconstruction programmes after the end of World War II. After the failure of neoclassical economics to provide capitalist economies with a quick way out of depression, it appeared increasingly clear that the development strategy of a country had to rest on direct public interventions at the sectoral and firm level aimed at stimulating particular lines of economic behaviour. For a developing country, the nature and level of state intervention may depend on the country's economic position relative to that of an advanced country (Gerschenkron, 1962). Moreover, many developing countries were unwilling to adopt the economic system of the colonialists, which added to the attraction of planning and intervention.

The Latin America structuralist school led by Prebisch (1950) argued that because of institutional barriers in developing countries preventing free factor mobility and productivity growth, economic development there would require the deliberate creation of conditions necessary for capitalism to work. These ideas received some support from Scitovsky's (1954) analysis of the need for the presence of several conditions necessary to achieve optimal dynamic resource allocation, such as complete and functioning markets, an absence of increasing returns, and complete tradability, which were generally not present in less developed countries (LDCs). The absence of full factor mobility under structural rigidity also meant that wages and exchange rates did not reflect the true opportunity costs of labour and foreign exchange.

Because of these structural rigidities and imperfect capital markets, the chances of the private sector undertaking the appropriate level of involvement to push the economy from an under-employment equilibrium towards its potential output and employment levels were arguably bleak. Hence, the Keynesians argued that the required level of investment in an underdeveloped economy is rather lumpy and large in comparison to savings flows or even to the national capital stock, and that the price mechanism which may provide signals for marginal changes cannot be relied on to guide big industrial decisions or to induce the resource transfer necessary for industrialization and economic development. This strongly supported the interventionist philosophy. Public interventions are required both in the form of support to investors (via protection, subsidies, cheap credit, etc.) and direct investment to break critical bottlenecks (Shapiro and Taylor, 1992). The greater extent of market failure in less developed as opposed to developed economies, therefore, provided the basic rationale for expanding the scope of state intervention. The Keynesian revolution, which cast doubt on the free market's ability to achieve optimal results, thus provided the states' leaders with arguments in favour of adopting centralized planning for economic development in LDCs. Theoretical arguments to justify import substitution regimes in LDCs received further support from the hypothesis of a secular decline in terms of trade for developing countries (Prebisch, 1950; Singer, 1950) by questioning the ability of the free market to achieve optimal results.

Yet, the leadership of a developmental state was strongly criticized as well. Bauer (1972, 1984), who led the counter revolution against the interventionist state after his disappointment with the performance of India's excessively interventionist state during the 1950s and 1960s, argued that government failure is likely to be worse than market failure and that state intervention in an economy creates more problems than it solves. Little et al. (1970) argued that the import-substituting industrial strategy implemented with a high level of effective tariff rates and quotas on imports was inefficient, as the incentives they created were highly unequal for different economic sectors. Krueger (1974) and Balassa (1971) were also strongly anti-import substitution, accepting state intervention mainly on the grounds of market failure. Later Krueger

(1983), with the help of empirical evidence, concluded that export-led growth created dynamic forces in an economy in excess of efficiency gains due to better resource allocation.

Kruger's analysis of the effects of state intervention in an economy via quantitative restrictions on trade exposed the rent seeking behaviour of the state. Firms compete for such state benefits as import licences and, thus, for their attached rents. Buchanan (1980), applying the technique of 'welfare triangles' showed the economic loss that results from rents in the presence of state regulation, while others argued that the emergence of monopoly and other distortions arising from state policy makes the deadweight loss even larger than the area of triangles identified by Buchanan. Following Krueger, Bhagwati (1982) argued that under state-imposed import restrictions, competition for rents which accrue to the winners of government largesse turns into widespread 'directly unproductive profit seeking' (DUP) activities – such as lobbying, bribe paying and incapacitating formal institutions by the interference of lobbying groups. Since any kind of state intervention creates the scope for rent seeking, it also greatly increases the risk of activities seeking government favour, overriding normal market activities. In such a situation, rent seeking by individuals, while being their rational behaviour, could lead to extremely sub-optimal outcomes for the economy. In addition to the possible distortions introduced by the intervention itself, real resources are squandered on non-productive activities instead of being used for producing goods and services.

Olson (1982) did not directly mention the words 'rent seeking', but he felt that in an interventionist and expanding state, economic decisions are unlikely to be taken in the collective interest of individuals due to bargaining costs and the problem of free riders, unless they are members of small groups. Such a coalition of self-interest persons is likely to try to redistribute income towards itself instead of working to raise efficiency and national income, the full benefit of which they will not receive. In stable societies, therefore, politics will be increasingly organized to cater to these interests. Consequently, inefficient income allocation will provide no incentive for Schumpeterian entrepreneurs to seek out technical innovation to accelerate overall economic growth. Olson here refers to political coalitions of self-interested individuals, which are most likely to be found in a decentralized governance system in a democracy rather than in an autocratic system. In the latter system it is more likely that the state itself – or rather the people who take decisions in the name of the state – turns into a special interest in its own right. North (1981), for example, admits that the interventionist state may become its own 'vested interest group', creating a trade-off between economic efficiency and state power. Lal (1983), a neoclassical author, believes that if the state possesses autonomy to some extent, a degree of authoritarianism is necessary to eliminate DUP activities.

The Demise of the Neoclassical State

The neoclassical attack against the expanding state was based on the assumption that markets function. Therefore, the state had only a minimal 'night watchman' role to play in the economy. Second, the advocacy of such a minimalist state was based on the assumption that a clear separation of powers existed between the legislative, executive and judicial branches of the state. We know already that the markets are full of imperfections. Unfettered markets tend to result in monopolies, cartels and other imperfections. Markets also create their own rent seeking groups and thereby alter the distribution of income. The overriding dominance of the legislature and judiciary by the executive in both developing and developed states has meant that the second assumption does not hold much ground either.

Furthermore, the neoclassical criticism of the interventionist developmental state was bolstered by the mistaken belief that the success of the export-oriented East Asian countries, such as South Korea and Taiwan, was due mainly to the non-interventionist nature of these states. In fact, the state in South Korea and Taiwan was highly interventionist (Clark and Roy, 1997; Wade, 1990). Export-oriented trading regimes may be as distortive as import-substituting ones and are also prone to the rise of Bhagwati's DUP activities, just as import-substituting trading regimes are, so the explanation to these countries' success is hardly their export orientation only.

Bauer's (1972) observation that government failure is likely to be worse than market failure and Lal's (1983) suggestion that a courageous, ruthless and perhaps undemocratic government is required to eliminate the rent-seeking and institution-maiming power of North's vested interest groups created by the state seem to refer to democratic governments. Hence, in the economic sphere, the neoclassicals seem to prefer the application of laissez-faire policy and substantial curb on the state's expanding role in the economy, but in the political sphere they seem to accept restrictions on individual freedom and concentration of power in authoritarian regimes such as those in South Korea and Taiwan. Although economists argue that all kinds of states create their vested interest groups, in democratic states the larger the number of political parties, the larger the number of such groups. At the same time, the East Asian authoritarian states were also interventionist and expanding states, and certainly not free from vested interests. Their success was due to not only the type of the state but also a unique set of other economic and non-economic factors which are not present in other developing countries even today.

From what has been discussed above, it can be argued that the laissez-faire state may have existed when the state was in its rudimentary form in the early stage of its evolutionary process. It certainly does not exist any more. But the developmental state of the 1960s and 1970s also does not exist today. The modern developmental state retains some of its interventionist roles and at the same time tries to enable the free market principle to operate and entrepreneurial dynamism to flourish in economic activities.

The neoclassical economists regarded the state as a black box, whose internal functioning was not a worthwhile subject for economic analysis (Blomqvist, 2002). But neo-utilitarian political economists attacked this view of the state on the ground that the consequences of state action were too important to leave the black box closed (Srinivasan, 1985). These consequences of state action emanate from the exchange relation between incumbents who require political supporters to survive and the supporters to provide continued support to the incumbent. These supporters require rent which may be provided to them through subsidies, loans, government appointments, job contracts or the provision of services, or alternatively by using their rule-making authority to create rents for favoured groups, restricting the ability of market forces to operate (Evans, 1992). After this, these supporters – whom we may call informal agents of the state or cadres of the political party in power – eliminate other potential office holders by incapacitating the formal institutions that the state itself created.

Examples of this incumbent and its cadre relationship can be found in the Indian province of Bengal which has been ruled by a dogmatic Marxist-led government for 30 years. Rent seeking is an outward manifestation of consumption. It can spread when the exercise of threat power by the informal agents or cadres of the state have weakened formal institutions originally created by the state to prevent rent seeking behaviour. When the leaders of the state also directly take part in the rent seeking activities and consume the surplus they extract, encourage private actors to shift from productive activities to non-productive rent seeking or fail to provide collective goods, they have no more regard for their society than a predator does for its prey. Consequently, such a state can legitimately be termed a predatory state (Lal, 1988).

However, many private actors may be paying rents to the state's agents to facilitate their productive economic activities in states where the formal institutions have also been kept alive to ensure the observance of formal rules and the collection of formal fees from private economic agents. In such situations, the rent seeking behaviour of the state apparatus increases the transaction cost of any economic activity but expedites the completion process of formalities. The result that is achieved from the completion of a particular economic activity may be sub-optimal, but that sub-optimal result would be better than no result at all. So when the state's rent seeking behaviour is relatively mild and is confined to certain types and areas of economic and social activity as well as being localized, then we have to agree with Margaret Levi's (1988) view that the state's predatory behaviour may, in fact, be a revenue-maximizing behaviour. The state maximizes revenue in ways that either promote development or impede it (Blomqvist and Lundahl, 2002). How the proceeds which are siphoned off are used is important as well.

The state's rent seeking behaviour can impede development seriously when it engulfs the entire fabric of the society and covers all social and economic transactions in a way that discourages productive economic activities. Examples are Bihar Province in India, where all formal institutions have virtually been destroyed, and to a considerable extent in Bengal Province where the agents of the Marxist-led government are master rent seekers. Many states in Africa and Latin America have also, from time to time, been predatory.

The term 'predatory' cannot always be used as an appendage to the developmental state, however. The idea of the 'productive predatory state' (Blomqvist and Lundahl, 2002) is based on the observation that the best alternative for a predatory regime is not necessarily to reduce the efficiency of the economy. When the state elite stands to gain more from sharing the fruits of development (e.g. through taxation) than from simply redistributing income to itself, it may well find it worthwhile to provide institutions that define property and contract rights, for example. An example of the productive predatory state is Indonesia under President Suharto, where the economy developed well and poverty was reduced dramatically, in spite of the fact that the president's family and cronies amassed fortunes through rent seeking.

Another issue that needs to be addressed is whether state power can be captured by rent seeking vested interest groups even in a neoclassical state. The role of a neoclassical minimalist state, which has already been discussed, is not as minimal as one may think. The faith of neoclassical economists in the ability of their state to prevent the growth of its vested interest groups and their rent seeking power rested on their assumption that the separation of powers between the legislature, executive and judiciary is maintained in their minimalist state. But this assumption does not hold in most countries in the world today due to the increasing dominance of the executive over the legislative and the judicial branches of the government. Even the most important task of the Smithian state, i.e. protection of inanimate property such as land and animate property such as human lives, as well as the enforcement of contractual agreements, cannot be performed successfully if the executive can influence the decision of the judges by exercising its power to appoint judges who are willing to carry out the executive's wishes. The Malaysian judicial system is an example of this. Moreover, even if judicial independence is maintained in a country, the verdict of judges on any issue cannot be enforced if the executive compromises the independence of the police force. Such a situation exists in most African and many Asian countries, as well as in Eastern Europe and Latin America.

Finally, the neoclassicists do not pay enough attention to the fact that markets do not work in a vacuum. The markets are deeply intertwined not only with formal institutions but also with informal ones such as cultural norms and social networks (Evans, 1992; Meier and Rauch, 2005) developed through the society's evolutionary process and often backed by state power. However, these norms and networks can also be influenced by the state to better perform even its minimalist task. Therefore, if markets must be surrounded by other kinds of social structures in order to function, then any attempt to free the market from the state may lead to the destruction of the institutional underpinnings that enable the exchange in the free market to take place. In fact, the road to the free market could not have been opened without substantial increase in centrally organized and controlled intervention by the state (Polanyi, 1957). The downfall of the Soviet Union is a case in point. The country became capitalist almost overnight, but at the same time the key institutions had all but broken down and were not quickly replaced by new ones. As a result, the economy took about 15 years to recover to the level of 1990.

Further support to Polanyi's view can be found in Weber's (1968) observation that the operation of large-scale capitalist enterprises depends on the availability of the kind of social and economic order that a modern bureaucratic state can provide. The intimate relationship between capitalism and bureaucracy, which is crucial to the success of capitalism, can only be found in a state where bureaucrats are concerned just with carrying out their assignments to realize the goals of the state. Such a bureaucracy existed in some East Asian autocratic developmental states where political leaders cannot threaten the job security of bureaucrats and technocrats (Clark and Roy, 1997; Wade, 1990).

The Modern Developmental State

The extravagant involvement of the developmental state in the production and supply of goods and services in the 1960s and 1970s does not exist in developing countries in the twenty first century. However, that does not mean that the developmental state is dead. On the contrary, the developmental state is alive and well, and bigger than ever (World Bank, 1997), but it is redesigning its role in the economy. Stern (1991), for example, argues that the role of the modern developmental state should not be minimal. Although the state's direct control over the productive capacity of the economy has been diminishing greatly, its role in other sectors has been increasing, as many activities require both private and public sector participation. The state has a further role to play to improve the functioning of the market and private sector activities, by building infrastructure and providing necessary regulatory frameworks, which allow the competition to work effectively, as well as by intervening selectively in industry and agriculture. Although some of these activities are controversial, such as industrial policy, nearly all existing states do all these things. The inevitable consequence is that the GDP share of the public sector must be substantial (Stern, 1991).

Even dealing with the issues mentioned above would require a great deal of state involvement in the economy. But the modern state should involve the society and market as well in the provision of basic services such as education, health and so on. The Taiwanese and Singaporean developmental states consistently followed this practice. To protect poor and unemployed people, the state may introduce unemployment insurance schemes, which can help smooth household income and consumption during a recession, or may implement (via private sector agencies) food-for-work programmes. Even in administrating unemployment insurance programmes, the state and market can cooperate. The private employers may, for example, deduct social insurance premiums directly from the wages of their employees. The competition in the product and factor markets among entrepreneurs and resource suppliers and in the state apparatus among bureaucrats is supposed to weaken the rent seeking power of the state's vested interest groups as well as the power of the business sector to exploit employees and the society.

But things do not always work out that well. For example, at the end of September 2006 in India, the Board of Industrial and Financial Reconstruction approved rehabilitation schemes for 695 sick companies in the private sector, 27 Central Public Sector Enterprises (CPSE) and 26 provincial (State) Public Sector Enterprises (SPSE) (GOI, 2007). Since the private sector enterprises are within the boundaries of various provinces, the relevant provincial governments also play a role to revive them. There are instances where selected private companies receive assistance to restart a sick company with a substantially reduced number of employees compared to before the enterprises collapsed. However, some of the new owners also have shown a tendency to spend part of the money, let the production continue for a while, and then to close down the factory and run. The primary reasons for the collapse of these enterprises under private sector control were exploitation of labour by unions and factory owners and outdated technology, as well as a lack of infrastructure. Therefore, a large part of the assistance granted by the state to the new owners of these companies is not likely to be used honestly to improve the competitiveness of the company.

The modern state also wants to retain control over some vital industrial sectors of the economy. To what extent an industry is 'vital' and should be government-owned is a moot point, however, and the situation varies from country to country. Moreover, government ownership may be difficult to relinquish in practice due to the lack of alternatives. For example, in India in 2005–06 the Central Public Sector Enterprises (CPSEs) accounted for 85 per cent of total coal production, 59 per cent of crude oil production and 75 per cent of petroleum of refining (GO1, 2007). Large-scale divestment of PSEs cannot occur in India because no private sector capitalist that takes over a loss-making PSE would accept keeping the whole baggage of unproductive employees on their pay roll. Second, union officials and their political masters would lose their handsome rents if divestment involved a substantial retrenchment of employees.

On the other hand, China has been able to dismantle a substantial proportion of its PSEs, which has led to the retrenchment of millions of employees, as special interests were not allowed to interfere. At the same time, its PSEs still retain a sizeable production capacity, although the market has penetrated deeply into the Chinese economy. The difference was that the political resistance against privatizing was not there in China because of the autocratic regime, but also because of the rapid growth of the private sector which was able to absorb most of the laid-off employees of the PSEs.

The Re-Emergence of the Keynesian State

However, the possibility of a rapid transition of an overarching developmental state of the 1960s to a minimalist developmental state in the twenty first century globalized economy was dealt a severe blow by the global financial meltdown which erupted in mid-2007, assumed serious proportions in early 2009 and plunged the global economy into a deep recession. Consequently, the much-maligned Keynesian theory (1936) became the primary policy for kick-starting the global economic recovery. Since late 2008, the state in many nations has begun to exert its control over banking and financial services, the operation of industrial enterprises, and fiscal and monetary policies, as well as over government expenditure programmes to create employment and increase consumption while trying to keep the anomalous free trade regime alive. The state's control over central banks' operation of monetary policy and commercial banks' lending policies has extended to the point where the independence of central banks and commercial banks in formulating monetary policy and commercial lending rate policies is no longer assured.

Printing money and distributing it freely to the people to spend in retail stores on consumer goods which are largely imported from China and other developing Asian countries does not accelerate the pace of economic recovery in the home country, as the size of the multiplier is reduced due to the large import content in the government-financed consumers' expenditure programmes. As Keynes was primarily interested in protecting the domestic economy from the devastating effects of the Great Depression, his policy prescription was designed to lift the domestic economy out of a depression by financing highly labour-intensive public works programmes to create physical assets with inputs produced and supplied largely by domestic industries. Since under free trade, a recession originating in a large open economy such as the USA affects all other economies, Keynesian policy does not seem to profess to be a champion of global free trade and free exchange rate regimes which can be manipulated by large export-oriented nation states to serve their national interests, particularly when the larger country is in a deep recession. Hence, what is necessary for the modern state is to facilitate the re-establishment of small and medium-sized industrial sectors which can become the largest providers of new employment opportunities within the country and to implement quickly many small-scale labour-intensive public works expenditure programmes, like the ones that were implemented in the 1940s in British India and which had very short lags between the project finalization time and the project implementation time.[1]

The current recession which initially was perceived to be a stagflation seems to have brought a profound change in the global community's perception of the future role of the state in economic development. Accordingly, one can now state with some confidence that the resurgent activist developmental state of the Asian style is not going to be thrown onto the back burner again any time soon.

NOTE

1. Such schemes which came to be widely known as 'Dry Dole Schemes' were implemented by the British Raj in India to construct new roads, new ponds, new irrigation canals and so on by employing hundreds of members of poor rural households. These Dry Dole Schemes, which were continued in independent India in the 1950s, 1960s and 1970s, were replaced by new schemes under Indira Gandhi's administration in the 1980s. One of the present authors (K.C. Roy) had the good fortune in his childhood to witness the massive scale of operation of these schemes in rural Bengal in the 1950s and the 1960s.

2. Institutional foundations of a developmental state

As discussed in Chapter 1, a modern developmental state is an initiator and a facilitator of a country's dynamics of development. Before we discuss the relevant enabling institutions for the state to initiate and propose the development process, we will make some general comments on the state's need for institutions.

In our discussion, we define institutions as those formal and informal rules by which a society operates, as well as the authorities and agencies that formulate, implement, and ensure the sanctity of these rules (World Bank, 2001, 2002; Roy and Sideras, 2006). The state may have to modify existing regulations or policies and also to create new ones as the situation demands in the process of the implementation of state policies. It also requires institutions to ensure an equitable distribution of gains resulting from economic growth among wider sections of the community. While appropriate institutional foundations to promote economic growth by creating greater employment opportunities for people will, ipso facto, reduce inequality in income distribution in the country, new institutions targeted at redistributing the national income may also have to be created.

Since the size distribution of income, which shows the amount of income received by the poor, middle class and the rich, and which is regarded as a direct measure of welfare, depends on ownership patterns of productive factors including the value of labour services, then any institution that enhances the return to labour will in general lead to a more equal distribution. This is because the large majority of the population is dependent on only their work input for their living.

In a globalized world, outward-oriented trade policies can increase the growth rate while inward-oriented policies are likely to lower it. But outward-oriented policies will have to be combined with non-inflationary macroeconomic policies as well as with a high savings and a low tax regime. The state also requires a pro-development, pro-open market outward-oriented political regime to formulate the right kind of policies and a competent bureaucracy to implement those policies. However, the formal rules and policies cannot deliver high growth and development outcomes without the cooperation of informal, social institutions (Nee, 1998). Also, sound judicial law enforcement institutions are a fundamental prerequisite for enforcing the rule of law and contractual agreements between the state and its citizens, as well as between the parties in business transactions.

Therefore, we can very well argue that hopes for development outcomes are best achieved when all institutions harmoniously cooperate. It is the responsibility of the state to ensure such cooperation among all relevant institutions. To initiate the development dynamics, the state sometimes may have to be directly involved in the production and supply of certain goods and services for which demand exists but current supply is limited or non-existent. In this way the state can entice private sector entrepreneurs to produce those goods and services thereby creating a competitive market for the goods. But if the state's political institutions are not pro-market, then the state enterprises can become monopolist suppliers of those products. Therefore, the effective functioning of government agencies depends crucially on a system of effective checks and balances on political power (World Bank, 2002). This is where the problem lies.

In small closed communities in rural areas such as those among India's north eastern hill tribes, informal institutions can govern the social and economic transactions, but with the expansion of trading between communities new formal institutions would be required to resolve conflicts. If these new institutions differ greatly from customary rules, people may not abide by the decisions of these institutions. Hence, it is suggested that a compromise between the old and new institutions be reached (Islam, 2002b). However, the experience of developing countries suggests that the new formal governance institutions may incapacitate the informal institutions and disregard the opinion of local people, which in turn would deliver growth outcomes which may be good for the leaders but bad for citizens (Roy and Prasad, 2007a, 2007b; Roy and Sidenko, 2007a).

In reality, many informal institutions in developing countries can be anti-growth and anti-development. Hence they are required to be replaced (cf. Olson, 1982). However, this may not be possible in a federal state with multiparty democratic government at both the federal and provincial level due to the lack of cooperation among the different layers of government institutions to reform or to abolish the anti-growth informal institutions.[1] In fact, although the maintenance of informal institutions adversely affects economic growth and development, the political party running the government may maintain the status quo as its primary objective to retain its hold on power at the next federal and provincial elections because even with a very low growth in gross domestic product (GDP), the governance regime and its informal agents can continue to earn handsome rents from their DUP (Bhagwati, 1982) activities. While the higher economic growth would also increase the size of rents, it may also act as a catalyst in the drive to force the governance regime out of power. Hence, the leaders are happy to live with low growth and the persistence of pervasive poverty among the population. The example of such a situation can be found in Bihar and Bengal Provinces in India and, outside Asia, in most African states. Hence before creating new formal institutions for a country, the leaders will have to examine the current set of such supporting institutions as customs and religious traditions, the basic level of education and skills possessed by the vast majority of the population, the level of available technology, the size of the domestic market, the complexity of current regulations and the level of corruption in the country.

The higher the complexity of regulation, the higher will be the potential level of bureaucratic red tape and corruption within the country. Consequently, a large segment of the country's population with weak political and economic power is, in effect, deprived of access to formal institutions.

Sometimes the state leaders may have to modify some informal institutions so that these cooperate with formal institutions to achieve the state's developmental goals. For example, in a country where in the rural sector the validity of most formal transactions cannot be guaranteed if they are not certified by the local customary law, despite these being certified by the formal law, the conflict between the formal and informal institutions may prevent these transactions from being completed. As a result, the country's development suffers. Hence, the government plays a central role in organizing dispersed interests and balancing competing interests to meet national goals (World Bank, 2003). However, changing informal institutions is difficult and time-consuming; sometimes the ruling elite is not very interested in reform at all, if there is a risk that its own economic interests would be impaired by the new order

LOWERING TRANSACTION COSTS

Therefore, the state in designing institutions of governance will have to aim to create those which will lower economic and social transaction costs. Economic transaction costs are inversely related to the degree of openness of the country to foreign trade and investment (Islam, 2002b). They can remain low if social transaction costs, which are mostly informal, are low. These transaction costs vary in inverse proportion to the level of acceptance by the civil society of the governance regime and its governance rules. The World Bank (2003) cites the example of the Ramkrishna Mission's role in West Bengal Province in India in implementing a number of social development projects in the fields of education and healthcare and thereby supplementing and strengthening the capability of the governance regime of West Bengal.

The society's acceptance of government rules depends among other things on the level of income and education of its people. With low income and a high level of illiteracy among the masses, it can be difficult for the state's citizens to enhance their economic and social welfare. Hence, in the absence of a genuine acceptance by the society of their legitimacy, the state's governance institutions cannot function effectively. Different countries at different levels of social and economic development would have different kinds of developmental needs and accordingly different kinds of institutions. To formulate and improve the quality of its governance institutions, the state has to understand the needs of its citizens (Chibber, 1997).

In a newly independent nation, due to low political institutionalization and its pre-independence existence as a colony, the pent-up demands and aspirations of different ethnic groups may come into conflict with each other. As a result, the most powerful group may try to capture the state power to fulfil the demands and aspirations of that group at the expense of other groups. A chaotic situation, which may develop, may prevent the development of a robust institutional set up (Nafziger, 2006) and can even lead to the breakdown of the newly emerging nation-state. Then instead of one state, each group may form a separate nation-state to realize the group's aspirations which may in fact be the aspirations and desires of the self-styled leaders of these groups and not of the majority of the members of those groups. To some extent such a situation has developed in East Timor, for example.

DETERMINANTS OF ENABLING INSTITUTIONS

Therefore a country's history, geographical location and current level of development among other factors tend to exercise a strong influence on the type of institutions it can design and adopt for all kinds of transactions.

History of Political Governance

The present authors' view is that history and geography shape a society's economic and political institutions and behaviour. The leaders can improve the performance of these institutions or can introduce new economic and political institutions to the society. But the new political institutions may not function well if the population at large has a long history of being ruled by a certain governance regime and has not been well prepared for their acceptance of the new regime. The perfect example is Russia. The breakup of the formal Soviet Union and the attempt by the self-styled leader and vested interest groups (North, 1981) to impose, under the cover of a democratic structure, a federal political governance regime as well as a semi-market economy on a society, which had been accustomed to a totalitarian regime and a command economy, created an upheaval in the society and a vacuum in the transaction process due mainly to the failure of the governance regime to put in place transitional institutions to minimize the adverse effects on the Russian society of a sudden change in institutional environment (North, 1987, 1990; Nee, 1998). The vacuum created in the transaction process led to the emergence of powerful mafia groups to carry out, on behalf of Russian citizens, economic transactions at an enormous cost to the society (Roy and Sidenko, 2007b). Russia's economic reform could not have been allowed to threaten the leader's ambition to stay in power and maintain control over the society (Fairclough, 2003; Huntington, 2003).

On the other hand, the self-proclaimed leader of vested interest groups of a country with a history of being ruled by a foreign colonial power may inspire people to join the elite group to wage a guerrilla war against the foreign ruler under the pretext of introducing a democratic political governance regime to eliminate the economic and social poverty of the masses. But after driving the foreign power out of the country, the leaders and their elite groups may maintain a facade of a democratic political regime but create a rule that enables the leaders and their vested interest groups to stay in power to plunder the country's wealth for their own benefits (Nafziger and Auvinen, 2003).

As a result, the pent-up aspirations of many ethnic groups are never fulfilled. This situation can cause upheaval in a newly independent country. Hence, the society after the change of governance regime may experience a type of economy and society it never experienced before under the previous regime. In a newly created democratic state, the explosion of mass participation in politics relative to the institutional capacity to absorb new participants will almost certainly lead to political instability as Huntington (1968) observed many decades ago. The new political regime, then, almost invariably seeks and receives international aid for many years to come. While the economic and social status of the majority of the population may not necessarily improve, the wealth of the members of the elite groups and of their informal agents increases greatly (Nafziger, 2006). One can find the presence of this situation in Zimbabwe and East Timor, to take some extreme examples. The elites as predators would have little interest in enforcing the rule of law and in enhancing the economic and social well-being of the population (Sandbrook, 2002).

It can therefore be argued that the imposition of a formal democratic governance regime on a developing society with no previous experience in such a political governance structure may in fact hinder the robust growth and development outcomes for which the new political regime was installed. Here we tend to disagree with Rodrick (2003) who suggests that, while growth spurts can be achieved under different political governance regimes, the sustenance and transformation of these spurts into a consistently higher standard of living are facilitated by democracy. In developing countries, the vested interest

groups tend to prop up their leaders to capture the state power through democratic elections. For representative democracy to work in a developing country,
the following preconditions must be met.

1. The overwhelming majority of the population of the country must be
    reasonably well educated. Each voter should be able to make an informed
    choice of the candidate he or she would like to vote for. Each voter should
    be free of intimidation by agents of political parties to force them to vote
    for candidates supported by these agents. Rigging an election process by
    agents of the political party in power, which is widely prevalent in nomi-
    nally democratic governance structures in developing countries, must be
    stopped.
2. The majority of the population must have economic freedom (i.e. adequate
    income-earning employment) so that they can exercise their voting rights
    freely.
3. The total population of the country should be small for the democracy to
    function smoothly, or at least, the relevant constituencies should be small
    enough.
4. People should have gained some experience in democratic governance
    even in a rudimentary form before the formal installation of democracy.
5. The number of political parties fighting an election battle to capture state
    power should preferably be two. This is necessary to ensure that one party
    has the absolute majority of members elected to the country's legislature.
    The party in opposition would also then be strong enough to make the
    government work effectively to implement the agenda for which it was
    elected by the people.

In Western Europe and in North America, such conditions were fulfilled when
democratic political governance regimes were installed. In England, the experiment in democracy developed during many years. It may arguably take even
a few hundred years for a democratic political governance system to establish
itself effectively (Mill, 1947).

In Eastern Europe the installation of democratic political governance regimes
has not worked very well because only a few of the above noted preconditions
were even partly met. This is the case in many Asian countries as well. The
attempt to unite populations of different regions with diverse linguistic, religious and ethnic backgrounds into a cohesive nation may not be successful
as resistance to the formation of a national identity may not be completely
done away with under the new political institutions (Lerner, 1958; Hunter,
1969; Foster, 1973). The movement from authoritarian to democratic rule is a
highly disruptive process (Sandbrook, 2002), which can easily trigger conflicts
among populations of different regions and ethnicities (Ottaway, 1995).

According to some commentators (Sandbrook and Oelbaum, 1997) who accept that institutional performance is shaped by traditions established over many years, the institutional change to democracy, which has to take place as a gradual process, may come about under pressure from aid donors even in countries with deeply rooted patrimonialism. In support of institutional change to democratic governance, others (Brandt and Turner, 2003) observe that in China, village-level elections, even when corruptible, tend to reduce rent seeking. But in newly formed federal states, with many layers of government, such an argument does not hold.

History of Political Order – Feuding States and Regionalism

Historically it has been found that if a country consisted of many feuding states, provinces, etc. with many languages, many religions, different ethnic groups and different cultural traditions, the allegiance of people to their respective states has tended to be stronger than their allegiance to the country.

A lack of homogeneity of population, languages, religion and culture which are crucial to the growth of the spirit of nationalism makes it difficult for the population of different regions to work unitedly towards the fulfilment of national developmental goals. In many traditional societies, people accustomed to a low-output economy prefer stability in their socio-economic status which is provided to them by their autocratic monarchs whose power is based on religious authority and custom. The imposition of a political governance regime on new provinces carved out of former sovereign states with deep-seated divisions in all elements fundamental to the growth of the spirit of nationalism and effective leadership may not unite them into a cohesive national entity. History would suggest that even the gradual transition process to a democratic governance system would have to be very slow.

History of Religious Orders

Religion can play an important role in the economic development of a country. Priests are regarded as the medium through whom the society could communicate with God. Many social activities of human beings, although legally valid, also had to be customarily valid, and priests were to decide the level and type of punishment for a person who violated that custom. Hence, monarchs and princes, whose authorities were supposedly sanctioned by God, systematically used religion through royal priests to impose rules of economic and social governance on their subjects. So if a benevolent autocratic monarch wanted to encourage domestic saving and investment, trade and commerce, agriculture and manufacturing activities within the kingdom by providing incentives to people, social acceptance of such activities was easier if the priests declared such activities as being divinely ordained. Thus historically all religions primarily showed their followers an appropriate way of life that they should follow. The (Hindi) Gita, the Bible and the Koran all teach the same basic philosophy.

After a decline in the authority of the medieval Roman Catholic Church, the Protestant Reformation of the sixteenth and seventeenth centuries promoted a new economic order which systematically began to regulate the religious and non-religious conduct of people by ascribing an 'inner worldly' ascetic value to such economic behaviours as frugality and deferred non-essential consumption to increase savings, investment and production, hard work for labour at low wages and free competition in the labour market.

All such activities were to be treated as service to God and obviously also to the employer (Weber, 1930). Religion, therefore, provided the necessary spiritual wherewithal for the rise of strong nation-states which provided a strong fillip to the growth of capitalism and entrepreneurial dynamics for more than 300 years from the sixteenth century to the early part of the twentieth century by building the necessary infrastructure for development, such as a domestic market and international trade free of barriers, a uniform monetary system, contract and property law, police forces to enforce law and order, and military force to defend countries' borders against external aggression.

Peoples' observance of many religious edicts and social mores prevents the occurrence of asymmetric information that can impede intertemporal transactions (Stiglitz and Weiss, 1981). Hence, some of the religious rules and social customs do tend to provide positive incentives for socially optimal behaviour. But many religious rules and social customs also, directly or indirectly, serve to maintain the status quo and prevent change. In Asia, the Confucian heritage was often invoked as a cause of economic stagnation – until the region began to develop rapidly. After that, Confucianism has been frequently mentioned as one possible cause of that success!

The adverse impacts on economic and social progress in a country of many religious practices and traditions assume more serious proportions when there are many religions and the total population is clearly divided on the basis of their religions. Some religious practices and social customs which discriminate against women (Roy et al., 1999; Roy and Sideras, 2006; Chai and Roy, 2006; Roy et al., 2008) and minorities, foreign nationals and other groups of people most certainly bring inefficient outcomes in growth, output and social development in a country. Discrimination against women and other caste-based and religion-based minorities, some of whom can be either McClelland's (1961) 'N-Achievers' or Hagen's (1962) 'Non-conformists', mars the prospect of the country's long-term welfare. In his 'stationary state' model, Schumpeter (1961) introduces the profit-motivated dynamic entrepreneur who begins to innovate. Such innovation which increases demand for new resources and raises the marginal productivity of these resources leads to the creation of new plants, new firms and new institutions, as well as to the eventual change of leadership. This is Schumpeter's 'creative destruction' which implies that a new economic, social and political order cannot be created without destroying the old order.

The rise of the developmental state would certainly depend to a great extent on its capacity to break old religious and social barriers which scuttle the attempt by the state authorities to enhance the economic and social welfare of their citizens (Olson, 1982). The history of religious orders, therefore, provides lessons as to what kind of governance institution – autocratic or democratic – would be able to inspire the entire population to get behind the state for the fulfilment of national development goals.

Geographical Location

Rodrick's (2003) research found that geographical location exercises a strong influence on the income level (as a proxy for economic development) indirectly by influencing the quality of institutions and that trade does have a positive effect on institutional quality. Thus, factor endowment, trade and current level of economic development seem to work in a complex process of interdependence that predetermines the type of institutional support that a developmental state requires to achieve its developmental goals.

Patterns of economic and social activities such as consumption, saving, investment, industrial and agricultural production, social customs and other cultural traits tend to differ from region to region within a country. Landlocked African countries in the tropics with persistently hot and humid climates and no direct access to sea routes or to overland routes to large markets have not been able to develop their agricultural sector, industrial sector and international trade (Gallup and Sachs, 1998; Hall and Jones, 1999). Even within the temperate zone, countries closer to the tropics tend to be less well off; and without a coast line a country's trade does not expand as isolation from major markets acts as a disincentive for local industries to increase investment to grow and to remain competitive. Agriculture sometimes cannot expand because of erratic climate and a lack of fertile land. Due to extremely hot weather, labour productivity also tends to remain low.

Lack of trade by eliminating the chance of interaction of the country's population with the outside world prevents the absorption of international best practices in production, consumption and social behaviours by the society and state apparatus. Consequently, low levels of economic growth and human development are likely to persist in such nations. Latin America also suffered from too much rigidity in its class and institutional structure. Therefore, even within a country with a reasonably long coast line, rigidities of old social and economic institutions will remain quite strong in vast inland regions where the mode of production will remain primarily agricultural. The presence of conservatism in social practices, low economic growth and human development will tend to keep peasant societies in poverty and enable vested interest groups to capture state power and to maintain their stranglehold on these regions for a long time.

The disadvantages of a country stemming from its adverse geographical location such as a location in the tropics and isolation from large markets do not necessarily prevent it from achieving growth and development because some of the burdens can be redressed to some extent by framing and adopting growth- and development-friendly policies and governance institutions. However, the locational disadvantage certainly creates difficulties and obstacles that make growth and development more difficult (Perkins et al., 2006).

The favourable influence on a country's trade pattern of its geographical characteristics such as its access to shipping routes and its location closer to major markets was even recognized by Adam Smith (1776). Even to this day countries with easier access to sea-based shipping along long coast lines tend to have larger exports and higher growth than landlocked countries, which face significantly higher transport costs as they have to pay for sea-based shipping as well as overland costs to and from the nearest sea port.

A number of studies (ADB, 1997; Radelet et al., 2001) have argued that favourable geography such as fewer landlocked countries, long coast lines and limited reliance on resource exports enabled the East and South-east Asian countries to grow faster. These factors seem to have contributed one percentage point to these regions' growth relative to the contribution of such factors to tropical Africa's growth and 0.6 percentage points relative to the contribution of such factors to Latin America's growth.

It can be argued that the prospect of a substantial benefit stemming from a country's geographical location tends to be stimulated by favourable historical precedents and to be weakened by adverse historical precedents. In tropical areas, where there was little immigration from colonialist countries, these established mainly extractive institutions giving little benefit to the local population. Where there was substantial immigration, like in South Africa, the institutions were often of better quality. A governance regime primarily interested in rent seeking and political predation would tend to preserve the adverse historical precedent regarding the country's openness to international trade and government institutions and keep the population in poverty. On the other hand, a favourable historical precedent would also tend to provide a strong fillip to the emergence of anti-growth and anti-development governance institutions.

THE FORMATION OF INSTITUTIONS TO PROMOTE GROWTH AND DEVELOPMENT

The responsibility for the formation of enabling institutions rests on the leaders of the governance regime which has captured state power. The leaders of the governance regime are required first to try to get the society to accept them as the legitimate rulers of the country. This is strongly influenced by how the leaders came to power. First, state power can be captured by a coup by a breakaway group of the country's military establishment who then ruthlessly suppress any dissent to their legitimacy to the seat of power. Second, some warlords with the help of their private military outfits may overthrow the incumbent government and capture state power. Third, a number of disgruntled people may form a rebel group opposed to the present regime, which can even be a colonial power, and overthrow the regime by resorting to guerrilla war against the incumbent government. In such a guerrilla war, the rebels often receive military and financial support from a foreign power pretending to be a 'good Samaritan' but with an ulterior motive to further its own economic and political interests after the victory of the rebel group in this conflict. Fourth, in a democracy, the incumbent political party holding state power can be thrown out of office in an election by a political party or by a coalition of political parties opposed to it. These are the most commonly used methods by which state power can be captured by vested interest groups (North, 1981, 1987, 1990) and coalitions of self-interested persons (Olson, 1982).

Establishing Legitimacy

Legitimacy, which refers to the acceptance by the society of the new governance regime, becomes easier to establish if the leaders of the new regime have made great personal sacrifices including the loss of lives of many of their followers to oust the previous oppressive regime from power. The society's endorsement of a rebel group as the legitimate ruler of the state then becomes axiomatic. However, such an endorsement may not last long, if the new governance regime cannot improve the socio-economic status of the wider political elite[2] and of peasants and poorer workers, or if it cannot demonstrate its capability to defend the country against any foreign aggression.

Socio-economic status of wider political elites
Improvement in the socio-economic status of wider political elites can only be achieved through the sustained increase in national income by implementing growth-promoting economic and social policies and by allowing entrepreneurial dynamism to flourish in the economy. Such elites played a powerful role in wealth creation and political governance in many countries in the seventeenth

to nineteenth centuries. Hence, it would be difficult for any ruling class to maintain its legitimacy for a long time without the support of this influential elite class (Nafziger, 2006).

Economic condition of peasants and poor workers

The best way to improve the economic condition of peasants and poor workers would also be to apply measures to increase the income and wealth of the country so that each section of the community can obtain a share of the increase in national wealth by increasing the tax on income and wealth of the wider political elite group and to transfer that additional tax revenue to the working class by bureaucratic action. Measures to supply essential consumption items such as staple foods and fuel to the poor at a very low price through a public distribution network can improve their well-being. On the other hand, local suppliers may suffer from the low prices.

Proven national defence capability

The state authorities are required to make the civil society convinced of its capability to defend the country against a foreign aggressor. To that end the state has to build up a strong military force and to establish a precedent of adequately dealing with an external threat.

The Legitimacy of a Democratically Elected Governance Regime

To democratically elected governance regimes in many developing countries and in Eastern Europe, the term 'establishing legitimacy' is a misnomer as political parties create their separate mafia groups and as political paraformal agents of the incumbent government with the help of the civilian police force routinely rig the election process to keep the incumbent government in power (e.g. Zimbabwe and the Central Asian states).

In Africa, the majority of the democratically elected regimes continue to hold elections to satisfy international norms of 'presentability' but ignore political liberties, the rule of law and separation of power (Nafziger and Auvinen, 2002, 2003). Hence, in many developing countries a regime capturing state power through a pseudo-democratic process can hold on to power without having to justify its legitimacy to the citizens which explains why democratization has taken place in many countries which have not achieved even a minimal rate of growth. Although Sen (1999) refutes one widely held view in East Asia that democratization is directly linked to the rate of economic growth and level of income of a country, it nevertheless is true that a genuine democratization in political governance cannot be achieved prior to a genuine democratization in economic governance which delivers robust growth and economic development outcomes which, in turn, make the population at large strong enough to challenge the legitimacy of a corrupt incumbent government. The East Asian states seem to rely on their economic achievements to justify their view on the democratization process.

INSTITUTIONAL SUPPORT FOR ROBUST GROWTH AND DEVELOPMENT

The Political Governance Regime

Whatever form the state takes, the governance regime must have a strong commitment to the national interest, have a value system about the justice and appropriateness of its actions (North, 1987), and be capable of formulating and implementing economic and social policies for the overall national welfare, even if such policies disadvantage some sections of the community. Such qualities as the honesty, efficiency and integrity of a good government are conditioned by such environmental parameters as cultural norms about the social and economic interactions for executing business transactions.

It has been argued (Friedman, 2005) that in the United States economic growth created conditions conducive to the strengthening of governance. The lessons from European history suggest that various connections exist between the economic and social transformations of the industrial revolution and the process of political modernization (Gill and Kharas, 2007). As the urban population and the country's middle class get better education and earn higher income, they make demands on the government for less corruption and more effective service delivery.

However if there is a history of economic growth being marred by a culture of corruption in economic and social transactions or by a culture of by-passing formal laws, rules and regulations in business transactions within the country or in neighbouring countries, then this historical experience is likely to greatly undermine the prospect of good governance as evidenced in African countries where the state, as Ake (1996) suggests, instead of being a public force, tends to be appropriated to the service of private interests by the dominant faction of the elite. The economic rents that are generated by economics of scale, then, will not lead to sustained growth if they are dissipated in corrupt governments (Gill and Kharas, 2007). If the political elite stands to gain more from development than from predation, it is likely to go for the former. But in order to benefit, those in power must rely on continued political stability. In an unstable political environment predation is the safer alternative, as there is no time to wait for long-run benefits (Blomqvist, 2002).

On the other hand, if a country is located in a dynamic region marked by a culture of good governance then the history of governance is likely to exert a blissful influence on the government of the country. But if a country is surrounded by neighbouring countries which were formerly parts of the same country, then the prevailing culture of governance in the neighbouring countries would tend to be very similar to what exists in the country itself (Roy and Tisdell, 1998).

The geographical area of the state, the structure of the state, the size of its population and the structure of the governance regime also can condition the performance quality of the government. Efficiently managing a large-sized state and a large population is more difficult than managing a small state and population. If the state is unitary, it has a better chance of being governed more efficiently than if it is a federal state or if the state is divided along ethnic or religious lines. If the government is autocratic, it can implement policies in a better way than if it is democratic. Good government can create well-functioning subsidiary institutions.

SUBSIDIARY INSTITUTIONS

Independent Technocracy and Bureaucracy

The independence of technocrats and bureaucrats from the influence of the political leaders is crucial for enhancing the quality of the performance of the governance regime. Technocrats include primarily economists and engineers who are specialists in and capable of formulating plans and programmes for improving a country's growth and development outcomes. Naturally, they work behind the scenes. Only by minimizing their contact with the civil society can their effectiveness be maintained and improved (World Bank, 1993).

They can then formulate national economic policies in a rational way. The bureaucrats, on the other hand, implement economic and social policies and programmes formulated by technocrats. They are in direct contact with the civil society to ensure the frictionless process of implementation programmes. The state's ability to support markets, capital accumulation and economic development depends on the bureaucracy being a coherent entity in which individuals see the furtherance of the nation's goals as the best means of maximizing their individual self-interest. This is a kind of corporate coherence which requires bureaucrats to be insulated from the demands of their political masters and of the surrounding society (Weber, 1968; Meier and Rauch, 2005).

One way of ensuring the insulation of technocrats and bureaucrats from political interference is to have a quasi-judicial body govern their recruitment, salary levels, and career rewards such as promotions and transfers. This may require the construction of a solid authoritarian governance framework as a prerequisite to the operation of the market and state power (Weber, 1968) which are the quintessence of a development state. In contrast, the chances of the effectiveness of technocrats and bureaucrats being severely undermined by their subjugation to their political masters tend to be quite high in many of those developing countries where democratic governance regimes are in control of the state power.

Government-Business Cooperation

Since in almost all states both public and private sector enterprises are crucial for the successful implementation of the state's development programmes and since the policies formulated by the government to implement such programmes will have considerable impact on the ability of these enterprises to undertake the necessary investment and production activities, it is important for the government to maintain regular liaison with the representative bodies of different business organizations before plans for development programmes are formulated and also during the period of implementation of such programmes as the state generally does not have the financial and technical capacity to execute successfully all development programmes. The developmental state model, by relying greatly on technocrats and bureaucrats to plan and implement development programmes, overlooked the central role of government-private sector cooperation (World Bank, 1993).

To ensure a successful coordination between the government and the business community, it is necessary to reassure this community that the private sector organizations would also benefit from higher economic growth. This can only be done by (i) maintaining a relatively honest and competent technocratic cadre insulated from day-to-day political interference and (ii) creating a business-friendly environment.

For achieving this environment, the following are necessary:

1. a simple as well as transparent legal and regulatory structure generally hospitable to business environment;
2. protection of private property, including personal lives of company personnel;
3. maintenance of competition in the markets for labour and other inputs of production;
4. equal treatment of domestic public and private sectors as well as foreign companies in regard to company taxes, business incentives and profit repatriation rules; and
5. provision of adequate infrastructural support such as roads, transport, telecommunication, power supply and so on.

Increasing opportunities for voice and participation in a government-business cooperation council can improve the capability of the state and reduce transaction costs by minimizing the scope for opportunistic action by a powerful minority to monopolize the direction of the government. The participation by stakeholders in the design and implementation of public services or other publicly funded programmes can improve both the rate of return and the sustainability of these activities.

However, the deliberative mechanism of the government-business cooperation council may not be effective in the long run if economic and social policies appear unresponsive to important societal demands. Unfortunately, genuine societal demands are unlikely to grow under democratic governments implementing the governing political party's manifesto, which does not necessarily correspond with these demands.

Education and Human Capital Formation

The availability of high-quality education within the country facilitates the creation of human capital, which in turn enables the government to create and maintain a competent and honest civil service (technocrats and bureaucrats). However, the maximum emphasis in the government's efforts to expand and improve the quality of the country's education system should arguably be placed on primary and secondary education, especially in the poorest countries. Even if the total budgetary expenditures on education as a proportion of the country's GDP remain constant, more resources should be available per child. More emphasis should be given to technical and vocational skill formation in post-secondary education even by importing educational services from developed countries (World Bank, 2003). Unfortunately however, in many developing countries the informal agents of democratically elected governments have infiltrated educational institutions and politically polluted the culture of education under which the genuine institutional performance of accountability to the society has virtually disappeared.

The largest proportion of the budgetary expenditures on education is often incurred to pay for ever increasing salaries and the number of administrative staff of educational institutions, while the smallest proportion is earmarked for improving the infrastructure such as buildings, classroom facilities, etc. In these cases, gross education funding should not be used as a proxy for the advancement in high quality education and human capital formation. Hence, a reordering of priorities in the education budget is required.

Growth of Savings and Investment

A country with a large pool of domestic savings will have less need for foreign investment to generate adequate capital to finance the large increase in investment necessary to generate high economic growth. But the rate of savings as a proportion of GDP can only increase if the government implements policies to achieve the following.

Avoidance of accelerating inflation
A mild rate of inflation by slowly increasing the level of prices and profit may be tolerated, however, and can encourage business enterprises to increase their level of investment expenditure in the economy (cf. Keynes, 1936).

Guarantee the security of banks
Bank security is essential to encourage small and medium-sized households and even small enterprises in the country to increase their saving. One way of achieving this goal is for the government to nationalize all privately owned banks. Such a course of action by eliminating competition among banks in the financial sector is likely to undermine their efficiency in the delivery of financial products to consumers and producers, but banks nevertheless have been nationalized in many developing countries. A better way to assure the security of banks would be to put in place strong and prudent regulation and supervision limits on competition and other institutional reforms.

Availability of small credit for the poor
Setting up so-called microfinance institutions has recently become a popular means for mobilizing capital for smallholders and small enterprises. These persons are not eligible for bank loans and cannot afford the interest rates charged by money lenders.

A positive real interest rate on bank deposits
A positive real interest rate on deposits with commercial banks and a low rate of tax on interest income earned from these deposits would encourage households and small and medium-sized companies to increase their level of saving which through commercial banks and other financial institutions, such as postal saving banks, can be channelled to investment activities within the country.

Land reform and income distribution
Land reform by transforming the rural sectors of a developing country from a large-sized to roughly an equal-sized landholder economy can improve land productivity via increased investment in land and immediately reduce the inequality in income distribution. Such a course of action can facilitate the rural society's acceptance of the legitimacy of the governance regime. However, such a type of land reform policy may not benefit a section of rural households which does not have enough capital to cultivate newly acquired blocks of land. For such households, working as tenant farmers is a better alternative. The experience from land reforms is diverse. In East Asia they

have been successful, while in countries like Zimbabwe and Iran they have been a failure. Also, the government must retain a sizeable proportion of land confiscated from landlords for its use for industrial development.

Culture

A culture influences a society's relationship with the state and its institutions. A homogenous culture accompanied by a homogenous religion and language can instil in people's minds the virtues of discipline in life, hard work, habits of thrift, obedience to superiors and of submission to the state's command, as well as the spirit of enlightened self-interest in economic activities. Such a culture provides one of the most enduring institutional foundations for robust growth and development in any developmental state.

CONCLUSION

After dealing extensively in the foregoing analysis with all important institutional foundations of a developmental state including the enduring influence of history and religion on a country's institutions, in Chapter 3 we will examine which of these aforementioned institutions have been present in the East Asian States and in the Subcontinental State of India.

NOTES

1. One perfect example is that of an attempt by the Indian government to construct a second runway at Calcutta International airport being scuttled by the presence within the airport precinct of an illegally constructed mosque on the land on which the runway is expected to be built. Despite the assurance by the federal government to the local Muslim community to relocate the mosque to a place close to its present location, the Bengal government is not willing to lend a helping hand to the federal government because of the fear of a backlash from the Muslim community at the next provincial election.
2. This wider political group includes political leaders, traditional princes, tribal chiefs, high-ranking military officers, senior civil servants and administrators, executives of public corporations, landowners, major business leaders and successful people from different professions.

3. Institutional foundations of East Asian and South Asian states

In Chapter 2 we have discussed at considerable length the determinants of enabling institutions with particular reference to a country's history of political governance and religious orders, as well as its geographic location and the types of institutions which make it possible for a developmental state to fulfil its goals. In this chapter we will comment briefly on the presence or otherwise in East Asia and South Asia of those enabling institutions allowing developmental state leaders to promote robust economic growth and socio-economic development in their countries. Three major topics are covered in this chapter. We begin by discussing the historical patterns of governance in these nations, then consider the institutional support that the various states have provided for economic development, and finally describe several governmental policies that have proved effective for stimulating development.

HISTORICAL GOVERNANCE

Japan

Japan's rise to an economic superpower began in 1868 under the monarch, Emperor Matsuhito (Meiji), who began to implement reforms to promote Japan's feudal society and economy to a modern industrial state – consisting of thriving manufacturing, mining, banking, transportation and agricultural sectors, financed, developed and controlled by big *zaibatsu* (financial houses) such as Mitsui, Mitsubishi and Sumitomo which continue to dominate the industrial structure to this day. Japan's transition to a rudimentary democratic governance structure began in 1955 with the formation of the Liberal Democratic political party. Although Japan's process of transformation to an economic and industrial superpower accelerated after 1954–55, it nevertheless began much earlier.

Japan's religious and cultural order greatly influenced the formation of growth and development-promoting institutions. Buddhism instilled in people's minds the virtues of diligence, discipline, tolerance, hard work and of the collective submission of the populace to the authority of the state. Hence, the Emperor, who was regarded as God's representative and was considered divine, was the supreme authority of the state and commanded total obedience of his subjects to his laws and dictates.

Buddhism also extols the efforts of its followers to seek knowledge, which is divine and which facilitates the process of attaining enlightenment. But the success of the Japanese system is likely due to the country's ability to emulate 'best practices' from the most developed countries without giving up its own cultural foundations. Starting with the Meiji Emperor, all subsequent leaders, including military dictators, adopted measures to send Japanese citizens to all parts of the world to seek knowledge and to hire European and American experts in many areas to come to Japan to teach Japanese workers, scientists and technicians about Western knowledge and methods of production, to make Japan a superpower. This historic emphasis on the expansion of education and the gathering of knowledge, and not on foreign capital inflow, was the single most important factor in Japan's ascendency to the top of the global technological ladder and in helping Japan to claim its rightful status as the world's second economic superpower (Clark and Roy, 1997).

Buddhism also produced a cohesive society where industry and labour formed a composite production and social unit, in which the labour force did not consider the capitalist as its enemy, thereby ensuring undisturbed industrial peace and uninterrupted production. The cohesiveness of the society is also achieved when people's customs, food habits and language are the same. Historically Japan's developmental state maintained a coherent and competent meritocratic bureaucracy, but also linked its functioning to informal networks between ministries and private sector entrepreneurs to ensure the successful implementation of the state's industrialization programme (Evans, 1992).

Also, throughout the Japanese development programmes' implementation process, consensus formation on any project implementation takes place through many informal networks and intermediate organizations (Okimoto, 1989). While this is a time-consuming process, it helps maintain industrial peace and good relations between all parties. But in this process, industrial labour organizations' role has been absent. Hence, informal networks and arrangements have been an important aspect of Japan's economic development. One language, culture and set of customs have also acted as a powerful force to unite the whole population into a single entity to stand behind the leaders in their pursuit of achieving national development goals.

Japan's geographical features might have contributed to a significant rise, historically, in Japan's maritime trade with Asia and the West. But that was not the case. While there were some sporadic visits by European priests and traders after 1543, these did not lead to any long-term expansion of Japan's trade with the West. Japan virtually maintained its isolation from the rest of the world until the 1853–54 treaty between Japan and the USA under which Japan opened her seaports to US trade.

Taiwan and Korea

Most East Asian countries, with the exception of Japan and Thailand, were colonized either by neighbouring countries or by European imperial forces such as Spain, Portugal, the Netherlands, France and Britain. The major imperial powers in the region – Russia, Japan and China – were also engaged in war among themselves to settle territorial disputes and to expand their respective spheres of influence over North-east Asia. Under the Treaty of Shimonoseki in 1895, which ended the Sino-Japanese war over Korea, China had to cede Taiwan and the Pescadores to Japan, which ruled Taiwan right up to the end of World War II. Japan left Taiwan after its defeat in World War II in 1945. The Nationalist Government in exile, led by Chiang Kai-Shek as the military general of the Nationalist army and the leader of the Kuomintang, the dominant political party, ruled Taiwan after 1949. In Korea too, Japanese rule continued up to the end of World War II.

During their rule, the Japanese developed the agricultural sector and built infrastructure, such as roads and other means of transport and communication, port facilities and so on, in both Korea and Taiwan. They also reformed social and economic institutions according to the Japanese system. Such infrastructure helped the new governments in both countries to kick-start the modern development process (Clark and Roy, 1997). These unitary states were ruled by military leaders for decades. The Japanese rule was a harsh one, however, especially in Korea. There was no democratic governance system in these states but one central government with one centre of power which could kill off any centrifugal tendencies originating in the society and implement economic development programmes with a minimum lag between the time when the blueprint for a programme was finalized and the time when it was implemented. Furthermore, provinces in both states had no sovereign powers and virtually acted as administrative units of the central government. Similar centres of power operated in Japan and in China operate to this day.

An adverse influence of the past history of oppression of the population by colonial rulers on the formation of new institutions was more than counterbalanced by the formation of pseudo-democratic, growth and development-oriented governance regimes in South Korea in the early 1960s and in Taiwan in the early 1950s. Both Taiwan and South Korea, in fact, adopted several Japanese practices in implementing their development programmes.

After Japan was defeated and its colonial rule ended in Korea, Soviet troops occupied the north, and American troops the south, leading to the creation of two hostile authoritarian regimes. After the Korean War began in 1950, the political governance structure and economic conditions remained unstable until General Park Chung Hee formed a new government in 1961. He concentrated on economic development with strong emphasis on industrial development and foreign trade. In pursuance of his economic development goals he, in trying to silence opposition to his rule, jailed many of his opponents, and freedom of speech and press were drastically curtailed. While a formal democratic structure was maintained, he ran a dictatorial regime, which did not allow any disruption to economic and industrial activities by the labour movement, and achieved great success in economic development.

Taiwan historically has been a land of family-based small entrepreneurs – along with large, state-owned enterprises. These small and medium-sized enterprises which have formed the backbone of the Taiwanese economy have developed a wide and intricate network of informal relationships between owners of production units, between producers and input suppliers, including labour in some form of horizontal and vertical integration (Clark and Roy, 1997). The unique feature of the history of political governance in Taiwan is that the state placed a strong emphasis on the central role of markets and of the private sector, including the informal private sector as the engine of growth. For that engine of growth to work, it is necessary for the state to create the enabling environment within which economic agents could operate (Fisher and Thomas, 1990). A big land reform in the early 1950s played an important role in this context (Gunnarsson, 1993).

The history of religious order had a profound influence on the economic and social behaviour of the population and the society in both nations. Buddhism inculcated in its followers' minds the virtues of tolerance to other people and their views and of practising non-violence in all economic and social transactions. On the other hand, Confucian philosophers espoused the virtues of benevolent government, rule by men of virtue and respect for learning, and the virtues of increasing savings for wealth creation. Good governance and economic development based on legalistic principles, honesty, love and filial piety were to bring harmony to the graded hierarchy of family, society and the state, and to nurture the growth of an organic whole. Such teachings helped the family and production unit to become a unified social unit. However, for this to happen it was necessary to regulate human conduct and to subordinate all personal freedom to the objective of creating a strong and prosperous state under a ruler of unlimited authority.

Among the Chinese, including the Taiwanese, the customary attitude of 'you mind your own business and let the authorities mind their own' has permeated the entire fabric of their economic, political and social transactions. With the adherence of the populace to the state's decrees assured, the autocratic and pseudo-democratic governments of these countries were able to build the right kind of growth and development-promoting institutional foundations in these countries. An organic relationship between the employer and labour existed not only in small and medium enterprises (SMEs) in Taiwan, but also in the big conglomerates or chaebol in South Korea. The work ethic and attitudes of labour have been influenced also by the right incentives provided by the state and entrepreneurs and by the availability of productive ideas (Smith, 1997; Wade, 1990).

Easterly and Levine (1997) argue that ethnic diversity tends to reduce economic growth and contributes to government failure. For example, it accounts for much of the poor growth performance of Sub-Saharan Africa. Others (Bates, 1981, 1983) argue that ethnically divided societies are more likely to adopt exceptionally inefficient project-based policies that can be targeted to co-ethnics. Most commentators seem to agree that ethnic diversity acts as a hindrance to economic growth. In the case of South Korea and Taiwan, ethnic and language homogeneity created an enabling environment for state authorities to create growth and development promoting institutions.

The long coast lines and relatively small size of both countries suggest that they would have historically been engaged in foreign trade. However, this seems not to have been the case as their economies were geared towards their common colonial master, Japan. Both countries however, became major trading nations after their economic development programmes began to be implemented after the mid-1950s. It would therefore seem that a country's past history may not always provide a clear indication of what kinds of new institutions would likely be created for the state to fulfil its developmental goals.

China and India: Similar Contexts

Both China and India have a similar turbulent history of political order. Both countries were ravaged by invasion of foreign warlords, dynastic conflicts and attacks by Western powers. Invading warlords butchered hundreds of thousands of people and plundered the wealth of both countries. Both countries had to cede their respective territories due to certain political arrangements over which the citizens and their leaders had very little control.

However, to the Chinese, ceding of territories was a temporary necessity, and they firmly believed that China's territorial integrity had to be restored. On the other hand, such a firm belief in India's territorial integrity rarely existed among Indian leaders and citizens. This was primarily due to the fact that India, historically, was like a confederation of many sovereign independent countries. Consequently such a spirit of nationalism as one can find in China could very rarely grow in a confederate India.

Both China and India have long navigable coast lines. The limited information that we have (Majumdar et al., 2009) of India's trade in ancient times would suggest that Alexander's invasion of India in 326 BC opened up India's trade with Greece. Later, trade also took place between India and Rome. Apart from these, trading journeys were undertaken by Indians to the coasts of Burma, Malaya, Ceylon, the Philippines and Babylon. Adam Smith (1776, 1976) referred to China, Bengal (India) and Egypt as major nations which sold their produce to the most expensive markets in the world. Another scholar (Raychaudhuri, 1968) provided a vivid account of China's and India's importance in the seventeenth and eighteenth centuries as two major Asian trading countries with rich merchant classes and well-built ships. However, during the Ming Dynasty in China the country turned inwards, and while trade took part mainly through the so-called Silk Road, trade exchange with the rest of the world was quite limited. India's major items of export were manufactures and some raw materials for European factories. During British rule, India's trade continued to prosper and Bengal maintained its importance as a major centre of India's international trade and commerce even though the British suppressed the development of the Indian manufacturing sector.

In the early 1950s, the new political regimes, which completely closed off both economies to the outside world, failed to utilize the advantages that the favourable geographic location of a country for creating robust growth-oriented institutions provides. However, China after 1980 and India after 1991 finally embraced an outward orientation in their economic policies, which enabled both countries to make greater use of their locational advantages for accelerating the pace of development. But the advantages of a favourable geography did not spread evenly across all regions. For example, in both China and India vast inland areas remain impoverished. In India, while Bengal under communist rule became increasingly inward looking and sank deeper into poverty and lawlessness, other southern and western provinces embraced all the institutions of outward orientation and market-led development and continued to achieve higher growth and development outcomes than the rest of India.

China

Throughout history, amidst changes in the dynastic political order, a deep undercurrent of a common governance goal passed through all regimes to unite all disparate and far-flung regions of China into one unified empire, with all powers formally residing with the Emperor. The rulers of the Chinese imperial dynasties cherished the same goal of creating a power-ful unified empire. However, the nineteenth century and the first half of the twentieth century witnessed two parallel trends: (i) a rapid deterioration of the imperial system, and (ii) a steady increase in foreign pressure from the Western powers and Japan for trade concessions and, more importantly, for territory. Dr Sun Yat-Sen's attempt to establish a Republican (Nationalist) Government led by his Kuomintang party was only partially successful, was never in full control of the country's whole territory and was swept away in the end by Mao Zedong's communist revolution in 1949. This event finally re-established a unified, powerful, monolithic and centrally controlled nation state in China.

In the history of political order in China, one school of thought which exercised lasting influence on Chinese civilization and political order was 'legalism' which called for the establishment of a social order based on strict and impersonal laws, and enforced by a wealthy and powerful state with a ruler wielding unquestioned authority over all aspects of the state's affairs. This aspect of legalism, requiring total obedience of the society to the commands of the state, which is an essential trait of Confucian culture, has helped China to realize its development goals, even during the late twentieth and early twenty first centuries, although Bramall (2009) tends to think that culture changes very slowly and hence the beneficial impact of Confucian culture on the Chinese society and economy may have been inflated. Nevertheless, one important point to note here is that in 1949, the territory that Mao took control of was almost – with the exception of Tibet, Taiwan, Hong Kong and Macau – an organic whole. This is where the major difference lies between the capabilities of the Chinese polity after 1949 and Indian polity after 1947 to formulate and implement their respective development programmes.

In China, Confucianism, Taoism and Buddhism did exercise strong influence on society. Confucianism and Taoism assimilated the fundamentals of Buddhism which places a strong emphasis on a human being's duty to a fellow human being and on the right path to escape from the hardships of life and to achieve salvation and eternal happiness. But it is Confucian teachings which had a profound impact on the formation of growth and development-promoting institutions (Clark and Roy, 1997) by emphasizing the need for (i) the establishment of an orderly, graded society, (ii) strict controls to regulate human conduct, (iii) strict laws and harsh punishments in the control of every aspect of human society, and (iv) the subordination of all personal freedom to the objective of creating a strong and prosperous state under a ruler of unlimited authority. These teachings over centuries guided human behaviour and social and economic practices. Thus, a totally centralized administration and pervasive state control over the economy and society could become an accepted fact after Mao's takeover of China from the Nationalist rulers, despite the fact that the Communist regime denounced Confucianism as such and tried to eradicate the old ways.

Confucian support for economic development, wealth creation and hard work by people might have encouraged the population at large to be very frugal in their consumption habits and to work hard to increase wealth whenever possible, irrespective of whatever kind of work place environment they were in. This became even more important after Deng Xiaoping's reforms from the late 1970s, which gradually increased individual freedom to accumulate some assets.

India

The history of political order in India is extremely important, as these features had a defining influence on the future performance capability of India's governments. First, historically, India as one country has existed only in name because, within its geographical boundaries, many kingdoms and principalities existed and were ruled by sovereign monarchs and princes and princesses. There was no democratic political governance; and the administration of these territories was centralized. People of different kingdoms spoke different languages and practised different customs.

Second, since the Aryan invasion began in the third millennium BC (Majumdar et al., 2009), foreign warlords at regular intervals attacked parts of the country, plundered its wealth, and slaughtered its population. Some established feudal dynasties, while others plundered parts of the country, killed many people and left with the loot. Alexander's invasion of India took place during 327–26 BC. The first Islamic invasion under the Afghan warlord Sabuktagin during 986–87 AD was followed by an invasion by Sultan Mahmud in 1001 AD and by many others, until Babur established the dynastic rule of the Mughals in 1526.

The Dutch, the Portuguese, the French and the British began to take control of parts of Indian territories from the sixteenth century onwards. Finally the East India Company took control of Bengal, India's most prosperous territory with a decent coast line for seafaring trade, by defeating the army of the Nawab of Bengal in the Battle of Plassey in 1757, thereby heralding the beginning in India of British rule which was to last for nearly 200 years up to August 1947. Such repeated invasion by foreign warlords and countries could not contribute to the maintenance of peace and stability necessary for increasing wealth and prosperity of Indians at large.

Third, none of the foreign invaders, including the British, was able to capture all territories within India. Even before the British left India, there were more than 600 princely kingdoms which could not be brought under the direct administration of the British Raj. Even when a foreign power attacked one kingdom within India, other rulers did not unite to put up a strong opposition to the invaders.

While a number of these foreign rulers implemented welfare programmes for their citizens, the most, by and large, built monuments to glorify their rule. The population at large within India in the nineteenth century and early part of the twentieth century lived under extreme poverty as the small scale textile industry was virtually destroyed by the British trade policy; and agriculture could not provide them subsistence income due to the vagaries of the monsoon. India's trade and commercial policy during the British rule was framed and used by the British government to extract net wealth from India and not to industrialize and develop the country (Saul, 1960; Roy, 1988).

Fourth, the political butchery of India began when the British, after keeping Burma for 52 years as a province of India, separated it in 1937. No sound political order interested in India's development would have done that. Then in August 1947, India was cut into three pieces by the stakeholders, several of whom were driven by their self-interest and a desire for self-aggrandizement. After the Cripps mission, which arrived in India in 1941 seeking a political solution to India's future political order, was sent back to Britain by Gandhi and Nehru, a greatly weakened Britain led by a delighted Churchill immediately adopted the policy of partition of India. Edwina Mountbatten, the wife of Viceroy Lord Mountbatten, played a big role in getting Nehru to agree to the political partition of India (Rakshit, 2009; Majumdar et al., 2009; Mukherjee, 2009). Lord Mountbatten was also successful in isolating Gandhi from Patel and Nehru (Puri, 2009).

Nehru and Jinnah, two extremely ambitious leaders, were desperate to be rulers of the two parts. These self-styled leaders who came from very wealthy families professed to represent the interests of both countries, while the main stakeholders, the masses, had no voice in the creation of two new political orders based on religion. The Governor of Bengal, Mr Herbert, prevented a coalition government combining Hindus and moderate Muslims from taking effect in Bengal in 1943. If such a coalition had been established there might not have been a partition of India (Mukherjee, 2009). Finally Gandhi did not voice any strong and forceful opposition to the Nehru–British–Jinnah plan for the partition of India, because he was outplayed by the British.

The British administration was a highly centralized political governance system and no experiment was undertaken in political democracy before India gained independence and adopted full parliamentary democracy with many political parties at both the federal and provincial levels. If Nehru and the Congress Party had provided the British in 1935 a plan for the experiment in provincial autonomy with a chance to succeed, then Indians would have gained experience in democratic practices; and India also might not have been partitioned.

In the absence of the truly national leader, Subhas Bose, who fled to Germany from India to raise a Nationalist army to drive the British out of India, there was no one who could unite the country to make it a powerful entity, and hence the spirit of nationalism could not grow in India as it had grown under the leadership of Chairman Mao in China.

Fifth, a democratic political order combined with a low level of political institutionalization in the country contributed to the rise of self-styled leaders from different ethnic minorities and other special interest groups professing to champion the causes of these groups and succeeding in carving out a new province for these leaders and their groups (Huntington, 1968). Consequently, at the time of India's independence there were 14 provinces, but now there are 29. Again, within each province, there is democratic political governance at the village level as well. Hence, the process of decision making is extremely slow, and it is very difficult for the government at the centre to quickly implement any law or development programme throughout the country.

The political party which captures power at the provincial level tends to ignore constitutional limits on its power and to maintain paraformal agents such as cadres of the communist party of India (Marxists) in Bengal, who act like private armed forces and continue to distort democratic institutions (Zakaria, 1997; Joseph, 1987; Barkan and N'gethe, 1998; Gyimah-Boadi, 1998). In several of these provinces, the party controlling the political power tends to act like a feudal lord (Bardhan, 1984, 1998).

The evolution of India's political order indicates a trend towards the further breaking up of current provinces into many ethnically based provinces. This is an outcome of the imposition of a democratic polity on a society which had no previous experience in democracy. Therefore, the beneficial influence of the history of India's political order on the evolution of growth and development promoting institutions has been marginal.

In India, religious conflict has clearly hurt the nation. The main rationale behind the division of India into three parts in August 1947 was the religious conflict between Hindus and Muslims which engulfed eastern and western India in 1946. The British administration in India indirectly and sometimes directly might have contributed to the rise of religious disharmony between Hindus and Muslims (Mukherjee, 2009; Majumdar et al., 2009). This division of the country on the ground of religious disharmony almost undermined the prospect of robust growth and development-promoting institutions for a long time and concentrated the government's efforts on secondary issues.

For a long time before Partition, neither Hinduism nor Islam was able to mould the social customs and habits and economic behaviour of its followers in a way which facilitated the creation by the state of appropriate institutions for development. For example, Hinduism, like Buddhism, teaches its followers not to indulge in material happiness and wealth creation because when we leave the earth, all possessions will be left behind (Chai and Roy, 2006). Such teaching could have had a dampening effect on an individual's marginal propensity to save. Many religious practices which came to be accepted as social customs were rigid and regressive and have not been conducive to growth and development. Nevertheless, this is hardly the only explanation. In other cultural and political contexts, particularly in the Diaspora, both Muslims and Hindus have proved to be very successful economically.

INSTITUTIONAL SUPPORT FOR GROWTH AND DEVELOPMENT

The Legitimacy of Governance Regimes

The leaders of the governance regimes which captured state power have historically been authorized by the society to create growth-promoting economic and social institutions in their own countries. But since their capability to complete the task successfully depends on the society's acceptance of the new regime, we briefly comment here on the perceived legitimacy of governance regimes which captured state power in East Asia, China and India.

Korea and Taiwan

The leaders of Korea and Taiwan made enormous personal sacrifices. The Korean War in the early 1950s devastated the country's economy, contributed to the loss of lives of millions of civilians and soldiers, and ended with a partition of the Korean peninsula into a communist-led North Korea and a South Korea that fell under the leadership of the authoritarian Yi Seungman (known in the West as Syngman Rhee). Korean society, tired of war and destruction, as well as the economic mismanagement of Yi, eventually accepted semi-military rule.

The Taiwanese government was a semi-military one, too, in the beginning. After General Chiang Kai-shek, having failed to halt the advance of Mao Zedong's communist armies, fled from China to Formosa Island (Taiwan) along with a large number of followers, he established the legitimacy of his government by ruthlessly suppressing any opposition of local Islanders to his rule as well as by implementing economic and social policies which promoted the role of market forces and entrepreneurial dynamism of the Islander elite class, as well as by undertaking land reform measures under which large blocks of land were broken up into small units and handed over to rural families to transform Taiwan's entire rural sector to a small landholder rural community. Both measures ensured an uninterrupted process of wealth creation and improved income distribution, moving forward in tandem. South Korean rulers also followed a similar policy of land reform (World Bank, 1993; Clark and Roy, 1997; Chai and Roy, 2006; Gill and Kharas, 2007; Meier and Rauch, 2005).

China

In China, after the civil war that erupted in 1946 between Kuomintang troops and Mao's rebels ended in 1949 due to the collapse of the Nationalist Government's resistance against Mao's forces, the communists, to establish legitimacy by eliminating all opposition by potential enemies to their rule, executed millions of so-called counter revolutionaries, among whom were hundreds of thousands of landlords.

To promote recovery and to redistribute gains from economic growth to the population at large, farmlands from landlords were seized and redistributed among peasants who were persuaded as well as forced to combine their land holdings into agricultural cooperatives which eventually operated as large communes to improve the savings rate and the efficiency of farm workers. All industries were brought under state control. At the social level, to make women equal partners in development, they were assured a position of equality with men and provided with equal rights with respect to employment, ownership of property and divorce.

India

The leaders of the Congress Party-led governance regime which took over the administration of India from the British Raj did not fight a long drawn-out and bloody conflict. There was very little bloodshed by Nehru and his close associates. Nehru was imprisoned by the British a few times, but that imprisonment was primarily used by the Congress Party to build Nehru's image as the only national leader to administer the country and to facilitate society's acceptance of the legitimacy of the Nehru-led governance regime.

The country's growth and development objectives were sought to be pursued through state ownership and control of all major means of production such as key industries and services, minerals and the major means of transport, while remaining private industries were heavily regulated. The resolution to this effect by the Congress Party in its Karachi Session in 1931 was described by Nehru, a Fabian socialist enamoured with Russia's industrialization, as a very short step in the socialist direction (Paranjape, 1964). This was, to Nehru, the only way that the population at large could get a share of the benefits of growth and development.

However, agriculture remained in private hands and land reform was not carried out, with the result that the Indian agricultural sector consisted of four categories of stakeholders: (i) landlords; (ii) tenant farmers; (iii) small landholders; and (iv) landless labourers. The result was that the agricultural sector could not become a catalyst for generating savings for industrialization and for a more even distribution of income. India's First Five Year Plan does not list economic growth and land reform as important measures to improve the socio-economic status of the peasants and poor workers, and to establish the legitimacy of the Nehru regime.

India's First Five Year Plan (GOI, 1957) had two objectives. The first was aimed at correcting the disequilibrium in the economy resulting from World War II and the partition of the country, and the second was aimed at kick-starting a process of balanced development which would ensure a rising national income and a steady improvement in living standards over a period. But the Plan document did not explain the nature of the disequilibrium and how it was to be corrected. Second, it was also not explained how the elites, peasants, the poor and other sections of the community would benefit from the rise in national income.

India versus East Asia

In East Asia and China, the governments played a crucial role in propelling the economies to a higher and higher growth trajectory. The state in these countries was unitary, and the governments were more or less authoritarian. The leaders, with a strong commitment to national interest and with an inbuilt value of fairness and justice, were able to formulate and implement policies, because the governments they were heading were autocratic. In India, the state is federal and there are 30 governments (one federal and 29 provincial, including territories). Even a democratic government would not be ipso facto harmful to a country's growth and development prospects, provided it is a unitary state, and there is one democratically elected government. But India is a federal state, with many governments elected by popular vote. There is a large number of political parties contesting elections of 30 governments. If Nehru had chosen to follow India's history of political order, he would have preferred a monarchy-style government with all power held by the centre and with the provinces ruled by appointed governors and not by democratically elected governments. But Nehru did not follow the lessons of history. Today, no law can be passed and applied, and no development programme can be formulated and implemented quickly and uniformly throughout the country because of India's dysfunctional democracy. On the other hand, all major East Asian states followed the lessons of history and accordingly formed appropriate political institutions to successfully implement their growth and development strategies.

Proven Capability to Defend the Country's Territory

Mao and his communist regime provided ample proof of their capability to defend the territorial integrity of China against foreign aggression, first by uniting the vast expanse of the far-flung Chinese empire under the rule of the centralized communist government after defeating the Nationalist army.

Then in its attempt to regain areas which it considered to be within the historic boundaries of China, the communist regime invaded Tibet in 1950 and forced Tibet to accept Chinese rule. Then, in 1959, Chinese troops penetrated and occupied 31,000 square kilometres of a common border territory with India. China considered these territories as its own.

In 1962 again, serious military conflict erupted between China and India when Chinese troops advanced on both the eastern and Ladakh borders of India. In both cases, Nehru failed to provide a strong leadership and to prove his regime's capability to defend the territorial integrity of the country against what Indians consider as Chinese aggression (Majumdar et al., 2009).

The total Indian territory currently under the control of the Chinese state stands at around 41,500 square kilometres. Now again the Chinese have laid claim to Arunachal Pradesh – a province of India in the North East, as Chinese territory. The Government of India's response to such Chinese claims has been mute. China considers this Indian province as a disputed territory, primarily because it does not accept the McMohan line which demarcated the border of India in 1915. However such border disputes have raised tension in both countries and are undermining their political and economic relations.

In 1947, after Partition, the state of Jammu and Kashmir was attacked by Pakistani warlords and their troops with the tacit support of the Pakistan Government. While Indian troops were forcing Pakistani troops to pull out completely from Jammu and Kashmir, Nehru decided to take this territorial dispute to the UN Security Council on 31 December 1947. More than 60 years have passed since then but the Kashmir problem remains unresolved.

Effective Technocracy and Bureaucracy

To ensure that a high rate of economic growth is achieved and sustained for a long period of time, as well as to ensure that the benefits of growth are passed on to the various groups of society, highly competent technocrats were recruited to formulate policies and plans for development and bureaucrats to implement those programmes of development in East Asia. The independence of the technocracy and the bureaucracy from interference in their activities by political leaders has been sought to be achieved by establishing a recruitment system based purely on merit and by providing a compensation package consisting of salary, other perks and prestige, guaranteed post-retirement income and security of tenure. These packages were similar to those offered by private companies to their top executives. Also promotion to higher positions was based strictly on merit and those occupying the highest positions received high rewards (World Bank, 1993).

Japan

It has been suggested (Johnson, 1982) that the greatest concentration of brain power in Japan has been in the Ministry of International Trade and Industry (MITI). Official agencies have attracted the most talented graduates of the country and the positions of those bureaucrats who are promoted to a very high level in those ministries are also the most prestigious in the country. Although bureaucrats in Japan follow a long-term career path and in performing their duties adhere to rules and established norms, they nevertheless make extensive use of their informal networks called *Gakubatsu* which is a network of classmates from elite universities from which the officials are recruited. These informal networks provide the bureaucracy with an internal coherence and corporate identity which the meritocratic process of the recruitment of bureaucrats alone would not have been able to achieve.

Korea and Taiwan

Despite having different state structures, different social bases of support and different policy strategies (Cheng, 1987), the policy initiatives facilitating industrial transformation in both South Korea and Taiwan were anchored by a coherent and competent bureaucratic organization which exhibits elements of Weberian embedded autonomy (Weber, 1968). Starting with Park's regime, the Korean bureaucracy has recruited its staff from among the most talented graduates of the most prestigious universities.

In Taiwan, the KMT set up a small number of elite policy organizations similar to Japan's MITI and Korea's EPB (Economic Planning Board) in terms of scope and expertise (Wade, 1990). Different sections of ministries are staffed by competent bureaucrats with knowledge and expertise in those particular areas. For example, the Council of Economic Planning and Development (CEPD) is staffed by an economic general staff, whereas the Industrial Development Bureau (IDB) of the Ministry of Economic Affairs is staffed mostly by engineers. These specialists, who are among the best and brightest in the country, were generally members of the KMT and graduates of Taiwan National University, which is the country's most prestigious university (Wade, 1990).

In Taiwan, the long bureaucratic tradition provided the KMT with a strong foundation on which to build the structure of a developmental state. The party organization provided political cohesion at the top of the ministries and the economic bureaucracy, with sufficient managerial expertise that laid out and managed development programmes. These bureaucrats, who were recruited through a meritocratic process and who largely came from Taiwan's elite universities, played a major role in managing the island nation's industrial policy (Wade, 1990).

Although the private sector in Taiwan was not, in the past, involved in economic policy networks to the same extent as it has been in Japan and

Korea, the current trend is to institutionalize decision making inputs from industrial organizations, finance companies and other private sector operators. Nevertheless, although the state in Taiwan is not isolated from the private sector, it seems to operate more effectively with a smaller set of public sector-private sector network ties than in Japan and Korea.

Other East Asia

Both in Singapore and Malaysia the civil service was originally largely moulded on the British system. In Singapore, bureaucrats are recruited strictly on the basis of merit through a very rigorous civil service examination process. However, lateral recruitment from other sectors is also allowed (Low, 1998; Cheung, 2003). These bureaucrats are paid high salaries which can even be greater than those received by ministers. In both Singapore and Malaysia, the social status of bureaucrats sometimes appears to be higher than that of ministers. The quality of the civil service is therefore very high. In Malaysia, the civil service examination system is of less importance because of the systematic positive discrimination of *bumiputeras* (indigenous people, mainly Malays) as positions are kept reserved for this group (Common, 2003).

India

In India bureaucrats are recruited through civil service examinations. The British Raj set up the Indian Civil Service cadre (ICS) to administer the Indian Colony; after the British left India, the name Indian Civil Service was changed to Indian Administrative Service (IAS). Within the IAS, there are different categories of administrative services for managing various public sector units such as the Indian Railway Service for managing Indian Railways; and the Indian Revenue Service for managing tax revenues and other financial matters. At the provincial level there are similar provincial services such as the West Bengal Civil Service (WBCS), Orissa Civil Service (OSC) and so on. Those who pass these examinations are employed in various departments of the respective provincial governments.

For managing economic affairs, there is the Indian Economic Service (IES). Those who pass the IES examination become technocrats and are employed at the Indian Planning Commission, the Department of Economic Affairs, and at the Ministries of Commerce and Trade. Those who pass these IAS and IES examinations and those who pass Provincial Civil Service examinations are immediately employed by federal and state governments. Their positions become permanent; and they cannot be sacked by their political masters. However, in recent years Indian Civil Service examinations at both the federal and provincial level have not been as stringent as those in some other Asian countries.

In recent years, the integrity of the IAS examination and the Provincial Civil Service examinations process appears to have been compromised. At the same time, the integrity and independence of bureaucrats at both the federal and provincial level seem less secure than in Japan, Korea and Singapore. The total size of the Indian bureaucracy, consisting of bureaucrats at the federal and provincial levels, is very large; and that size itself acts as a powerful deterrent to its effectiveness as a cohesive unit for quick action. While bureaucrats' employment cannot be terminated, they can be transferred to distant regions of the country by their displeased political masters. Even the parliament can attack civil servants' integrity. The role played by parliament and political parties in undermining morale in public sector enterprises and in administrative services generally has, however, been almost unique to the Indian scene (Bhagwati and Desai, 1971).

Because of a lack of coordination between different ministries, any solution to a particular issue which requires clearance from several ministries may be considerably delayed. Even within each ministry, the same file has to move from one desk to a few others before it can be transferred to another ministry. Because of such inordinate delays in the decision making process, no quick solution to any urgent matter can be expected. Hence, to cope with large burdens, the administrative structure grows in size, and as its size increases, it becomes slower in its operations (Hanson, 1966).

India versus East Asia
The ineffectiveness and inefficiency of the Indian bureaucracy cannot be attributed solely to its generalist nature, lack of coordination between bureaucrats of different departments and so on. During nearly 200 years of British rule, ICS officers consisting of both Indian and British personnel excelled in their jobs and kept the British administration running smoothly. The power and prestige enjoyed by those bureaucrats was similar to those enjoyed by bureaucrats in Japan, Korea, Taiwan and Singapore. Therefore the question that needs to be asked is why bureaucracy appears to be so efficient in East Asia compared with that in India, and why the integrity of bureaucrats is compromised in India and not in East Asia.

In answer to those two questions, one can argue that in East Asia, the extremely rigorous selection process, combined with the power, prestige and high salary associated with the position, tends to keep bureaucrats honest and prevent the occurrence of an unholy alliance between bureaucrats and political leaders. Bureaucrats' compensation packages also compare very favourably with those offered to executives in private sector companies.

In India, the salaries of civil service personnel were not comparable to those of executives in private sector organizations. That anomaly has been rectified in recent years. But the power and prestige of bureaucrats have waned considerably, and their independence and integrity also may have been compromised by the intrusion of political factors into the bureaucratic decision making process (Rudolph and Rudolph, 1987; Taub, 1969). The widespread nature of bureaucratic controls, leading to the inevitable corruption of some sections of the bureaucracy and of politicians in power, made for many attacks on the integrity of politicians and civil servants at the federal level by self-appointed watchdogs in Parliament as early as in the 1960s (Bhagwati and Desai, 1971).

The prevailing work ethic and culture are also important factors. East Asian culture, which regards civil servants highly, does possess an advantage in building bureaucracies. Under Confucianism, passing a civil service examination or getting a civil service promotion becomes similar to being inducted into a hall of fame. It provides a signal to the community at large that these service holders are special human beings.

In India, there is no Confucian culture. There are two major religions and several minor ones. Since religion influences culture, with many religions, a uniform culture has failed to emerge in India. Moreover political parties are primarily responsible for encouraging the society, including bureaucrats, not to adhere strictly to their cultural values. Governments can create an environment for the promotion of an appropriate culture to achieve high growth and development.

In East Asia, democratic governance is more or less missing, except in Japan. Most governments are autocratic and there is one centre of power. Therefore political leaders, once in government, do not have to worry about losing their jobs soon. Thus they can be genuinely interested in formulating and implementing programmes for national development. But in India there are democratically elected governments formed by a coalition of political parties at the federal and provincial levels. The number of provinces has increased from 14 in the 1950s to 29 in 2011. Therefore, there are in the country 30 sets of bureaucratic structures, of which 29 are at provincial administration and one is at federal administration. Since governments, particularly at the provincial level, can easily stay in power by vote rigging, they have a tendency to use bureaucrats and the police force to help capture votes at the next election. Therefore, political leaders and political parties are primarily responsible for incapacitating the institution of bureaucracy in India.

Douglass North (1987), in explaining the four important determinants of transaction costs, placed a great deal of emphasis on the need for parties undertaking any economic transaction to have some conviction about the justice and appropriateness of the society and economic system they are operating in. If ministers and other political leaders at all levels of government who are directly involved in economic and social transactions possess some conviction about justice while transacting business, the integrity, independence and efficiency of bureaucrats will not be compromised. East Asian political leaders by and large do seem to possess such a sense of justice and a strong ideological conviction which drive them towards achieving their national development goals.

In Korea a grouping of junior military officers who came to power under Park's leadership was driven by a strong ideological conviction and was united by reformist convictions, close interpersonal ties and *Gakubatsu*-like network ties originating in the military academy (Meier and Rauch, 2005). The leverage provided by their own corporate solidarity helped these military officers holding top positions in the government to both strengthen and discipline the bureaucracy. But in Korea there is no such multi-party democratic government as in India.

As opposed to other East Asian countries, there is no independent bureaucracy in China. The civil service at all levels is always subject to the will of the Party, and the party officials are the ones that are the real decision makers. The integrity of the bureaucracy cannot thus be assured. However, bureaucrats and political leaders alike are driven by a spirit of nationalism. Therefore achieving national goals became a matter of paramount importance to political leaders and bureaucrats, even if the system must be less than perfectly efficient. In India, such a spirit is lacking among most political leaders.

Ethnicity, Race and Culture

A nation's social institutions also shape its developmental potential quite significantly. Bauer (1984) attributed a country's growth to its reliance on the free market and to some intangible characteristics which are natural to certain ethnic groups. Bauer held the view that, given the same liberal social environment in a foreign country, Indian emigrants would be less ingenious, energetic, resourceful and industrious than Chinese emigrants (Srinivasan, 1984). While scholars tend to disagree with this view, they feel that certain traits of a population do change to fit the evolving needs of social and productive structures. However, this change is brought about by a strong authoritarian government. It has the capability to minimize the adverse effect of ethnicity on people's work ethic and industry, and to engage them in creating wealth instead of transfer activities.

In East Asia, such governments have historically existed; and also there is homogeneity in ethnicity and race in Korea, Taiwan and China. In India, there is no single, strong, authoritarian government in which the sovereign power resides. Among the 29 provincial governments, the primary objective has been to stay in political power by capturing the votes of different ethnic groups. This involves encouraging ethnic divisions within the country and even ethnic and race-related violence, and by allowing these groups the freedom to break laws and to disrupt productive activities. This has encouraged the growth of transfer activities within the country. In contrast, homogeneous ethnicity and race combine with homogeneous language to create one national identity, which is beneficial for economic growth and for the population. This has happened in China, Korea and Taiwan, but not in India.

While Confucian teachings inculcated in people's minds the virtues of respect for and obedience to superiors, respect for knowledge, high savings and deferred gratification, promotion of wealth, observance of state laws, and so on, the influence of the teachings of Hinduism on Indians was minimized by the actions of their leaders and their semi-formal agents to promote rent seeking and transfer activities in democratic India.

Business-Government Relations

Japan

The East Asian countries historically have encouraged private sector enterprises to undertake growth-promoting investment activities, while the state has continued to play a powerful role in the development dynamics of all the major East Asian countries. The relationship between private sector enterprises and the government has taken a more formal shape in Japan and South Korea than in Taiwan. The state has provided a transparent and simple legal as well as regulatory environment for private sector entrepreneurs to increase their level of investment in these economies (World Bank, 1993). To that end, governments established cooperative relations with big businesses, as well as with labour, by setting up a support network for small and medium-sized enterprises (SMEs). The support network for SMEs included, among other things, financial support to improve technology to help them capture export markets and direct help from the government to identify importers of consumer goods and the types of goods that they want to import. Japan's industrial policy has depended fundamentally on the ties connecting MITI (Ministry of International Trade and Industry) and major industrial powerhouses (Okimoto, 1989). The business–government relationship is reinforced by the presence of retired senior MITI personnel in key positions in major private corporations as well as in industry associations and quasi-governmental organizations which form the intermediate organizational network and informed policy networks, within which deliberations take place to reach consensus on all issues affecting the trade and industrial development of the country. While some (Samuels, 1987) may argue that the effectiveness of the Japanese state as a facilitator of development has depended on the stability and complexity of its interaction with private sector businesses, others (Meier and Rauch, 2005) tend to present the view that the internal bureaucratic coherence has been an essential precondition for the Japanese state's effective participation in external networks for the following reasons:

1. The state could not have been able to participate in external networks if MITI were not a highly competent and cohesive organization.
2. The state could not have been able to get private sector entrepreneurs to engage actively in deliberations to reach a consensus in major industrial and trade matters, if MITI were not an autonomous unit capable of setting its own goals and of ensuring, with the support of its staff, the realization of those goals.

Our view is that both state and external networks have been proactive in developing and nurturing this government-business relationship in Japan.

Korea, Taiwan and Singapore
In Korea, although Park during the early period of his presidency was not favourably disposed to the involvement of private capital in the country's development, he soon began to realize the need for and the importance of dynamic entrepreneurs and expert managers to promote industrial development in Korea. Since private entrepreneurs did not have enough capital to develop industries, they also had to rely on the state to supply that capital. The state also wanted its capital to be concentrated in a fewer hands which will facilitate the implementation of its strategy for industrial transformations. Thus was established a symbiotic relationship between the Korean state and giant private sector chaebol (Mee, 1987; Soo, 1987). However, in this relationship, which has not been institutionalized in the same way as that between MITI and private sector corporations in Japan, networks and other intermediaries played no role and the state was the dominant partner. Since the early 1990s, the Korean state has been trying to downgrade this relationship of interdependence to reduce the opportunities for chaebol to seek favours from the government, while the chaebol for their part used their increased economic power to resist government policies (Haggard and Moon, 1990).

In Taiwan, although the relationship between the state and the private sector business has not been institutionalized as in Japan or even to the same extent as in Korea, the Taiwanese state has nevertheless not been isolated from the private sector (Gold, 1986). During the three decades from the early 1950s to the late 1970s, the state directed its efforts to building up state-operated enterprises (SOEs) which were to take the leadership role in the country's industrial development. The state provided support to export-oriented private sector firms to become competitive in the global market. In the 1950s, it picked up the textile industry and in the 1970s, the semiconductor industry, both of which had considerable export potential, for its support. Such support was provided through Industrial Development Bureau (IDB) officials who provided administrative guidance and through SOEs, which provided entrepreneurial guidance (Wade, 1990). Then the state also spent a considerable amount of its resources to set up an agency called the China Export Trade Development Council (CETDC) with the primary objective of creating opportunities for hundreds of small and medium-sized enterprises (SMEs) to upgrade and adapt their technology to capture the US and other industrial countries' market.

From 1980 onwards, the officers of the CETDC's New York office were engaged in field research to find out the country of origin of import of various consumer goods into the US market, as well as the prices and designs of these products. After they identified those products which Taiwanese firms could produce at prevailing import prices in the US, these officers sent the information to the relevant firms and asked them to send their samples and price lists to the CETDC office in New York. After these officers received the samples, they approached the relevant importers with those samples for their reaction. If it was positive, they sent the contact details of these importers to the firms in Taiwan which had supplied the samples (Smith, 1997).

Wade (1990) found the existence of this interaction between state agencies and private firms in negotiations between raw material suppliers and final goods producers in textile companies in the synthetic fibre industry. The main reason for such interaction was to ensure the process of backward integration into intermediary products. Thus, the progress of textile goods towards achieving export competitiveness would not be undermined by conflicts between import suppliers and final output producers in the textile sector. At the same time, one has to note that the Taiwanese state wanted to preserve its autonomy as well as maintain market competition. Both of these goals could be achieved by maintaining an informal public-private network, not by a deeper and more formalized network as in Japan and Korea (Meier and Rauch, 2005).

In Singapore, public and private sector participation in policy-making takes place in several ways, such as private citizens serving on government statutory boards as directors or serving as members on government committees to review policy and to make recommendations to the government. Also, the government invites comments from professional bodies on specific issues.

India

In India there has not been a formal institutionalized network between the state and private sector businesses as in Japan. But some form of informal relationship seems to exist. There were two major reasons for the lack of such formal relationships. First, although historically India was a land of private enterprises, a culture of apathy and hatred towards private sector capital began to grow after the adoption by the government of India of the Second Industrial Policy Resolution (IPR) in 1956, which re-emphasized the importance of the public sector and the necessity to regulate the growth of the private sector in light of the shift to a more explicitly 'socialistic' stance by the government led by Nehru, who changed his earlier favourable opinion about private sector capital and expressed support for the increasing role of the public sector in the evolution of his socialistic society (Bhagwati and Desai, 1971). The relationship of the state with the private sector capital began to change for the better mainly from the mid-1980s onwards.

Second, since all provinces have jurisdiction over land, the respective provincial governments have their own provincial linkages with private sector informal networks to attract private investments to their respective territories. The federal government makes policy decisions regarding the private sector's involvement in the industrial development of the country. Also, the Confederation of Indian Industry (CII) meets with relevant ministers from time to time to explain what new measures are needed for the industrial sector to grow and achieve success in the export market.

The Indian Planning Commission has also created its own expert group consisting of academics, business leaders and so on to seek its advice on matters relating to the formulation of planned programs for development. Hence, the government–business relationship is not as structured and dense as it is in Japan and Korea and or even Taiwan.

EFFECTIVE POLICIES FOR PROMOTING DEVELOPMENT

Universal Education

All the East Asian countries have placed stronger emphasis on education than countries in South Asia and Africa during the post-war era. Expansion of education among children enhances a country's capacity for technology adoption, which accelerates the rate of increase in technology-induced human capital, which in turn raises the return to human capital, which further increases investment in human capital, thereby continuously increasing the human-capital augmented population, reducing population growth and accelerating the rate of technological progress even further (Gaylor and Weil, 1999). This virtuous cycle has certainly increased the contribution of total factor productivity (TFP) to the overall GDP growth of these countries.

Primary school enrolment rates in East Asian countries have generally been higher than predicted for their level of income. In 1960, the number of students enrolled in primary school as a percentage of the age group was 94 for Korea, 87 for Hong Kong, 111[1] for Singapore, 96 for Malaysia, 83 for Thailand and 71 for Indonesia, but only 61 for India (World Bank, 1980). In 1965, in China, 89 per cent of children in the relevant age group were enrolled for primary education (World Bank, 1980). The share of GNP used for public expenditure on education was high for Malaysia and Singapore, and moderate for the other East Asian countries; the proportion of the education budget allocated to basic education has been high for all major East Asian countries. Also in 1965 at the primary level, the student–teacher ratio was lower for several East Asian countries than for India. The ratio for Hong Kong and Singapore at 29 was marginally higher than Australia's 28, but lower than France's 30, the Netherlands' 31 and Spain's 34 (World Bank, 1990).

The other interesting trend that we notice is that the emphasis placed even in 1965 on girls' primary education in Singapore, Korea and Hong Kong, where the enrolment of girls in primary education was quite high and even higher than the emphasis placed in some advanced countries such as the United Kingdom, Finland, Sweden and Switzerland. Enrolment rates for girls at the primary level (those aged 6 to 11 years) surpassed 90 per cent by 1956 in Taiwan. These results are consistent with the historical cultural veneration of the Chinese for education. Koreans and Indians also historically had veneration for education, but Koreans achieved greater success in education expansion than India, although the share of total expenditure (by federal and provincial governments) on education in India's GDP is not so low.

Land Reform and Income Distribution

Japan, Korea and Taiwan

In South Korea and Taiwan, the primary objective of land reform was to establish the legitimacy of the incumbent government. Land reform, by transforming the rural sector into a smallholder economy, was to help increase agricultural productivity and wage goods production, reduce inequality in income distribution, create employment opportunities for the unemployed, increase savings for the country's industrialization, and also provide cheap labour and land for the establishment of small-scale labour-intensive manufacturing units. However, Mellor and Johnston (1984) argue that it is only in a so-called unimodal development strategy in which a broad base of smallholders are the central focus of agricultural research and extension services and also receive the major proportion of revenue earned from agriculture that agriculture can play such a role.

However, small-scale agriculture also needs significant amounts of technical and financial support from the public sector to realize these objectives. In East Asia as well as in India, the state undertook infrastructure investment for technological change, technology transfer and adoption in agriculture – which has resulted in increases in growth rates in basic food production since the mid-1960s (Mellor, 1998).

In Japan, land reform was carried by the occupation regime to create small peasant proprietors who could help establish a democratic Japan. The payment to landlords for confiscated lands amounted to virtually nothing after the real value of the currency was greatly eroded due to inflation (Dore, 1959).

In Korea after the Korean War, the Rhee government confiscated large tracts of agricultural land from *yangban* (landlords) by paying compensation which was insignificant relative to the capitalized value of land. It was fixed at 150 per cent of the value of the annual harvest and spread over a number of years. These tracts of land were broken up into plots of three hectares each. However, substantial reduction in the domestic price of staples, due to the import of cost-free food from the United States under food-aid programmes and the transfer of surplus staples to the government at a very low price forced many farmers to leave their farms and migrate to urban areas where small-scale labour intensive manufacturing units were able to absorb them as cheap labour. In the 1960s, however, the government allocated close to 30 per cent of its budget to agricultural development, which considerably reduced the rural–urban divide (Cypher and Dietz, 2009).

In Taiwan too, the Kuomintang regime, with a political will and aided by an able bureaucracy, was able to implement a comprehensive land reform programme, named the land-to-the-tiller programme (Smith 1997; Clark and Roy, 1997) during the 1950s in three stages. In the first stage there was rent reduction; the next stage consisted of confiscation of land from landlords and sale as well as transfer of lands to peasants at a very nominal price. Finally, surplus land holdings above a stipulated minimum had to be transferred by landlords to peasants in exchange for stocks in state-owned enterprises. The land reform was a major factor in the extremely rapid growth of agricultural productivity in this period. This land reform also laid the initial foundation for the later industrialization of Taiwan by creating resources that were transferred to the industrial sector.

China

In China, the process of land reform took a different shape and character from that in Japan, Korea and Taiwan. Prior to land reform in the 1950s by the communist government, about 40 per cent of cultivable land was tilled by peasants who paid 50 per cent of their main crop to their landlords as rent, while landlords contributed nothing to improve the quality of land or the economic condition of peasants (Perkins et al., 2006).

After Mao's takeover of China, the government collectivized production, controlled prices and monopolized the distribution system (Lynn, 2003). By 1958, a substantial proportion of households, roughly 120 million, were arranged into 24,000 communes to ensure that irrigation, infrastructure and crop production were well organized. But the productivity of agriculture remained low and a large decline in production between 1959 and 1961 contributed to starvation which led to the deaths of about 30 million people, and a major policy change only took effect after Mao's death in 1976. This policy change consisted of three features:

1. Control over production was transferred from communes to house-holds under the 'Household Responsibility System'. This transfer was completed in 1983.
2. While the state still retained its power to buy and sell agricultural produce, it also allowed the private sector to engage in such activities.
3. Finally, the government became concerned about the low procurement prices of agricultural produce and raised procurement prices.

However, higher grain prices to sustain incentives for farmers led to increased production but also to an increase in subsidies for food consumption. Alternatively, when the grain prices were reduced, the grain output fell as farmers switched to the production of other crops. This trend is to some extent similar to a primitive cobweb process as depicted in the well-known cobweb theorem. In India too, similar problems have been caused by the continuation of differential prices for procurement and retail sale of food grain (Chai and Roy, 2006). Eventually procurement and resale prices of grain were freed in China in 1993.

China's agricultural reform is also entwined with small village enterprises. The number of such enterprises has increased greatly since 1983 when the government allowed private sector investment in these enterprises, although most enterprises are still collectively owned by townships and villages. Such enterprises produced more than 60 per cent of total rural non-agricultural output in the early 1990s. Also, the priority in such enterprises was not so different from that in large SOEs (Jefferson, 1999; Mood, 1997). While agricultural output seems to outstrip population growth, which is low in China, productivity remains low because of high labour intensity, despite significant improvement in technical progress in the farm sector (Dong et al., 2006). China's strong commitment to achieving and maintaining self-sufficiency in food production and supply may have contributed to the massive increase in per hectare usage of chemical fertilizer which in turn eventually will contribute to declining yield and soil fertility, and significant environmental damage via pollution of water (Smil, 2004; Bramall, 2009).

India

The issue of land reform in India is too complex to be explained easily. First, since India's independence in 1947 under the federal structure of the country, the federal government does not have any jurisdiction over land which is under the exclusive jurisdiction of provinces. Hence, there is no single political institution (i.e. one government) which can formulate a policy of land reform in India, nor one able bureaucracy which could implement a land reform programme. Second, the land tenancy system, which prevailed during the British rule and which continued for quite some time in post-independence India, is no longer the predominant form of land tenure today. With the demise of the tenancy system, landlords also departed from India's agricultural sector in many provinces.

Third, there is no presence of sizeable plantation agriculture. Thus the major proportion of agricultural land is distributed among smallholder peasant families. Virtually the entire agricultural sector in India is under private control. In Bengal in the late 1960s, a coalition government with communists as one partner tried to implement land reform by confiscating surplus land from families holding in excess of five acres and then distributing the land to landless labourers. But this scheme did not work too well for the following reasons:

1. Those landless labourers, who received free land from the government, did not have enough savings or income to purchase all the inputs necessary for the cultivation of those plots of land and also income to pay for foods and other necessities. Hence the farmers' 'wage goods constraint' prevented these new owners from utilizing their blocks of land effectively.
2. Some of these blocks of land which were transferred to landless villagers were not fertile enough for growing food and non-food crops.
3. Aggrieved owners, whose lands were in the process of being confiscated, filed lawsuits against the Bengal Government in the High Court and took injunctions against the government's attempt at confiscating so-called excess land. Also, any grain output in excess of the quantity that a family could legally keep was confiscated by the government at a price which was predetermined by the government but which was well below the market price. The determination of the excess quantity was not based on a scientific estimation of the total grain output of a family. Hence, these aggrieved farmers again filed law suits in the High Court against this unjustified act of the Bengal Government and brought an injunction against such government action.[2]

In other provinces, no serious attempt had been made to enforce land reform laws. In Bihar, while the federal government awarded substantial areas of land to Harijan (untouchable) caste members, nothing happened in practice as real power in Bihar is in the hands of upper-caste members of large land-owning families, who prevented Harijans from establishing their legal rights over those lands (Perkins et al., 2006; Bardhan, 1984). In both Bihar Province and Upper Province (UP), the large landholder families form a feudal class which wields considerable power in provincial and national politics in the Indian democracy.

Generally, agricultural productivity remained low in India due to the lack of incentives, ever-increasing prices of essential inputs, lack of knowledge about the appropriate input mix and shortage of water. However, in the aftermath of the introduction of green revolution technology in Indian agriculture during a ten-year period from 1968 to 1978, the output of food grains increased considerably (Roy and Lougheed, 1979; Chai and Roy, 2006). But in later periods, due to lack of continuous innovation, output productivity did not increase. Like China, India also had a strong commitment to achieving self-sufficiency in food grain production and supply, and that commitment was realized.

India has hardly any small-sized village enterprises producing non-agricultural output as in China and Taiwan. Hence, the rise in rural income per capita and in rural saving was not pronounced. There is also some leakage in the process of the transmission of rural savings to investment finance for industrialization because of leakages of a part of rural savings into expenditures on the purchase of gold jewellery, land, wedding ceremonies and medical care, or even simply the hoarding of cash. One of the reasons why the agricultural sector has not been rejuvenated by provincial governments in India is the desire to retain the votes that the agricultural sector provides for any provincial government during election time by keeping this sector and its population in an impoverished state. In fact, the switching of ownership titles in the countryside without any accompanying agricultural development strategy is likely to lead to failure and is not a real land reform (Cypher and Dietz, 2009).

CONCLUDING REMARKS

In conclusion, we have to agree with the widely prevalent view that high growth and development-promoting institutions have been present in greater measure in East Asia and China than in India. However, we also have to accept the fact that the partition of India into three parts in 1947 by the British Raj and the adoption at the federal and provincial level by the Congress party of a democratic governance system, which eventually became highly decentralized, greatly circumscribed the Indian state's capacity to grow and develop as consistently as East Asia and China. East Asian countries including China were not butchered by any imperial power, and they did not adopt the same Indian-style political governance system. In terms of the model developed in this chapter, India's pattern of historical governance produced much less effective institutions than emerged in East Asia and, consequently, resulted in less supportive policies for its development project.

These extensive discussions in the first three chapters on the role and institutional foundations of developmental states have now set the stage for the discussion of specific growth and development issues in East Asia and South Asia in the subsequent chapters.

NOTE

1. Census data may understate the number of people in an age group, thus creating ratios of over 100 in a few countries with very high enrolments.
2. One of the present authors, Roy, had the misfortune of being forced to take such a legal action in 1969 against the Bengal Government for its attempt to forcibly confiscate a substantial quantity of grain output from his ancestral home in Bengal, although the total output was within the limit prescribed by the government's regulations.

4. Trade, technology and industrialization in the Asian states

All countries promoting trade free of all restrictions as advocated by Smith ([1776] 1976) can increase their own economic wealth and thereby can also increase the wealth of the global economy. By 'free of restrictions' we refer to the total absence of all tariff and nontariff barriers to trade. If a country continues to maintain a large and rising surplus in its trade with other countries, then its currency will appreciate in value vis-à-vis those currencies of importing countries. Consequently, although free trade does not necessarily guarantee that the trade will be automatically balanced, at least free trade aided by an appropriately flexible exchange rate system can help a country running a deficit in its trade with another country to increase its income from its exports to and reduce its payments for imports from the trading partner maintaining a surplus with it.

However, even if the currency of the country running a deficit in its trade with another country is depreciated, it may not increase export income if the foreign demand for its exportable goods is less than one. This is the situation with which India has been confronted in late 2011. Currently, India's burgeoning trade deficit has been accompanied by substantial depreciation of the Indian rupee against all major currencies of the world. Even then, there does not appear to be any perceptible and justifiable increase in India's export income. Furthermore, the depreciation of the rupee at an alarming rate has significantly increased India's cost of import payments. This seems to have further widened the size of India's global trade deficit. Hence, the depreciation of the currency of a country running a deficit in its trade with another country may not necessarily correct the country's trade imbalance.

This is the situation that exists in global trade today; and it is also this situation which the present authors firmly believe is at least partly responsible for the occurrence of the global financial meltdown which began in July 2007. In a highly integrated global economy, some countries can continue to gain from trade at the expense of other countries only if other countries continue to lose and do not mind losing in their trade. But such a situation can continue to benefit only a small number of countries for a certain period of time, because eventually those countries with large deficits will be forced to cut down on their budget deficits and trade deficits by imposing tariff and other restrictions on imports in order to restart the development of import-competing industries.

If the combined GDPs and the size of the domestic markets for consumer goods of countries with large trade deficits are substantial, such actions will greatly undermine the growth and development of the global economy, as a substantial reduction in the import demand of these countries will eventually bring down the trade surplus and economic growth of those few countries maintaining large trade supplies for a long time.

We presented this view in order to highlight the divergence between what Asian countries did and what, according to the pure theory of trade, they should have done to implement their trade and industrialization policies.

TRADE, TECHNOLOGY AND INDUSTRIALIZATION IN ASIAN COUNTRIES: OVERVIEW

Most leading Asian countries adopted a mixed foreign trade regime under which aggressive export promotion policies were combined with a varying degree of tariffs on the import of different consumer goods and a zero tariff on the import of capital and intermediate goods for use in export-oriented industries. While such a concession of duty free imports of machinery and equipment was available to firms in both the state and private sectors in East and South-east Asian countries, in India concessions of any type were available mainly to state-operated enterprises (SOEs), many of which were import-substituting industries producing goods mainly for domestic consumption under the draconian trade regime maintained by Nehru and his daughter, Indira Gandhi, between 1956 and 1984 (Bhagwati and Desai, 1971; Bardhan, 1984; Bhagwati, 1993; Lal, 1988, 1995; Srinivasan, 2000; Joshi and Little, 1994; Basu, 2004; Chai and Roy, 2006).

Although India's trade regime began to become more outward-oriented after 1985, all major East, South-east and South Asian economies were far more export-oriented; and in 2006–07 (before the onset of the financial meltdown) they were even more export-oriented than in the early 1990s. The state played a major role in the trade and industrialization of all the major economies by maintaining a stable macro-economy and granting export subsidies, duty free import facilities, concessional loans, aid in the acquisition of technology and so on.

Bradford (1986) and Kohli (2004) have lent strong support to the view that there is hardly any important example in the developing world where industrialization has proceeded very far without the intervention of effective states which can provide industries with the much-needed help to overcome the disadvantages emanating from capital insecurity, technological backwardness, labour market rigidities and the power of corporations, which may like to enter a captive market created by tariff walls with a view mainly to make profit in the host countries' domestic markets. This state intervention in the trade and industrialization process for almost 30 years helped the Indian economy to be more self-reliant and innovative than probably it would have been if there had been no state intervention (Burton, 1989, 1998; Bardhan, 1984; Panagariya, 2008). Korea too, which opened up its economy long before India did, has been better-off in terms of the development of its indigenous technology because it relied less on foreign corporations than many other countries and, instead, used 'national champions' to spearhead its industrialization drive (Burton, 1989, 1998).

The Linkages Among Trade, Technology and the Industrialization Process

The acquisition of technology has helped the Asian countries' export-oriented industrial sectors to upgrade their technologies continuously to remain competitive in the global market for durable and non-durable consumer goods, capital and intermediate goods. Adoption of upgraded technology in export-oriented firms has helped lower the unit cost of production. The productivity of labour, with the same wages and improved technology, has increased. Hence, the use of improved technology and of technology-induced human capital (Gaylor and Weil, 1999) has helped these Asian countries to produce and export goods with higher value-added technology content and thereby to raise their export earnings.

The acquisition of technology and knowledge in Asia has taken place through the following channels:

1. import of technology via FDI (foreign direct investment);
2. development of indigenous technology via research and development;
3. expansion of general education, science and engineering education;
4. the process of learning from experience; and
5. acquisition of trade secrets by informal means.

Continuous upgrading of technology in the production of goods and services has been the hallmark of industrial policy in the major Asian economies.

Trade Openness, Trade Patterns and Technology Upgradation

Trade openness
It is difficult to determine the effect of a specific trade policy on a country's economic growth because the effect results from the application of a package of

policies of which one specific policy is a component (Pritchett, 1996; Perkins et al., 2006). Hence, despite the imposition of a high level of import tariffs in several Asian countries, they achieved great success in raising export incomes and economic growth rates, whereas other countries in other regions achieved lesser success on both fronts despite lowering considerably their import tariff levels in the 1990s. Hence, what matters in a country's outward orientation is the 'right' kind of policy mix that can be different for different countries.

To gauge the extent of a country's outward orientation in its trade policies, the following indicators (Sachs and Warner, 1995; Perkins et al., 2006) can be used:

1. A high and increasing share of the value of trade in a country's GDP.
2. A country's average tariff rate is less than 40 per cent.
3. Its nontariff barriers including quotas cover less than 40 per cent of imports.
4. The premium on unofficial parallel market exchange rate does not exceed 20 per cent.
5. There is no state monopoly controlling the export of any major item.
6. The country is not a socialist economy.
7. The country maintains a freely floating exchange rate and macro-economic stability with a mild rate of inflation.
8. Unnecessary regulatory burdens, bureaucratic costs and red tape which raise the cost of doing business are reduced.
9. The country maintains, particularly for labour and credit, flexible (competitive) factor markets under which wages and interest rates are determined by the market demand for and supply of labour and capital.

The share of total trade in GDP rose again for all countries after the 1997 East Asian Crisis which temporarily stalled the growth of trade. In 2006, the share of total trade value in GDP of all these countries was more than 30 per cent. The simple mean tariff on imports of all products was below 17 per cent for all these countries, although the simple mean tariff on the import of primary goods was higher than that on the import of manufactured goods. It is difficult to identify nontariff barriers, but these are generally imposed on imports of food and other agricultural products. The number of complaints filed by several importing countries with the WTO against exporting countries on the grounds of unfair trade practices may be an indicator. But generally, if the major proportion of a country's total imports consists of the import of capital and intermediate goods destined for investment in the production sector of the economy, then nontariff barriers will not pose a serious concern for the country.

The premium on unofficial parallel market exchange rates has not exceeded 20 per cent in any of those countries in recent times. Although, except for

Japan and Singapore, the other countries have not yet adopted full convertibility in their capital accounts, restrictions on the outflow of capital are moderate, and the exchange rates, while not freely floating, are nevertheless quite flexible, except in China. Except for China and Vietnam, the other countries are not socialist, although some of them have not completely done away with socialist policies.

Two main features of the trade policies of the major Asian countries which stand out are as follows:

1. Most developing countries placed tariff and nontariff restrictions on imports of most consumer goods, and some countries even barred the import of certain essential consumer goods. Such restrictions, although less severe now, are still continuing. They were accompanied, however, by duty free imports of capital and intermediate goods for use in export-oriented manufacturing industries, as well as by other export-promotion measures which enabled firms to capture new export markets by lowering the export price of their products below a price which did not cover the average cost of production per unit of output (Clark and Roy, 1997).
2. The currencies of all countries remained undervalued against the US dollar throughout the 1990s and the early part of the 2000s. In 2007, the Chinese yuan was appreciated against the US dollar (Batson, 2010).

The Plaza Accord of 1985 (World Bank, 1993) contributed to the depreciation of the US dollar against the Japanese yen by about 20 per cent. Recently, Japan appreciated the value of the yen, which reduced Japan's exports to the United States. Hence, some undervaluation of their currencies against the US dollar seems to have been an important component of the trade policies of the major Asian countries.

Trade patterns
Trade patterns and technology upgradation in Asia are interlinked. A main feature of this trade pattern is a strong emphasis on intra-industry trade, which is fuelled by the growth in intra-regional trade (UN, 2009; Athukorala, 2007). A sizeable proportion of Asia's total trade value is derived from the export and import of capital and intermediate goods, which indicates that these countries are attempting to move up the technology ladder to produce and export upgraded technology-intensive goods. Also, the higher share of capital and intermediate goods should indicate these countries' success in achieving that goal. A very large proportion of this export and import trade is taking place among countries within the region. Within East Asia and China the share of intra-industry trade has risen rapidly since 1990 while the share of inter-industry trade declined. This intra-industry trade exhibits two trends – (i) horizontal

trade, referring to trade in products that are similar in function but possess difference in value, in terms of design and other minor features, and (ii) vertical trade, referring to products at a different level in the value chain (Gill and Kharas, 2007). The emergence of integrated industrial networks is a feature of East Asia, due to widely differing comparative advantages, but does not yet encompass India to any great extent.

Technology upgradation

Technology upgradation has been taking place in Asian countries by: (i) acquiring technology and knowledge from abroad via FDI; (ii) exports under long-term original equipment manufacturing (OEM) contracts for multinational corporations or MNCs (mainly in East and South-east Asia); (iii) the purchase of part of technology and knowledge via acquisition of patents, licences, trademarks, designs, patterns and disclosures of knowledge (Gill and Kharas, 2007), as well as by endogenous innovation through knowledge-imbedded human capital (Romer, 1994), R&D activities and the process of learning-by-doing (Arrow, 1962). Such endogenous innovation places technological progress at the forefront of the development process (Grossman and Helpman, 1991). For the formation of knowledge-imbedded human capital and for facilitating technology innovation and adaptation, the state as well as the private sector has played a role in all the major Asian economies.

Foreign direct investment has been an important source for the acquisition of technology for most Asian countries from MNCs which also would have provided export-oriented MNC subsidiaries with information about the type of products in terms of design and quality that foreigners want and would have established distribution channels in foreign markets. These are a kind of infrastructure bottleneck which in East Asia was partly dealt with by the state. Most Asian countries included in this study have performed favourably on the following conditions (Gampat and Weeratunge, 2008) necessary to facilitate FDI inflow:

1. growth rates of real GDP, real per-capita income and size of GDP;
2. degree of openness to trade;
3. corporate tax rates and import tariffs;
4. quality of infrastructure;
5. level of corruption, government stability and capacity to attract FDI;
6. the strength of the rule of law and security of private property; and
7. the level of labour market rigidities – such as union dominance over wage rates, labour hours and supply of labour, etc.

There is also the implicit assumption that normal production hours in factories and all other economic and social transactions intended to create wealth will not be disrupted frequently by political parties and their paraformal agents (unemployed mafia) by calling a strike, rally, parade, demonstration and so on, as well as even by threats to the lives of company personnel.

Industrial Policy and Industrialization in Asia

Industrial policy in East and South-east Asia has been greatly shaped by the adoption by these countries of highly outward-oriented trade regimes and by their reliance on FDI, so that a restructuring of comparative advantage takes place. Hence, a strong impetus has been provided to the growth of export-oriented industries so that Factory Asia's[1] (UN, 2009) total exports to the rest of the world are far greater than the total exports of Latin America, South Asia, Eastern Europe, Russia, the Middle East, North Africa and Sub-Saharan Africa combined. The share of total exports in GDP in the region is more than 50 per cent. The dramatic growth in export-oriented industries in this industrialization process has been the principal source of economic lifeblood of Factory Asia.

The Flying Geese model
The Flying Geese is a model (or rather, a metaphor) originally put forth by Akamatsu (1961, 1962), outlining the dynamics of industrialization in a region consisting of countries at different stages of development. By using Akamatsu's model, one can see how FDI from Japan became a channel for it to recycle its comparative advantage to the rest of Asia (see Blomqvist, 1996). In Akamatsu's model, the flying geese stop flying at the exporting stage of the product cycle of an industry. However, after the exporting industry has lost its comparative advantage, it shifts its production to other low-cost countries in emerging East Asia (Gill and Kharas, 2007). As Japan developed new tech-nologies and production capabilities, it shifted these techniques first to the four tiger economies, South Korea, Taiwan, Hong Kong and Singapore. Since the primary reason for this relocation was cheaper labour costs, the production facilities subsequently began, in turn, to move to South-east Asia and then China as labour costs became higher in those tiger economies. Although this theory explains the catch-up by developing countries to the developed coun-tries, it cannot fully explain how the industrial structure can become more technology-intensive. However, that cannot happen anyway without catching up first. In Factory Asia, small and medium enterprises (SMEs) and the service sector enterprises also have played a powerful role in employment generation, export promotion and technology upgradation in the industrialization process. These will be discussed later in this chapter.

The flying geese, however, could not fly to India because, although the country has become more outward-oriented since the early 1990s, the degree of its trade openness is still considerably lower than that of other countries covered in this study. While in East Asia, the state's incentive schemes for promoting exports were heavily biased towards export-sector industries; these schemes made it relatively unprofitable for manufacturing-sector industries to produce for domestic consumption. But in India even today, the state's incentive schemes, which are not as pervasive as in East Asia, seem to be directed considerably towards the industries producing for domestic consumption. This factor, combined with the failure of India to fulfil most of the above-mentioned important conditions necessary to attract MNCs to the country to develop export-oriented industries, forced the MNCs to engage with their Indian joint venture partners to manufacture durable and semi-durable non-essential consumer goods to cater to the needs of domestic consumers.

The only foreign company which entered India with the intention of producing motor vehicles for the domestic market, Suzuki Motors of Japan, has also been quite successful in the export market. A substantial proportion of India's imports of intermediate goods, chemical products and industrial machinery continue to be directed to industries producing goods for domestic consumers, however. This is an indication of technology upgradation for inward-oriented industries. In India, the term that is used to describe small and medium enterprises or SMEs is MSEs (Micro and Small Enterprises). The official statistics provide information on those MSEs which are registered firms, but there are also many thousands of MSEs in the informal and non-traded sector which operate throughout the country in all major towns and cities, and which provide employment to millions of labourers and add to the country's income. The income generated in this sector is not included in the official estimate of India's GDP. Therefore India's GDP figure is considerably underestimated. In both the formal and informal sector MSEs, which produce for domestic consumption, the process of learning from experience and from spillover effects of knowledge is very evident.

Technology upgradation cannot take place in these MSE businesses because they are too small in size and capital, but innovation is taking place in design and other minor improvements. In the Information and Communication Technology (ICT) sector, which is highly export-oriented, foreign capital has played a role, but endogenous innovation has played a big role in technology upgradation.

Another factor which makes the inflow of FDI look large is the value of Indian rupees, which are heavily depreciated against the US dollar. In 1971, one US dollar could buy five Indian rupees. In 2010, one US dollar could buy more than 40 Indian rupees. Hence, an inflow of 500 million US dollars' worth of FDI to India would, after conversion, make it 20 billion Indian rupees' worth of FDI. But the same 500 million US dollars inflow to China would make about 5 billion Chinese yuan of FDI, which represents a small amount of FDI in China. Therefore, even if most conditions of FDI inflow are met, the total amount of FDI in US dollars would remain low, in comparison with that amount which flows to China, Singapore, Hong Kong and so on. By and large India, even now, does not seem to have put in place a clear export-oriented industrial policy. Even if such a policy is ever formulated, it could not possibly be implemented under India's political governance structure, which is unable to promote fully the growth of competition, openness, export promotion and wealth creation activities.[2]

DIRECTION AND PATTERN OF TRADE

Tables 4.1 to 4.7 illustrate important aspects of the foreign trade of China, India, East Asia, and South-east Asia.[3] It can be seen from Table 4.1 that China's total exports to the world increased from 326 billion US dollars in 2002 to 1.42 trillion US dollars in 2008, thereby recording a massive increase of more than 300 per cent. The trade balance, which remained in surplus throughout this period, reached 297 billion US dollars in 2008, from only 31 billion in 2002. The total value of exports for the period stood at 5.74 trillion US dollars and the total favourable balance of trade stood at 929 billion US dollars. China's trade with the advanced economies for the whole period from 2002 to 2008 stood at 1.27 trillion US dollars primarily because this list includes Japan, Hong Kong, Taiwan, Korea and Singapore, all of which maintained substantial surplus in their trade with China. This trend is reflected in Table 4.2 which illustrates China's trade with Japan and China's trade partners in emerging Asia. As the table shows, China recorded a large trade deficit with all these countries except the Philippines and Hong Kong which had a massive trade deficit with China. This massive surplus in China's trade with Hong Kong reflects Hong Kong's major role as China's entrepôt trade gateway. The last row of the table shows that, if we exclude China's trade with Hong Kong, then for the whole period of 2002–08 China displayed a massive trade deficit of a total of 1.40 trillion US dollars in its trade with Japan and the other major Asian partners.

Table 4.3 shows the direction of India's foreign trade for the period 2002 to 2008. The important as well as the distressing feature of this table is that in comparison to China, which recorded trade surpluses with all regions except Japan and East Asia, India recorded a large deficit in its global trade with all regions. India's total value of world exports increased by nearly 300 per cent, the value of its global imports increased by nearly 435 per cent and its adverse trade balance increased by nearly 1,270 per cent. However, Table 4.4 (row 6) shows that during the same period the value of India's exports to its East Asian neighbours and partners, including Japan and Korea, increased by nearly 650 per cent and its deficit in its trade with neighbours increased by almost 1,180 per cent. The important thing to note here is that both China and India are far

Table 4.1   Direction of China's foreign trade (value in US $billions)

		2002	2003	2004	2005	2006	2007	2008	Total	% change 2002–2008
		1	2	3	4	5	6	7	8	9
I	**Total world trade**									
1	Total export	326	438	593	763	970	1,219	1,429	5,738	+338.3
2	Total import	295	413	561	660	792	956	1,132	4,809	+283.7
3	Trade balance	+31	+25	+32	+103	+178	+263	+297	+929	+858.1
II	**Trade with developed countries**[a]									
4	Export to	266.43	354.80	476.57	605.862	748.18	902.69	1015.27	4369.81	+281.1
5	Import from	217.86	292.613	386.97	433.081	503.77	594.05	671.78	3100.12	+208.3
6	Trade balance	+48.56	+62.19	+89.59	+172.77	+244.40	+368.64	+343.48	+1269.69	+607.3
III	**Emerging and developing countries**[b]									
10	Export to	58.53	82.70	115.66	154.76	218.64	312.90	410.20	1356.41	+600.8
11	Import from	62.20	94.60	134.96	170.19	213.61	274.76	365.98	1317.33	+488.4
12	Trade balance	–3.66	–11.89	–19.29	–16.43	+5.03	+38.13	+44.22	+39.08	n.a.
IV	**Other countries**[c]									
19	Export to	0.778	0.86	1.01	1.72	2.49	2.56	3.38	12.80	+334.4
10	Import from	0.38	0.51	0.78	0.73	0.99	1.68	1.65	6.75	+334.2
21	Trade balance	+0.34	+0.34	+0.35	+0.98	+1.50	+0.87	+1.72	+6.14	+405.9

Notes:

[a] Includes Hong Kong, Korea, Singapore and Taiwan.
[b] Includes countries in Africa, the rest of developing Asia and others.
[c] Includes Cuba and North Korea.

Source: IMF (2009a), *Direction of Trade Statistics Yearbook 2009*, Washington, DC: IMF, pp. 141–143.

Table 4.2   *China's trade with Japan and emerging Asian partners (value in US $billions)*

	2002	2003	2004	2005	2006	2007	2008	Total	% change 2002–2008
	1	2	3	4	5	6	7	8	9
Japan									
Export to	48.48	59.42	72.48	84.09	91.77	102.11	116.17	569.58	+139.6
Import from	53.48	74.15	94.33	100.46	115.81	133.90	150.80	1772.19	+182.0
Trade balance	−5.0	−14.72	−20.85	−16.37	−24.04	−24.04	−34.63	−1202.61	−572.6
Korea									
Export to	15.50	20.09	27.81	35.11	44.55	56.12	73.90	273.13	+376.8
Import from	25.58	43.13	62.25	76.87	89.81	104.04	112.17	513.87	+338.5
Trade balance	−10.1	−23.03	34.43	−4.75	−45.26	−47.94	−38.27	−240.74	−278.9
Hong Kong									
Export to	58.48	76.28	100.87	124.50	155.43	184.28	190.77	2600.65	+226.2
Import from	10.78	11.11	11.80	12.23	10.79	12.82	12.94	70.85	+20.0
Trade balance	+47.70	+65.17	+89.07	+12.37	+144.64	+171.46	+177.83	+2529.80	+272.8
Taiwan									
Export to	6.59	9.00	13.54	16.55	20.74	23.48	25.88	115.80	+292.7
Import from	20.08	49.36	64.77	74.65	87.14	100.98	103.33	510.33	+414.6
Trade balance	−23.49	−49.35	−63.42	−58.09	−66.40	−77.50	−77.44	−394.53	−229.7
Singapore									
Export to	1.30	1.94	3.37	5.06	5.90	7.04	7.70	32.26	+492.3
Import from	1.40	1.92	2.45	3.17	4.95	7.46	13.15	34.53	+839.3
Trade balance	−0.10	−0.02	+0.92	+18.9	+0.95	0.42.	−5.45	−2.17	−5350.0
Malaysia									
Export to	0.75	0.85	0.97	1.14	1.26	2.25	2.82	10.06	+276.0
Import from	1.38	1.90	2.17	2.38	4.578	5.82	8.15	26.40	+490.5
Trade balance	−0.62	−1.04	−1.20	−1.24	−3.31	−3.57	−5.33	−16.34	759.7
Thailand									
Export to	0.69	0.80	0.85	1.03	1.35	1.71	2.31	8.75	+234.8
Import from	0.39	0.55	0.77	1.12	1.61	2.16	3.68	10.30	+843.6
Trade balance	+0.30	+0.25	+0.08	−0.09	−0.26	−0.44	−1.37	−1.54	−556.6
Philippines									
Export to	0.41	0.35	0.37	0.47	0.56	0.61	0.59	3.39	+43.9
Import from	0.11	0.12	0.16	0.22	0.18	0.19	0.21	1.22	+90.9
Trade balance	+0.29	+0.23	+0.20	+0.25	+0.37	+0.41	+0.38	+2.16	+31.0
Japan and Emerging Asia without Hong Kong									
Export to	72.99	92.49	120.45	143.49	165.16	193.34	229.40	1,001.10	+214.29
Import from	102.44	17.14	226.98	258.90	304.09	354.54	391.52	2,409.57	+282.19
Trade balance	−29.44	−78.65	−106.52	−115.41	−139.93	−161.23	−162.11	−1,408.47	−450.65

Note: Emerging Asia in this table includes Korea, Hong Kong, Taiwan, Singapore, Malaysia, Thailand and Philippines.

Source: IMF (2009a), *Direction of Trade Statistics Yearbook 2009*, Washington, DC: IMF, pp. 141–143.

Table 4.3   Direction of India's foreign trade (value in US $billions)

	2002	2003	2004	2005	2006	2007	2008	Total	% change 2002–2008
1. Total world trade									
Total export	50.37	61.13	75.38	98.21	120.60	153.96	198.26	7,507.91	+293.61
Total import	58.91	74.07	99.83	139.88	176.66	235.18	315.09	1,099.62	+434.87
Trade balance	-8.54	-12.94	-24.45	-41.67	-56.06	-81.22	-116.83	-341.71	-1268.03
2. Trade with developed countries[a]									
Export to	30.54	35.54	42.41	55.61	64.52	77.42	95.73	401.77	+213.46
Import from	27.59	35.19	44.59	60.67	75.78	99.94	132.80	496.56	+381.33
Trade balance	+2.95	+0.35	-2.18	-5.06	-11.26	-22.42	-37.07	-94.79	-1356.61
3. Emerging and developing countries[b]									
Export to	19.09	25.19	32.52	42.27	55.67	75.32	101.15	351.21	+429.86
Import from	14.45	18.85	27.40	38.23	88.85	133.31	180.09	501.18	+1146.30
Trade balance	+4.64	+6.34	+5.12	+4.04	-33.18	-57.99	-78.94	-140.97	-1801.29
4. Other countries[c]									
Export to	0.86	0.38	0.43	0.32	0.38	1.20	1.37	4.94	+59.30
Import from	16.86	20.01	27.83	40.84	11.95	1.91	2.18	121.16	-87.07
Trade balance	-16.0	-19.63	-27.40	-40.52	-11.57	-0.71	0.81	-116.22	n.a.

Notes:
Row 1 = 2 + 3 + 4
[a] Includes Hong Kong, Korea, Singapore and Taiwan.
[b] Includes all countries in Africa and all others in Asia and Latin America.
[c] Includes all others and Cuba and North Korea.

Source: IMF (2009a), *Direction of Trade Statistics Yearbook 2009*, Washington, DC: IMF, pp. 264–266.

Table 4.4   India's trade with Asian partners excluding China (value in US $billions)

	2002	2003	2004	2005	2006	2007	2008	Total	% change 2002–2008
1. Japan									
Export to	1.77	1.74	1.91	2.39	2.76	3.60	5.98	20.15	+237.85
Import from	1.91	2.46	2.92	3.85	4.46	5.89	8.68	29.97	+354.45
Trade balance	−0.14	−0.72	−1.01	−1.46	−1.70	−2.29	−2.70	−9.82	−1,828.57
2. Korea									
Export to	0.60	0.73	0.91	1.63	2.34	2.76	5.98	14.98	−896.67
Import from	1.42	2.50	3.10	4.30	4.74	5.73	9.87	31.66	+595.07
Trade balance	−0.82	−1.77	−3.09	−2.67	−2.40	−2.97	−3.89	−16.68	−374.39
3. Taiwan									
Export to	0.52	0.54	0.57	0.62	0.84	1.53	2.12	6.74	+307.69
Import from	0.63	0.74	0.98	1.31	1.60	2.22	3.30	10.78	+423.80
Trade balance	−0.11	−0.20	−0.41	−0.69	−0.84	−0.69	−1.18	−4.04	−972.72
4. Singapore									
Export to	1.30	1.94	3.37	5.06	5.90	7.04	7.70	32.31	+492.30
Import from	1.40	1.92	2.45	3.17	4.95	7.46	13.15	34.50	+839.28
Trade balance	−0.10	+0.02	+0.92	+1.89	+0.95	−0.42	−5.45	−2.19	−5350.0
5. Malaysia									
Export to	0.75	0.85	0.97	1.14	1.26	2.52	2.82	10.31	+276.0
Import from	1.38	1.90	2.17	2.38	4.57	5.82	8.15	26.37	+490.58
Trade balance	−0.63	−1.05	−1.20	−1.24	−3.31	−3.30	−5.33	−16.06	−746.03
Total (1–5)									
Export to	6.66	8.51	11.90	17.31	21.01	27.64	43.09	136.12	+647.0
Import from	9.34	9.52	17.69	24.93	36.13	51.81	77.81	227.23	+733.08
Trade balance	−2.72	−1.01	−5.79	−7.62	−15.12	−24.17	−34.72	−91.11	−1,176.47

Source: IMF (2009a), *Direction of Trade Statistics Yearbook 2009*, Washington, DC: IMF, pp. 264–266.

more deeply integrated in their trade with East Asian partners than in their trade with the rest of the world.

The significance of this point is clearly brought out in Tables 4.5A and 4.5B. Table 4.5A presents the share of intra-Asian regional trade in the total trade of each country. It can be seen that the share of each country's exports to the region continued to increase with the exceptions of China's exports to the region which showed a marginal decline in 2008 from a high share of 51.4 per cent which it enjoyed in 2001. India, Korea, Taiwan, Singapore and Malaysia consistently increased the share of their exports to the region in their total export trade from 29.3, 46.5, 53.2, 59.5 and 56.9 per cent in 2001 to

34.2, 49.0, 66.3, 71.0 and 65.2 per cent in 2008. The share of imports from the region in their total import trade during the same period presents a similar picture, with the exception of Taiwan, whose regional imports remained about 55 per cent of the total throughout the decade. In 2008, China, Singapore and Malaysia had sourced more than 50 per cent of their total in global imports from their East Asian neighbours. For India and Japan, while this share in 2008 remained below 50 per cent, at 36 and 49 per cent, they were quite significant. Accordingly, the share of intra-regional trade in total trade remained below 50 per cent for Japan, China and India but above 60 per cent for Singapore and Malaysia and almost 60 per cent for Taiwan. This trend is a reflection of a burgeoning intra-industry trade involving all the countries of the region which includes both China and India.

This growth in intra-regional trade has also meant a gradual decline in the dependence of China, India and East Asia on the developed countries. This trend is presented in Table 4.5B, which shows that the indicator values of the relative dependence in the exports of Japan, China, India, Taiwan, Singapore and Malaysia declined from 2.2, 7.1, 4.6, 1.1, 1.1 and 1.5 in 2001 to 1.1, 4.5, 2.2, 0.5, 0.5 and 0.9 in 2008. For China and India, this drop in indicator value amounted to 35.0 and 52.2 per cent respectively. A similar declining trend is noticed in the relative dependence of these countries on imports from developed countries and on the total trade with developed countries. Again, during the same period, the rates of decline in dependence on the developed countries for imports were 48 per cent for both China and India. The rates of decline in relative dependence on total trade with developed countries during the same period were 41.3 and 31.3 per cent.

Hence, both China and India are far more integrated with the East Asian region in their trade relations than with developed countries in 2008 than they were at the turn of the twenty first century. However, as shown in Table 4.5B section 4, despite its deeper integration with the East Asian region, India's net beneficial achievement from its global trade has been very poor as reflected in the share in GDP of its trade balance which remained negative throughout the period from 2001 to 2008. This negative trade balance reached 6.5 per cent of GDP in 2006. In comparison to the positive trade balance enjoyed by all other countries in the region, India's negative trade balance makes very discouraging reading.

Further evidence of deeper integration of each of these countries with the region in trade is presented in Table 4.6A which shows that the intra-regional trade growth for India increased from 6 per cent in 2001 to nearly 41 per cent in 2006. In 2008, the corresponding growth rates for Japan, China, India, Taiwan, Singapore and Malaysia stood at 15.2, 14.5, 32.1, 3.2, 15.8 and 12.6 per cent, respectively.

Table 4.5A   Share of intra-regional trade in total trade of each country (%)

	2001	2002	2003	2004	2005	2006	2007	2008
1. Export to the region								
Japan	37.2	39.8	43.3	44.8	45.1	44.8	46.5	49.0
China	51.4	50.8	49.3	48.3	46.9	45.6	45.8	45.2
India	29.3	32.6	34.6	35.2	34.7	34.0	33.9	34.2
South Korea	46.5	47.7	52.6	51.8	53.0	53.2	53.6	49.0
Taiwan	53.2	57.7	60.4	63.1	65.0	65.5	66.6	66.3
Singapore	59.5	60.8	65.1	66.0	67.4	68.9	70.2	71.0
Malaysia	56.9	57.8	59.0	59.6	60.1	59.5	61.8	65.2
2. Import from the region								
Japan	45.9	46.8	48.6	49.7	49.7	48.8	49.6	48.9
China	52.7	54.8	55.9	55.8	57.0	56.4	55.7	53.2
India	25.9	24.7	29.8	28.0	28.5	36.6	37.9	35.7
South Korea	49.2	51.3	51.7	52.9	52.3	51.4	52.9	n.a.
Taiwan	54.7	57.0	58.3	58.3	53.5	57.2	55.2	51.9
Singapore	55.0	56.5	58.2	57.8	57.0	57.0	56.3	54.7
Malaysia	58.4	61.0	61.9	62.5	63.0	61.7	63.5	62.7
3. Intra-regional trade in total trade								
Japan	41.2	43.0	45.7	47.0	47.2	46.7	48.0	48.9
China	50.3	50.3	49.5	48.6	47.7	46.3	46.2	45.1
India	27.5	28.3	32.0	31.1	31.0	35.5	36.3	35.1
South Korea	47.8	49.4	52.2	52.3	52.7	52.3	53.3	n.a.
Taiwan	53.8	57.3	59.5	60.8	61.7	61.6	61.3	59.3
Singapore	57.3	58.7	61.9	62.2	62.6	63.3	63.7	63.0
Malaysia	57.6	59.3	60.3	60.5	61.0	60.5	62.1	64.1

Sources:
UN (2009), *Asia-Pacific Trade and Investment Report 2009*, Bangkok: UN, pp. 195–198.
IMF (2009a), *Direction of Trade Statistics Yearbook 2009*, Washington, DC: IMF, p. 265.
CEPD (2009), *Taiwan Statistical Data Book 2009*, Taipei: CEPD, pp. 227–230.

Despite India's impressive record in participation in intra-regional trade growth, the actual value of total trade for India with the region in 2008 was $175 billion as compared with $383 billion, $1,248 billion, $295 billion, $415 billion and $228 billion for Japan, China, Taiwan, Singapore and Malaysia. Hence, along with the rate of growth in trade, the total value of trade and, more particularly, a large and rising trade surplus are of fundamental importance for a country's exports and total trade to act as its engine of growth and for it to enhance its economic and political clout in the world. Naturally, with a low value of total trade and a rising trade deficit, India's economic clout in the world is significantly less than that of China.

Table 4.5B   Relative dependence on developed countries for trade (%)

	2001	2002	2003	2004	2005	2006	2007	2008
1. Relative dependence on exports to developed countries[a]								
Japan	2.2	1.9	1.6	1.5	1.4	1.4	1.2	1.1
China	7.1	6.5	6.7	6.3	6.1	5.7	4.9	4.5
India	4.6	3.7	3.2	2.4	2.5	2.3	2.4	2.2
South Korea	1.9	1.7	1.4	1.3	1.2	1.1	1.0	n.a.
Taiwan	1.1	0.8	0.7	0.6	0.6	0.6	0.5	0.5
Singapore	1.1	1.0	0.8	0.7	0.7	0.6	0.5	0.5
Malaysia	1.5	1.3	1.3	1.2	1.2	1.0	1.0	0.9
2. Relative dependence on imports from developed countries[b]								
Japan	1.0	0.9	0.8	0.7	0.7	0.6	0.6	0.6
China	3.1	2.5	2.1	1.9	1.6	1.5	1.5	1.6
India	2.5	2.4	2.0	1.8	1.8	1.3	1.1	1.3
South Korea	2.1	2.0	2.0	1.8	1.6	1.4	1.3	n.a.
Taiwan	2.5	2.4	2.2	2.0	2.0	1.8	1.7	1.6
Singapore	1.3	1.1	1.0	0.9	0.9	0.8	0.8	0.9
Malaysia	1.7	1.5	1.3	1.2	1.0	1.0	0.9	0.9
3. Relative dependence on total trade with developed countries[c]								
Japan	1.5	1.4	1.2	1.1	1.0	1.0	0.9	0.8
China	4.6	3.9	3.6	3.3	3.0	2.9	2.7	2.7
India	3.3	3.0	2.5	2.1	2.1	1.7	1.6	1.6
South Korea	2.0	1.8	1.6	1.5	1.3	1.2	1.1	n.a.
Singapore	1.2	1.1	0.9	0.8	0.7	0.7	6.7	0.7
Malaysia	1.6	1.4	1.3	1.2	1.1	1.1	1.0	0.9
4. Global trade balance as a percentage of GDP[d]								
Japan	+1.3	+2.0	+2.1	+2.4	+1.7	+1.5	+2.1	+0.77
China	+1.7	+2.1	+1.5	+1.7	+4.4	+6.4	+7.7	+6.90
India	−1.6	−1.7	−2.4	−4.1	−5.7	−6.5	−6.4	−1.80
South Korea	+1.9	+1.9	+2.5	+4.3	+2.9	+1.8	+1.5	+0.65
Singapore	+6.7	+9.9	+25.4	+22.9	+24.7	+24.2	+22.4	+26.88
Malaysia	+16.1	+15.3	+20.2	+17.2	+19.8	+18.9	+15.7	+16.77

Notes:
[a] Indicates the ratio of exports of goods directed to the EU, the US and Japan to the exports of goods and services to ASEAN, China and India.
[b] Indicates the ratio of imports of goods and services from the EU, the US and Japan to the imports from ASEAN, China and India.
[c] Indicates the ratio of trade with the three developed markets to each country's trade with ASEAN, China and India.
[d] The ratio of 1 indicates equal dependence on both regions for trade. While the ratio of greater than 1 indicates greater dependence on developed markets, that of less than 1 indicates lesser reliance on developed markets and greater reliance on regional markets.

Sources:
IMF (2009a), *Direction of Trade Statistics Yearbook 2009*, Washington, DC: IMF, pp. 142, 265.
IMF (2009b), *International Financial Statistics Yearbook*, Washington, DC: IMF, pp. 236–238, 422–425, 391–393, 437–440, 487–488, 646–648.
UN (2009), *Asia-Pacific Trade and Investment Report 2009*, Bangkok: UN, pp. 195–202.
CEPD (2009), *Taiwan Statistical Data Book 2009*, Taipei: CEPD, pp. 227–230.

Table 4.6A   Intra-regional trade growth (%)

	2001	2002	2003	2004	2005	2006	2007	2008	Value of total i-r trade in US$billions 2008
	1	**2**	**3**	**4**	**5**	**6**	**7**	**8**	**9**
Japan	−13.8	10.8	23.2	23.9	5.9	8.1	14.6	15.2	382.80
China	6.6	23.3	36.6	34.3	22.3	21.1	22.7	14.5	1,247.72
India	6.0	21.9	39.2	30.3	34.5	40.9	19.5	32.1	174.90
South Korea	−11.2	11.7	25.0	28.6	14.9	15.5	16.9	n.a.	n.a.
Taiwan	3.9	12.9	16.2	28.9	9.6	11.7	8.6	3.2	294.53
Singapore	−12.8	4.2	29.3	26.2	16.1	20.2	10.8	15.8	414.81
Malaysia	−11.5	10.4	10.2	25.1	11.4	12.3	14.6	12.6	227.60

Sources:
UN (2009), *Asia-Pacific Trade and Investment Report 2009*, Bangkok: UN, p. 194.
CEPD (2009), *Taiwan Statistical Data Book 2009*, Taipei: CEPD, pp. 222–226.

The US's and India's Trade with China

In the light of the recent global debate on the burgeoning trade deficit of the United States with China and on its implications for the international value of the Chinese yuan, we have presented in Table 4.6B the export and import trade of the US and India with China, as both countries have continuously suffered from rising trade deficits. Column 8 of row 3 of the table shows that the total deficit in the US trade with China for the period from 2002 to 2008 stood at $1.45 trillion accounting for 33 per cent of America's global trade deficit (row 6, column 8). Row 4 of the table shows that exports to China accounted for only 20 per cent of the US's total imports from that country in 2008. India's total trade deficit with China for the whole period stood at nearly $47 billion (column 8 and row 9). More significant is the fact that the share of India's exports to China compared to its imports from China declined from 66.15 per cent in 2001 to 53.34 per cent in 2008 implying that the capacity of India's exports to China to pay for its imports from China continuously weakened (row 10).

Trade Balance and Exchange Rates

Substantial surpluses in its trade with the US, Europe, India and other countries have enabled China to accumulate a large amount of foreign currencies. The maintenance of a favourable trade balance and the consequent substantial inflow of foreign currency into China via portfolio investment and investment in construction activities have pushed China's foreign currency reserves to more than $2.5 trillion. Hence, pressure is mounting on China to revalue its yuan against the US dollar so that exports to China from the US, the EU

Table 4.6B   *The US's and India's trade balance with China (value in US $billions)*

	2002	2003	2004	2005	2006	2007	2008	Total
	1	**2**	**3**	**4**	**5**	**6**	**7**	**8**
China								
1. US exports to	22.05	28.41	34.72	41.83	55.22	65.23	71.45	318.94
2. Imports from	133.49	163.25	210.52	259.83	305.78	340.11	356.319	1769.33
3. Balance of trade	−112.44	−134.84	−175.80	−218.00	−250.56	−274.88	−284.86	−1450.38
4. as % of 2	16.50	17.40	16.50	16.10	18.10	19.20	20.10	18.00
US								
5. Global trade deficit	−509.00	−581.00	−709.00	−829.00	−882.00	−854.00	−866.00	−4,401.00
6. 3 as % of 5	21.90	23.90	24.80	26.30	28.40	32.20	32.90	33.00
India								
7. Exports to China	1.72	2.71	4.17	6.47	7.91	10.19	18.49	51.67
8. Imports from China	2.60	3.73	6.07	9.92	15.81	24.69	34.66	98.14
9. Trade Balance	−0.88	−1.02	−1.90	−3.45	−7.90	−14.50	−16.17	−46.48
10. 7 as % of 8	66.15	72.65	68.69	65.22	50.03	41.27	53.34	52.64
11. Global trade balance	−8.39	−12.94	−24.45	−41.67	−56.05	−81.22	−116.82	−341.57
12. 9 as % of 11	10.48	7.88	7.77	8.27	14.09	17.85	13.84	13.42

Source: IMF (2003, 2009a), *Direction of Trade Statistics Yearbook*, Washington, DC: IMF, pp. 512, 260.

and other countries can increase as well as imports to the US and other countries from China decrease, thereby reducing the size their imbalance of trade. Pegging the Chinese yuan to the US dollar since 2008 has enabled China to maintain the competitive advantage of Chinese goods in the US market.

Our research (IMF, 2009b) shows that after 2002, the value of the yuan and of the US dollar against the IMF's Special Drawing Rights (SDRs) moved in the same direction. In some years the yuan depreciated at a marginally higher rate than the rate of depreciation of the US dollar. Also, after 2005 the appreciation of the yuan against the US dollar was only marginal. But in 2008 the yuan was pegged to the US dollar with a view, among other things, to maintaining the real value of China's massive dollar assets. Hence, the general consensus is that the Chinese yuan is not sufficiently appreciated against the US dollar, so as to provide the US with the opportunity to increase its exports to China and to reduce its huge trade deficit. However, it is unlikely that China will move away immediately from the system of currency pegging and float the currency (Solomon and Batson, 2010).

But correcting the misalignment of currencies is only one part of the solution. The other parts of the solution lie in further reduction in the level of protection on imports to China from the US as well as the removal of discriminating rules limiting the ability of foreign companies to carry on investment and production in China in competition with domestic companies. Also, and more importantly, the US government needs to take measures to ensure that domestic consumers cut down their debt-financed consumption expenditures considerably. As long as the domestic demand in the US exceeds its domestic supply, there will, of course, be a current account deficit by definition.

The US government also needs to ensure that domestic small and medium-sized manufacturing industries have strong government support to restart their production lines. In the end, it is due to the policy of American corporations that US companies left their homeland in droves for China to make large profits for themselves and virtually decimate their domestic manufacturing sector. Hence, the responsibility for the current deficit in America's trade with China must lie a great deal with US companies, too. A great deal of the bilateral deficit is, as a matter of fact, created by American companies located in China, not by Chinese companies.

The value of Indian rupees is determined against a basket of currencies. But the value of the rupee against foreign currencies fluctuates almost freely in response to the demand and supply of the currency in the market. All other Asian currencies are less controlled than the yuan is currently, although most of them are not completely free-floating.

China, for its part, put in place a few of Adam Smith's ([1776] 1976) basic institutions such as the protection of property and the elimination of restrictions on the use of factors of production such as labour, raw materials and so on. The People's Republic of China (PRC) also created foreign investment and trade-promoting infrastructure and institutions in the form of road, rail, air and sea communication, high-class port facilities, power supply, low restrictions on the repatriation of profits, low corporate tax rates, guarantees of the uninterrupted deregulation of factory hours and wages, and the elimination of trade union activities in both product and factor markets. Nevertheless, one may argue that the ethics of fair trading institutions require that countries accumulating large trade surpluses increase their imports from countries incurring large deficits in their trade balance so that large imbalances in global trade are reduced. In this respect China and all other countries with large trade surpluses have some responsibility to increase their imports from countries with large trade deficits substantially.

Terms of Trade and Mean Tariff Level

In Table 4.7A we present indices of the terms of trade of the major countries covered in our study, although we present terms of trade indices for only four countries because of data constraints. As the table shows, terms of trade indices for Japan, South Korea and Singapore were higher than 100 before 2005 and lower than 100 after 2005, but the reverse was true for India. The reason for such a trend in India's terms of trade after 2005 is that during this period the prices of commodities and metals, such as agricultural products, minerals, gemstones and gold, have been rising; and India was an exporter of agricultural commodities (see Table 4.8 below), gemstones, jewellery and so on. But despite this, India's trade balance did not improve.

Table 4.7A   Terms of trade indices of major Asian countries (2005 = 100)

	2002	2003	2004	2005	2006	2007	2008
Japan	122.1	116.1	109.4	100.0	90.5	86.1	74.1
India	84.2	91.4	81.9	100.0	105.3	121.1	n.a.
South Korea	120.1	112.7	108.0	100.0	93.4	91.1	78.8
Singapore	108.9	103.1	103.1	100.0	99.8	90.8	89.9

Source: IMF (2009b), *International Financial Statistics Yearbook*, Washington, DC: IMF, pp. 84–85.

Although not a very good measure of a country's import restrictions, the simple mean tariff, as presented in Table 4.7B, provides us with a broad indication of the import trade regime of the countries covered in our study. It would appear from the table that India, South Korea and Malaysia maintained considerable restrictions on imports of all products and quite high levels of tariffs on the import of agricultural products. Such a high rate of tariff for India on agricultural goods was a reflection of India's need to protect its 700 million villagers who primarily sustain their livelihood from agriculture. In 2009–10, the rates came down further as the peak rate of customs tariff in India in 2007–08 stood at 10 per cent and the mean tariff at 9.7 per cent (GOI, 2008). Korea and China also maintained a relatively high level of mean tariff.

However, since India has been incurring a substantial trade deficit (see Table 4.5B above), it has more justification for maintaining a relatively higher level of mean tariff than China and South Korea which have been accumulating large trade surpluses as a share of their GDP (see Table 4.5B above). But the almost exclusive reliance of Indian villagers on agriculture for their survival could have been lessened by facilitating the growth of hundreds of thousands of micro and small enterprises in the vast hinterland of rural India, as Taiwan and China did. This was Gandhi's dream (Narayan, 1962; Roy, 1986) which could not be realized because of Nehru's obsession with the plan of creating a self-reliant giant industrialized India.

Table 4.7B   Simple mean tariff in Asian countries

	All products		Primary		Manufactured	
	2005	2007	2005	2007	2005	2007
Japan	2.7	2.9	5.0	11.4	1.3	2.9
China	8.9	10.0	8.9	9.0	8.9	8.9
India	16.8	17.0	24.4	25.2	15.7	15.9
South Korea	9.1	15.8	21.2	20.8	7.3	6.6
Singapore	5.0	7.0	5.5	5.6	4.9	4.9
Malaysia	11.6	14.5	3.0	2.8	3.7	8.5

Sources:
World Bank (2008), *World Development Indicators*, Washington, DC: World Bank, pp. 340–342.
World Bank (2009b), *World Development Indicators*, Washington, DC: World Bank, pp. 352–353.

TECHNOLOGY ACQUISITION AND UPGRADATION

Since trade and FDI are the most important means of technology acquisition and upgradation, which in turn define and direct a country's industrialization process, we will now examine the process of technology acquisition and upgradation in China, India and East Asia. The commodity composition of a country's imports is a clear indicator of a country's effort to upgrade its technology.

China and India

For China, during 2000–04, a clear shift took place in exports, from light manufacturing products such as textiles, apparel and leather goods to more technologically sophisticated, capital-intensive manufactures which included heavy capital goods as well as innovative telecommunication and electronic machinery. Also within the consumer goods category, there has been a marked shift from traditional labour-intensive, less durable consumer goods exports to more durable consumer goods exports, such as refrigerators, television sets, room air conditioners, washing machines, cellular phones, personal computers and so on.

During 2006–08, on average, the exports of all manufactures accounted for more than 94 per cent of China's total exports, as shown in Table 4.8. During the same period China's exports of machinery and equipment accounted for slightly over 47 per cent of total exports. This share included exports of all these technologically upgraded and sophisticated products. For India during the same period, exports of manufactured goods consisted of about 65.5 per cent of total exports, but machinery and equipment accounted for only 12 per cent of total exports. Hence China's share of machinery and technology-intensive exports in total exports was four times higher than India's share of the same items.

Fifty-three per cent of India's total exports consisted of low-skilled labour-intensive manufactures. Also, exports of agricultural products consisted of low-skilled labour-intensive products which accounted for more than 17 per cent of India's total global exports but only 3.6 per cent of China's total global exports during 2006–08. Therefore, the very low share of machinery and technology-imbedded equipment in India's total imports and exports relative to the high share of such products in China's import and export trade would suggest that China is far superior to India in technology acquisition for the upgradation of its industrial sector.

Consequently, the share of other labour-intensive technology-imbedded non-essential products as well as that of agriculture and related products in China's

Table 4.8   Commodity composition of trade (major items and percent in total)

	2000–2004 average		2006–2008 average	
	Exports	Imports	Exports	Imports
1. Agricultural and related products				
China	5.2	7.7	3.6	14.8
India	12.0	4.1	17.4	18.1
2. Mining and fuel				
China	4.1	13.7	1.9	12.4
India	9.3	30.2	16.4	34.5
3. Total manufacture including chemical products				
China	90.1	77.9	94.4	72.6
India	78.3	65.7	65.5	46.3
4. of which machinery and equipment				
China	40.6	45.0	47.2	42.4
India	13.2	11.6	12.0	21.6
5. All other manufactures including unclassified				
China	49.5	32.9	47.2	30.2
India	65.1	54.1	53.5	24.7
6. of which garments and textiles				
China	18.3	4.4	n.a.	n.a.
India	16.9	NA	n.a.	n.a.
7. of which unclassified				
China	NA	NA	n.a.	n.a.
India	2.1	18.4	n.a.	n.a.

Source: UN (2009), *Asia-Pacific Trade and Investment Report 2009*, Bangkok: UN, pp. 2003–2004.

total export income have fallen during the period from 2000 to 2008. During the same period, the share of similar manufactured goods in India's total export income has remained almost stationary, whereas the share of agriculture in India's total export income has also declined considerably. Although during the period of 2006–08 the share of India's imports of technology-imbedded machinery and equipment in her total import payment was double the share of such products in the total import payment during the period 2000–04 (Table 4.8), the share of machinery and technology-intensive goods in China's total import payment during this same period was double that of such imports in India's total import payments. However, the 2006–08 share was lower than the 2000–04 share of such imports in China's total imports. This may reflect an increasing capability to manufacture such products in China.

Foreign Direct Investment

The share of FDI in gross fixed capital formation and the import penetration share of GDP are indicators of a country's progress in technology upgradation. It can be seen from Table 4.9 that the share of FDI in gross fixed capital formation for China and India were 9.7 and 4.2 per cent in 2001. For both countries the share fell during 2003–05. In 2008, the share of FDI in India's fixed capital formation reached a high level of 9.8 per cent.

Overall, throughout the period of 2001–07 the share of FDI in China's gross fixed capital formation was more than double the share of FDI in India's gross fixed capital formation except in 2000. Also, the import penetration was significantly higher in China than in India. These trends are also illustrated in Table 4.9, which presents important indicators for China and India of their integration with the global economy. Since imports of machinery and equipment constitute the major component of FDI, the Chinese and the East Asian export-oriented economies with high shares of trade in GDP also have recorded a high share of FDI in fixed capital formation and high percentage of import penetration. It can be seen from Table 4.10 that the average share of machinery and transport equipment in the total imports of Japan, South Korea, Singapore and Malaysia stood at 23.2, 30.1, 51.2 and 50.1 respectively during 2006–08. The import penetration expressed as the percentage share of imports in total domestic demand for Japan, South Korea, Singapore and Malaysia stood at 14.5, 37.9, 93.3 and 21.2 per cent respectively (UN, 2009).

Intra-Industry Trade

A high share of manufactured goods consisting of components and final goods in the total trade of China and East Asia (Tables 4.8 and 4.10) shows a clear trend of convergence in the composition of intermediate and final goods'

Table 4.9   Indicators of integration with the global economy: China and India

	2001	2002	2003	2004	2005	2006	2007	2008
1. Share of total merchandising trade in GDP (%)								
China	37.56	41.72	50.65	55.33	62.16	64.42	62.75	57.96
India	19.87	21.16	22.23	25.38	29.81	32.23	31.75	38.29
2. Share of non-trade sector GDP (%)								
China	62.44	58.28	49.35	44.67	37.84	35.58	37.25	42.04
India	80.13	78.84	77.77	74.62	70.19	67.77	68.25	61.77
3. Share of total service trade in GDP (%)								
China	5.47	5.92	6.21	6.96	7.07	7.21	7.45	7.07
India	7.74	8.02	8.24	10.63	12.76	15.23	12.87	12.78
4. Import penetration[a] (share of import in total domestic demand)								
China	20.60	23.08	24.63	28.51	29.90	30.63	29.50	27.07
India	10.50	11.50	12.00	13.90	16.70	17.93	17.90	21.80
5. Net FDI inflow (billions of US dollars)								
China	44.24	49.30	47.07	54.93	79.12	78.09	138.41	147.79
India	5.47	5.62	4.32	5.77	6.67	17.45	22.97	41.55[b]
6. Share of FDI in gross fixed capital formation (%)								
China	9.69	9.40	7.40	7.00	8.40	6.90	10.00	n.a.
India	4.18	4.66	2.92	2.91	2.64	5.88	4.40	9.75
7. Share of FDI inflow in GDP (%)								
China	3.33	3.38	2.86	2.84	3.53	2.92	4.08	3.41
India	1.13	1.11	0.73	0.83	0.82	1.91	2.00	3.39

Notes:
[a] Total domestic demand = GDP – Exports + Imports.
[b] UN (2009), *Asia–Pacific Trade and Investment Review 2009*, Bangkok: UN, p. 207.

Source: IMF (2009b), *International Financial Statistics Yearbook 2009*, Washington, DC: IMF, pp. 236–238, 391–393.

exports and imports within the region. This trend is a reflection of the growing importance of intra-industry vertical and horizontal trade as well as of significant progress in technology acquisition and upgradation. Such items as power-generating equipment, industrial machinery, telecommunications equipment and road transportation machinery are exported to and imported from China, Malaysia and Singapore and so on (Athukorala and Yamashita, 2005). Television sets and other consumer electronics with product differentiation in superficial as well as genuine features are exported from and imported to the same countries within East Asia.

The current process of integration in East Asia in trade technology acquisition seems to be changing the character of the old net working model under

Table 4.10 *Commodity composition of East Asian trade (in %, average of 2006–2008)*

	Japan	South Korea	Singapore	Malaysia
Exports				
1. Agricultural and allied products	1.8	2.0	2.3	12.1
2. Mining and fuel	1.5	6.5	15.1	15.4
3. Total manufactures	96.7	91.4	82.5	72.6
4. of which machinery and equipment	63.0	58.7	54.4	44.9
5. All other manufactures including unclassified	21.3	33.6	28.1	27.7
Imports				
1. Agricultural and allied products	15.9	10.7	3.4	14.0
2. Mining and fuel	30.3	27.5	22.2	9.5
3. Total manufactures	53.9	61.8	74.5	81.5
4. of which machinery and equipment	23.2	30.1	51.2	50.1
5. All other manufactures including unclassified	30.7	31.7	23.3	31.4

Source: UN (2009), *Asia-Pacific Trade and Investment Report*, Bangkok: UN, pp. 203–204.

which first Japan and later the NIEs manufactured and exported high-quality components and capital goods to new developing East Asian countries for assembling these into final goods for their eventual export to the US and other developed countries (Gill and Kharas, 2007). During the decade of 2000, a car with a 'made-in-Japan' sticker included components manufactured in the East Asian countries as well as in other countries. For example, the Japanese car Honda is now assembled in Thailand with components sourced from many countries. Due to the significant rise in intra-industry trade and in intra-regional trade in East Asia, the major export-oriented countries of this region have been able to increase their market share in the same products conjoined with China.

In India too, motor vehicles, television sets, microwave ovens, refrigerators and so on are made with components sourced from East Asian and other countries. Hence, technology upgradation via trade also is taking place in India in the same way, albeit with considerably less export orientation in the Indian manufacturing sector than in the Chinese and East Asian manufacturing sectors. As illustrated in Table 4.6A above, this trend is reflected in the sharp increase in the rate of growth in India's trade with East Asia from 6 per cent of its total trade in 2001 to 21 per cent in 2002 and to 39 per cent in 2003. But the same intra-regional trade effects are not being felt in India's trade with its near neighbours. This trend also indicates that economically as well as geographically, India is far more integrated with China and East Asia than with its South Asian near neighbours, which were integral parts of India for millennia.

Myanmar and Pakistan were split off from India in 1938 and 1947 and East Pakistan (Bengal in undivided India) became independent Bangladesh in 1971. These smaller states possess the same anti-growth and inward-oriented institutions as India; they also harbour politics of mutual distrust (Roy and Tisdell, 1998). For technology upgradation through trade, the flying geese effect and the favourable contagion effect are spreading from Japan to China and India as well as from China to the smaller East Asian countries.

Nevertheless, because of prevailing institutional restrictions on exports, the Indian economy is significantly less integrated with the global economy than the Chinese and East Asian economies. Hence, the urge is strong to acquire and adopt cutting-edge technology in industries to manufacture goods, which can compete successfully in the world market with similar exportable goods from China and from India's export-oriented Asian neighbours, among indigenous industries and MNCs operating in the Indian manufacturing sector.

Tradeable Sector-Led Technology Upgradation

A country's capacity to achieve success in technology upgradation and technology-imbedded industrialization is greatly conditioned by the size of its merchandise trade sector. Panagariya (2007) argues that industrial output is far more tradeable than services. If in a country the share of industry in GDP is low, it can slow down the growth rate; this low share also leads to a low trade-to-GDP ratio which slows down the growth in trade. Since FDI is drawn primarily to the manufacturing industry to take advantage of lower wages, a low share of the manufacturing industry and total industrial sector in GDP leads to a low inflow of FDI to the country, which in turn contributes to a low inflow of technology for their industrialization.

However, the problem is that when efforts of a country's political leaders to open up the economy to external competition are greatly circumscribed by a prevailing inbuilt bias in the political structure against outward orientation and trade openness, the inflow of technology will be directed to manufacturing industries producing goods for the domestic market only. The proportion of advanced technology in the total technology import would tend to be minimal. Therefore, the size of the export-oriented manufacturing sector in the country is more important than the overall size of the industrial sector for trade-oriented industrial policy implementation.

Nevertheless, we have expanded Panagariya's (2007) argument by including in Table 4.11 a few more indicators to examine the importance of the tradeable sector in China, India and East Asia's trade-oriented industrialization. It can be seen (column 1) that for Japan, which is currently the third largest economy in the world, the share of industry in GDP declined from 34 per cent in 1995 to 30 per cent in 2007. For China this share increased from 47 to 49 per cent; for India only marginally, from 28 to 30 per cent; for Taiwan it declined from 33 to 25 per cent; for Singapore it declined from 35 to 31 per cent; and for Malaysia it increased from 41 to 48 per cent. The share of manufacturing sector in GDP for China was 34 per cent compared with 16 per cent for India in 2007. All other countries included here recorded more than a 16 per cent share in GDP in this area in 2007. The share of the service sector in GDP (column 3) at 52 per cent in 2007 for India was quite robust and higher than China's 40 per cent, but this sector's contribution to boost the efforts for technology upgradation and industrialization is marginal, as Panagariya noted.

The important indicators to examine are the share of merchandise exports and imports in GDP (col. 4), the share of FDI in GDP (column 6) and the share of Most Favored Nation (MFN) duty free imports in total imports (column 7). In 2007 India's share of merchandise trade in GDP at about 31 per cent was significantly lower than China's 64 per cent, Korea's 75 per cent, Taiwan's 119 per cent, Singapore's 337 per cent, Malaysia's 173 per cent, and almost equal to Japan's 30 per cent. In 2007, India's share of FDI in GDP at 2 per cent was significantly lower than China's 4 per cent, Singapore's 19 per cent and Malaysia's 5 per cent.

The share of MFN duty free imports in total imports provides a measure of a country's trade openness. In 2006, India had only 10 per cent of total non-agricultural products as MFN duty free imports, whereas Japan allowed 81 per cent, China 44 per cent, Korea 36 per cent, Singapore 100 per cent and Malaysia 79 per cent of their total non-agricultural imports to enter the country as MFN duty free. For the imports of agricultural goods, India's allowance of 7 per cent of imports as MFN duty free compared unfavourably to 42 per cent for Japan, 8 per cent for China, 99 per cent for Singapore and 76 per cent for Malaysia.

Evidence of the validity of Panagariya's (2007) hypothesis can also be found in the share of import penetration in the total domestic demand of China and India (Table 4.9 above). Row 4 of the table shows that the share of imports in total domestic demand of India has consistently been lower than that in the total demand of China throughout the period from 2001 to 2008.

R&D Activities and Learning-by-Experience

Learning-by-experience contributes to innovation and technology upgradation. R&D activities by firms constitute a form of capital investment for long-term returns in innovation. But such expenditures are influenced by a number of factors, prominent among them being macro-economic stability, cost of

Table 4.11 Tradeable sector-led technology upgradation and industrialization

	Share of industry in GDP (%) (1)				Share of manufacturing in GDP (%) (2)				Share of services sector in GDP (%) (3)				Share of merchandise exports and imports in GDP (%) (4)				Share of service trade in GDP (%) (5)				Share of FDI in GDP (%) (6)			Share of MFN duty free imports (%) 2006 (7)	
	1995	2006	2007	2008	1995	2006	2007	2008	1995	2006	2007	2008	1995	2006	2007	2008	1995	2006	2007	2008	2006	2007	2008	Ag.	Non-ag.
Japan	34	30	30	n.a.	23	21	21	n.a.	64	69	68	n.a.	n.a.	28	30	31	4	6	6	6	0	1	0	42	81
China	47	49	49	49	34	34	34	34	33	40	40	40	39	66	64	59	6	7	7	7	3	4	3	8	44
India	28	28	30	29	18	16	16	16	46	55	52	54	18	32	31	41	4	7	15	14	2	2	4	7	10
Korea	42	40	39	37	28	28	28	28	52	57	58	60	50	72	75	92	9	13	14	18	0	0	0	6	36
Taiwan	33	27	28	25	25	23	24	22	65	71	71	73	76	112	116	119	n.a.	n.a.	n.a.	n.a.	n.a.	n.a.	n.a.	n.a.	n.a.
Singapore	35	32	31	28	27	27	25	21	65	68	69	72	288	367	337	362	55	93	93	89	20	19	12	99	100
Malaysia	41	50	48	n.a.	26	30	28	n.a.	46	41	42	n.a.	171	187	173	161	30	29	31	27	4	5	3	76	79

Sources:
UN (2009), *Asia-Pacific Trade and Investment Report*, Bangkok: UN, p. 206.
World Bank (2008), *World Development Indicators*, Washington, DC: World Bank, pp. 202–204, 210–212, 314–316, 352–354.
World Bank (2009b), *World Development Indicators*, Washington, DC: World Bank, pp. 84–86, 208–210, 216–218, 232–234, 328–330, 364–366.
World Bank (2010), *World Development Indicators*, online.
UNDP (2008), *Human Development Report 2007–2008*, New York: UNDP, pp. 270–272.
CEPD (2009), *Taiwan Statistical Data Book 2009*, Taipei: CEPD, pp. 60–61, p. 216.

capital, openness, competition and infrastructure. User costs of capital which include the (i) real interest rate, (ii) depreciation, and (iii) tax allowances tend to have a negative relation to the growth of R&D stocks in both developed and developing countries (Jaumotte and Pain, 2005; Lederman and Maloney, 2003). The availability of credit from sources external to the firm seems to enhance the capacity and desire of a firm to innovate. Similarly a high corporate profit tax discourages innovation-related activities (Ayyagari et al., 2006; Jaumotte and Pain, 2005; Gill and Kharas, 2007).

FDI, Interest and Bank Credit

Since FDI is an important means of technology transfer to boost domestic R&D activities in developing countries, restrictive trade and investment policies in some countries have posed a major hindrance to technology transfer to domestic firms.

A moderate lending rate of interest and availability of sufficient loans from financial institutions are important requirements for the private sector to invest in R&D activities. Lending rates have been significantly lower in China than in India. The lending rate is also an indicator of macro-economic stability and inflation level in a country. In Table 4.12, we present the bank lending rates in China, India and other countries.

It can be seen from the table that lending rates in India were substantially higher than those in the other countries. India's rates were well above 10 per cent where the rates in Japan remained below 2 per cent. Since the year 2001, one can then ask whether the share of R&D expenditures in GDP has been higher in Japan compared with that in other countries included in this study. We will look at Japan's expenditure on R&D later. However, it is worth noting here that since Japan was the leading country in technology innovation and transfer to East Asia, it has already reached the highest stage of technological development. Naturally, a steady share of R&D expenditure in Japan's GDP will be sufficient for Japan to maintain its technological superiority.

In China during 2000–04, the average credit to private sector businesses accounted for 118 per cent of average GDP for the period (Gill and Kharas, 2007). In India during the 11-year period from 1997 to 2007, the average bank credit for all economic activities accounted for about 60 per cent of average GDP for the period (GOI, 2008; IMF, 2009b). Since this total credit by the banking sector includes credit for all kinds of economic activities to state and private sector borrowers, the share of average credit extended to large private sector firms in average GDP for the period would have been smaller.

However, in China the share of total bank credit to private enterprises including thousands of small and medium enterprises is very small compared with the very large share of total loans by banks to state enterprises under

Table 4.12   Lending rates per annum in China, India and East Asia (%)

	2001	2002	2003	2004	2005	2006	2007	2008
Japan	n.a.	1.86	1.82	1.76	1.67	1.66	1.88	1.91
China	5.85	5.31	5.31	5.58	5.58	6.12	7.49	5.31
India	12.08	11.92	11.46	10.92	10.75	11.19	13.02	13.31
Korea	n.a.	6.77	6.24	5.90	5.59	5.99	6.55	7.17
Singapore	5.66	5.37	5.31	5.30	5.30	5.31	5.33	5.38
Malaysia	7.13	6.53	6.30	6.05	5.95	6.49	6.41	6.08

Source: IMF (2010), *International Financial Statistic Yearbook 2010*, Washington, DC: IMF, pp. 229, 388, 421, 437, 488, 656.

government direction. Consequently, the bank lending rate is subsidized and not determined by market forces (Bardhan, 2010), as is the case in India.

It can be seen from Table 4.13 that in 2006 for India, the average tariff rate of 16.8 per cent was considerably higher than such rates in all other countries covered in this study. The share of merchandise trade in GDP was slightly over 32 per cent compared with nearly 67 per cent for China, 72 per cent for Korea, 386 per cent for Singapore and 194 per cent for Malaysia. Except for Japan and Korea, the share of FDI in GDP, which stood at only 1.9 per cent in India, was considerably lower than the share of FDI in GDP for all other countries in the same year. The share in GDP of domestic credit to private sector business, which was 45 per cent in India, was well above 100 per cent for most of the other countries. The commercial bank lending rate per annum for loans, at slightly over 11 per cent per annum, was significantly higher than such rates in all other countries during the period. The total tax rate as a percentage of business profit reached nearly 71 per cent for India and 74 per cent for China. Finally, the inflexibility of the labour market, expressed by the 'rigidity of employment' index, stood at 30 for India, 24 for China, 37 for South Korea and only 17 for Japan.

Hence by all accounts, the presence of the above-noted favourable factors to boost expenditure on domestic R&D activities was not as robust in India as in China and East Asia. Consequently, we would expect that expenditures on R&D activities to generate innovation and expenditures on education would have been smaller compared with those in China and East Asia.

Expenditures on R&D Activities and Education

In Table 4.14 we present government expenditures on education and R&D activities in China, India and East Asia. Column 1 of Table 4.14 shows that the public sector's expenditure on information and communication technology as

Table 4.13   Factors influencing expenditures on R&D activities, 2006

	Japan	China	India	Korea	Singapore	Malaysia
	1	**2**	**3**	**4**	**6**	**7**
1. Openness to trade and competition:						
(a) Average level of tariff (%) 2006	2.7	8.9	16.8	9.1	0.0	6.2
(b) Trade as % of GDP, 2006						
(i) Merchandise	28.1	66.6	32.4	71.5	386.2	193.7
(ii) Services	5.8	7.3	15.2	13.8	91.6	30.2
(c) Net FDI inflow as % of GDP, 2006	0.0	3.0	2.0	0.0	20.0	4.0
2. Domestic credit to private sector businesses as % of GDP, 2006	182.0	113.6	45.0	102.0	98.6	108.1
3. Domestic credit provided by banks, % of GDP, 2006*	307.7	136.9	63.4	107.1	72.6	119.4
4. Gross inflow of international finance	n.a.	2.6	4.2	n.a.	n.a.	7.0
5. Bank lending rate (%) per annum, 2006	1.7	6.1	11.2	6.0	5.3	6.5
6. Taxes payable by business: total tax rate as % of profit, 2006	52.0	73.9	70.6	34.9	23.2	36.0
7. Competitive labour market: rigidity of employment index; 0–100 (least to most rigid)	17	24	30	37	0	10

Note: * This credit includes all kinds of loans granted by banks to both private and public sector activities.

Source: World Bank (2008), *World Development Indicators*, Washington, DC: World Bank, pp. 246–248, 268–270, 276–278, 284–286, 288–290, 312–314, 320–322.

a proportion of GDP for 2007 for India was lower than such share of expenditures in the GDP of all the other countries. From column 2 of the table we can see that the R&D expenditure as a proportion of GDP on average during 2000–06 at 0.7 per cent for India was the second lowest and at 3.4 per cent for Japan was the highest. For China this share, at 1.4 per cent, was also modest. The share of public expenditures on education in GDP for all other countries, except Malaysia (6.2 per cent), was below 5 per cent during the period from 2000 to 2007. The expenditures of the central government on education as a proportion of GDP for China during 2006 and 2007 was, at 1.3 and 1.2 per cent, the lowest of the shares of these countries. India's shares were marginally higher than those of China. Tertiary students in science, engineering and construction as a proportion of total tertiary students on average during 2000–05 remained at 19 per cent for Japan, 22 per cent for India, 40 per cent for Korea and 40 per cent for Malaysia. Hence, we have to admit that the monetary contribution of the public sector to the growth of R&D activities in India was extremely low. However, since the figures for China and India refer to the expenditure of the central government only, the actual situation is likely to be somewhat less dismal than the figures would lead us to believe.

In China, Japan and East Asia during the first half of the decade of 2000, the business sector's contribution to total expenditures on R&D activities was around 60 per cent, 75 per cent and 55 per cent respectively (Gill and Kharas, 2007). One way of gauging the contribution of the business sector to R&D activities in India is to look at the proportion of total FDI inflow to the service sector, computer software and hardware, telecommunications, automobile industry, drugs and pharmaceuticals and metallurgical industries in which the technical capacity of R&D activities can be strengthened to absorb knowledge from abroad so as to make it useable for local adaptation and able to act as a catalyst for indigenous innovation. During a seven-year period from April 2000 to November 2007, FDI inflow to the service sector, computer software and telecommunications as a proportion of total FDI inflow to India stood at 38.4 per cent, but those shares of the automobile industry, drugs and pharmaceutical and metallurgical industries were only 2.4 per cent, 0.8 per cent and 4.2 per cent respectively. Consequently, the contribution of these three sectors to India's export income has been marginal. So for India too, the contribution of the business sector to total expenditures for R&D activities seems to have been higher than that of the public sector (GOI, 2008).

It is appropriate for any developmental state to minimize the effects of adverse externalities arising from the presence of an imperfect capital market and the problem of appropriability in knowledge-based FDI. The state in Japan, South Korea and Taiwan has greatly enhanced the capability of private sector firms to increase R&D activities by dealing with those problems (Cypher and Dietz, 2009; Meier and Rauch, 2005). The Indian state, however, has not followed an aggressive policy in this regard. Moreover, the tax exemption on income spent on R&D activities by the private sector firms has been moderate.

The Process of Technology Upgradation

The process of technology upgradation has to be looked at in two ways:

1.   methods of technology upgradation; and
2.   sources of innovation.

Table 4.14 *Indicators of information technology, R&D and education*

| | Information and communication technology expenditure (% of GDP) | | Research and development expenditure (% of GDP) | | Public expenditure on education[a] | | | | | | Student enrolments | |
| | 1 | | 2 | | % of GDP 3 | | | % of government expenditure 4 | | | Net secondary enrolment rate (%) 5 | Tertiary students in science, engineering & construction (% of tertiary students) 6 |
	2006	2007	1997–2002	2000–2006	2002–2005	2006	2007	2002–2005	2006	2007	2007	2000–2005
Japan	7.9	7.2	3.1	3.4	3.6	3.7	3.5	9.8	9.8	9.5	99.0	19.0
China	5.4	7.9	1.2	1.4	1.9	2.5	3.0	13.0	1.3	1.2	n.a.	n.a.
India	6.1	5.6	0.8	0.7	3.8	3.8	3.2	10.7	3.4	4.1	n.a.	22.0
Korea	6.6	7.1	2.5	3.2	4.6	4.6	4.4	16.5	16.5	15.3	96.0	40.0
Taiwan	n.a.	n.a.	2.0	2.3	4.2	4.0	4.0	20.6	21.6	21.8	n.a.	n.a.
Singapore	9.3	6.5	2.2	2.4	3.0	3.0	n.a.	n.a.	10.8	15.3	n.a.	n.a.
Malaysia	6.7	6.8	0.7	0.6	6.2	6.2	n.a.	25.2	n.a.	18.0	69.0	40.0

Note: [a] refers to expenditure of central government only for China and India.

Sources:
UNDP (2006), *Human Development Report 2006*, New York: UN, pp. 262–265.
UNDP (2008), *Human Development Report 2007–2008*, New York: UN, pp. 265–267 269–672, 273–275.
World Bank (2008), *World Development Indicators*, Washington, DC: World Bank, pp.76–78, 308–310, 270–272.
World Bank (2009b), *World Development Indicators*, Washington, DC: World Bank.
World Bank (2010), *World Development Indicators*, online.
IMF (2008), *International Financial Statistics Yearbook*, Washington, DC: IMF, pp. 116–117, 217–220.

Methods of technology upgradation

In East Asia in general, technology upgradation appears to have been taking place by introducing new product lines, upgrading current product lines and introducing new technology. During the first half decade of the 2000s, on average 59 per cent of all firms upgraded their product lines; 44 per cent of all firms introduced new product lines; and 38 per cent of firms used new technology in their production process. Hence, the upgradation of existing product lines was the most commonly used method for technology upgradation (Gill and Kharas, 2007).

Sources of innovation

Since the upgradation of existing product lines also involves the use of new technology-imbedded machinery, it would appear that the largest proportion of firms in East Asia used newly imported machinery to achieve technological innovation. Innovation in technology was also achieved by host country firms in cooperation with technology-exporting firms from the home country of the FDI hiring key personnel of technology-exporting firms and by developing and adapting innovation indigenously within host country firms. During the first half of the decade, the share of the firms using those last three sources of innovation in several East Asian countries, including Malaysia, in total firms was almost 35 per cent (Gill and Kharas, 2007).

For China, the importation of new machinery and equipment and the hiring of personnel play a big role in the country's upgradation of technology. The upgradation of technology is also taking place in product lines by innovation undertaken within firms. In India the importance of the import of new technology has been quite low. During 2000–04 the importation of new machinery and equipment accounted for only 11.6 per cent of total imports in India compared with 44.6 per cent in total imports for China. During the 2006–08 period, the share of such imports in total imports accounted for 21.6 and 42.4 per cent, respectively.

Indigenous innovation, therefore, played a key role in technology upgradation in India's industrial and service sectors. As already discussed, imported technology was directed primarily to the non-financial service, computer software and hardware, and telecommunications sectors. These sectors, along with motor vehicles, drugs and pharmaceuticals, are the ones in which indigenous innovation appears to be taking place quite significantly with the help of FDI, learning-by-experience and the spillover effects of knowledge-based externalities (Cohen and Levinthal, 1989; Meier and Rauch, 2005; Cypher and Dietz, 2009).

Since, in electronic hardware, computer software and automobile manufactures, FDI played an important role in technology upgradation in India, we present in Table 4.15 the share of exports in electronic hardware and computer software production and in automobile production during 2002–03 and 2006–07. It can be seen from the table that the share of exports in electronic hardware and computer software manufactures reached more than 62 per cent in 2006–07 from 53 per cent in 2002–03. Within automobile production, the shares of total automobile exports and passenger car exports reached 7.5 and 16.9 per cent in 2004–05 from 4.9 and 11.7 per cent in 2002–03. The Indian government did set up the National Automobile Testing and R&D Infrastructure Project (NATRIP) and also implemented the Automotive Mission Plan (AMP) for ten years from 2006–16 to make India a preferred destination for the design and manufacture of automobiles and automotive parts (GOI, 2008). However, unless these measures can substantially increase automobile exports in total automobile production, India's industrialization programme, as far as automobiles are concerned, will remain inwardly oriented.

In the early and mid-2000s, 72 per cent of domestic firms in the four smaller East Asian countries upgraded their product line with the help of R&D activities. However, the success in achieving good results from R&D activities depends on the availability in adequate numbers of science and technology-induced labour to make use of in the production process of more technologically advanced imported machinery and equipment, as well as of indigenous innovations. The shortage of such labour is currently being felt in China's export-oriented industries, which are utilizing upgraded technology to manufacture high value-added products. This is a constraint in Malaysia, too, while Korea, Taiwan and Singapore fare much better. Moreover, this type of knowledge quickly tends to become obsolete: the qualifications and technological knowledge of those who are currently unemployed are becoming irrelevant to the knowledge and skill required to make use of the upgraded technology (Callick, 2010).

On the other hand, despite having a good number of science and engineering graduates, the private sector businesses in India could not achieve success in R&D expenditure outcomes because of (i) the continuing presence of considerable inward orientation in trade and industrial policy, (ii) the state's not so

Table 4.15   Share of exports in production: electronics and automobiles (%), India

	2002–2003	2003–2004	2004–2005	2005–2006	2006–2007
Electronic hardware and computer software	53.3	54.9	57.9	59.8	62.4
Total automobiles	4.9	6.6	7.5	8.3	9.1
Passenger cars	11.7	15.0	16.9	16.3	14.7

Sources:
GOI (2007), *Economic Survey*, New Delhi: GOI.
GOI (2008), *Economic Survey*, New Delhi: Oxford University Press.

proactive role in dealing with the problems of imperfect capital markets and the appropriateness of knowledge-based FDI inflow, and (iii) the high bank lending rate since the early 2000s.

INDIA AS A GLOBAL INFORMATION TECHNOLOGY SERVICES HUB

In Table 4.16 we present some identifiable outcomes from technology acquisition and upgradation. It can be seen from the table that in patent applications filed, India's achievement appears to be better than that of Singapore and Malaysia but worse than those of Japan, China and South Korea. In terms of royalty and licence fees received, India's achievement is only better than that of Malaysia, but in high-tech exports which is the most important indicator of a country's success in technology acquisition and upgradation, India's achievement is far less than those of all the others.

In value terms, in 2007 India's high-tech exports amounted to only about $5 billion compared with $121 billion for Japan, $337 billion for China, $111 billion for South Korea, about $106 billion for Singapore and $65 billion for Malaysia. For 2008, in commercial service trade, India's export income of $103.2 billion compares favourably with Singapore's $71.9 billion and Malaysia's $29.5 billion, but very unfavourably with Japan's $147.1 billion, China's $143.7 billion and South Korea's $160.6 billion. Therefore, such results tend to confirm our observation that lack of a sufficient outward orientation in India's export trade has greatly undermined its capacity to acquire sophisticated technology and to upgrade existing technology in its industrialization process. Considering the large size of the Indian economy, the situation is, in fact, still worse than it seems, looking at the absolute figures.

Hence, the question that naturally arises is whether India can achieve the status of a global leader in Information and Communication Technology Enabling (ICTE) services, since this is what many economists predict (Bardhan, 2010). We will make some passing comments on this issue.

Fundamental Requirements

India's IITs (Indian Institutes of Technology) and other engineering universities such as Bengal Engineering University and Jadavpur University and regional engineering colleges and institutes, such as the Indian Institute of Science, produce high-quality technical and science graduates. English as the medium of instruction and a strong emphasis on mathematics and science at the school and college levels have created a strong comparative advantage in the supply of technical labour for India (Dev, 2008). However, India is facing

Table 4.16 Identifiable outcomes from technology acquisition and upgradation

	Patent applications filed				Royalty and licence fees				High-technology exports				Commercial service trade (value $million)	
	Residents		Non-residents		Receipts ($millions)		Payments ($millions)		$millions		% of manufactured exports			
	1		2		3		4		5		6		7	
	2005	2007	2005	2007	2006	2007	2006	2007	2006	2007	2006	2007	2008 Export	2008 Import
Japan	359,382	333,498	67,696	62,793	20,096	23,229	15,500	16,678	126,618	121,425	22	19	147,112	165,592
China	93,172	153,060	80,155	92,101	205	343	6,634	8,192	271,170	336,988	30	30	143,704	461,278
India	6,795	4,521	10,671	19,984	112	112	949	949	3,511	4,944	5	5	103,171	53,289
South Korea	121,942	128,701	38,979	43,768	2,011	1,920	4,487	5,075	92,945	110,633	32	33	160,622	92,790
Singapore	435	696	8,170	9,255	730	716	10,470	9,905	134,133	105,549	58	46	71,935	76,342
Malaysia	522	n.a.	670	4,269	26	36	1,052	1,195	63,411	64,584	54	52	29,543	29,285

Sources:
World Bank (2010), World Development Indicators, online.
World Bank (2009b), World Development Indicators, Washington, DC: World Bank, pp. 312–314.
World Bank (2008), World Development Indicators, Washington, DC: World Bank, pp. 314–316.
UN (2009), Asia-Pacific Trade and Investment Report, Bangkok: UN, pp. 189–190.

competition from such nations as China, Ireland and the Philippines in the supply of low-cost labour with adequate technical qualifications (Joshi, 2006). While the labour costs in the ITS and ICTE sectors have been rising rapidly, the estimated attrition rate of 55 per cent would appear to be higher than those in China and the Philippines. The attrition is higher among female employees in ITS and ICTE services. There is still resistance within the Indian society against young unmarried girls working night shifts. The vast majority of Indian parents still obey the customary law of getting their daughters married to a suitable groom. After marriage, they tend to lose their freedom; and Becker's (1973) 'altruistic dictator' decides their future (Roy et al., 2008). Consequently, an acute shortage in the supply of technical personnel in the ITS and ICTE sector is expected to occur in India within the foreseeable future (NASSCOM, 2005). Hence, with the shortage of the supply of technical labour, the average wage rate for such labour will continue to rise, thereby making India a relatively less attractive destination for outsourcing activities from Europe and the USA. The consistent appreciation of the Indian rupee against the US dollar in recent years has also made Indian goods, including software services, in overseas markets more expensive than before.

Adequate infrastructure is the second crucial precondition for the successful development of the ITS sector. In power supply, the deficit in terms of peak availability and of total energy supply at the end of 2007 stood at around 15 per cent and 8.4 per cent (GOI, 2008). But the deficit in Eastern India was more severe because of the shortage of a supply of coal to power stations due to pilferage by political party mafias. Also peasants and households in the rural sector illegally use power to irrigate their lands and light their houses by stealing electricity from power lines. Hence, the intermittent supply of electricity does not allow these service sector operations to run smoothly for 24 hours a day for seven days a week. Also road and port networks are in a state of disrepair (GOI, 2008). The government of India hardly made any attempt to correct these adverse externalities that the ITS and ICTE sectors suffer from. The state does not have the capacity to enforce the rule of law in the society, and the possibility of intrusion in the service sector by militant unions looms large.

These unfavourable externalities raise the transaction costs of doing business in these areas and thereby raise the prices of the products they export. The government has, however, implemented a special incentive package scheme to encourage investments for setting up semiconductor fabrication and other micro- and nano-technology manufacturing industries, under which the average rate of incentives admissible is 22.5 per cent of capital expenditure for the first ten years for all those units located in special economic zones (SEZs) and out of such zones (GOI, 2008).

In Table 4.17 we present the annual growth of overall commercial service trade of China, India and East Asia during 2001–08. It can be seen from the table that

India's exports of commercial services recorded a growth of 60 per cent in 2004. But the rate of growth decelerated form 2005 onwards. In 2008 the growth in the export of commercial services of China, India and East Asian countries suffered in the wake of the global financial crisis. But the growth rate of such exports of China has exceeded India's export growth in services from 2007 onwards.

In answer to the question 'Can India attain the status of a global ITS hub?', one can conclude that there are many difficulties, given India's current institutional environment within which all business enterprises operate. China, besides already being a global manufacturing hub, can eventually attain the status of a global IT services hub as well (Joshi, 2009). In the areas of knowledge of the English language, India's superiority is now also being challenged by China. However, although there has been a significant increase in the number of Chinese youths trained in English since the late 1990s, the total number of the English-speaking population that India possesses is the second largest in the world after the United States.

Indian companies in the ITS and ICTE sector are keenly aware of the possibility of China becoming the global ITS and ICTE hub. Hence, they are diversifying their exports in establishing new service lines such as R&D and engineering services, consulting services in many areas including medical and legal, system integration, application development and maintenance, traditional IT outsourcing and horizontal services in finance, accounting, administration, customer interaction services and in human resources administration and research. Indian companies are also now applying IT in core businesses, banking, insurance, manufacturing, pharmaceuticals, pathology, travel and hospitality, animation, media and entertainment while retaining their original support services in business process outsourcing (BPO), knowledge process outsourcing (KPO), engineering process outsourcing (EPO) and human resource outsourcing (HRO) (Joshi, 2009). Thus, the remarkable horizontal and vertical intra-industry integration in the service sector in India is comparable to the similar trend in manufacturing which we have discussed earlier in this chapter.

Hence, in conclusion we can argue that to sustain India's leadership in the ITS and ITES sectors, the Indian state has to ensure that:

1. there is a growing supply of qualified English-speaking manpower adequate enough to satisfy the needs of the industry;
2. the quality of services delivered by companies continues to conform to international standards;
3. strong emphasis is placed on information security practices;
4. the quality of telecommunications and other infrastructure, including power, roads, ports, etc. approaches international standards; and
5. the state policy is so designed and implemented as to promote the entrepreneurial freedom and growth of industry (Karnik, 2005).

Table 4.17 Commercial service trade (annual % change)

	Total exports to the world								Total imports from the world							
	2001	2002	2003	2004	2005	2006	2007	2008	2001	2002	2003	2004	2005	2006	2007	2008
Japan	−6.6	2.2	1,708.0	25.6	13.2	6.2	10.1	11.2	−7.0	−0.2	3.1	21.7	−0.9	1.0	10.9	10.0
China	9.5	19.2	17.6	33.6	19.2	23.6	32.8	20.4	9.0	18.5	18.9	30.4	16.2	20.3	29.0	22.1
India	6.5	12.4	22.8	60.0	37.5	35.2	29.2	12.3	−0.8	4.0	16.4	44.0	29.5	23.0	93.4	−31.3
South Korea	−4.8	−2.3	16.1	27.1	7.8	10.6	26.3	17.1	−1.4	11.1	10.4	23.6	17.7	17.1	21.4	11.0
Singapore	−2.6	7.7	22.9	28.8	13.2	15.4	14.3	3.0	7.8	5.2	19.9	25.1	11.1	14.6	13.6	5.4
Malaysia	3.7	2.9	−11.8	30.4	14.6	11.3	35.0	0.2	−0.5	−1.2	4.2	12.3	15.0	7.1	21.3	1.7

Source: UN (2009), Asia-Pacific Trade and Investment Report, Bangkok: UN, pp. 189–190.

SMES IN EXPORT PROMOTION AND TECHNOLOGY UPGRADATION IN ASIA

Throughout Asia, small and medium-sized industries have played a powerful role in the export-led development strategy. But their role has been different in different countries. They were even important in Japan's developmental state, despite the stereotype that the Japanese economy has been dominated by large conglomerates or keiretsu (Friedman, 1988).

China and India

Reliable data on the production, export and employment creation by small and medium enterprises in China and India are not available. In China, many small enterprises are owned by rural towns and villages, and are accordingly known as town and village enterprises (TVEs). In India, micro-enterprises are added to SMEs and hence are termed MSMEs. In both countries – and more importantly, in India – there are millions of micro and small enterprises which operate in the informal sector and are not officially registered, and hence no statistics are available on the performance of these enterprises.

TVEs were the primary source of revenue for town and village governments up to the mid-1990s, after which they were, in compliance with constitutional recognition of the importance of the private sector in the Chinese economy, increasingly privatized. With increasing marketization of the economy, rapid entry of new firms increased the demand for and the prices of factor inputs, which raised the operational cost of TVEs and lowered their profit margins. After the reform of the monetary and banking systems, banks independent of government control became less accessible to TVEs for credit (Meier and Rauch, 2005; Jefferson, 1999; Mood, 1997). Also, since loss-making TVEs no longer had a chance of being protected by their respective village and town governments, they had to cut down their costs of production and produce more efficiently to maintain their minimum profit levels to stay in business. The entrepreneurial dynamism was more widely prevalent in TVEs in the coastal region, where the beneficial effects of agglomeration, combined with better transport and other communication facilities as well as easy access to markets, enabled them to raise their share in China's total industrial output, which at the turn of the twentieth century reached around 40 per cent from about 22 per cent in the late 1970s (Perkins et al., 2006). Although these small labour-intensive manufacturing enterprises have limited capacity to increase their contribution to the value added in manufacturing industries, they nevertheless have made a contribution to the country's export income.

In India the classification of small and medium-sized industries tends to follow the conventional definition under which: (i) units with one to four workers are classified as micro (cottage) industries which are by and large family-owned and family member-operated enterprises and which can be found in textiles, shoemaking, jewellery manufacturing, etc.; (ii) units with five to 19 workers are classified as small-sized enterprises; (iii) units with 20 to 99 workers are said to be medium-sized enterprises; and (iv) units with 100 and more workers are classified as large-sized industries (Perkins et al., 2006).

In accordance with India's industrial and labour laws, if there is a minimum of 20 workers on a company's payroll, that company must be registered under the relevant act and be placed under the organized industrial sector. Once this is done, labour union leaders move in and force the 20 or more labourers to join the relevant union as members. Union thuggery, stoppage of work and high wage demands for less than normal hours of weekly work make it extremely difficult for these medium-sized enterprises to survive, grow and increase their export income.

On the other hand, the large number of micro and small enterprises is, up to now, outside the purview of the federal and provincial government law and union thuggery. They are all under the unorganized and hence informal sector. They operate from their homes in villages (textiles and shoemaking) or on street sides in towns and cities. They operate for long hours each day and are able to cut down their cost of production to sell their products at any price that the market offers. Although in India's Five Year Plan documents (GOI, 1957), the importance of small-scale industrial sector was always recognized, no real help in terms of credit, marketing, etc. was provided to these enterprises. Large public sector banks are reluctant to extend loans to the informal sector, just as TVEs in China's rural areas have experienced. These are the enterprises which Gandhi wanted to promote in rural India (Schumacher, 1962; Roy, 1986), but in his vision of a giant industrial India Nehru could see the role of small-scale industries only as providers of employment and explorers of the possibility of creative efforts (Paranjape, 1964). MSEs surely are involved in creative efforts as their dynamism is reflected in not only their capacity to face cut-throat competition in the product market and grow, but also in their innovative capacity and in their horizontal expansion in product diversification.

For example, millions of sarees are produced each year in silk and cotton textiles. But one could hardly find two sarees with exactly the same design and print, although there can be several sarees with the same print and design in different colours. While jute manufacture and export has lost its pre-eminent status in India's agro-based industries in recent years, fine jute fibres are being mixed with cotton fibres to make fine fabrics for designer apparel for females. Similar horizontal expansion is also taking place in small-scale leather manufacture and jewellery manufacture.

During a period of five years from 1 April 2002 to 31 March 2007, the total employment provided by MSEs stood at 143.9 million and, on average, the employment figure was 28.8 million workers. The total number of these enterprises was 12.8 million and their contribution to the total manufacturing sector output was 39 per cent on 31 March 2007. On average, between 1 April 2002 and 31 March 2007, MSEs accounted for 30 per cent of the total export income of India. Also, during the same period, on average the share of exports in total output value of this sector stood at around 31 per cent. Furthermore, the exports of micro, small and medium-sized enterprises together during 2000– 01 and 2006–07 on average accounted for more than 38 per cent of the total exports of the country (GOI, 2005, 2008).

The government of India has now initiated measures to address the concerns of the MSEs relating to credit availability, fiscal support, cluster-based development (similar to agglomeration-based development in China's TVEs), infrastructure, technology and marketing. Also, to force these enterprises to face market-based competition, the deletion of products from the list of items reserved for production by MSMEs has been continuing (GOI, 2008).

Singapore and Malaysia

At independence in 1963, Singapore's industrial sector was undeveloped, as domestic entrepreneurs concentrated on entrepôt trade and other services. Since the British military, a significant employer, was about to leave the country, the government was hard pressed to do something in order to secure the livelihood of citizens. To do so it followed a two-pronged strategy. On the one hand it made an effort (in hindsight a very successful one) to attract FDIs from large multinational companies. On the other hand, it turned the shipyards and other facilities left behind by the British into state-operated companies, what became the so-called government-linked companies (GLCs). In the process, however, the government forgot the small domestic entrepreneurs. These, in turn, were suspicious of the government, which they saw as biased against them, and were also reluctant to cooperate for fear of excessive government control. While all this has changed considerably during the last couple of decades, it left a mark on Singapore's industrial structure that is clearly visible even today. Domestic private companies, although often quite successful, are still mostly small, often working as subcontractors for the large MNCs. Developing this sector, often through leveraging knowhow brought in by MNCs, is today part of Singapore's explicit industrial strategy. The country has also become an important foreign investor in its own right (Blomqvist, 2005:37–40). However, a big problem for the smaller companies is the fact that the competition for good employees is hard and the small companies have difficulties competing with the MNCs and the government.

Malaysia, contrary to Singapore, is a resource-rich country where the two main legs of the economy were tin and rubber during the colonial period.

However, at independence, the economic future of the country appeared to be bleak. There was no industrial tradition; and the country seemed to be potentially unstable due to ethnic fragmentation (Lim and Nesadurai, 1997). Industrialization started late: only in the mid-1980s did the GDP share of manufacturing become larger than that of agriculture.

Like Singapore, Malaysia chose to rely on FDI to a great extent, although the FDI-induced boom came some 20 years later. FDI poured in partly as a response to increasing costs in more advanced Asian countries; and Malaysia became one of the leading host countries for FDI in Asia. This period was interrupted by the Asian economic crisis in 1997–98, and although the growth resumed after that, it has not been as fast and smooth as before. Moreover, the emergence of China and other low-cost production bases puts Malaysia in a precarious position where many foreign investors may consider pulling out of the country, as the country's cost competitiveness deteriorates. Meanwhile, the effects of FDI on domestic industrial capabilities have reportedly been limited (Rasiah, 2006), which limits the possibilities for Malaysia to upgrade its industrial structure and thus increase its real competitiveness.

SMEs in Malaysia (firms with less than 150 full-time employees) contribute significantly to the country's manufacturing production and employment. In 2000 their share of manufacturing value added was 26 per cent and their share of employment was nearly one-third. Many of these firms are active in low-tech sectors oriented towards the domestic market, like food and beverages. Others are subcontractors of large MNCs, which may give them some opportunities for learning new technologies but at the same time make them dependent on a small number of customers, sometimes one single company. Thus SMEs' share in exports was only some 20 per cent, which is lower than in many other countries. According to a number of studies, the growth of the SME sector is limited by the lack of financing, low productivity, poor access to management and technology, and many government regulations. These difficulties seem to persist despite the fact that the government has initiated many programmes in order to improve their lot (Saleh and Ndubisi, 2006). Moreover, an ethnically-based bias may play a role, as many small entrepreneurs are ethnic Chinese while the government tends to favour the indigenous (Malay) part of the population.

Taiwan

Small and medium enterprises (SMEs) provided the dynamism for Taiwan's export boom from the 1960s through to the 1980s. Their flexibility and entrepreneurship allowed them to take advantage of changing market conditions, and they proved to be surprisingly capable of upgrading to the production of advanced electronics goods (Hu and Schive, 1998; Lam, 1992; Lam and

Clark, 1994; Wu and Huang, 2003). They then were able to take advantage of the growing integration across the Taiwan Strait during the 1990s by moving production to China (Naughton, 1997). However, over the last two decades they have become increasingly squeezed between low-cost producers from developing nations and much larger and more sophisticated corporations in the developed world (Wu and Huang, 2003). Moreover, because they are small and dispersed, their political influence in Taiwan is fairly limited, making it hard for them to get aid from the government (Tan, 2008).

The SMEs have clearly made a substantial contribution to Taiwan's rapid economic development. During the late 1970s and early 1980s, for example, they constituted just under half of manufacturing production and over 80 per cent of commercial sales (Wu, 1988). In terms of employment, SMEs employed 61 per cent of all Taiwanese workers in 1976, and this figure increased to 78 per cent in 1997. As far as the share of exports is concerned, in 1981 SMEs accounted for 68 per cent of all exports, though this figure dropped to a still high proportion of 49 per cent in 1997 (Wu and Huang, 2003).

The SMEs in Taiwan pursue highly entrepreneurial strategies that Danny Lam (1992) has termed 'guerrilla capitalism'. Guerrilla capitalism includes extreme flexibility in rapidly filling even small orders, attention to quality and design, audacious bidding, participation in complex networks of subcontracting, and only partial observation at best of government regulations and international laws, such as those regarding intellectual property rights. The SMEs have also demonstrated a remarkable capacity to innovate and upgrade their operations. Thus, while guerrilla capitalism took off in the textile and shoe industries in the 1960s, such entrepreneurs moved into low-tech electronics assembly in the 1970s; and some were able to upgrade into more sophisticated high-tech production in the 1980s (Lam, 1992; Lam and Clark, 1994).

The success of the SMEs is explained by several of their organizational characteristics. The use of an extensive network of subcontracting relationships among all competitors in an industry was a surprisingly common pattern in Taiwan. Therefore, although it is true that the winning contractor benefited the most from a lucrative foreign order, that firm was able, in effect, to have the slack capacity of the entire industry available to it through subcontracting. This prevalence of subcontracting networks was facilitated by the prevailing pattern of ownership because almost all firms in a particular industry owned each other's shares. Subcontracting enhanced the efficiency of the market in two ways. First, it allowed the winning contractor to make above-normal profits through their knowledge of the local industry. Thus, they would normally subcontract to firms that had surplus capacity which they would sell at marginal rather than full cost. Second, it kept other firms in business and allowed them to become more efficient through 'learning-by-doing'. In other words, rather than a zero-sum game typical of the bidding process in the West, in Taiwanese business the winner took the most, but the loser also benefited from having less lucrative, but still profitable, subcontracting work. This process explains how a layer of small firms could circumvent the limitations that would normally be placed on them by under-capitalization and the inability to handle large orders. This intricate subcontracting network, therefore, made Taiwanese industry able to respond more as a unified organism rather than as discrete units (Lam, 1992).

The dynamic of moving from textiles to electronics in the late 1960s and 1970s also involved applying the principles of guerrilla capitalism to acquiring technology transfers from the foreign multinational corporations (MNCs) that initially dominated Taiwan's electronics industry, especially the export sector. Ironically, the drive for an indigenous industry was fuelled by the rapid growth of MNC assemblers and component makers. As with any industry experiencing rapid growth, there was a large turnover of labour and management as new arrivals acquired skilled managers by hiring talent from established firms. Thus, every new entrant created more and more opportunities for both the trained local staff and the expatriate staff of the established firms. Local managers soon realized that, in fact, the MNC operations were not highly sophisticated. Managers who worked in assembly operations, therefore, quickly saw that there was little that was beyond their own capability to set up with relatively little capital. Naturally, many of them jumped at the opportunity and left their MNC employers to establish assembly operations on their own (Kuo, 1998; Lam, 1992).

By the early 1980s, however, the SMEs were already beginning to be challenged in global markets as Taiwan's industrial development increasingly priced its companies out of labour-intensive production. Thus, the SMEs were forced either to upgrade into sophisticated knowledge-intensive production or to move offshore, primarily to China. Their role in the economy quickly began to deteriorate. For example, their share of total exports dropped from a high of 70 per cent in 1982 to a respectable proportion of 49 per cent in 1997 (Wu and Huang, 2003) and then to a much lower level of 28 per cent in 2006 (SMEA, 2008).

THE INSTITUTIONAL ENVIRONMENT TO PROMOTE BUSINESS AND TRADE

Any kind of business activity undertaken for the production of goods and services for either domestic consumption or the export market can only prosper in a country in which an enabling institutional environment exists. The important growth and development-promoting institutions have been discussed extensively in Chapters 2 and 3. In Tables 4.18A, 4.18B and 4.19, we present some important indicators for assessing the relative ease with which activities can be carried out.

Rows 1 to 3 of Table 4.18A show that in both China and India, the total tax rate eats away more than 70 per cent of total profit and that the corporate marginal tax rate stands at 25 and 30 per cent. However, for Singapore, this marginal corporate tax rate is only 18 per cent. Rows 4 to 6 show how many bureaucratic procedures a firm has to complete, how much time it takes to complete those procedures and how much the cost of completion of those procedures is as a proportion of the country's per capita income. The time and cost required to start a business appear to be the lowest in Singapore and highest in India. To start a business it takes 70 per cent of per capita income in India compared with 8.4 per cent in China, 16.9 per cent for South Korea, 0.7 per cent for Singapore and 14.7 per cent for Malaysia. For registering property, the number of procedures to be completed is only 6 transactions for India but the number of days required to complete this process is 45 for India, compared with 9 days for Singapore, 11 for South Korea, 14 for Japan, 29 for China and 144 for Malaysia. The number of procedures to be completed to build a warehouse ranges from the lowest of 11 for Singapore to 20 for India and to the highest at 37 for China. But the time required to complete construction ranges from the lowest of 34 days for South Korea, to 187 days for Japan, 224 days for India, 261 days for Malaysia and to the highest, 336 days, for China.

The number of procedures to be completed and the number of days required to enforce a business contract range from 21 steps and 150 days for Singapore to 30 steps and 316 days for Japan, 35 steps and 230 days for Korea, 34 steps and 406 days for China, to 30 steps and 600 days for Malaysia; however, India requires 46 steps and 1,420 days. To resolve insolvency and close a business via law court, it takes only 7 months in Japan, 9 months in Singapore, 1.5 years in South Korea, 1.7 years in China and 2.3 years in Malaysia, but 10 years in India. No wonder foreign investors have been less attracted to locate manufacturing activities in India.

How difficult it is to comply with hire-and-fire rules in the employment of labour is indicated by indices ranging between 0 implying least rigid and 100 implying most rigid. This index stands at 0 for Singapore, 10 for Malaysia, 17 for Japan, 27 for China, 30 for India and 45 for South Korea. Hence labour employment conditions in China are the fourth most rigid and are slightly less rigid than in India, but even then China received the largest amount of average inflow of FDI per year. Further comments will be made on employment rigidity below.

In Table 4.18B we present entrepreneurs' opinions about the business environment in China, India and East Asia. Since these entrepreneurs are aware of the ground realities of doing business in these countries, their opinion is highly relevant in judging the degree of ease with which business can be conducted in these countries. On most issues, both China and India have fared badly. For example, in China and India, company and management officers meet tax officials 14 times and 31 times per year, respectively. In 73 and 48 per cent of

Table 4.18A   Institutional environment for business activities

	Japan	China	India	South Korea	Singapore	Malaysia
Tax policies, 2006–08						
1. Total tax rate, % of profit (2008)	31	80	72	34	28	35
2. Highest marginal individual tax rate	40	45	30	35	20	28
3. Corporate	30	25	30	25	18	28
Starting a business, 2008						
4. Number of procedures	8	14	13	10	4	9
5. Time required, days	23	40	30	17	4	13
6. Cost as % of per capita income	8	8	70	17	1	15
Registering property, 2008						
7. Number of procedures	6	4	6	7	3	5
8. Time required, days	14	29	45	11	9	144
Dealing with construction permits, 2008						
9. Number of procedures to build a warehouse	15	37	20	13	11	25
10. Time required to build a warehouse, days	187	336	224	34	38	261
Employing workers, 2008						
11. Rigidity of employment index, least (0) to most (100) rigid	17	27	30	45	0	10
Enforcing contracts, 2008						
12. Number of procedures	30	34	46	35	21	30
13. Time required, days	316	406	1,420	230	150	600
14. Protecting investors, disclosure, 2008						
(0 = least to 10 = most disclosure)	7	10	7	7	10	10
15. Closing businesses, 2008						
(Time resolving insolvency, years)	0.6	1.7	10	1.5	0.8	2.3

Source: World Bank (2009b), *World Development Indicators*, Washington, DC: World Bank, pp. 278–280, 290–292.

firms, unofficial payments to public officials are part of the picture in these countries. About 50, 59 and 44 per cent of firms in China, India and South Korea do not report the details of all sales to their respective taxation departments. Clearing an export consignment through the red tape of the customs department takes 7, 7, 5 and 16 days in China, South Korea, Malaysia and India, respectively. Generally, entrepreneurs' opinion on most issues relating to the business environment in India appears to be unfavourable.

The recognition of the ownership of innovations through ISO certification was accorded to 36, 23 and 18 per cent of firms in China, India and South Korea. Indigenous innovation has received a strong boost in the high-technology sector

Table 4.18B   Enterprise survey results on environment for business activities

	China 2003	India 2006	South Korea 2005	Malaysia 2006
1. Regulations and taxes				
a) Time dealing with officials (% of management time)	18.3	6.7	3.2	7.3
b) Average number of times management met with tax officials	14.4	31.0	2.4	5.2
2. Permits and licences				
Time required to obtain operating licences	11.8	n.a.	n.a.	n.a.
3. Corruption				
Unofficial payments to public officials (% of time)	72.6	47.5	14.1	n.a.
4. Crime				
Losses to theft, robbery, vandalism, and arson (% of sales)	0.1	0.1	0.0	0.3
5. Informality				
Firms that do not report all sales for tax purposes (% of firms)	49.5	59.2	43.7	n.a.
6. Gender				
Firms with female participation in ownership (% of firms)	n.a.	9.1	19.1	n.a.
7. Finance				
Firms using banks to finance investment (% of firms)	9.8	19.4	11.5	23.8
8. Infrastructure				
Value lost due to electrical outages (% of sales)	1.3	6.6	n.a.	1.8
9. Innovation				
ISO certification (% of firms)	35.9	22.5	17.6	8.6
10. Trade				
Average time to clear exports through customs (days)	6.7	15.6	7.2	4.8
11. Workplace				
Firms offering formal training (% of firms)	84.8	15.9	39.5	22.5

Source: World Bank (2009b), *World Development Indicators*, Washington, DC: World Bank, pp. 272–273.

in China via government purchase of high-technology products and equipment from domestic manufacturers, thus undermining foreign-based companies' chances to capture a part of this market (*The Australian*, 2010). Although offering formal training to workers at workplaces enhances the capacity of the 'learning-from-experience' process to improve labour efficiency, the chances of endogenous innovation and technology upgradation within enterprises in India's record are abysmal. For example, 89, 40 and 23 per cent of firms in China, South Korea and Malaysia offer training of workers at workplaces, but only 16 per cent of firms do that in India.

PROBLEMS CONFRONTING INDIA'S INDUSTRIAL SECTOR

While there are undoubtedly many problems that Indian and foreign entrepreneurs are confronted with in their effort to promote India's export and industrial production, we will comment on the few regulations which adversely affect India's efforts to attract a large inflow of FDI, to manufacture exportable goods at globally competitive prices by hiring labour at a deregulated labour-market wage rate, to get factories running without interruption caused by labour strikes and power shortages, and to get export and import consignments clear through sea and airports speedily.

1. Foreign investors are not allowed to purchase more than 51 per cent of the equity in Indian companies in most areas of investment. This rule is an important factor which prevents a large inflow of FDI into India.
2. If a company, whether indigenous or foreign, with more than 100 labourers wants to close down its business, it will have to seek the permission of the provincial government, which in most cases is not willing to give it. The implications of this rule are twofold:
    a) A profit-maximizing foreign enterprise intending to invest in India can only operate safely it if keeps in its payroll a labour force of less than 100 so that the company can close down the business and withdraw its capital safely.
    b) If it has to maintain a labour force of less than 100, then according to official classification, it is granted a status of a medium-sized enterprise which cannot employ large-scale production techniques and, hence, cannot enjoy the benefits of economic scale so necessary to produce output at the lowest cost per unit to remain competitive at the export market as well as to maximize profits.

The sole objective of such bizarre rules is obviously the preservation of employment of the industrial labour force even at the risk of driving indigenous and foreign capital out of India's industrial sector.

Industrial Sickness

As a consequence of the inability of the government of India to put in place an exit policy, in 2007 the number of applications of companies applying to the Board for Industrial and Financial Re-construction for the conversion of their status to sick industries and accordingly for the sanction of Rehabilitation Schemes for these companies reached 7,158, out of which 5,301 references were accepted (GOI, 2008). The overwhelming bulk (96 per cent) of these successful references came from private sector enterprises and only a small proportion (4 per cent) from public sector enterprises under the jurisdiction of federal and provincial governments.

Man Days Lost in Workplace

One of the primary reasons for industrial sickness is man-days lost due to strikes and lock-outs in industrial enterprises. But the total man-days lost would not necessarily relate to any dispute within enterprises as leaders of political parties and labour unions can call a strike any time without any economic reason. From January 2002 to 30 November 2007, the total man-days lost in enterprises reached 136.33 million, of which 36.03 million days were lost due to strikes by the labour force and the rest due to lock-outs (GOI, 2008). However, millions of man-days are also lost due to *bandhs* (strikes) called by political party leaders and enforced on the civil society and public and private sector businesses by political party thugs. Naturally, the labour cost per unit of output in India has to be higher than that of similar output in China where migrant low-skilled workers in export-oriented electronic industries earn, on average, a basic salary of US$130 per month (*The Australian*, 2010), which is equivalent to about Indian rupees 4,800, an amount which is considerably lower than a factory worker in a similar industry in India earns per month. But the monthly wage of labourers in certain types of production facilities in China is considerably lower than US$130 per month. For example, in Fushan, in a factory manufacturing Honda's transmission mechanism, labourers are paid US$22 per month (*The Australian*, 2010). Even labourers in India's agricultural sector are paid around Rs4,000 per month in cash and more than Rs1,000 in kind per month.

Inflexibility of Labour Markets, Female Labour and Infrastructure

The labour force led by the most virulent trade unions in the industrial and service sectors in India is probably the world's most violent. Such a situation was created by both the federal and provincial governments needing the support of trade unions to secure votes at elections to capture state power. There are about 45 laws dealing with employment conditions, such as wages, job security, industrial disputes, safety at jobs and so on. Furthermore, apart from providing employees in large state-owned and private sector enterprises with pension facilities and health insurance, the management of these enterprises is also required to inform official labour exchanges of any labour vacancy that may occur and of any change that occurs in companies' demand for labour. In the organized industrial sector, it is quite difficult for a company to retrench its labour, even when it is in financial trouble and incurring losses.

In this scenario, why would an export-oriented MNC come to India when it is far better off in China and East Asia?

Agriculture

Due to (i) its stagnant growth, (ii) a high level of protection by Western countries on imports of agricultural products, and a high level of tariffs imposed by India on the import of agricultural products, (iii) a fragmented internal market for agricultural goods, and (iv) the almost total absence of mass manufacturing involving low-wage and low-skilled rural labour, India's agricultural sector failed to boost the country's total export earnings and the share of total trade in GDP significantly (Sally, 2009).

Female literacy

Adult literacy rates provide a good indicator of the capacity of a country's masses to absorb at least the technology required by low-skilled labour in the production of simple non-durable manufactured goods and agricultural goods. Female labour is particularly suitable for such production. But during 2005–07, the female literacy rate was 56 per cent in India, compared with 90 per cent in China and Malaysia and 92 per cent in Singapore (World Bank, 2009b). During the same period, the male literacy rate in India was close to 80 per cent. Such a low level of female literacy has prevented female labour's conversion to a technology-induced labour force. This in turn has undermined India's capacity to increase the contribution of total factor productivity to its GDP (Winters, 2004).

With a low female literacy level, India is less able to access global finance for its low-skilled, labour-intensive, export-oriented manufacturing sector. Furthermore, advances in technology since the mid-1990s have led to the emergence of supply chains and to the growth of offshoring in intermediate goods and services, which were non-tradeable earlier and which now can absorb a substantial proportion of the country's literate female labour force (Coe, 2007). India, with its low level of female literacy, has difficulties taking advantages of these new developments.

Infrastructure

The current state of India's infrastructure is awfully inadequate for the needs of a growing export trade sector. For manufactured goods, there is a supply chain of intermediate goods sourced from different parts of the country and from overseas. The smooth running of this supply chain, final assembly plants and completion of final trade procedures for export requires good roads, a rail network and port facilities. However, these are in very bad shape. Consequently, it takes on average 24 days for an export consignment to travel from India to the United States, whereas it takes on average 15 days for a consignment to reach the US from China (Wilson and Kein, 2006).

Table 4.19   Trade facilitation environment

	Japan	China	India	South Korea	Singapore	Malaysia
1. Time for completing trade procedures (days)						
2005	11	21	40	12	4	16
2009	11	23	19	8	4	16
% change	0	10	−53	−33	0	0
2. Cost of completing trade procedures (constant 2000 US dollars)						
2005	934	326	967	835	359	375
2009	848	435	794	618	373	375
% change	−9	34	−18	−26	4	0
3. Import–export facilitation bias[a]						
Time bias	1.1	1.1	1.0	1.0	0.6	0.8
Cost bias	1.1	1.1	1.0	1.0	0.6	1.0

Note: [a] The import–export facilitation bias shows the ratio of the time to import to the time to export for the 'time basis' and the ratio of the cost to import to the cost to export for the 'cost basis'.

Source: UN (2009), *Asia-Pacific Trade and Investment Report*, Bangkok: UN, p. 209.

Also, the pre-berth waiting time of ships carrying container traffic in India's ports is longer than the waiting time of ships in ports in China and East Asia because of poor labour efficiency and poor road and rail container evacuation infrastructure from ports to the country's hinterland (GOI, 2005). In 2007, this waiting time increased to 10 hours on average in India ports. As pre-berth waiting time has increased, the average turnaround time of container ships has also increased to 36 hours in comparison to 10 hours in Hong Kong, due primarily to the delay in the evacuation of cargo resulting from bad road conditions and rail networks linking Indian ports to the hinterland (GOI, 2008).

Further delay for export consignments to leave Indian ports is caused by the time it takes for them to obtain clearance from customs. As row 10 of Table 4.18B above showed, the average time required for export consignments to clear through customs was 16 days in India in 2006, compared with 7 days in China in 2003, 7 days in South Korea in 2005 and 5 days in Malaysia in 2006. Such delays significantly undermine the competitiveness of Indian ports relative to that of Chinese and East Asian ports.

Trade facilitation environment
In Table 4.19, we present the trade facilitation environment in terms of three indicators in China, India and East Asia. It can be seen from row 1 of the table that the number of days required to complete trade procedures in 2009 was lowest for Singapore at 4 days and highest for China at 23 days. For India,

the number came down from 40 days in 2005 to 19 days in 2009. The time for completing trade procedure relates to the average time to export or the time to import goods. For exporting goods, such procedures include the time for packing goods at the warehouse to the time when the vessel departs from the port. For importing goods, it is the time from the entry of the vessel at the port of entry to the time of goods delivery at the warehouse.

In row 2, we present the cost of completing trade procedures in 2000 constant US dollars for China, India and East Asia. The cost of completing trade procedures refers to the cost of completing export and import trade procedures for a standardized cargo of goods by sea transport (UN, 2009). This cost for India declined from US$967 in 2005 to US$794 in 2009. For China and Singapore, it increased from $326 and $359 to $435 and $373. For Japan, it declined from $934 to $848. Despite a decline of 18 per cent, the cost of completing the trade procedure was about 83 per cent higher in India than in China. Row 3 shows that for Japan, China and India, the time spent on completing procedures for exporting was higher than that for completing procedures for importing, but for Singapore and Malaysia, it took less time to complete exporting than importing trade procedures. For Japan and China, the cost to complete export trade procedures was higher than for import trade procedures; for India, South Korea and Malaysia, the cost ratio did not show any bias, but for Singapore the cost to export was lower than the cost to import. Apart from the delay in getting documents completed and cleared by relevant government authorities, the other important issue which can greatly undermine a company's reputation as a reliable exporter or importer is the uncertainty of the likelihood of imports or exports arriving at their destination on time. Since export-oriented firms operate in a highly competitive environment, the failure to deliver exports on time may lead to the cancellation of all future orders by importing companies. Such a problem is more serious for Indian exporters and importers than for their counterparts in China and East Asia.

Another factor which makes it difficult for India's exports to increase rapidly is the lack of the strict implementation of measures of quality control of products by some exporters. This problem mostly exists in some manufactured goods, such as leather goods and shoes, and also in other semi-durable goods manufactured for both domestic and international markets. A similar problem has occurred in some goods manufactured by Chinese firms under contract to supply companies in USA and Europe, as well as in goods destined for developing country markets.

Why Does India Lag Behind China?

Panagariya (2007) argues that since industrial output is far more tradeable than services, a low share of industry in GDP is likely to slow down the rate of economic growth and this low share of industry in GDP also leads to a low trade to GDP ratio, which slows down the growth in trade. The low share of industry and trade in GDP also means a low level of inflow of FDI to labour-abundant countries such as India for its use in manufacturing industries to take advantage of lower wages compared to other countries for labour-intensive manufacturing activities.

Decomposition of Panagariya's thesis

By decomposing Panagariya's (2007) thesis, we have come up with the following virtuous circle. Economic growth driven by an increasing share of investment directed to export-promoting industries increases industry's share of a country's GDP and also increases the country's export income and foreign exchange earnings. This creates a favourable trade balance and raises the share of a country's global trade in GDP, which together increase the inflow of FDI in upgraded technology and knowledge to the export-oriented manufacturing and service industries, which in turn enables the industrial and service sectors to produce more technology-induced goods to further increase the country's export and foreign exchange income, favourable trade balance, share of trade in GDP and rate of economic growth. This cycle starts all over again with higher economic growth driven by the export-promoting industrialization strategy which, by raising the share of industry in GDP and by creating backward linkages, connects the centre to the periphery of the country and brings millions of people out of poverty, as we have witnessed in China and East Asia.

In Table 4.20 we present the share of industry and other sectors in GDP of China, India and East Asia between 1995 and 2007. It can be seen from the table that for China and India, the share of industry in GDP increased from 47 and 28 per cent in 1995 to 49 and 30 per cent in 2007. For all other countries, except Malaysia, the share in 2007 was lower than that in 1995. But to comprehend the contribution of a country's industry to its export expansion, technology upgradation and economic growth, one has to look also at the share of manufacturing industry in the country's GDP. This is where India is far behind China, as the table shows that in 2007 the share of manufacturing industry in the GDP of China and India stood at 32 and 16 per cent, respectively. All the other countries recorded a larger share of manufacturing in GDP that year than India did. The share of services in GDP in 2007 for China and India was 40 and 52 per cent. It would therefore seem that India tried to bypass the manufacturing industrial sector and leapfrog to the service sector.

Following Panagariya's thesis, we can see from Table 4.20 that India has indeed lagged behind China and East Asia in the manufacturing industry's share in GDP. Consequently, India is also lagging behind China and East Asia in the share of trade, FDI, fixed capital investment and of import penetration in GDP, as illustrated earlier in Table 4.9. The reason is that while the production

Table 4.20   Share of industry and other sectors in GDP (%)

	Japan	China	India	South Korea	Taiwan	Singapore	Malaysia
Agriculture							
1995	2	20	26	6	3	0	13
2006	1	12	18	3	2	0	9
2007	2	11	18	3	2	0	10
Total industry							
1995	34	47	28	42	33	35	41
2006	30	48	28	40	27	35	50
2007	30	49	30	39	28	31	48
Manufacturing							
1995	23	34	18	28	26	27	26
2006	21	33	16	28	23	29	30
2007	21	32	16	28	24	25	28
Services							
1995	64	33	46	52	64	65	46
2006	69	40	55	57	71	65	41
2007	68	40	52	58	71	69	42

Sources:
World Bank (2008), *World Development Indicators*, Washington, DC: World Bank, pp. 202–204.
World Bank (2009b), *World Development Indicators*, Washington, DC: World Bank, pp. 208–210.
CEPD (2009), *Taiwan Statistical Data Book 2009*, Taipei: CEPD, p. 60.

of consumer goods in the manufacturing industrial sector in China and East Asia was geared to satisfy foreign demand for consumer goods, in India it was overwhelmingly geared to satisfy domestic demand for consumer goods since the implementation of Nehru's policy of self-reliant development in 1956. Even today, the trade and national macro-economic and labour-market policies and provincial-level policies of India are not overtly supportive of export-oriented, labour-intensive manufacturing industries and export-promotion activities (Sally, 2009; GOI, 2008; Panagariya, 2008), in contrast to China and East Asia.

The primary causes

1. All the reasons presented earlier in this chapter are of secondary importance and are symptoms of a deeply rooted malaise that has crippled the Indian economy since 1956–57. The malaise is the decision made by Indian leaders led by Nehru after India's independence to accord political freedom and democratic governance the status of primacy over economic freedom, entrepreneurial dynamism, free market rules in product and factor markets, and wealth creation activities as opposed to transfer activities. This democratic governance with many political parties has

been highly decentralized from the federal to the provincial and village levels, so much so that today there are millions of democratic governance systems for every kind of economic and social activity spread throughout the country, thereby making the country completely ungovernable and dysfunctional. China and East Asia accorded economic freedom, entrepreneurial dynamism, free market rules and deregulated product and factor markets the primacy of status over political freedom and highly decentralized dysfunctional democratic governance.

2. The superiority of China and East Asia over India in export promotion, technology upgradation and overall development has resulted from those countries' capability to attract a substantial proportion of outsourcing of the production of all kinds of manufactured goods and manufacturing industries from the developed countries, as well as to capture outsourcing of high-end knowledge-based products in the service sector. But India has been able to capture only a decent proportion of the production of high end knowledge-based products in Information Technology Services (ITS) and Information and Communication Technology Enabling (ICTE) services.

3. The outsourcing of manufactured goods and facilities to China from the West has meant that foreign companies operating in China have their own well-established marketing networks in their home countries. Hence, China did not have to undertake measures to establish marketing channels. Even giant retail stores, such as Wal-Mart in the USA and Myer and Coles in Australia, have established arrangements with Chinese manufacturers to manufacture goods under their own brand names.

In India, very little of such outsourcing of manufacturing industries has taken place. The term 'outsourcing' now applies to both the industrial and service sectors in today's globalized world. The primacy of politics over economics under a democratic governance mechanism, as expected, has contributed to a significant rise in transfer activities and only a moderate rise in wealth creation activities in India.

CONCLUSION

We have discussed above the primary reasons for India's failure to catch up with China and also East Asia in export promotion, technology upgradation and export-led industrialization. It is true that the Indian state, led by its political-bureaucratic elite, continues to remain unreformed as it maintains the status quo, which provides the political elite with a hassle-free life. The much-needed economic reforms cannot take place without a reform of the state

(Sally, 2009), but the reform of the state can perhaps never take place because of the following:

1. The Indian state is being continuously broken up into smaller provincial units based on religion, language and ethnicity. Hence, there is no unified demand from Indian citizens that the state leaders establish, on a regular basis, their legitimacy to govern the country and provinces by protecting the civil society from incidents that lead to the loss of human lives and property.
2. The leaders of the state do not need to secure on a regular basis their customary right to govern the country by creating wealth, preventing transfer activities and distributing wealth created by high economic growth among all sections of the population of the country.
3. Almost all the top leaders of the state in recent years are, among other things, in the age group of above 70 years; they seem to lack the initiative and drive expected of leaders.

In all these areas, China and East Asia are far ahead of India.

NOTES

1. Factory Asia includes greater China consisting of the People's Republic (PR) of China, Hong Kong and Taiwan, as well as Korea and ASEAN (Association of Southeast Asian Nations).
2. One of the present authors' (Roy) private conversation with several entrepreneurs in India reveals that businesses can operate quite successfully in India provided adequate infrastructure is made available to them and there are no government and trade union restrictions on factory hours, labour wages, no stoppage of factory work due to any kind of strike and *bandh*, as well as a government guarantee of the security of business property and of their personal lives, which are also considered as private property in democratic India.
3. Refers to Cambodia, Thailand, Malaysia, Indonesia and the Philippines.

5. Growth and income distribution in the Asian states

In Chapter 4, we presented an in-depth analysis of the institutional environment for promoting business activities in the major Asian states. The same unfavourable institutions which adversely affect a country's effort to promote exports, technology acquisitions and business activities also prevent a country from achieving better economic growth outcomes. In this chapter we will first examine the main features of GDP growth, proceeding then to the issues of sustainability, macro-economic management and income distribution.

ECONOMIC GROWTH

China and India

In Table 5.1 we present the main features of the growth in GDP and its components in China and India between 2002 and 2008. It can be seen from row 1 of the table that the real GDP of China, estimated at 2005 prices increased from $US1,657.23 billion in 2002 to $US3,362 billion in 2008 thereby representing an increase of 102.9 per cent. For India it grew from $US573.79 billion in 2002 to $US1,077.26 billion in 2008, thereby representing an increase of 87.7 per cent. From row 2, it can be seen that China's real GDP, which was 2.9 times higher than India's real GDP in 2002, became 3.12 times higher in 2008. The widening gap between China's and India's GDP seems to imply that the gap between India's potential and actual GDP will not be closing as rapidly as the gap between China's potential and actual GDP. The average growth rate for China and India during eight years between 2000 and 2008 was 10.4 and 7.9 per cent, respectively.

Rows 3 to 9 present the contributions of household consumption expenditures (C), government consumption expenditures (G) and private investment expenditures (I) to GDP. It can be seen from row 3 that the contribution of household consumption expenditures to GDP has consistently been close to 20 percentage points higher for India than for China. The share of government consumption in GDP (row 4) has consistently been higher for China than

Table 5.1 *Growth in GDP and its major components*

		2002	2003	2004	2005	2006	2007	2008
		1	**2**	**3**	**4**	**5**	**6**	**7**
1. Real GDP	China	1,657.23	1,822.8	2,0005.41	2,237.08	2,579.56	3,041.49	3,362.00
(US$billions at	India	573.79	649.85	724.04	813.31	868.93	1,046.21	1,077.26
2005 prices)								
2. Real GDP		2.90	2.80	2.77	2.75	3.00	2.90	3.12
ratio: China's								
to India's								
3. Household	China	43.68	41.84	39.92	38.68	37.97	35.93	34.55
consumption as	India	63.25	61.84	58.68	57.55	55.89	55.00	54.74
% of GDP (C)								
4. Government	China	15.88	15.17	14.51	14.52	14.21	13.94	13.54
consumption as	India	11.87	11.26	10.73	10.47	10.20	10.17	11.58
% of GDP (G)								
5. Total	China	59.56	56.01	54.43	53.40	52.18	49.87	48.09
consumption	India	75.10	73.10	69.41	68.02	66.09	65.14	66.32
as % of GDP								
(C+G)								
6. Total savings	China	40.44	43.00	45.51	46.80	47.82	50.13	51.91
(S) as % of	India	24.90	26.90	30.59	31.98	33.91	34.86	33.68
GDP								
7. Total	China	37.85	40.87	43.25	44.01	44.53	42.84	44.40
investment (I)	India	25.06	25.93	30.35	33.66	34.44	37.60	38.32
as % of GDP								
(fixed capital+								
inventory)								
8. Investment in	China	36.25	39.38	40.72	42.19	42.53	40.89	41.89
fixed capital as	India	23.83	25.00	28.45	31.02	31.80	34.00	34.80
% of GDP								
9. Investment in	China	1.60	1.49	2.53	1.82	2.00	1.95	2.43
inventory as %	India	1.23	0.93	1.90	2.68	2.64	3.60	3.52
of GDP								
10. Incremental	China	0.23	0.30	0.40	0.29	0.22	0.41	0.32
capital/output	India	0.30	0.42	0.41	0.40	0.44	0.33	0.30
ratio								

Sources:
IMF (2010), *International Financial Statistics Yearbook 2010*, Washington, DC: IMF, pp. 332, 637.
IMF (2009b), *International Financial Statistics Yearbook 2009*, Washington, DC: IMF, pp. 238, 393.

for India, but the gap between the two has narrowed from about 4 percentage points in 2002 to about 2 percentage points in 2008, thanks mainly to the greater success of the Chinese government in trimming the size of government expenditures. But when we look at the total contribution of household and government consumption expenditure (C+G) in GDP, we can see that in 2002, the share of total C+G in GDP stood at 75.1 per cent for India, but only 59.6 per cent for China. In 2008, the share of total C+G in GDP declined to 48.1 per cent for China and 66.3 per cent for India. These figures would, there-fore, tend to justify the perception among economists that India's growth has been driven more by consumption expenditures and other endogenous factors than by investment expenditures and exogenous factors stemming from export expansion and technology acquisition (BMI, 2010; Cypher and Dietz, 2009; Luce, 2007).

The total share of investment expenditures (fixed capital and inventory) in GDP (row 7) for China rose from 37.9 per cent in 2002 to 44.4 per cent in 2008, whereas for India, the share rose from about 25.1 per cent in 2002 to 38.3 per cent in 2008. But the share of investment in fixed capital (row 8), which plays a more crucial role in generating and sustaining a high rate of growth than the share of total consumption in GDP, was the main driver of China's high rate of economic growth.

The importance of investment in fixed capital in China's GDP growth is evident from its share in GDP rising from 36.2 per cent in 2002 to nearly 42 per cent in 2008, thereby recording an increase of 5.8 percentage points. For India, too, this share rose rapidly from 23.8 per cent in 2002 to 34.8 per cent in 2008, thereby recording an increase of 11 percentage points. Consequently, if India's infrastructure development programmes do really get implemented then gross fixed capital formation (GFCF) can grow by slightly over 10 per cent per annum. On that assumption, it is estimated that the share of GFCF in GDP for India will surpass that for China by 2016 (BMI, 2010). However, this is unlikely to happen because of the lack of finance of the debt-ridden government, the lack of private sector capital, and the presence of bureaucratic red tape, as well as the lack of support of many inward-oriented provincial governments. Although an increasing proportion of investment in both coun-tries has been financed by domestic savings as evidenced in the rise in share of domestic savings in GDP for China and India (row 6) from 40.4 per cent and nearly 25 per cent in 2002 to nearly 52 per cent and 33.7 per cent in 2008, a substantially larger proportion of investment was financed by foreign savings in the form of industrial machinery and other technology-imbedded imports in China's highly outward-oriented economy than in India's semi-closed and inward-oriented economy.

Nevertheless, the capital/output ratio (row 10) increased more rapidly in India from 0.30 in 2002 to 0.42 in 2003 and to 0.44 in 2006 than in China where it rose from 0.23 in 2002 to 0.30 in 2003, and declined to 0.22 in 2006. The primary reason for the rapid rise in the capital to output ratio in India is that considerable investment opportunities accumulated throughout the 1990s, thereby creating a greatly increased return to capital. In China, however, investment opportunities were continuously utilized since the 1980s with large inflows of foreign capital.

Other Countries

The total growth of real GDP in Korea, Malaysia, Singapore and Taiwan were 26, 99, 45 and 27 per cent, respectively. These figures correspond to an average growth rate of 4, 12, 6.5 and 4 per cent. With the exception of Malaysia these figures are not remarkably high. However, and again with the exception of Malaysia, these are more mature economies for which the growth rates are quite respectable, particularly as they were all affected badly by the global information technology crisis in the early 2000s.

The share of household consumption in these four countries is in most cases lower than that of India but higher than the corresponding figure for China. Government consumption, in turn, is mostly between 10 and 15 per cent (with the highest figure for Korea), which is also roughly between the figures of China and India. The combined share of private and government consumption was, in 2007 before the crisis of 2008, 69, 58, 47 and 69 per cent of GDP for Korea, Malaysia, Singapore and Taiwan. In Singapore, this figure is close to that of China, while the other ones are similar to that of India. Investment in fixed capital is lower than that of both India and China, varying from about 30 per cent in Korea to just over 20 in most years for Malaysia and Singapore. Domestic savings are high in all these countries, varying in 2007 from 30–31 per cent in Taiwan and Korea to 50 per cent in Singapore. Investments could thus be easily financed out of domestic savings, although FDI is important for technology transfer.

Sustainability of Growth in India

India's reliance on domestic consumption expenditures to maintain a high growth rate makes the sustainability of such growth quite uncertain for a number of reasons. We will look into this matter in some detail below. A key factor explaining the fragility of consumption-based growth in India is the low level of consumption of the rural sector, which is still much more important than in most other Asian countries.

Due to the almost total absence of small-scale, labour-intensive manufacturing industries in the rural sector, the vast majority of the country's workforce (about 52 per cent) relies on agriculture, petty trading and casual jobs directly or indirectly to earn their livelihood. The shift of rural labour from agriculture to non-agricultural work has been very slow because of strict labour laws. In rural areas less than 5 per cent of farm produce is processed to add value and a significant proportion of fruits and vegetables rot due to the lack of adequate storage facilities. Since the federal government depends on the support of a number of coalition partners, most of whom have an inward-oriented culture and a negative attitude towards liberalization of foreign investment rules for investment in retail trade, the government has failed to attract large multinational retail giants such as Wal-Mart to India's retail trade sector. These retail giants could have provided adequate storage facilities, paid a better price to farmers and also invested in creating backward linkages in processing, transport, etc.

Because agriculture in India is mostly under private sector control and under the jurisdiction of provincial governments, the direct involvement of the federal government in agriculture has been limited. Consequently, whatever groundwater is available has been appropriated by large landholders. Small farmers' survival depends on a timely monsoon, the absence of which in 2008–09 brought down the growth rate of agricultural output to 1.6 per cent in 2008–09 from 4.9 per cent in 2007–08. This growth rate of 1.6 per cent is considerably less than 4 per cent, which according to the government of India is necessary for the country to achieve and maintain a growth rate of 9 to 10 per cent (EIU, 2008b).

The share of agriculture in total gross fixed capital formation, which is an indication of the level of mechanization of agriculture, was in 2007–08 only 5.7 per cent. This can also partly explain why the rate of growth of agricultural output was so low.

Land and Production in Agriculture

For India and China, the share of agricultural land in total land area stood at 61 and 59 per cent respectively during 2005 and 2007, but the land area under cereal production at 99.79 million hectares for India was considerably higher than the 86.05 million hectares for China during 2006–08. But despite 13.7 million hectares more land being devoted to agriculture in India than in China, cereal yield in kilograms per hectare in India was 16.3 per cent less than in China (World Bank, 2010); and the food production index value during 2005–07 (at 1900–2001 = 100) was 16 per cent less than in China. While the income of landholder households and of landless labourers in India has increased during the last decades, their expenditure on non-essential consumer goods would not have increased to the extent necessary to drive the economic growth rate upwards. Hence, the consumption expenditure of the urban and semi-urban population played a crucial role in pushing India's economic growth rate upward.

While land reforms and increasing productivity in agriculture played a very important, if even decisive, role in the economic rise of Korea, Taiwan and Malaysia, their importance as an engine of development is much less today (see Table 5.2 below), despite the fact that agriculture is very efficient in all of them. The one exception is Malaysia, where cash crops still play an important role and are actively supported by the government. However, the country's leading cash crop of the past, rubber, has lost in importance. The overwhelmingly dominant crop today is the oil palm, where demand has lately been fuelled by the increasing interest in bio-fuels. Singapore, of course, has no rural sector to speak of.

Investment Expenditures and Sectoral Growth

Economic growth driven mostly by investment expenditures becomes more sustainable if it is fuelled by production to satisfy foreign demand for the home country's exports rather than by production to satisfy domestic consumers' demand for home country manufacturers. In other words, economic growth driven by investment expenditures will be more sustainable in an export-oriented economy in which most regulations on factor and product markets are eliminated and adequate infrastructure is built. Foreign exchange earnings from exports pay for the country's imports and leave a surplus which builds up the country's foreign exchange reserve. The Chinese economy fulfils these conditions and accordingly its growth, driven mostly by investment, is more exogenously determined and more sustainable than the growth of the Indian economy, which is driven more by consumption expenditures and is more endogenously determined. Although the share of investment in India's GDP increased from 25 per cent in 2002 to 38.3 per cent in 2008, much of the investment was directed to the production of goods for domestic consumption. Hence, the lack of sufficient increase in export income to pay for its imports has led to a continuous increase in the size of the trade and current account deficits.

Hence, we have to conclude that while India so far has been able to maintain a high rate of growth in real GDP, averaging about 8 per cent per year since 2002, such a rate of growth may not be as sustainable as China's growth in real GDP that averaged about 10 per cent from 2002 to 2008. The greatest danger to the sustainability of India's domestic demand or consumption driven growth is posed by the persistence of Chenery and Strout's (1966) trade gap and foreign exchange gap, as well as the government budget gap.

In Table 5.2 we present the contribution of value added to GDP from the agriculture, industry and service sectors. For both China and India, agriculture's value added to GDP declined respectively from 15 and 23 per cent in 2003 to 11 and 18 per cent in 2008. In the smaller Asian countries discussed in this book, agriculture is of little importance as a driver of development, although it may be significant for other reasons, such as food security. The one exception is Malaysia, whose cash crop-dominated agriculture has important industrial linkages and is, if anything, increasingly important.

Table 5.2   Contribution of sectoral value added to GDP

	2003	2004	2005	2006	2007	2008
	1	2	3	4	5	6
Agriculture						
China	15	15	13	12	12	11
India	23	22	19	18	18	18
Korea	4	4	3	3	3	3
Malaysia	9	9	8	9	10	10
Singapore	0	0	0	0	0	0
Taiwan	2	2	2	2	2	2
Industry						
China	53	51	46	47	48	49
India	26	26	28	28	29	29
Korea	37	38	38	37	37	36
Malaysia	47	49	50	50	47	48
Singapore	32	33	31	31	29	26
Taiwan	28	28	27	27	28	25
Services						
China	32	35	41	41	40	40
India	52	52	54	55	53	53
Korea	60	58	59	60	60	61
Malaysia	44	42	42	42	42	42
Singapore	68	67	69	69	71	74
Taiwan	70	71	71	71	71	73

Sources:
World Bank (2005, 2006, 2007), *World Development Report*, New York: Oxford University Press.
World Bank (2008, 2009b, 2010), *World Development Indicators*, Washington DC: World Bank.
CEPD (2009), *Taiwan Statistical Data Book 2009*, Taipei: CEPD, p. 60.

For China, the industrial sector's value added to GDP declined from a high of 53 per cent in 2003 to 49 per cent in 2008, while for India this share increased from 26 per cent in 2003 to 29 per cent in 2009. That the gap between the respective contributions of industry to GDP in China and India narrowed from 27 per cent points (53–26) in 2003 to 20 percentage points (49–29) in 2008 is indicative of the robust growth in industrial output in India since 2002–03. Overall the industrial sector's contribution to GDP for India is still lower than that for many East Asian countries. Table 5.2 shows that Korea and Malaysia have larger industrial sectors than India, while Singapore and Taiwan are fairly comparable to India due to their huge service sectors. Within the industrial sector the private sector plays a dominant role in all countries, including China. But for India this private industrial sector has to play a bigger role in manufacturing such that manufactured output can grow by 15 to 17 per cent per year. This would be necessary in order to reach the government of India's target of manufacturing industry's output accounting for 25 per cent of GDP (EIU, 2008b). Moreover, India's manufacturing sector must move away from the production and exports of low technology-imbedded and low value-added products to high technology-imbedded and high value-added products, which is what China's manufacturing industries have been doing (EIU, 2009). Many of these industries in China and the other East Asian countries are wholly or partly foreign-owned, which points at the strategic importance of FDI as an engine of export-led growth.

The contribution of the service sector's value added to GDP increased from 32 per cent and 52 per cent in 2003 to 40 per cent and 53 per cent in 2008 for China and India. China's service sector has increased the contribution of its value added to GDP by eight percentage points compared with a one percentage point increase in India's service sector's value added to GDP. The main reason for such disparate performance of the service sectors is that while big banks dominate China's service sector, the major proportion of its value-added growth has been sourced from the booming retail sector, tourism and logistics industry. We also see a catch-up from the days of the planned economy, where the service sector was disproportionally small, like in the other socialist countries. Of the other Asian countries, this sector in Malaysia is comparable to that of China, while Korea, Singapore and Taiwan, being more developed economies, each sport a much larger services sector. Especially in the latter two countries, services are likely to become even more dominating over time, although their governments do emphasize the importance of preserving a relatively big and healthy industrial sector.

In India's service sector, which is the main driver of economic growth, the IT sector's value-added contribution to GDP has been very high. Its share in GDP reached 5.2 per cent in 2007–08. However, only 40 per cent of 5,000 Indian IT companies operate internationally (EIU, 2008b). Within this 40 per cent there are many foreign MNCs. So a part of the export income from IT service exports will be remitted to foreign MNCs' parent offices. To increase significantly the export income of IT and ITE services, a good proportion of the 60 per cent of total companies involved in servicing the domestic market will have to expand their operations to overseas markets.

FISCAL AND MONETARY MANAGEMENT

Since sound fiscal and monetary management by maintaining a surplus or balanced budget can help a country achieve and maintain a robust rate of economic growth, we now will analyse the central government's budgetary transactions and interest rates in China and India in some detail. Some figures are presented in Table 5.3A. After that we will briefly look into the situation in other Asian countries.

Row 1 of Table 5.3A shows that the revenue deficits in the central government's budgets as a proportion of GDP for China consistently declined from 2.3 per cent in 2002 to 1.4 per cent in 2008. For India it declined from 4.7 per cent in 2002 to 2.6 per cent in 2007 and increased sharply to 5.8 per cent in 2008, a direct fallout of the global financial crisis. While the Chinese economy was more severely affected by the financial crisis than the Indian economy, the share of the central government's revenue deficit in GDP remained at 1.4 per cent in 2008, a rate which has been maintained since 2006. China's huge foreign exchange reserves helped it finance hundreds of billions of dollars' worth of development projects during the financial crisis. India, in turn, had to borrow from the private sector to finance its stimulus package because its export trade as a percentage of GDP is small and because it has been running a consistent trade deficit. So the argument that because India's non-traded sector accounts for about 60 per cent of its GDP, it has minimized the severity of adverse effects of the financial crisis, is not justified.

The relative effectiveness of sound budgetary management is also illustrated in row 2 of Table 5.3A, which shows that the share of revenue in the expenditures of the central government of China has consistently risen from 88.1 per cent in 2002 to 94.5 per cent in 2005 before declining slightly to 91.2 per cent in 2008. For India's central government, the share of revenue in expenditure increased from 72.7 per cent in 2002 to almost 97 per cent in 2007 and then declined to 68.9 per cent in 2008. Generally throughout this period, the size of the revenue gap to cover expenditures has been considerably smaller for the central government in China than for the central government in India. Interest payments on government debt as a percentage of government expenditure are an indicator of the size of a country's public debt. As shown in row 3, for China and India, the share of interest payment in the expenditure of the central government were 5.3 and 28.7 per cent in 2002. In 2008 the respective shares were 4 per cent and 24.1 per cent.

Subsidies and grants imposed a severe burden on central government budgets of both countries. But because the size of interest payments on China's public debt was small, the central government was left, after the payment of grants, with an adequate amount of financial resources to deal with important social and economic development issues. For the government of India, after the payment of interest on government debt and payment of subsidies and grants, little resources were left to deal with important social and economic development issues. As shown in row 4 of Table 5.3A, grants and subsidies accounted for 63.7 per cent and 55.9 per cent of government expenditures in China and India in 2002.

Table 5.3A   The central government's budgetary transactions and interest rates: China and India

	2002	2003	2004	2005	2006	2007	2008
1. Cash (revenue) surplus/deficit as % of GDP							
China	−2.28	−2.14	−2.11	−1.52	−1.40	−1.42	−1.40
India	−4.73	−3.70	−3.20	−3.20	−3.30	−2.60	−5.80
2. Revenue receipts as % of expenditure							
China	88.10	88.30	88.50	94.50	93.50	90.40	91.20
India	72.70	76.10	80.40	81.80	84.40	96.50	68.90
3. Interest payment as % of expenditure							
China	5.30	6.72	4.20	4.10	4.04	4.00	4.00
India	28.70	27.76	25.51	23.40	22.20	21.34	24.10
4. Payment of subsidies and grants as % of expenditure							
China	63.73	61.00	63.14	61.20	62.00	60.00	60.00
India	55.91[a]	57.93[a]	15.10[b]	42.80[a]	43.09[a]	36.00[a]	54.00[a]
5. Total net incurrence of liabilities as % of GDP							
China	2.60	2.35	2.00	1.63	1.43	1.10	1.10
India	5.14	3.50	2.80	4.20	3.80	3.20	4.90
6. Bank lending rate (%)							
China	5.31	5.31	5.58	5.58	6.12	7.47	5.31
India	11.92	11.46	10.92	10.75	11.19	13.02	13.31
7. Deposit rates (%)							
China	2.00	2.00	2.25	2.25	2.52	4.14	2.25
India	6.80	5.40	5.40	5.90	7.30	7.40	8.00
8. Money market rate (%)							
China	n.a.	2.90	3.40	2.90	2.70	3.40	n.a.
India	n.a.	4.50	4.80	5.30	6.00	6.00	n.a.
9. Inflation rate (%)							
China	5.70	2.60	7.00	3.70	3.60	7.70	7.20
India	3.80	3.40	5.50	4.20	4.90	4.90	7.00

Notes:
[a] includes grants and subsidies
[b] includes only subsidies

Source: IMF (2009b), *International Financial Statistics Yearbook 2009*, Washington, DC: IMF, pp. 283, 393.

For example, in 2002, expenditures on interest payment and on subsidies and grants accounted for 84.6 per cent of total central government expenditures in India. Hence, only 15.4 per cent of total expenditures was directed to deal with all the other functions of the government which includes payment for defence services. But in the same year, for China's central government, after paying for interest on public debt and for subsidies and grants, which together accounted for 69 per cent of total central government's expenditure, 31 per cent of the expenditure was left to pay for expenses to discharge all other government functions including defence services. In 2008, the share of interest payments as well as subsidies and grants accounted for 80 and 64 per cent of the total expenditures of India's and China's central government budgets. Such a drastic fall in the share of revenue in the total expenditures of India's central government was a direct outcome of the fiscal expansion during the second half of 2008 and of the fall in the collection of indirect taxes, resulting from across-the-board reductions in excise duties undertaken to minimize the adverse effects of the financial crisis on the economy. Better management of the government's budget and higher tax revenues in China left larger amounts of financial resources for expenditures on defence, education, health, social and public services, etc.

Because the size of India's gross public debt is substantially larger than that of China, the share of the net incurrence of liabilities in GDP has been significantly larger for India than for China (row 5). Important interrelated indicators of the soundness of a government's management of public finance are the size of the public debt in GDP, the size of revenue surplus or deficit in GDP and the size of fiscal surplus or deficit in GDP. If these deficits are kept within a reasonable limit – say 3 per cent of GDP – it becomes easier for the central bank to perform its primary task of controlling inflation.

In rows 6, 7 and 9, we present commercial bank lending rates, deposit rates and inflation rates. Since the primary objective of monetary policy in any country is to ensure a robust growth in real GDP at stable prices, it is necessary for the monetary authorities to ensure that interest rates on loans extended and deposits received by banks are neither too high nor too low to encourage the business sector to borrow and the household sector to increase its deposit with banks. While a high rate of interest may be necessary to keep the inflation rate under control, it also increases the cost of borrowing, thereby discouraging investment in productive business activities. As the table shows, the bank lending rate in India has been more than double the rate in China for several years (row 6). However, bank lending rates which reached 13.3 per cent in 2008 from 11.9 per cent in 2002 were the official prime lending rates, which were above the market rates of interest at which loans were offered by banks. But since these market rates were different for different banks and different for different loans with different maturity periods, it was difficult to obtain an average market rate of interest charged by banks for loans.

The inflation rate (row 9) in both China and India moved up and down respectively to reach 7.2 per cent and 7 per cent in 2008 respectively. With a high inflation rate, the maintenance of a positive real deposit rate (nominal deposit rate less inflation rate) can increase bank deposits and the level of domestic savings. But, although the real deposit rate in China was negative and in India marginally positive, the share of domestic savings in GDP of both countries increased greatly. Hence, the increase in domestic savings in both countries appears to be more a function of cultural habits and concern for the effective management of future risks in life than one of a positive real bank deposit rate.

China

In China, although government expenditures have risen after 2007, all the deficits have been kept within the limit of 3 per cent of GDP as evidenced from the share of revenue deficits in GDP and the share of interest payment on the public debt in government expenditures in Table 5.3A. Due to the legitimate concern of the central government that grants directed to local governments would not be spent wisely, substantial increases in expenditures on grants were avoided. Recent estimates suggest that out of the massive stimulus package of US$586 billion which was launched at the end of 2008, the new expenditures were kept within the range of 1 per cent to 2.5 per cent of GDP (EIU, 2009).

China's central bank used monetary policy more effectively in recent years than during the reform period by raising the official interest rates several times during 2006 and 2007 to prevent the economy from overheating, but then began to make the policy expansionary by lowering the bank rate and the reserve ratio, and by expanding credit quotas to banks in the wake of the financial crisis. These expanded quotas helped mostly state-operated enterprises (SOEs), but disadvantaged SMEs which create employment for millions of Chinese labourers and form the backbone of China's rise to an economic superpower.

India

One indicator of the fiscal health of an economy is whether the primary balance expressed as the fiscal balance minus interest payments remains in surplus so as to allow the country's debt to rise to a sustainable management level and to ensure that the interest payments on public debt should remain below 3 per cent of GDP. For India the fiscal balance (total expenditure minus total receipts less borrowings and other liabilities) was in deficit; and, consequently, the primary balance (fiscal balance minus interest payment) was also in deficit (GOI, 2009; EIU, 2008b). Although the Fiscal Responsibility and Budget Management Act of 2004 placed a limit on the central government's borrowing and made it mandatory for the government to close the revenue deficit by 2009 (EIU, 2008b), in reality it will take a much longer time for the government to fulfil that mandate. A variety of measures are necessary to raise revenue: increasing the coverage of the income tax net beyond the current size of the income tax-paying population of 32 million; reducing expenditures by privatizing loss-making PSEs; reducing the size of public sector employment; discontinuing the hefty pay raises to unproductive employees including teachers in schools, colleges and universities with monotonous regularity; and reducing the size of grants to provinces, much of which end up in pockets of vested interest groups. However, it would be extremely difficult to implement these measures at the federal and provincial levels, where there are many coalition governments that are driven by the politics of vote-buying and, thus, necessarily indulge in boundless fiscal profligacy.

The Reserve Bank of India, which had consistently aimed to achieve price stability and to ensure a smooth flow of credit to the economy, gradually had to raise interest rates in the 2000s as inflationary pressures resulting from a significant rise in commodity prices began to be felt in the economy. However, in recent years the Bank has lost much of its independence due to political interference in its power to implement appropriate monetary policy.

Other Countries

Although China has recently emerged as a major global player and is quite dependent on its foreign trade, the smaller Asian countries are much more open economies and are thus more vulnerable to disturbances in the global economy. This became painfully clear during the Asian Financial Crisis in 1997–98 and the IT crisis in 2000–02, which hit all these counties very hard. Despite this, these countries have been largely capable of pursuing a prudent fiscal and monetary policy, not having run into major financial difficulties, at least not after the 1980s. For easy comparison, Table 5.3B provides the same information on government finances and money markets as Table 5.3A for China and India, for Korea, Malaysia, Singapore and Taiwan.

Singapore's government finances are in excellent shape, and the government sits on large reserves, intended to be used in cases of emergency. In fact, some of these reserves were used during the financial crisis of 2008–09 in order to soften the impact of the crisis. Public construction works have been regularly used as a countercyclical measure, as have tax reductions and reductions in the mandatory payments to the Central Provident Fund (the administrator of the country's pension system). More important, however, is the fact that the number of foreign workers is very large, which makes it possible for the government to adapt the labour force very quickly in the face of a changing demand for labour. Monetary policy in Singapore has mainly targeted the exchange rate, rather than the rate of interest or economic activity. This makes sense because in a very import-dependent country like Singapore, price developments can be efficiently controlled through the exchange rate (Blomqvist, 2005, p. 18).

After a period of very strong fiscal expansion in the early 1980s, the government of Malaysia ran into a serious deficit problem and had to

Table 5.3B   The central government's budgetary transactions and interest rates: Korea, Malaysia, Singapore and Taiwan

	2002	2003	2004	2005	2006	2007	2008
1. Cash (revenue) surplus/deficit as % of GDP							
Korea	3.61	1.69	0.00	0.01	0.01	0.02	0.02
Singapore	−0.50	6.79	6.49	8.42	7.62	12.74	5.64
Taiwan	−3.46	−3.40	−2.41	−1.55	−0.65	−0.37	n.a.
2. Revenue receipts as % of expenditure							
Korea	128.1	115.9	112.2	110.5	110.2	120.4	120.5
Singapore	96.6	147.8	142.3	165.4	154.8	200.0	0.96
Taiwan	83.3	83.8	88.1	92.2	96.5	98.0	n.a.
3. Interest payment as % of expenditure							
Korea	5.78	4.83	5.77	5.85	6.42	6.63	6.83
4. Payment of subsidies and grants as % of expenditure							
Korea	43.4	40.3	36.0	36.8	37.1	45.9	42.5
5. Total net incurrence of liabilities as % of GDP							
Korea	−3.5	−3.7	−1.8	−0.5	−0.5	−2.5	−2.5
Singapore	1.9	8.0	8.6	5.9	4.0	12.4	7.5
6. Bank lending rate (%)							
Korea	6.77	6.24	5.90	5.59	5.99	6.55	7.17
Malaysia	6.53	6.30	6.05	5.95	6.49	6.41	6.08
Singapore	5.37	5.31	5.30	5.30	5.31	5.33	5.38
7. Deposit rates (%)							
Korea	4.95	4.25	3.87	3.72	4.50	5.17	5.87
Malaysia	3.21	3.07	3.00	3.00	3.15	3.17	3.13
Singapore	0.91	0.51	0.41	0.44	0.57	0.53	0.42
8. Money market rate (%)							
Korea	4.21	4.00	3.65	3.33	4.19	4.77	4.78
Malaysia	2.73	2.74	2.70	2.72	3.38	3.50	3.47
Singapore	0.96	0.74	1.04	2.28	3.46	2.72	1.31
Taiwan	1.63	1.38	1.75	2.25	2.75	3.38	2.00
9. Inflation rate (%)							
Korea	3.2	3.5	3.0	0.7	−0.1	2.0	2.9
Malaysia	3.2	3.3	6.0	4.6	3.9	4.9	10.3
Singapore	−1.0	−0.1	4.4	1.1	1.8	7.0	1.7
Taiwan	−0.3	−1.3	−0.9	−0.6	−0.7	0.3	−2.4

Sources:

IMF (2010), *International Financial Statistics Yearbook 2010*, Washington, DC: IMF.
CEPD (2009), *Taiwan Statistical Data Book 2009*, Taipei: CEPD, pp. 17, 153, 177.

implement a structural adjustment policy, reducing the direct involvement of the government in industrial and commercial activities. Instead it emphasized supporting private initiatives related to promoting economic development. As a result, the share of public expenditures in GDP decreased from 44 per cent in 1982 to 21 per cent in 1997, while the total debt of the federal government was down to 32 per cent of GDP, as compared to 103 per cent in 1986. Moreover, the government actually ran a consistent fiscal surplus for five years, during 1993–97. The government finances were thus in a strong position when the crises of 1997–98 and 2000–02 set in (Bank of International Settlements, 2003).

Malaysia's financial markets were liberalized and modernized relatively early, in the 1970s and 1980s. In the realm of monetary policy, Malaysia is known as a prudent but unconventional player, not afraid of intervening with whatever means available in order to stabilize the economy and promote development. Like Singapore, management of the exchange rate is a main target of monetary policy in Malaysia, apart from price stability (McCauley, 2006). In the wake of the Asian Financial Crisis the country's banking system came close to a collapse. Against the advice of the IMF and the international community the country adopted controversial policy measures, such as the temporary freezing of foreign assets and pegging the Malaysian ringgit to the US dollar (Mahani, 2002). Contrary to the expectations of most 'experts', these measures turned out to be quite successful, not least because they allowed a low interest rate to be combined with a stable exchange rate.

Korea was one of the major victims of the Asian Financial Crisis of 1997–98, but it recovered its economic dynamism quite quickly. In the short term, its budgetary response to near economic collapse was immediate and quite significant. The government increased spending and, once the peak of the crisis was over, taxes and expanded its previously very limited support of needy Koreans by substantially increasing funds for social development and for aiding local government. Thus, despite its being forced to accept a large IMF loan in late 1997, Korea clearly rejected the IMF model of fiscal austerity and governmental downsizing, giving a much higher priority to the welfare of its citizens. At that time there were significant fears that this might lead to dangerous fiscal imbalances. For example, the government's deficit averaged nearly 3 per cent of GDP for the three-year period of 1997–99. Yet, as Table 5.3B shows, slight surpluses have been run since then. Consequently, by 2007 the ratio of government debt to GDP was only 36 per cent which is quite respectable by OECD standards (Jung and Clark, 2010).

Taiwan's fiscal pattern was almost the opposite of Korea's in that its government has run a significant deficit over the last decade. Still, this deficit dropped steadily from 3.46 per cent to 0.37 per cent of GDP between 2002 and 2007, suggesting that the country is in relatively good shape. However, the government is clearly constrained by an inability to raise revenues which, given the centralized nature of intergovernmental budgetary relations, has created a growing crisis in local government finances (Lee and Clark, 2010). Taiwan's financial system presents a similarly ambiguous picture. Taiwan's traditional financial system appears to have been paradoxical. On the one hand, the most important parts of the system were rigid, state dominated and clearly discriminatory toward the dynamic SME sector. On the other hand, informal practices, such as the curb market of informal loans, helped produce an extraordinary record for savings, investment and economic dynamism. Indeed, it has been argued that this system produced 'prosperity from countervailing perversities' which prevented the various dysfunctional incentives of the system from becoming too powerful (Clark, 1997). Furthermore, the lack of financial reform through the 1990s has been given credit for Taiwan's escape from the Asian Financial Crisis of 1997–98 with relatively little damage, because the country remained comparatively insulated from the international financial system (Chu, 1999; Tan, 2001). More recently, however, democratization has led to a growing politicization of financial policy and regulation (Tan, 2001, 2008).

INCOME DISTRIBUTION

While one way of reducing the inequality in income between the rich and the poor in any developing country is by the transfer of income from the rich to the poor, the superior method is to raise economic growth of the country. This is because it would require an enormous adjustment in the distribution of income to achieve the same addition to the living standard of the poor which an additional percentage point of sustained growth could achieve. The World Bank's (2003) estimate of the income distribution in 80 countries during the late 1990s found the relationship between inequality in income and GDP per capita to be like Kuznets' (1955) inverted U, skewed to the right. Oshima's (1994) study found that technological change, by creating increasing employment requiring diverse skills, although making a large number of labourers well-off, also makes many redundant, thereby increasing inequality and contributing to the skew shape of the inverted U.

In Table 5.4A we present income distribution statistics for China and India. Data on the Gini index and percentage shares of household income by percentile groups of households were not available for recent years. Nevertheless, the Gini indices show that income inequality was considerably higher in China than in India between the late 1990s and mid-2000s. Also, the other interesting trend to be noted is that the Gini index and per capita income increased from 40.3 and \$US750 in 1998 to 46.9 and \$US1,290 in 2004 for China. During the six-year period, per capita income increased by 540 US dollars and the Gini index by 6.6 points. Such a substantial increase in income inequality is in conformity with Kuznets' curve. But between 2004 and 2005 there was an increase of 450 US dollars in per capita income and a decline in the Gini index by 5.4 points. Hence, the trend in the Gini index in China between 1998 and 2005 does not seem to follow a consistent trend of rising inequality in income. On the other hand, the Gini index in India fell from 37.8 in 1997 to 36.8 in 2004–05. The per capita income, during these seven years, increased by only 190 US dollars and the Gini index declined by one point. The decline in inequality in income when the per capita income is rising can be caused by a targeted redistribution of national income to the poorest income groups of households by the governments in both China and India via provisions for the supply of food and healthcare, state-provided educational facilities and so on.

As column 4 of Table 5.4A shows, on the basis of official data, in 1998 and 2005 China's lowest 10 per cent group of households obtained no more than 2.4 per cent of national income whereas India's lowest 10 per cent income group of households obtained 3.5 and 3.6 per cent of household income in 1997 and 2004–05. Also the ratios of the highest 10 per cent income group and the highest 20 per cent income group of households to the lowest 10 per cent income group and the lowest 20 per cent income group of households were considerably higher in China than in India (cols. 12 and 13).

Ahluwalia et al. (1979) and Ahluwalia (1974) defined income inequality in a country to be: high if the income share of the poorest 40 per cent is less than 12 per cent of GNP; moderate, if it is between 12 and 17 per cent; and low, if it is 17 per cent and above. Applying this test to determine the relative levels of inequality, we find that in India during 1997 and 2004–05 the income share held by the lowest 40 per cent income group were 19.7 and 19.4, well above the 17 per cent which is the minimum for inequality to be accepted as low. In Korea the figure was 22 per cent in 1998 (see Table 5.4B), and the figure was a fairly comparable 19 per cent in Taiwan in 2009. In contrast, the poorest 40 per cent of the population received only 12 and 14 per cent of household income, respectively, in Malaysia (1997) and Singapore (1998). By applying the same test, we find that the inequality in income distribution in China has been moderate and, therefore, higher than in India. A study (GOI, 2010) found that while the bottom quintile in India has seen a robust rise in income in comparison with its benchmark starting income, it has obtained a smaller share of the aggregate growth in income.

Official figures may not always tell the whole truth, however. Another study (*The Australian*, 2010) found from a survey of income of 4,195 households from all geographic regions of China that the actual annual disposable income per capita of the top 10 per cent income group of households was $US23,000, which was three times the amount indicated in the official surveys, and that the average household income revealed was 90.4 per cent higher than what the official data revealed. The study also found that 63 per cent of the 'grey

Table 5.4A: Trends in income distribution: percentage share of household income by percentile groups: China and India

1	2	3	4	5	6	7	8	9	10	11	12	13
Country	Survey year	Gini index	Lowest 10%	Lowest 20%	Second 20%	Third 20%	Fourth 20%	Highest 20%	Highest 10%	Lowest 40%	Ratio of col. 10 to col. 4	Ratio of col. 9 to col. 5
China	1998	40.3	2.4	5.9	10.2	15.1	22.2	46.6	30.4	16.1	12.7	7.9
	2004	46.9	1.6	4.3	8.5	13.7	21.7	51.7	34.9	12.8	21.8	12.0
	2005	41.5	2.4	5.7	9.8	14.7	22.0	47.8	31.4	15.5	13.1	8.4
India	1997	37.8	3.5	8.1	11.6	15.0	19.3	46.1	33.5	19.7	9.6	5.9
	2004–05	36.8	3.6	8.1	11.3	14.9	20.4	45.3	31.1	19.4	8.6	5.6

Sources:
World Bank (2001), *World Development Report*, New York: Oxford University Press, pp. 282–283.
World Bank (2008–2010), *World Development Indicators*, Washington, DC: World Bank.

Table 5.4B   Trends in income distribution: percentage share of household income by percentile groups: other countries

1	2	3	4	5	6	7	8	9	10	11	12	13
Country	Survey year	Gini index	Lowest 10%	Lowest 20%	Second 20%	Third 20%	Fourth 20%	Highest 20%	Highest 10%	Lowest 40%	Ratio of col. 10 to col. 4	Ratio of col. 9 to col. 5
Korea 1998		32	3	8	14	18	23	37	22	22	7.3	4.6
Malaysia 1997		49	2	4	8	13	21	54	38	12	19.0	13.5
2004		38	3	6	11	16	23	44	29	17	9.7	7.3
Singapore 1998		42	2	5	9	15	22	49	33	14	16.5	9.8
Taiwan 1953												20.5
1961												11.6
1976				9	14	17	23	37				4.1
2007				7	12	17	24	40				5.7

Sources:
World Bank (2010), *World Development Indicators*, Washington, DC: World Bank.
CEPD (2009), *Taiwan Statistical Data Book 2009*, Taipei: CEPD, pp. 84–85.
Clark (1989), *Taiwan's Development*, Westport, CT: Greenwood, p. 173.

income' or 'black money' amounting to $US1.5 trillion, or 30 per cent of China's GDP, was captured by the wealthiest 10 per cent income group of households. All kinds of corrupt practices which arose from the misuse of power by government officials for personal gains contributed to the rise in the size of the black money. Naturally, if this black money could be unearthed, the Gini index would be closer to what we find in most Latin American countries, and the income inequality would be considerably higher than what is officially revealed. Hence, India seems to have been more successful than China in escaping from Kuznets' inverted U-curve relationship between income inequality and economic growth (Chai and Roy, 2006).

One important aspect of a study of income inequality between poorer and richer income groups of households is that it extends to intra-household inequality in the distribution of consumption to male and female members of low-income and high-income families. Several studies for India (Lakshmanasamy and Roy, 2010; Roy, 2006; Roy, 2008) found that in households belonging to the poorest income group at very low levels of income, the allocation of foods, status and independence by Becker's (1973, 1974, 1991) altruistic dictator (family head) to female members is not discriminatory. Discrimination against females does seem to rise as families' total pooled income continues to rise.

For the other Asian countries the picture is sketchier because of the lack of time series except for Taiwan. Some figures are provided in Table 5.4B. The general picture is that the income distribution in Korea and Taiwan is more equal than in both China and India. Singapore and Malaysia both have a more unequal income distribution than both China and India (World Bank, 2010). In both cases, the societies are more egalitarian than India and China, however, because of high social mobility. In the case of Singapore the large number of expatriates among the permanent residents may contribute to the seemingly high level of inequality.

The longer data series on Taiwan provides a more detailed picture of that country's impressive record of 'growth with equity' (Fei et al., 1979). Taiwan departed markedly from Kuznets' (1950) inverted-U pattern in which development and industrialization first produce greater inequality before ultimately leading to more equal income distributions. Rather, as indicated by the ratio of the richest fifth of the population to the poorest fifth in Table 5.4B, inequality dropped dramatically during even the first stages of industrialization in Taiwan during the 1950s and 1960s as the income ratio plummeted from 20.5 in 1953 to 11.6 in 1961 to 4.1 in 1976, a level low by even the standards of the developed world. This resulted from a radical land reform that created a nation of smallholders, the early implementation of primary universal education, an industrialization pattern that emphasized small and medium-sized enterprises (SMEs) in both urban and rural areas, and the stand-offish relations between business and the government which inhibited rent seeking (Clark, 1989; Fei et al., 1979). After the mid-1970s, though, inequality increased steadily as its basic industries were increasingly forced offshore, following a widespread pattern among developed nations (Clark and Tan, 2011).

The Rural–Urban Divide

We can argue that the rural–urban divide tends to get subsumed in the poor–rich divide, on the basic assumption of the Kuznets curve hypothesis that there is little inequality in income in the poor rural sector relying on agriculture. Hence, inequality in income distribution is due to inequality in income in the urban sector resulting from income inequality between informally and formally employed workers (Rauch, 1993).

In China, during the phenomenal growth of town and village enterprises (TVEs), inequality in income in the rural sector increased between those relying exclusively on agriculture and others relying on jobs at TVEs. On the other hand, remittances to rural families from a substantial proportion of 130 million factory workers who were laid off by loss-making PSEs between 1995 and 2002 but got absorbed in factories along the eastern coastline increased the income of the rural sector and thereby tended to contract the rural–urban divide.

After 1995, the gap between rural and urban income in China widened as reflected in the rise in the Gini index from 38.8 in 1995 (Chai and Roy, 2006) to 40.3 in 1998 (column 3 of Table 5.4A). The magnitude of the gap between rural and urban incomes in China is caused by (i) the government's policy of controlling the pace of migration from labour surplus regions to the labour scarce eastern coastal regions to achieve self-sufficiency in food grain supply, (ii) the high cost of relocation including limited access to social services for unregistered newcomers in urban areas, and (iii) the government's policy of lifting the urban standard of living by subsidizing the urban cost of living via the provision of low-cost capital for urban enterprises, low-cost housing for urban residents, as well as generous healthcare insurance and pension schemes (Meier and Rauch, 2005). While the rate of growth of the real net per capita rural income decelerated in the late 1990s, there was an increase by 51.9 per cent between 2000 and 2007 due, among other things, to a reduction in agricultural taxes and higher grain prices. Nevertheless, the gap between rural and urban incomes widened further as there was a 96 per cent rise in the real net urban per capita income during the same period (EIU, 2009). Consequently, the income gap between coastal regions, which are highly urbanized and industrialized, and the interior is quite significant.

In India, a similar trend in income disparity is noticed between the high-performing coastal provinces such as Gujarat, Maharashtra, Karnataka, Tamilnadu and Andhra Pradesh as well as Delhi and Haryana and low-performing Upper Province (UP), Middle Province (MP), Bihar, Coastal

Orissa, West Bengal and the seven North Eastern Hill provinces mired in poverty, unemployment, violence and political thuggery.

Despite such problems the technological change in agriculture, which began in the late 1960s, improved the income of landless labourers and rich farmers (Baker and Jewitt, 2007). Although small landholder farmers may not have derived so much benefit as the large ones, their income level was nevertheless higher than before the introduction of the green revolution technology in Indian agriculture. Higher grain prices, combined with subsidized prices of fertilizer and seeds, cost-free water and tax-free agricultural plots, undoubtedly helped to reduce the income disparity between the rural and urban sectors. Also, the migration of rural labour to urban slums and the remittances of income to their rural families, combined with the availability of some basic foods and fuels at subsidized prices to poor landless families, helped reduce the rural–urban income gap.

The gap between rural and urban areas is also important in Malaysia, where agriculture still constitutes 10 per cent of GDP (see Table 5.2 above). More importantly, the rural–urban divide in Malaysia is closely related to the multiracial character of the country that became a consequence of massive immigration of Chinese and Indian labourers during the colonial period. With the indigenous groups, mainly Malays, dominating in the rural areas and the Chinese in the urban ones, the 1960s saw increasing cleavages between town and country, between ethnic groups and also within those groups. Economic policies were at that time geared towards import substitution but achieved little in terms of employment, while in the rural areas the emphasis was put on productivity rather than redistribution (Jomo and Gomez, 1997). The consequent tensions took the form of interracial resentment. The fact that Malaysian politics was, and is, organized according to ethnic lines contributed to this; and the tensions, in turn, probably strengthened the compartmentalization of politics in ethnically-based parties (Jomo and Gomez, 1997).

Because Malays were the largest ethnic group, this and some constitutional provisions gave them a dominating political status and power over the government apparatus, which has always been a source of discontent among the other ethnic groups. The Malays, in turn, resented the Chinese business community, which dominated the economy and whose success they regarded as being at their expense, although most Chinese were not very well-off either. The ratio of Chinese to Malay median income increased, however, from 2:1 in 1957–58 to 2.2:1 in 1967–68 (Rasiah, 1997). The smaller Indian community was and is rather divided, between well-to-do professionals and a poor majority eking out their livelihood from menial labour. The social unrest exploded in racial riots in 1969. These events became a defining factor in the country's subsequent economic policy.

Because of the problems just mentioned, managing the ethnic cleavages became a paramount trait of all economic policy-making in Malaysia. The aim of the so-called New Economic Policy (NEP), introduced in 1970, was to relieve ethnic tensions through a programme aiming at the redistribution of wealth (Rasiah, 1997). In practice this meant favouring the Malay part of the population through granting the Malays privileges not available to members of other races. This was supposed to be a temporary policy, but the main features of the NEP became a permanent feature in Malaysian economic politics, even though the programme in itself expired in 1990. Any suggestion to tamper with the 'Malay rights' is met with loud protests, even today. Ironically, the policy of affirmative measures has not been a great success, although the income share of the Malays has risen. The great beneficiaries have rather been the Malay elite rather than the ethnic group as a whole; and the complicated rules have created ample opportunities for rent seeking and corruption.

Singapore, for all practical purposes, lacks a rural sector. The agricultural sectors in Taiwan and Korea are now quite small at 2–3 per cent of GDP (see Table 5.2 above), with agricultural and rural areas clearly lagging. Similarly to Malaysia, regionalism is quite important in Korean politics (Kang, 2002); and ethnic and regional divisions form the major political cleavage in Taiwan (Copper, 2010). In both these countries, however, what is important is some combination of region or ethnicity rather than rural or urban location per se.

CONCLUSIONS

In the end, we have to conclude that since all economic and social policies and their implementation are functions of the political governance regime, the difference between the high growth performance of highly outward-oriented China and good growth performance of semi-outward-oriented India is entirely attributable to the differences in relative strengths of the powerful, centralized, highly activist but corrupt governance regime in China and the weak, highly decentralized, corrupt and much less activist governance regimes in India. The highly efficient uncorrupted polity and bureaucracy of Singapore bears witness of what solid institutional environment can achieve, while the picture in Malaysia is more complicated because of the prominent role of racial management that has always been a central part of Malaysian politics. In addition, the states in Korea and Taiwan played a major role in leading their rapid development trajectories (Clark and Roy, 1997), as will be discussed in more detail in Chapter 7.

6. Poverty and human development in the Asian states

The term poverty, as used here, does not refer to the lack of supply of foods and other basic necessities which an individual or a family wants to purchase but to the lack of means at the disposal of a person or a family to procure foods, clothes, shelter, healthcare, education and other items of necessity (Sen, 1981). It then becomes the responsibility of every state to make these items of necessity available to people living under such poverty. However, even those who have the means to acquire foods and other necessities may also be prevented from acquiring those necessities by unfriendly social and political institutions, cadres of the political party running the government in a democracy like India, Zimbabwe and in other countries. Examples are women and adolescent girls in general, tribals, low-caste family members (in several provinces in India), and members of religious minorities (in Pakistan, Afghanistan and several other countries in the Middle East)[1] (*The Statesman Weekly*, 2011). This is a kind of deprivation which is an important dimension of poverty. Poverty in the form of extreme deprivation is also evident in poor people's lack of political power and voice (particularly of women) and in their vulnerability to sickness, economic dislocation resulting from sudden loss of jobs, personal violence (particularly against women) and natural disasters.

Powerlessness and voicelessness, which together constitute the extreme form of deprivation, can keep the state or a particular province in a federal state in a perpetual state of voicelessness and helplessness even in a democracy where the political party in power converts the governance regime into a magnificent cipher and runs the administration of the country or the province by armed cadres. In such a case very little economic development activity can take place. The society gets divided into two blocs – those who support the political party in power and those who oppose it. Much of the government largesse is transferred to the ruling political party under *guanxi* communism and very little is used for development activities. The whole country or the province suffers from extreme poverty and deprivation. This situation has prevailed in the Indian province of West Bengal, where the Marxist Communist Party of India (CPM) has ruled the province for 34 years.[2] While such dimensions of poverty cannot be quantified, we can nevertheless contend that poverty can be expressed as unfreedom (Sen, 1985) and unfreedom as unhappiness (Roy, 1986). The elimination of unfreedom therefore brings happiness to the society. Isn't the attainment of this happiness, the ultimate goal of human development? (Roy et al., 2008).

In this chapter we comment briefly on economic poverty and other deprivation levels, and on the following other important aspects to human development in the Asian countries covered in this study:

1. employment;
2. demography and health; and
3. education.

EXTREME POVERTY

From row 1 of Table 6.1, which outlines several important aspects of extreme poverty, it can be seen that during the period 2000–08, the proportion of total population living below the national poverty line was 2.8 per cent in China, whereas in India, the proportion stood at 28.6 per cent (UNDP, 2010). In China, the huge expansion of industrial activities in giant special economic zones along the eastern coastline since the middle of the first decade of this century enabled millions of young members of the labour force to move from China's rural heartland to eastern coastal industrial towns to obtain employment and thereby to lift their families at home above the national poverty line (Meier and Rauch, 2005). Furthermore, the rapid expansion of town and village enterprises (TVEs) right up to the mid-1990s enabled a good proportion of rural labour force to be absorbed in these TVEs (Meier and Rauch, 2005; Byrd and Lin, 1990).

Nevertheless, unemployment and underemployment beset those who are of a mature age and are left behind in villages in China (EIU, 2009). Income poverty, which is also more prevalent in rural areas and in smaller towns than in urban areas and in large cities such as Shanghai and Beijing in China, is evidenced from the difference between urban income of US$1,812 per year and average rural income of US$544 in 2007 (EIU, 2009). Since the majority of population within the 10 percentile income group would be from rural areas, the actual per capita income of this poorest group of population would not differ much from our estimated amount of US$416 in 2005 as shown in row 5 of Table 6.1. One estimate suggests that during 2000–08, the proportion of employed people living below US$1 per day in total employment in China stood at 18.6 per cent (UNDP, 2010).

Table 6.1   *Aspects of extreme poverty*

(1)	China (2)	India (3)	Japan (4)	Korea (5)	Malaysia (6)	Singapore (7)
1. Population below national poverty line (2000–08): in %	2.8	28.6	negligible	negligible	negligible	negligible
2. Population below International poverty line; less than US$1 per day (1990–2005): in %	9.9	34.3	n.a.	n.a.	15.5.	n.a.
3. Share of the lowest 10 percentile income group of people, in national expenditure: in %[a]	2.4 (2005)	3.6 (2004–05)	4.8 (1993)	n.a.	2.6 (2004)	1.9 (1998)
4. The size of the lowest 10 percentile group of population	130 million (2005)	108 million (2004)	12.5 million (1993)	n.a.	2.5 million (2004)	0.3 million (1998)
5. Per capita expenditure of the lowest 10 percentile income group of population: In US dollars	$416.30	$175.40	$1,2185.60	n.a.	$1,208.00	$6,206.00
6. The size of the lowest 10 percentile income group of population, 2008	132.50 million	114 million	12.8 million	n.a.	2.7 million	0.48 million
7. Human Poverty Index : (2006)						
(i) Rank[b]	29	62	12	n.a.	16	7
(ii) Value (%)[c]	11.7	31.3	11.7	n.a.	8.3	5.2

Notes:
[a] Figures in parentheses indicate years for which data were available.
[b] Lower rank indicates greater achievement in poverty reduction.
[c] Lower percentage in value indicates lower level of human poverty.

Sources:
UNDP (2008), *Human Development Report 2008*, New York: UN, pp. 238–241.
UNDP (2010), *Human Development Report 2010*, New York: UNDP.
World Bank (2010), *World Development Indicators*, Washington, DC: World Bank, pp. 94–96.
World Bank (1995), *World Development Report*, New York: Oxford University Press.
World Bank (2000), *World Development Report*, New York: Oxford University Press.
World Bank (2006), *World Development Report*, New York: Oxford University Press.
World Bank (2007), *World Development Report*, New York: Oxford University Press.

For India, while the proportion of population below the national poverty line averaged 28.6 per cent during the 2000–08 period (UNDP, 2010), the Indian Planning Commission, based on the information provided by the National Sample Survey Organization (NSSO), estimated the percentage of population living below the national poverty line to be 21.8 in 2008 under the Mixed Retail Period (MRP) consumption distribution method (GOI, 2010). However, the method of estimation of households living below poverty level in rural and urban areas uses per capita expenditure of Rs356 per month in rural areas and Rs539 per month in urban areas as well as per day per capita intake of 1,820 calories in rural and urban areas. This has not changed, while the prices of food have increased greatly and the amount of calories that many people in rural and urban areas need to consume have increased to 2,400 and 2,100 calories in rural and urban areas. Accordingly, the availability of subsidized food and other essential goods (GOI, 2010, 272–275) to the poor below the poverty line remains confined to those poor who consume only 1,820 calories while others who are equally poor and consume 2,400 and 2,100 calories, incurring expenses of Rs700 and Rs1,000, in rural and urban areas are excluded from the BPL (below the poverty line) list. Accordingly, to get a correct estimate of the proportion of population living BPL, the per capita expenditure amount will need to be increased to Rs700 and Rs1,000 per month and the required BPL calorie consumption amount to be raised to 2,400 and 2,100 calories for both rural and urban sectors. If this happens, then the proportion of people living BPL would appear to be even higher. There is also another problem here (GOI, 2010). The data that the NSSO collects may also not be correct, because the families living in the rural sector and in urban slums in India (as well as in other countries in Asia and Africa) are not likely to reveal the correct amount of monthly per capita income or expenditure to NSSO officers. Second, the vast majority of population living in the rural sector in India does not have regular income and cannot predict what the per capita expenditure per month would be.

Given this situation, it is also entirely possible and highly likely that these people and those in urban slums systematically understate their per capita income and expenditures per month. In that case the actual proportion of population living BPL expenditures in India could be lower than what NSSO data reveals. One estimate (Radhakrishna et al., 2011), based on the official poverty line, puts the number of people BPL at 300 million. But as we have pointed out, the estimation of the poverty line is flawed. The UNDP (2010) estimated that during 2000–08 the proportion of employed people living on less than US$1 per day accounted for 51.4 per cent of the total employed people in India.

However, in the other four countries a small population, higher per capita income and more efficient administrative machinery have virtually eliminated this extreme poverty. In Malaysia, for example, the proportion of employed people living on less than US$1 per day accounted for only 0.6 per cent of total employed people during 2000–08.

In Japan, Korea and Singapore it is unlikely that there would be a considerable number of people living on less than US$1 per day income. But within the three other countries, certain percentages of the population live below that limit. In China, this percentage was about 10 per cent, in India about 34.3 and in Malaysia it was about 15.5 for the 15-year period from 1990 to 2005. As India recorded a consistently high rate of economic growth, we would expect that the percentage of people living on less than US$1 per day would be considerably smaller than in 2005.

In rows 3, 4 and 5, we present the nature of extreme poverty that the poorest 10 percentile group of the population in these countries experience. It can be seen from row 3 that the command of the poorest 10 percentile income group of households on total national expenditures stood at 2.4 per cent for China (2005), 3.6 per cent for India (2005); 4.8 per cent for Japan (1993), 2.6 per cent for Malaysia (2004) and only 1.9 per cent for Singapore (1998). However while the share of the lowest percentile income group of people in national expenditures is small in Malaysia and Singapore, the size of population within this lowest 10 percentile income groups is also small as shown in row 4 of the table. Also, since both countries experienced a high level of economic growth, the per capita expenditure of these 10 percentile group of population at $1,208 for Malaysia and at $6,206 for Singapore remained quite high. But for China and India the 10 percentile income group of people amounted to 130 million in China (2005) and 108 million in India (2004). Also, since China recorded consistently higher economic growth than India, the per capita expenditures of the lowest 10 percentile income group of population in China also at $416.30 was considerably higher (137 per cent) than India's $175.40. Assuming that the command over total national expenditures of the lowest 10 percentile income group of people in 2008 had remained the same as in 2005, we have shown in row 6 that the size of the population increased by 6 million in India, but only by 2.5 million in China, 0.3 million in Japan, 0.2 million in Malaysia and 0.2 million in Singapore.

Hence, the higher rate of population growth in India than in other countries increased the size of the population in the lowest 10 percentile income group of population by 6 million in 2008 from 108 million in 2004. The implication of the data presented in Table 6.1 is that extreme poverty cannot simply be ameliorated by achieving higher economic growth alone. This growth has to be accompanied by implementing measures for the creation of income earning opportunities for these people, by redistributing income in favour of the poor and by reducing population. Row 7 of the table shows that among all countries, India ranked 62nd in terms of the level of human development achieved whereas China ranked 29th, Japan 12th, Malaysia 16th and Singapore 7th. Accordingly, in percentage value terms, the human poverty level in India was higher than in all the other countries covered in this table.

LABOUR FORCE PARTICIPATION

It can be seen from row 1 of Table 6.2 that the shares of employed persons of ages 15 and above in the total population for all six countries in 2008 were lower than those in 1991. One factor which contributed to this fall in shares of employed persons in the total population was the global financial crisis which began to hit the global economy from the second half of 2007. However, China's share at 71 per cent was still considerably higher than India's and Japan's share of 56 and 54 per cent, respectively. Japan was already in near recession when the global financial crisis affected all economies and China had already surpassed Japan as Asia's leading manufacturer of consumer goods. India's archaic labour laws, militant trade unions, maze of bureaucratic regulations and corrupt political system made it impossible for it to become a major manufacturing country in Asia.

Hence, while the recession also affected China, its manufacturing sector activities were not severely disrupted as the Chinese government injected hundreds of billions of dollars into the economy and export-oriented industries that were still operating. The implication for India of a decline in the share of employed in total population of ages 15 and older is that the dependency burden, which was 0.44 in 2008, fell heavily on a smaller proportion of employed people. This dependency ratio will be discussed in more detail in a separate section.

The male labour force participation rate (row 2 of Table 6.2) in 2008 was high for China, India and Malaysia at 78 per cent, 81 per cent and 80 per cent respectively. But the female labour force participation rates for India at 34 and 33 per cent in 1991 and 2008 were abysmally low compared with 73 and 68 per cent for China. For Malaysia, female labour force participation rates at 43 and 44 per cent were lower than those for China but higher than those for India. In Malaysia the 'ideology of seclusion' nowadays has little leverage, but combined with a relatively high level of per capita income it might have prevented some women in Muslim families from taking up socially recognized and socially visible extra-household income earning activities. However, hundreds of thousands of young girls have been employed in factories producing consumer electronics and other sophisticated manufactured goods. In India too, this ideology prevents Muslim women and women who belong to upper Hindu castes from taking part in extra-household income earning employment activities. This trend is particularly evident in rural areas in India where the

Table 6.2 Some features of labour employment and population

	China 1991	China 2008	India 1991	India 2008	Japan 1991	Japan 2008	Korea 1991	Korea 2008	Malaysia 1991	Malaysia 2008	Singapore 1991	Singapore 2008
1. Share of employed in total population (% of ages 15 and above)	75	71	58	56	61	54	59	58	60	61	64	62
2. Labour force participation rate (% of ages 15 and above)												
Male	85	78	85	81	76	69	73	72	80	80	79	75
Female	73	68	34	33	50	49	47	50	43	44	51	54
3. Female population as percent of total population	–	48.1	–	48.3	–	51.3	–	50.6	–	49.2	–	49.7
4. Population of working age as percentage of total population (ages 15 and over)	–	72	–	63	–	65	–	68	–	65	–	73
5. Average annual rate of growth of population (in %), 2008	–	0.6	–	1.3	–	0.3	–	0.3	–	1.5	–	1.5
6. Size of population (in millions)	–	1,377.7	–	1,141	–	127.7	–	48.6	–	27	–	4.8

Source: World Bank (2010), *World Development Indicators*, Washington, DC: World Bank, pp. 46–48, 62–64, 66–68, 74–76.

power of social customs and taboos supporting the intra-household confinement of women in most Hindu families has not weakened much. This forcible confinement of rural women within their marital homes is tantamount to the deprivation of women's freedom to do what they want to (Sen, 1999; Roy et al., 2008; Roy, 2008; Chai and Roy, 2006).

An increase in the share of women in the labour force increases their chance of earning income which they can use to obtain greater bargaining power in resource allocation within the household and the chances of lowering the birth rate as well as improving the well-being of their children.

But as row 3 in Table 6.2 shows, the systematic abortion of female foetuses by parents wanting to have male children has led to the share of female population in total population falling well below 50 per cent in both China and India (Sen, 1992; Klasen, 1994; Coale, 1991; Dreze and Sen, 1989; Roy, 2008). In 2008 these shares stood at 48.1 and 48.3 for China and India. Ideally, the share of female population in the total population should be above 50 per cent. The deprivation of a female foetus of its natural right to be born and grow up to be a human being has certainly circumscribed the capability of these two countries to achieve genuine human development. The ratio of females per 1,000 males was 933 in 2005 for India. This ratio would have come down further since then (EIU, 2008b). In Japan, where rules of patriarchy also govern the intra-household relations between men and women, the share of women in the total population has remained well above 50 per cent, while the figures for Malaysia and Singapore are close to 50 per cent. The decline in the female population as a percentage of a country's total population can lower the size of a country's working age population and that may undermine a country's effort to achieve a robust human development.

Despite the problem of missing women that plague both China and India, the share of working-age population in the total population stayed at 72 per cent for China compared with only 63 per cent for India, although India's population growth rate is more than double that of China's. The availability of such a large working-age population has enabled China's giant export-oriented industries to capture global markets and fuelled China's high rate of economic growth consistently over three decades (Sen, 1992).

Since India's working age population within the age group of 25 to 45 is considerably larger than the size of the population in the same age group in China, India would be able to maintain its high economic growth rate over a longer period than China, but only if it can create enough job opportunities to absorb these people within this age group. Hence, for achieving significant progress in the elimination of absolute poverty and in achieving substantive progress in human development, India has to lower its population growth rate rapidly.

Some Special Features of the Employment Situation: China and India

Since employment provides income to a person who can exchange it to obtain the bundle of goods necessary to improve living conditions, in row 1 of Table 6.2 we have presented an estimate of the share of employed people in the total population in all six Asian countries. Among these who are employed there are millions of people who are employed in market activities in the informal and unorganized sector. India's agricultural sector constitutes the major component of the informal sector where the production of goods and services and employment of labour are not governed by either state regulations or by collective agreements (Ghosh, 2011).

An estimate (Harris-White, 2004) places India's unregistered and informal market workforce at 93 per cent of the total workforce. Hence the unemployment statistics that are available to us are from the organized sector labour force and cannot be accepted at face value as an estimate of the true situation. Even in the modern sector, informal employment (casual) accounts for about 40 per cent of total employment. Since export processing zones (EPZs) did not prosper in India to the same extent as in China, the opportunity for labour to move from agriculture and other informal sectors to firms in EPZs did not exist in India to the same extent as in China.

China's unemployment statistics are also poor and unreliable, so official jobless statistics cannot be accepted as accurate. Even when one-third of labourers in state-operated enterprises (SOEs) lost their jobs during the late 1990s and early 2000s, the official unemployment statistics did not record this loss of employment. Millions of labourers, particularly women, migrated from the rural sector to the EPZs in China's eastern coast for employment at factories at extremely low pay of even US45 cents per hour (Cypher and Dietz, 2009). The rate of unemployment in both China and India began to decline from 2003 onwards. In China the rate declined from 10.3 per cent in 2003 to 9.2 per cent in 2007 (EIU, 2008a, 2009) and in India from 8.4 per cent in 2003 to 7.2 per cent in 2007 (EIU, 2008b), before the global financial crisis contributed to a perceptible rise in unemployment in the short term in both countries.

East Asia

A very substantial difference exists between Japan, on the one hand, and the smaller economies of East and South-east Asia, on the other, in the employment trends over the last two decades. For Japan, the collapse of its economic 'bubble' in 1989 ushered in continuing recession and stagnation. Consequently, the share of those aged 15 and older who were employed dropped significantly from 61 per cent to 54 per cent between 1991 and 2008, a rate slightly lower than India's. The figure, however, also reflects the unfavourable age structure of the Japanese population. In contrast, the employment ratio stayed almost constant in Korea (59 per cent to 58 per cent), Malaysia (60 per cent to 61 per cent) and Singapore (64 per cent to 62 per cent). In Taiwan the proportion of adults who were employed only declined slightly from 58 per cent in 1991 to 56 per cent in 2008 (Council for Economic Planning and Development, 2009:33).

A closer look at the Taiwan case is instructive because it points to a problem that is masked by the aggregate data. In particular, the fairly constant percentage of adults who were employed over the last two decades hides fundamental changes that were occurring in the structure of the country's labour force in terms of both economic sector and educational attainment. Over the last two decades, the service sector has expanded from 47 per cent to 58 per cent of total employment. In contrast, agriculture's share dropped sharply from 13 per cent to 5 per cent, while industry's slipped from 30 per cent to 27 per cent. The change in the educational levels of the labour force was even more dramatic. In 1991, 53 per cent of the work force had a junior high education or less, while 18 years later this had been more than cut in half to 25 per cent. In contrast, the proportion of employees who had at least a junior college education more than doubled from 17 per cent to 40 per cent (Council for Economic Planning and Development, 2009:35, 37). This has both good and bad aspects for Taiwan. Positively, there are more jobs requiring advanced skills and training. However, those who have lost their jobs in agriculture and semi-skilled manufacturing have little, if no, chance of attaining them. Consequently, Taiwan's past pride in 'growth with equity' seems no longer merited, as income inequality has jumped considerably over the last three decades (Clark and Tan, 2011).

In Malaysia and Singapore the situation is different inasmuch as both countries depend on immigrant labour on more or less temporary work permits. By regulating the number and type of such permits the governments are able to stabilize the employment situation for their own citizens. However, both countries are afflicted by the same type of structural problem as described above in the case of Taiwan. Due to their increasingly advanced industrial structure, there is limited use for unskilled labour, so older and less-educated workers often find it difficult to land a job. The government, especially in Singapore, has tried to address this problem by providing training courses for older and low-skilled workers.

POPULATION GROWTH

As shown in row 5 of Table 6.2, among all the countries covered in this study, the rate of population growth in India and Malaysia, despite experiencing declining trends, has still remained well above 1 per cent. But both countries have achieved robust rates of economic growth. The conventional economic wisdom would suggest that the reason for the slower rate of decline in population growth can be found in the incomplete nature of the demographic transition in these two countries. The death rate in both countries has been low compared with the birth rate. Hence the gap between birth rate and death rate (i.e. net birth) rate per 1,000 people in 2008 stands at 16 in both India and Malaysia (see Table 6.3). What is more interesting to observe is that in Malaysia the death rate and birth rate per 1,000 people in 2008 were lower than those in India.

Table 6.3   Trends in demography and reproductive health

	China 1	India 2	Japan 3	Korea 4	Malaysia 5	Singapore 6
1. Total fertility rate						
(Number of births per woman)						
1990	2.3	4	1.5	1.6	3.7	1.9
2010	1.8	2.5	1.3	1.3	2.4	1.3
2. Adolescent fertility rate						
(births per 1,000 women), 2008	10	67	5	6	13	4
3. Net addition to population						
(per 1,000 people), 2008	5	16	0	4	16	6
4. Dependency ratio, 1990	0.51	0.71	0.43	0.44	0.7	0.37
(% of working-age population)						
2010	0.39	0.55	0.58	0.37	0.51	0.35
5. Contraceptive use (% of mature women ages 15 to 49), 2003–08	85	56	–	–	–	–
6. Pregnant women having received prenatal care (in %), 2003–08	91	74	–	–	79	–
7. Births attended by skilled health care staff (% of total), 2003–08	98	47	100	100	98	100
8. Prevalence of anaemia (% of pregnant women), 2000–06	29	50	15	23	38	24
9. Maternal mortality (per 100,000 live births), 2000–08	37	301	–	–	30	–

Sources:
World Bank (2010), *World Development Indicators*, Washington, DC: World Bank, pp. 46–48, 62–64, 132–138.
UNDP (2010), *Human Development Report*, New York: Palgrave Macmillan, pp. 184–186.

The rate of decline in birth and death rates is considerably influenced by the rate of change in fertility which in turn is greatly influenced by the effectiveness of family planning programmes, the rise in family income, economic status and the effectiveness of programmes for the expansion of women's education. The effects of these factors can be seen in changes in the fertility rate in Table 6.3 below; the total fertility rate (number of births per woman) in 2010 remained at 2.5 for India and 2.4 for Malaysia, compared to 4 and 3.7 in 1990. It is undoubtedly true that with a low population (27 million in 2008), it has been easier for the Malaysian government to implement more effectively family planning programmes than for the India government. On the other hand, the attitude of the government towards an increasing population has been favourable in Malaysia, for a number of reasons.

China's population is larger than that of India. However, China has been more successful in drastically reducing its population growth rate and fertility rate. Why is that? For China, the entire programme of family planning consisting of 'one child per couple' policy information campaign to urge couples to follow this policy, of providing an adequate supply of contraceptive to couples and of economic incentives for those couples adopting the only child policy was implemented entirely by the employees of communes, whose duty was to fulfil the objective of the government population control policy. Hence, considerable sincerity and efficiency of commune officials were exhibited in the course of the implementation of China's policy of drastically lowering population growth.

In India the task of the implementation of the family planning programme rested on public service personnel at the provincial level. These public service officials, however, did not have the same efficiency and sincerity in implementing family programmes as those in China. The information campaigns to educate couples about the need to use condoms and other devices during intercourse to keep the fertility rate low were not seriously undertaken. Illiteracy and religious taboos prevented the vast number of India's Muslim couples from undertaking population planning control measures. The effectiveness of family programmes can be reasonably gauged from the following three indicators:

1.   adult females' fertility rate;
2.   adolescent girls' fertility rate; and
3.   contraceptive use by women.

Contraceptive Use and Fertility

As for other important indicators of the quality of women's reproductive health, India's achievement is far inferior to those of the other five countries. During 2003–08, on an average, 56 per cent of Indian women within the age group of 15 to 49 and a substantially higher percentage of married women used contraceptives. During the same period, among pregnant women, 91 per cent in China, 79 per cent in Malaysia and 74 per cent in India received prenatal care. During the same period also in China 98 per cent, in Japan 100 per cent, in Korea 100 per cent, in Malaysia 98 per cent and in Singapore 100 per cent, but in India only 47 per cent of total births of children were attended by skilled healthcare personnel.

During the period of 2000–06, 29 per cent of pregnant women in China, 15 per cent of those in Japan, 23 per cent of those in Korea, 38 per cent of those in Malaysia, 24 per cent of those in Singapore and 50 per cent of those pregnant women in India were found to be suffering from anaemia. This is due to the inability of the Indian state to provide adequate care to pregnant women during both the antenatal and postnatal periods. The maternal mortality rate in India during 2000–08 stood at 301 per 100,000 live births, while the fertility rate for women in India in 2010 declined to 2.5 from 4.0 in 1990; in Malaysia in the same year, the rate declined to 2.4 from 3.7 in 1990; in China the rate declined to 1.8 in 2010 from 2.3 in 1990; in Korea, the rate declined from 1.6 in 1990 to 1.3 in 2008; in Japan, the ratio also declined to 1.3 in 2008 from 1.5 in 1990; and in Singapore, the fertility rate also declined to 1.3 in 2010 from 1.9 in 1990. Thus the fertility rate of 2.5 in 2010 for Indian women is still higher than that rate in all the other five countries. Moreover, since the adolescent fertility rate which estimates the total birth per 1,000 women aged 15 to 19 stood at 67 for Indian girls in 2008, it is very difficult for India to achieve a perceptible reduction in women's fertility rate, population growth and absolute poverty level because its adolescent fertility rate compares very unfavourably with 10 for China, 5 for Japan, 6 for South Korea, 13 for Malaysia and 4 for Singapore (World Bank, 2010).

Implication of Adolescent Fertility

The maternal mortality ratio and adolescent fertility rate are the two most important determinants of women's reproductive health. A rise in the adolescent fertility rate prevents the female fertility rate from falling rapidly. A girl giving birth to a child at the age of 18 has 27 years left of her fertility period during which she can give birth to many children. The practice of arranging marriages for daughters at the age of 18–19 by their parents in order to discharge their social responsibility, even against their own and their daughter's wishes, to comply with customary dictates of village elders and to avoid social humiliation, is quite common in the vast hinterlands of rural India where more than 700 million people live (Chai and Roy, 2006; Roy, 2008). The power of such customary rules and other extra-household environmentalities can be weakened by: (i) the state making marriage of couples at 18–19 years illegal and strictly enforcing these rules on rural households as well as on households in urban *bustees* (slums) living in squalid conditions; (ii) the rapid expansion of general education and broad-based community education to encompass boys, girls and adults; (iii) creating employment opportunities for the vast and swelling army of the disguised unemployed; and (iv) allowing the social benefits of globalization to rapidly penetrate the rural sector of India. Although these forces of globalization have already begun to lessen the power of social taboos and other derogatory customary rules on rural women (Roy, 2006), the process has been slow because India is still not as globalized a country as China and the East Asian countries are, and there are considerable institutional restrictions on the economic freedom of households and business enterprises. Consequently, in China and East Asia, greater social freedom, economic freedom and the rise in income and education level have kept the marriage of couples at 18–19 at a very low level, as well as the fertility rate and population growth rate. The rise in income has to be combined with the rise in education level of couples and the expansion of education to all members of the extended family they belong to. A study by Sujaya (2011), which concurs with the argument that we have presented here, shows that among four categories of women – (a) illiterate; (b) scheduled caste; (c) scheduled tribes and; (d) others (who are wealthier, better educated and belong to upper caste) – the first cohabitation of an illiterate women with her husband occurred at an age of 16.3 years. The first cohabitation of a woman with her husband from a scheduled caste took place at the age of 17.1. For a woman of scheduled tribes it occurred at the age of 17.8. For a woman from the 'other category' (i.e. an upper caste), it occurred at the age of 18.9, almost 19 years.

Also, the total fertility of illiterate women at 3.47 was found to be the highest and that of a woman from the other category (the upper caste) at 2.66 was found to be the lowest among all four categories of women. The neo-natal fertility of illiterate women on average at 38.2 was found to be the highest and that of women from the 'other category' at 27.5 per cent was found to be the lowest among all four categories.

Dependency Ratio

The high dependency ratio that reduces the level of savings of the working members of families, puts extra pressure on income earning family members to make additional provision of food, healthcare and other social services in urban centres as well as in rural areas and, consequently, has prevented the share of population below poverty level from falling rapidly in India. As shown in Table 6.2, in 2008, the dependency ratio of population in China, India, Japan, Korea, Malaysia and Singapore stood at 0.40. 0.59, 0.52, 0.54, 0.36 and 0.47,[3] respectively. This dependency ratio in India is higher than those in the other five countries. The working-age population (aged 15–64) as a proportion of total population which in 2008 stood at 63 per cent for India, compared unfavourably with 72 per cent in China, 65 per cent in Japan, 68 per cent in Korea, 65 per cent in Malaysia and 73 per cent in Singapore (World Bank, 2010).

However, China has also been experiencing a rise in the rate of growth of the population of ethnic minorities well above the rate of growth of the Han population. Some minority groups such as Tibetans and Mongols have been granted exemption from the one-child policy. Furthermore, the consistent underreporting of births to local officials by Chinese couples since the one-child policy became effective has contributed to the underestimation of the net addition to the total population and hence the estimation of the population growth rate. Consequently the dependency ratio in China, which was lower than that in India in 2008, is expected to rise as the proportion of China's population of age 65 and over will increase to 22 per cent in 2030. At that time, the ratio of working age population to those aged 65 and above is likely to fall from 9.7:1 in the mid-1990s to 4.2:1 in 2030. In seven years, the proportion of population over 65 years increased from 7 per cent in 2000 to 9.4 per cent in 2007 (EIU, 2009), although this aging process is still occurring at a slower rate than in Japan, where the proportion of population of aged 65 and over in total population increased by 2.4 per cent each year. No wonder that China places so much emphasis on maintaining the high economic growth rate over as long a period as possible.

MULTIDIMENSIONAL POVERTY

In 2010 the Human Poverty Index was replaced by the Multidimensional Poverty Index (MPI) which includes income poverty as well as deprivations suffered by individuals, households and larger groups jointly in education, health, nutrition, liveable housing facilities, social inclusion and active participation in political, social and economic decision making process.

The construction of the MPI, inspired by Sen's (1985) work on commodities and capabilities, estimates the intensity of poverty by deriving the share of people who are multidimensionally poor and the average number of deprivations each poor household experiences. Therefore, a household suffering from deprivation in two to six indicators out of a total of ten can be found to be multidimensionally poor. Hence in a country where the welfare state provides poor households with many social goods free of cost, the share of people who are multidimensionally poor may be lower than the share of people below US $1.25 per day in the total population. In Table 6.4 we present trends in multidimensional poverty in China and India.

Columns 3 and 10 in Table 6.4 enable us to compare the multidimensional poverty and income poverty that persist in both China and India. Although

Table 6.4 Trends in multidimensional poverty (2000–08)

Country	MPI	Population in multidimensional poverty (MPI)		Population at right of MP (%)	Population with at least one severe deprivation in			Population below income poverty line	
		Head count (%)	Intensity of deprivation (%)		Education (%)	Health (%)	Living standard (%)	PPP $1.25 per day (%)	National Poverty Line (%)
1	2	3	4	5	6	7	8	9	10
1 China	0.056	12.5	44.9	6.3	10.9	11.3	12.4	15.9	2.8
2 India	0.296	55.6	53.5	16.1	37.5	56.5	58.5	41.6	28.6
3 Ratio of row 2 to row 1	5.3	4.45	1.2	2.6	3.44	5	4.71	2.61	10.21

Source: UNDP (2010), *Human Development Report 2010*, New York: UNDP, pp. 161–163.

data on such poverty in the other four countries covered in this study were not available, we believe that MPI and income poverty would be marginal in these countries. During 2000–08, the proportion of population living below the national poverty line accounted for only 2.8 per cent but that of population under Multidimensional Poverty (MP) accounted for 12.5 of total population in China. The average percentage of deprivation experienced by people in MP stood at 44.9 per cent (row 4) in China. For India, during the same period, the percentage of the total population living below the national poverty line and of those living in MP stood at 28.6 per cent and 55.6 per cent. The ratios of column 3 to column 10 at 4.46 for China and at 1.94 for India show that the gap between the MP and income poverty is higher in China than in India. But when we compare in row 3 the achievement of China with that of India on all indicators, China's achievements are far superior to India's in all the indicators of MP alleviation.

EDUCATION FOR HUMAN CAPITAL FORMATION

The successful structural transformation of economically poorer countries from a production pattern based mostly on the agricultural sector to one based on the industrial and services sectors is heavily dependent on their success in achieving a high rate of economic growth. The endogenous growth theory (Romer, 1994) placed significant stress on the need for a country to increase its stock of human capital to achieve that high rate of economic growth by expanding the level of average education (primary and secondary level) and improving the quality of higher education (tertiary) to build up an adequate supply of scientists, engineers and technicians who can utilize technological advancements to shape their country's development profile (Cypher and Dietz, 2009). The tertiary education which, therefore, is meant for those who are meritorious should be promoted by incentive schemes such as scholarships, job assurance after completion of education and so on, and should not be dominated by academic lobby groups such as teachers unions, which are branches of bigger unions of major political parties in democracies. So the major proportion of the total expenditure of the state on education (about 75 per cent) (Cypher and Dietz, 2009) should be spent on the expansion of and improvement in the quality of primary and secondary education, and on reducing gender-based and rural versus urban inequality in education.

Economists supporting public choice theory (Halsey et al., 1997), which lends support to the view that the quality of education is more important than the quantity, have expressed serious concern at the present trend of substantial rises in the cost of education. Much of this increase is due to very high salaries, which teachers would not have received if their salary had been left to

Table 6.5 Progress in educational attainment

	China	India	Japan	Korea	Malaysia	Singapore
1. HDI rank	89	119	11	12	57	27
2. Adult literacy rate (% of ages 15 and older), 2005–08	93.7	62.8	n.a.	n.a.	92.1	94.5
3. Population with at least secondary education (% of ages 25 and older), 2010	38.4	22.2	71.9	75.3	50.5	59.1
4. Primary enrolment ratio; gross (% of primary school age population), 2004–09[a]	112.1	113.1	102.2	103.7	97.9	n.a.
5. Secondary enrolment ratio; gross (% of secondary school age population), 2001–09[a]	74	57	100.7	97.5	69.1	n.a.
6. Tertiary enrolment ratio; gross (% of tertiary college age population), 2001–09	22.1	13.5	57.9	96.1	29.7	0
7. Dropout rates; all grades; gross (% of primary school cohort), 2005–08	0.4	34.2	n.a.	1.6	7.8	n.a.
8. Primary school student–teacher ratio (number of students per teacher), 2005–08	18.3	40.7	18.8	24.1	17.5	20.1

Note:
[a]Census data may understate the number of people in an age group, thus creating ratios of over 100 in a few countries with very high enrolments.

Source: UNDP (2010), *Human Development Report 2010*, New York: UNDP, pp. 192–195.

be determined by free market forces. This is the case particularly in democracies, where teachers led by their trade unions form a powerful political force. Consequently, little money may be left to improve the infrastructure of educational institutions and to enhance students' welfare.

In the light of this discussion, we now comment on educational attainment in all six countries in our statistical analysis. In Table 6.5 (row 2), we have outlined the progress achieved by these nations in the expansion of education. The table shows that during 2005–08, the adult literacy rate was maintained at almost 94 per cent of all ages 15 and older in China. So the illiterates and semi-illiterates accounted for only 6.3. In Malaysia and Singapore the rates were 92.1 and 94.5 per cent, whereas in India the rate was 62.8. This meant that during the same period of 2005–08, the total number of illiterates and semi-illiterates accounted for 37.2 per cent in India.

In 2010 in India, the population with at least secondary education accounted for 22.2 per cent of the population of ages 15 and older (row 3) compared with 38.4 per cent in China, 71.9 per cent in Japan, 75.3 per cent in Korea, 50.5 per cent in Malaysia and 59.1 per cent in Singapore. In terms of gross primary enrolment ratio (row 4), all the countries have done quite well except India. The same trend can also be seen for India in secondary enrolment (row 5). The tertiary enrolment ratio at 13.5 for India during 2001–09 was considerably lower than that for all other countries (row 6).

The drop out of students in primary schools (row 7) during 2005–08 for India at 34.2 per cent compares very unfavourably with the 0.4 per cent rate in China, 1.6 per cent in Korea and 7.8 per cent in Malaysia. The primary school student–teacher ratio during 2005–08 at almost 41 students per teacher in India was more than double that ratio in China, Japan, Malaysia and Singapore. Even the Korean ratio of 24 students per teacher looks significantly better than the Indian ratio.

However, this broad picture as presented in Table 6.5 masks some regional variations in educational attainments. For example, the population under illiteracy and semi-illiteracy is higher in rural areas and some provinces in China, such as Tibet and in nine other remote provinces. Truancy and absenteeism have plagued students' regular attendance at schools in these regions. Concerns also persist about the quality of teaching and of students under the rote-learning teaching used in China (EIU, 2009).

In India too, truancy and absenteeism are widely prevalent among children coming from poor economic backgrounds and from low-caste families in rural areas. In India, the truancy is more prevalent among girls because of their need to extend support to their mothers in discharging household chores. But in urban *bustees* (slums), truancy is more prevalent among boys, whereas girls are found to be extremely keen to pursue their studies.[4] The quality of education imparted by teachers to students at the tertiary level (colleges and universities) is generally poor as the recruitment process of teachers at all levels is non-transparent and heavily influenced by political power plays.

In India, the pay commission determines the salaries of employees of public sector organizations, including civil service personnel. Its job is just to raise the salary level and not to question whether the rise in salary is justified. Once this salary increase is announced, it is automatically accepted by provincial governments; and teachers at all levels of education are rewarded with the same rate of increase in salary. The average salary of public sector employees increased by 178.5 per cent from Rs193,554 per year in 2001–02 to Rs538,985 per year in 2008–09. But during the same period, the corruption perception index (CPI) (960 = 100) increased by only 44.5 per cent (GOI, 2010). Thus, a major proportion of total public expenditures per student is used to finance the salary costs of school, college and university teachers, top administrators and of lower-level employees and smaller amounts are spent on primary and secondary education, as Table 6.6 demonstrates.

The table shows that in India, 55 per cent of GDP per capita was spent on tertiary students in 2008 who during the 2001–09 period accounted for only 13.5 per cent (Table 6.5) of tertiary college-age students. Malaysia also spent nearly 60 per cent of GDP per capita on tertiary students who accounted for nearly 30 per cent of total tertiary college-age students (Table 6.5). But Malaysia has a shortage of skilled personnel, which justifies such expenditure. However, nearly all other countries justifiably spent more on primary and secondary education. Furthermore, the statistics on school enrolment may not be an accurate indicator of the expansion of education in developing countries particularly in South Asia, where the chances of providing false information to those who collect these statistics by public officials in rural areas are quite high.

Table 6.6   Public expenditures per student, 2008

	% of GDP per capita		
	Primary	Secondary	Tertiary
India	8.9	16.2	55.0
Japan	21.9	22.4	19.1
Korea	17.2	22.2	9.5
Malaysia	10.8	n.a.	59.7
Singapore	11.2	16.6	26.9

Source: World Bank (2010), *World Development Indicators*, Washington, DC: World Bank, pp. 102–104.

The persistent gender-based inequality in achievement in education adversely affects economic growth and robust human development. In 2008, the primary education completion rates in China for males and females were 98 and 102, in India, 95 and 92, in Korea 101 and 97, and in Malaysia 97 and 96. So generally all these four countries have made good progress in this area. During 2005–08, in China the adult literacy rate for males and females above ages 15 and older were 97 and 91; in India the rates were 75 and 51; in Malaysia, the rates were 99 and 90 and in Singapore, the respective rates were 97 and 92 (World Bank, 2010).

A Case Study of Women's Education in Taiwan

In Taiwan, women only averaged 8.8 years of schooling at the turn of the century compared to 10.2 for men. This is clearly a holdover from the past, though, when school attendance was much more limited than the almost universal secondary education that exists today. In 2005, for example, of those girls in the relevant age groups, 98 per cent were enrolled in primary schools and 93 per cent in secondary schools, almost exactly the same figures as for boys. Indeed, there is little difference between the school attendance of girls and boys in Taiwan through four-year colleges and universities, although a clear male bias in graduate education remains.

The attainment of increased and increasingly equal education for women in Taiwan is crucial because a good education is almost required to broaden one's possibilities and achieve independence and empowerment. Traditionally before industrialization, most families in Taiwan had been reluctant to invest in education for their girls who were regarded as 'spilled water' because they left the family upon marriage. Consequently, educational opportunities were vital if women were to develop their skills and resources. At the beginning of Taiwan's industrialization drive, educational opportunities were quite limited; and very substantial gender inequality existed in the education system. For example, in 1951 the average man had attended school for four years, while the average woman had only a year and a half of education.

The government instituted compulsory primary school at the beginning of the country's development drive; and compulsory schooling was expanded to nine years in 1968. Universal education paid for by the government is obviously very advantageous for girls because it overcomes cultural prejudices against girls going to school. In 1969, just after the increase in compulsory schooling, there was nearly universal schooling for both girls and boys through to the age of 11. For older children, however, the proportion of those in school dropped considerably, and serious gender inequality existed for those who continued their schooling. For example, only little more than half (54 per cent) of the girls aged 12–14 were in school compared to nearly three-quarters (70 per cent) of the boys. Clearly, the patriarchal traditional culture was acting in a biased manner to limit the resource endowments of many girls and women in Taiwan.

Two decades later, as Taiwan emerged as an industrialized society, the picture was much more positive. School attendance for both girls and boys had increased substantially. Furthermore, the decided gender inequality that existed in the educational system had been overcome as well. Indeed, by 1988 women had become a little more likely than men to have continued their education beyond 15 years of age. Consequently, the tremendous expansion of educational opportunities for women during the post-war era is widely seen as making a major contribution to women's empowerment in Taiwan (Clark and Clark, 2002).

UNFREEDOM, EMPOWERMENT AND HUMAN DEVELOPMENT

China and India

'Unfreedom' refers to the lack of intra-household and extra-household freedom of a person to acquire skills and other means to satisfy basic economic needs such as food, shelter, clothing and so on, and to engage in intra-household and extra-household activities without being subjected to discriminatory treatment by the family head or the society on the basis of the religion, sex, caste and economic status of that person.

Thus, a person who is economically poor and is a member of a minority religious community is likely to experience greater difficulty in acquiring knowledge and skills than another person from the majority religious community and with a similar economic background. Also, a woman is likely to experience more severe discriminatory treatment than a man of the same economic background and religious minority group background from members of the religious majority group, bound by convoluted social norms greatly influenced by religious dictates and by economic and political institutions, in her attempt to acquire the same skill and endowment as the man.[5] Furthermore, while an economically poor man and a woman due to their birth in a low social caste or in a minority religious community are likely to find it more difficult to exchange their skill and endowment for income earning jobs than those from an economically rich, upper-caste and religious majority group community, the level of discrimination that the poor woman is likely to face will be greater than that faced by the man (Roy et al., 2008; Roy, 2008; Chai and Roy, 2006).

In Pakistan, for instance, both poor women and men from Christian and Hindu minorities tend to suffer from such discrimination. Therefore, such discrimination, which is tantamount to 'deprivation', is the outward manifestations of 'unfreedom'. The deprivation here expresses itself in different ways. In China the Uighur minority does not seem to enjoy the same opportunities as the Han Chinese in acquiring knowledge- and skill-based endowments and in exchanging those acquired skills in obtaining the same employment as the Han Chinese in those economic activities which are suited to their skills. In Tibet too, Tibetans seem to suffer from similar levels of unfreedom and deprivation that those members of Uighur community suffer from: some extreme forms of deprivation which express themselves in victim women's voicelessness, powerlessness and helplessness (Roy, 2008).

Violence Against Women

As noted above, some extreme forms of deprivation, which cannot be quantitatively measured, express themselves in victim women's voicelessness, powerlessness and helplessness (Roy, 2008). This may result from considerable physical punishment meted out to women of low caste by upper-caste village elders for no fault of the women.[6] Within the marital household, a bride, even if she is educated, employed and bringing income to the groom's family has to endure harassment, insult and other forms of torture by her in-laws on the pretext that members of her marital home failed to fulfil their dowry obligation. Many such victims of assault were ultimately murdered by their in-laws. The voicelessness and powerlessness of many such women lead them to commit suicide. The statistics of dowry-related deaths are unlikely to be correct as many such deaths are not reported. The data from the National Health Survey (*The Statesman Weekly*, 2007) put the percentage of women in urban areas and villages who experienced trauma due to physical violence against them at 62.2 and 58.9 in Bihar, whereas the all India average rate of domestic violence against women in rural areas stood at 40.2 per cent in 2007. In 2008, the total number of reported cases of torture of women reached 75,930, a rise of 7.1 per cent over the previous year. In Bengal, where the treatment of women is generally fairer than in other provinces, there were 13,663 reported cases of domestic violence, which was the highest in the country in 2008 (*The Telegraph*, 2010).

In China, while generally violence against women is less than in India, discrimination against girls is more prevalent in China than in India due to the Chinese society's adherence to the patrilineal and patrilocal kinship system as well as to the one-child policy (Chai and Roy, 2006). While land is periodically contracted out to households on the basis of the principle of granting each member of a family a portion of total allocated land, the family also uses a portion of the land allocated to a girl member after she leaves her natal home as a married woman.

Thus, historically the customary preference for a son and the one-child policy combined together led millions of couples to abandon female children and take recourse to abortion of female foetuses and to the maltreatment of their daughters (World Bank, 1995; Chai and Roy, 2006). However, China's rapid economic growth, export-oriented industrialization and the consequent spread of urbanization during a period of three decades since the early 1980s allowed millions of young girls to move out of their village homes to take up income earning employment in urban industrial centres as well in rural enterprises, thereby enabling them to send part of their income to their village homes as well as to lead self-reliant lives in urban centres away from the clutches of rural prejudice and customs (World Bank, 2001). Furthermore, after the communist government took control of China, the Chinese legal system, under the influence of Marxist ideology, accepted women's status and rights to be equal to those of men. Although the abolition of the commune system made women's position inferior to that of men, rural economic reforms since the late 1970s and early 1980s improved women's position in the rural society which was being increasingly urbanized (Gao, 1994). Furthermore, the marriage law of 1950, which has been strictly enforced and widely accepted by the Chinese society, banned arranged marriage, polygamy, bride price and child-marriage as well as allowing Chinese women the right to choose partners, demand divorce from their husbands, inherit property and retain a part of control over their children's lives (World Bank, 2001). Hence, by and large, the level of deprivation and powerlessness of and of violence against women would be less in China than in India, but in rural China the gap between the legal and customary rights has not been entirely eliminated. Hence, under patrilineal inheritance, daughters' share in rural residences and in other properties has been routinely ignored (Chai and Roy, 2006).

East Asia

Taiwan has an industrial (and increasingly post-industrial) economy and a primarily urban society. Consequently, women have gained substantially more opportunities in education and employment; and women's subjugation in the family to both husbands and mother-in-laws has decreased considerably as well. Yet, the patriarchal norms of the country's Confucian culture still create significant 'unfreedom', especially for older rural women (Farris, 2000). For example, while the gender gap in education has narrowed dramatically in terms of aggregate data (see above), pronounced gender discrimination can still be found in Taiwan's educational system. For example, primary and secondary textbooks contain many gender stereotypes; and there is gender segregation in college majors with women concentrated in the humanities and social sciences but greatly underrepresented in science and technology (Hsieh, 1996).

In Singapore and Malaysia, the situation as to gender equality is fairly good, although not perfect due to remaining undercurrents of patriarchal social philosophy; and social norms and traditions may still overrule the law in some cases. However, there are no socio-cultural norms to prevent women from taking part in paid employment (Jamilah, 1996), which automatically contributes to strengthening their independence. Malaysian and Singapore women are also well educated, on average, which works in the same direction. In Malaysia, the situation varies somewhat between the states, the status of women being more restricted in states governed by the Islamic party. Furthermore, it varies between races, since inheritance rules are different for Muslims and non-Muslims. Early marriage is infrequent; only 5 per cent of women between 15 and 19 are or have been married. Polygamy is now prohibited but still exists, as marriages entered before the law came into force are recognized (CEDAW, 2004).

In Singapore only 1 per cent of women aged 15 to 19 were or had been married. Family matters are regulated partly through civil law, partly through Sharia law (for Muslims), which means that polygamy is not outlawed. Singapore women enjoy a high degree of civil liberties as well as economic independence, according to the law (CEDAW, 2004). The remaining gender gap manifests itself in more subtle ways. For example, it still appears to be more difficult for foreign male spouses of Singaporeans to settle down in the city state, compared to female spouses.

The Empowerment Status of Women

Empowering a woman refers to endowing that woman with the capability to take control of her own and her children's lives. Acquiring that capability requires education and skills, or physical strength to earn income from employment and from the woman's own assets such as land, dowry and so on. But the implicit assumptions here are that: (i) the parents of a girl will pay for the education and skills the girl wants to acquire; (ii) she will be able to exchange her skill for an income earning job appropriate to her knowledge and skill in a transparent, unbiased and corruption free selection process; (iii) the girl will be allowed by her parents to take up that employment even if the location of employment is at a considerable distance from the natal home; (iv) the society and adult members of her household will accord her the same freedom and status as accorded to male members of her family in her interaction within and outside the confines of her natal home; and (v) that girl or her sisters will get an equal share of their ancestral property along with their brothers. Also, for a married woman whose parents have provided her with education and skills and have paid dowry to her marital home, to be able to attain empowerment the five assumptions will have to remain valid. However, none of these five assumptions is totally valid in any of the countries covered in this study, although the 'ideology of seclusion' is not strictly enforced by the society on young girls and women, who often enjoy enough freedom in their engagement in economic and social affairs within and outside their homes.

In China, the stricter enforcement of the Chinese marriage law of 1950, which eliminated arranged marriage and the practice of dowry payment and upheld women's right to divorce their husbands, has gone a long way towards enhancing women's freedom. Furthermore, the Chinese Constitution of 1982 granted women rights equal to those granted to men in all economic and social transactions, and directed the state to apply the principle of equal pay for men and women for the same job. The Women's Rights Protection Law, which became effective in 1992, also acted to enhance women's empowerment status

(Woo, 1994). Nevertheless, the facts that a son enables a family to gain another piece of land when he marries and that the disbandment of the commune system has forced parents to rely on their sons to look after them during their old age have acted to prevent improvement in women's empowerment status in rural China (Roy and Chai, 1999).

The current sex ratio (*The Australian*, 2011) at premarital age of 1.15 men for 1 woman testifies to the continuation of discrimination against girls and women and of abortion of female foetuses in China. Families accumulate savings to pay for their sons' education and to help them obtain high incomes to secure good brides. It is the 'groom price' which is prevalent in China.

In India all of the above noted assumptions are not valid. Such important sources of discrimination against women as arranged marriage and bride price are present. Women's right to choose their partners is still not widely accepted in the Indian society. Two extreme manifestations of gender inequality can be found in the child mortality rate for males and females per 1,000 live births and also in the maternal mortality rate per 100,000 live births which was 301 in 2003–08 in India. Although the Hindu Succession Act of 1956 (Roy, 2008) granted sons and daughters equal rights to their ancestral home and other properties, the Indian State also maintained the coparcenary system under which the right of a daughter to her ancestral home and other ancestral properties was denied. Also, the Hindu law states that a woman can enjoy a lifelong interest in ancestral property only as a widow or as a daughter in a son-less family. The Islamic law also gives only partial availability of income earning employment opportunities for women. These are considerably less in India than in China due primarily to lack of adequate expansion of labour-intensive manufacturing industries and of market openness in India's semi-closed economy.

In India's rural sector, the mode of cultivation of land has not been modernized, and there is a marked absence of horticultural activities and small-scale light manufacturing activities. Women from lower-caste families and tribal families tend to take up employment in agriculture as casual day labourers, whereas those from upper-caste, landholder families mostly tend to remain engaged in intra-household non-market work. Hence, it is in these relatively well-off rural families that the rule of patriarchy continues to be enforced. In well-off families in smaller urban centres, where there is primarily petty trading and other service but no manufacturing activities, women's chances of getting employment are very limited; and the ideology of seclusion governs women's engagement in intra-household and extra-household activities.

In China, to help women come out of their home and to be easily absorbed in the workforce, the state created collective dining halls, nurseries, sewing collectives, laundries, hair salons, shoemaking shops and knitting shops in cities and industrial centres throughout the country. Also, the government trained an increasing number of women workers as model workers to act as role models for fellow workers. These role models were also promoted to higher administrative positions (Gao, 1994; Chai and Roy, 2006). Such initiatives by the government can rarely be found in India.

Women's Income and Land Rights

The current literature (Becker, 1973, 1974, 1991; Agarwal, 1997; Chai and Roy, 2006; Roy, 2006, 2008) tends to place strong emphasis on measures to increase women's income and assets such as cultivable land, education and even jewellery (which can be a source of capital in business ventures) to increase a woman's control over the resources she owns and in intra-household decisions about the allocation of food, nutrition for children, work roads, reproduction and her freedom of movement and of social engagement outside the home.

Some studies (Kabeer, 1998; Pitt and Khandker, 1998) on the effects of micro-loans on poor female borrowers' economic status within their families found that access to micro-loans increased their control of non-land assets and enhanced their role in household decision making. This control over money also enabled them to engage in extra-household market-based and other activities without requiring permission from their husbands or other family heads. While these studies refer to poor women in Bangladesh, doubts are also being raised about the effectiveness of these loan programmes in reducing economic poverty. But Chai and Roy (2006) found that wives earning cash income from petty trading and from working on other householders' land do not significantly improve their status within the confines of their homes in rural India. The authors also noted that landless tribal women going out of their homes to collect non-market income or market-based income did not lose their extra household freedom of movement. But immediately after these women entered their homes, their income and freedom came under the control of the household head. Also, Lakshmanasamy and Roy (2010) found that in India premarital investments in women, in the form of education and dowry (source of capital), are not likely to improve women's position within their marital homes as they seem to possess little bargaining strength in household resource allocation decisions, even with sizeable assets and income (well-paid employment) under their control. A survey (*The Australian*, 2011) conducted in six countries including China and India found that in India 86 per cent of the men interviewed felt that women's job in the household is to care for children and to attend to household chores and 37 per cent of them admitted to using physical violence against their female partners on a regular basis.

Hence, it would appear that income earning jobs, land, jewellery, education and so on may lessen the level of discrimination against women by men, but these cannot ensure that these women will be empowered. This empowerment, in the true sense of the term, can only be achieved when women attain the same substantive freedom as men in all intra-household economic, social, human capital formation, reproductive and other household decision making and actions, as well as the same substantive freedom of movement, speech and of other interactions with both men and women in the society outside their homes (UNDP, 2010).

Unfortunately, in India, women's capability to enjoy this substantive freedom both inside and outside their homes is governed more by customary law than by the formal law of the state. Here, even with the state granting women the same freedom as men, women are still required to secure from society their customary right to be treated equally with men in all kinds of activities (Roy, 2006). In India, such customary laws are changing more slowly than in Chinese and other East Asian societies. One of the reasons is that in the latter cases, interaction with the Western society in trade, investment, culture and human migration has been more pervasive and intense than the Indian society's interaction with the West in these areas. In 2008, the total female population of India stood at 550.6 million, accounting for 48.3 per cent of the total population of the country. Out of this total female population, 374 million lived in villages and rural towns. Since women in rural India enjoy less freedom to improve their social, educational, health and economic status than women in urban India, achievements in the empowerment indicators and in human development indicators remain extremely poor as demonstrated in Tables 6.7, 6.8A and 6.8B, below. Doubts are also being now raised about whether Indian women do really want to attain empowerment (Roy, 2008).

Empowerment Indicators

Several important empowerment indicators, which are presented in Table 6.7, provide us with an indication of the level of freedom that women in the six Asian countries are enjoying in making and implementing decisions to exercise full control over their own lives and those of their children. The concept of freedom of choice is very broad, as it refers to the freedom to choose and consume economic and environmental goods. The capacity to choose and consume a product is governed by the availability of the product in the market and by the purchasing power of the consumer. However, the supply of adequate quantities of economic and social goods and sufficient consumers' income to enable them to make a choice of what to buy and in what quantities depends on whether the economy is operating on free-market rules, the state is not imposing restrictions on people's freedom of choice, and the society is bold enough to disband its antiquated customs and taboos to enable individuals freely to choose and consume the social goods they want.

Table 6.7 Selected empowerment indicators

	China	India	Japan	Korea	Malaysia	Singapore
1 Satisfaction with freedom of choice (% satisfied)						
(a) total	70	66	70	55	83	73
(b) female	68	60	75	56	83	73
2 Presence of democracy; score (0–2)[a], 2008	0	1	2	2	1	1
3 Human rights violations; score (1–5)[b], 2008	4	4	2	1	2	1
4 Press freedom (index)[c], 2009	84.5	29.3	3.3	15.7	44.3	45.0
5 Number of seats for females in Parliament (% of total seats), 2008	21.3	9.2	12.3	13.7	14.6	24.5
6 Political engagement (% of people expressing opinion to bureaucracy), 2008	–	12	22	22	11	12
7 Gender Inequality Index (GII)[d]						
(a) rank (2008)	38	122	50	12	20	10
(b) value (2008)	0.405	0.748	0.493	0.273	0.310	0.255

Notes:
[a] 0 refers to non-democratic; 1 to democratic with no alteration; 2 to democratic with alteration.
[b] 1 refers to a few human rights violations; 5 refers to most human rights violations.
[c] a lower score indicates greater freedom of the press.
[d] the score 0 implies that women are mostly equal to men and 1 implies that women fare as poorly as possible in all measured dimensions.

Source: UNDP (2010), *Human Development Report 2010*, New York: UNDP, pp. 68–71, 156–158, 164–167, 176–178.

The proportions of the total population and of the total female population who are satisfied with their freedom of choice are considerably smaller in India and Korea than in the other four countries (Table 6.7, row 1). On the 'presence of democracy' (row 2) Japan and Korea have earned the highest positive score and China the highest negative score, with India, Malaysia and Singapore earning a medium positive score. On human rights violations (row 3), both China and India have fared badly, whereas in Korea and Singapore very few human rights violations seem to occur.

On press freedom (row 4), Japan, Korea, Malaysia and India seem to grant far greater freedom than Singapore and China. As to women's participation in parliament (row 5), expressed as a percentage of total parliamentary seats occupied by women, Singapore stands out as number one followed by China, and India stands as number six. Furthermore, only a small proportion of the total population took part in political engagement by interacting with bureaucracy in all countries except China (row 6). In gender equality (row 7), India with index number 122 ranks last and Singapore with index number 10 ranks first among these six countries. Accordingly, in gender inequality value, India with a 0.748 score ranks last and Singapore with a 0.255 value ranks first among these six countries.

The data on the empowerment indicators in Table 6.7 contain some interesting and important exceptions to the general pattern that we have found among the economic and social indicators for these Asian nations. Normally, there is a decided correlation between a country's affluence and how well it scores on most measures of economic, social and political development and performance (Lipset, 1959). For the Asian countries in this analysis, therefore, one would expect Japan to have the best record and India the worst, with China somewhat better than India and the other East Asian nations between Japan and China. In terms of general democracy and human rights, this pattern is generally replicated with the very significant exception of India's democratic (but not human rights) accomplishments. In particular, India is equivalent to Singapore and Malaysia on the levels of democracy and political engagement, and actually has a greater degree of press freedom. In contrast, India is much worse than all the East Asian countries and no better than China on human rights violations.

The indicators of the status and empowerment of women, however, display much more idiosyncratic violations. As noted previously, India has a very low ranking on the gender inequality index. However, the comparison in Table 6.7 shows that China's overall rank of 38 is much closer to the East Asian nations than to India. That is, its ability to reduce gender inequality is somewhat better comparatively than its performance on most of the other social and economic indicators considered in this section. The most striking aspect of the gender inequality data, however, is the poor record of Japan, which is the wealthiest and longest-functioning democracy by far in East Asia, two characteristics that are generally associated with promoting the status of women. Instead, Japan's highly patriarchal culture has quite clearly resulted in continuing discrimination against women in the economic, social and political realms (Reischauer, 1988). This is especially striking in view of the evident progress that has occurred in the other Confucian cultures in China, Singapore and South Korea.

In the area of women's political representation, India's poor record of women holding only 9 per cent of parliamentary seats does not look so bad in a relative sense, because women's representation in the national legislature is also under 15 per cent in Japan, Korea and Malaysia. While it is 21 per cent in China, the authoritarian regime there makes the value of this better representation questionable. In contrast, Taiwan has achieved a fairly good record on this dimension as well. For example, in the latest election for its Legislative Yuan in 2008, women won 30 per cent of the seats (Central Election Commission, 2008).

The ability of women to gain elective political office in Taiwan is the cumulative result of a special feature of the country's election system dating back to the early post-war period. About 10 per cent of legislative and assembly seats were 'reserved' for women in multi-member constituencies (i.e. the woman with the highest number of votes would be awarded the seat even if male candidates outpolled them). Even during the authoritarian era, most elections were quite competitive between factions within the ruling Kuomintang. Consequently, women had to develop political skills and constituency skills to win elections that were vital to their own factions; and over time, therefore, women became independent political actors in their own right. By the late 1980s and 1990s, women were winning more than their reserved quotas for most offices; and they continued to do so even when the election system was changed and the reserved-seats system was discontinued (Clark and Clark, 2002).

Nevertheless, the evidence tends to suggest that with a wide-ranging decentralization process taking place around the world, there has been a perceptible increase in people's perceived freedom to choose. In many countries, while at the national level a formal democratic structure is increasingly being entrenched, at the subnational level, right down to village level, local participatory systems of development, women, as well as identity-based and economically and politically poor groups, are becoming more visibly engaged in political and social actions (UNDP, 2010). However, when the number of substitutes in economic, social goods and the system of politic control available to a citizen is limited in a country, people's perceived freedom to choose is also limited.

OTHER DIMENSIONS OF DEVELOPMENT AND FREEDOM

Human Development Indicators

As illustrated in Tables 6.8A and 6.8B, in GDP per capita, life expectancy at birth, adult literacy rate, gross school enrolment ratio, mean years of schooling, and expected years of schooling, India stood out to be the poorest achiever among all six countries. Consequently the deprivation scores of Indians resulting from their failure to achieve high scores in the indicators of human development are also higher than the deprivation scores of citizens of the other five countries. In row 3 of Table 6.8B we present the human development index (HDI) value, deprivation scores and HDI rank. Here also we can see that in the HDI value, while Japan and Korea scored 0.884 and 0.877, India and China scored 0.519 and 0.663. In deprivation scores, India and China's 41.9 and 34.5 compare very unfavourably with Japan, Korea, Malaysia and Singapore's scores of 6.8, 7.6, 24.3 and 11.5.

Accordingly, India with the HDI rank of 119 was placed second among the bottom ten countries and China with the rank of 89 was placed in fourth position among the top ten countries within the medium human development category. Japan, Korea and Singapore were within the very high human development category of 47 countries, whereas Malaysia was placed in the high human development category.

The Corruption Perception Index

The not so impressive performance of India and of China in human development indicators can, to a great extent, be attributed to the prevalence of pervasive corruption in these two countries. The primary source of corruption is the public sector bureaucracy and its political masters who administer each country. Gradually the corruption spreads to the private sector and permeates all kinds of transactions in the society as public officials taking bribes provide a customary validity to the practice of rent seeking in the whole society. For India in addition, the democratic governance with many political parties at the federal, provincial and village level has strengthened the culture of incapacitating all formal institutions of good governance and of staying in power by buying votes at elections (Roy and Sidenko, 2007b).

The corruption perception index, institutional non-compliance scores and citizens' experience of corruption for all six countries presented in Table 6.9A demonstrate clearly that in China, India and Malaysia, corruption indices at (row 1) 3.5, 3.3 and 4.4 respectively imply the presence of an extremely high level of corruption as with their index scores of less than 5 they belong to the

Table 6.8A   Trends in principal human development indicators

	China		India		Japan		Korea		Malaysia		Singapore	
	2003	2008	2003	2008	2003	2008	2003	2008	2003	2008	2003	2008
1. GDP per capita (current $US)	1,100	3,266	564	1,016	33,713	38,456	12,634	39,039	4,187	8,214	21,492	37,906
2. Gross school enrolment ratio												
(i) % of age group	69	69.3	60	61	84	87	93	99	71	67.7	87	0
(ii) Deprivation score[b]	48.4	47.3	58.1	56.6	32.3	26.1	22.6	13	46.2	46.4	29	0
3. (i) Adult literacy rate (% of age 15 and above)	90.9	93	61	66	n.a.	n.a.	97.9	n.a.	88.7	92	92.5	94
(ii) Deprivation score[b]	10.4	9.9	44.7	45.9	0	0	16.4	0	13.9	11.3	8.6	85
4. (i) Life expectancy at birth (in years)	69	73	63.3	64	82	83	77	80	73.2	74	78.2	81
(ii) Deprivation score[b]	28.4	25.6	41	48.7	0	0	10.9	7.7	19.3	23.1	7.2	5.1

Notes:
[a] relates to 2006.
[b] a lower value indicates improvement in human development and decline in deprivation level.

Sources:
UNDP (2006), *Human Development Report 2006*, New York: UNDP, pp. 266–268.
World Bank (2008), *World Development Indicators*, Washington, DC: World Bank, pp. 80-82.
World Bank (2010), *World Development Indicators*, Washington, DC: World Bank, pp. 106–108, 144–146.
World Bank (2010), *World Development Report*, Washington, DC: World Bank, pp. 377–379.
World Bank (2005), *World Development Report*, New York: Oxford University Press, pp. 256–257.

Table 6.8B   Additional indicators and index of human development (HDI), 2010

	China	India	Japan	Korea	Malaysia	Singapore
	1	**2**	**3**	**4**	**5**	**6**
1. Mean years of schooling,						
(i) years	7.5	4.4	11.5	11.6	9.5	8.8
(ii) Deprivation score	45	72	10	9	27.2	33.3
2. Expected years of schooling						
(i) years	11.4	10.3	15.1	16.8	12.5	14.4
(ii) Deprivation score	56.2	63	33.3	23	49.4	37.7
3. Human Development Index						
(i) Value (HDI)	0.663	0.519	0.884	0.877	0.744	0.846
(ii) Deprivation score	34.5	41.9	6.8	7.6	24.3	11.5
(iii) HDI rank	89	119	11	12	57	27

Note: Lower deprivation scores imply a lower level of deprivation for a country's population in achievements in human development.

Source: UNDP (2010), *Human Development Report*, New York: Palgrave Macmillan, pp. 143–146.

133 most corrupt countries in the world. Among the six countries discussed here, India appears to be the most corrupt and Singapore to be the cleanest. China's corruption status is slightly better than that of India. Consequently, the institutional non-compliance score (row 2) of India and China at 6.7 and 6.5 are highest and the score for Singapore at 0.7 is the lowest of the countries' scores. The implication is that the formal institutions of good governance have been far more severely incapacitated by paraformal mafia groups of the political parties in power in India and China than in the other four countries included in this study. Citizens' experience recorded in row 3 and expressed as a percentage of total respondents answers to three questions showed that while in all six countries the level of corruption increased between 2007 and 2010, 74 per cent and 46 per cent of respondents answered that the corruption in India and China had increased and only 10 per cent and 25 per cent of respondents felt that the corruption level had declined. In Japan and Malaysia too, the largest proportion of respondents felt the corruption level had increased.

Human Development and Human Happiness

The increase in the human development indicator values for each of the six countries between 2003 and 2008, as demonstrated in Tables 6.8A and 6.8B above, provides a clear indication that these countries have achieved considerable

Table 6.9A   Corruption perception index and citizens' experience of corruption, 2010

	China	India	Japan	Korea	Malaysia	Singapore
	1	**2**	**3**	**4**	**5**	**6**
1. Corruption Perception Index						
(10 = highly clean; 0 = highly corrupt)	3.5	3.3	7.8	5.4	4.4	9.3
2. Institutional non-compliance score						
(10 minus the country score)	6.5	6.7	2.2	4.6	5.6	0.7
3. Citizens' attitude to and experience of corruption (2007–10)						
(i) Percent of citizens reporting (%)						
(a) Corruption level decreased	25	10	14	24	19	28
(b) Corruption level did not change	29	16	40	44	35	33
(c) Corruption level increased	46	74	46	32	46	38

Source: Transparency International (2011), *Research Surveys*, Berlin: Transparency International, www.transparency.org/policy_research/surveys_indices/CPI/2010

progress in human development, although the progress recorded by Japan, Korea, Singapore and Malaysia appears to be greater than that recorded by China and India. Consequently, its effect will be felt on the human well-being and happiness of citizens of these countries. Table 6.9B illustrates, in terms of several indicators, the well-being and happiness achieved by citizens of the six countries. This table aims to capture peoples' perception of well-being and happiness achieved, given all the institutional constraints within which they led their lives. During 2006–09, while in 'overall satisfaction' Indians recorded the lowest score, in 'purposeful life' they scored the highest score. Similarly, in 'standard of living', the Chinese recorded the lowest score. But in the 'negative experience' index, which appears to be the most crucial indicator, Indians with a score of 26 scored better than all others; and the Chinese with a score of 17 seem to have the most negative experiences about many things in their lives. So the main issue that needs to be discussed is whether the improvements in the empowerment, human development and well-being indicators in a country achieve real happiness for the people. Alternatively, since all these indicators relate to material aspects of human lives, one could ask whether the so-called perceived happiness of people is apparent and not real happiness. Also, people's perceived happiness may change to unhappiness if they are made aware of the availability of better substitutes for the products they are currently consuming (Sen, 1985). Thus, for example, the so-called current perceived material happiness of Tibetans would have fallen far short of their potential perceived material happiness in 2008 when they were made aware of the fact that their per capita household consumption expenditure was

Table 6.9B   Human well-being and happiness indicators

	China	India	Japan	Korea	Malaysia	Singapore
	1	2	3	4	5	6
1. Overall life satisfaction,						
(0, least satisfied; 10, most satisfied), 2006–09	6.4	5.5	6.8	6.3	7.7	6.7
2. Satisfaction with aspects of wellbeing, 2006–09:						
(a) Jobs (% of employed respondents who are satisfied)	78	74	73	68	86	88
(b) Personal health (% of respondents who are satisfied)	80	85	68	71	87	95
(c) Standard of living (% of respondents who are satisfied)	60	61	64	71	68	79
3. Elements of happiness, 2006–09:						
(a) Purposeful life (% of "yes" responses)	–	91	76	80	95	90
(b) Treated with respect (% of "yes" responses)	87	72	60	63	88	81
(c) Social support network (% of "yes" responses)	79	66	89	79	81	84
4. Negative experience index, 2006–09						
(0, most negative; 100, least negative)	17	26	21	23	20	19

Source: UNDP (2010), *Human Development Report 2010*, New York: UNDP, pp. 176–178.

only one-quarter of that in the coastal region of Guangdong (UNDP, 2010). Furthermore, the gap between the current perceived material happiness and potential perceived material happiness of the population of Guangdong will widen when they find out their per capita consumption expenditure is lower than that of the population of Beijing and its surrounding region.

The proportion of people in the total global population who have the capability to be genuinely happy is very small, because a consumer's material happiness turns to unhappiness if, after completing a transaction for the purchase of a good, they are made aware of the availability of the product at a considerably lower price than the one they paid. The loss in the consumer's surplus has now become bigger as the gap between the perceived potential surplus and the perceived current surplus has widened. To get out of the current state of unhappiness, the consumer tries to rationalize their behaviour by arguing that the product is of high quality, the store selling that product has a very good reputation and so on. Thus, people who are always in pursuit of material wealth and happiness tend to be in a perpetual state of unhappiness. As a result, economically poor families and individuals and those slightly above the national poverty line income or expenditure in e.g. Tibet, Laos or Bhutan have a greater chance of achieving real happiness than those economically well-off families in China and other countries.

Real Happiness

Since the objective of human life is often considered to be happy living, then to realize that objective, one requires placing a limit on one's material wants (Narayan, 1960; Schumacher, 1962; Roy, 1986; Roy et al., 2008). It is only then that the person can achieve real happiness which is a particular state of mind, a state of contentment in which there is no more urge for the pursuit of further accumulation of wealth and goods of material consumption; and the mind is not restless (Kamenka, 1972). But the most fundamental requirements for citizens of any country to achieve real happiness are the following:

1. They must have complete political freedom of speech, movement, assembly and be able to be openly critical of the state's policies and actions without any fear of reprisals from the state's agents. This freedom is Gandhi's 'Swaraj' which also includes the freedom of mind, body and spirit.
2. Their two most important private properties – their personal lives and their shelter – must be protected and then their basic minimum needs must be met by the state.
3. The state, by changing its laws and incentive structure, must directly promote the production and consumption of a more simple lifestyle and related goods.
4. The society also is required to embrace some elements of Gandhi's spiritualism, which abhors the citizens yearning for more material wealth and non-essential consumer goods driven by greed.

Young Marx, like Gandhi, also felt that the prime role occupied by money in the functioning of the political economy is greatly responsible for turning man into a dependent being, into a commodity. Since money makes a man forget his own power it becomes the higher good, and the person who possesses it also becomes a commodity (Kamenka, 1972). True freedom (political, economic, social and spiritual) is therefore the quintessential requirement for everything that a human being may want to achieve in life – empowerment, human development and genuine human happiness (UNDP, 2010). Only in a properly functioning democracy with democratic elections and political parties can citizens have a chance of enjoying this true freedom. Among the six countries covered in this study, only Japan, Korea and India are fully functioning democracies, although India's functioning is beset with many difficulties. Nevertheless, political freedom, including freedom of speech, freedom of assembly and the freedom to be able to attack the government publicly for its failures in any area of economic and social development enjoyed by Indians is almost unparalleled in the developing world. But of course the per capita income of India is considerably lower than in the five other countries. This is precisely one of the prime reasons for Indians, by and large, to be easily contented with limited amounts in a materialistic lifestyle. The religion and culture which is greatly influenced by religion also played an important side in cultivating in the minds of Hindus in India and Buddhists in Japan, Korea and China the virtues of humility and abstinence of any excess consumption of material goods. On the other hand, in China, Confucianism espoused the virtues of wealth creation and a materialistic lifestyle for China's majority population, the Han Chinese. In India though, the economic freedom of the populace is considerably less than that of the populace in all other countries covered in this study.

Thus, if a production possibility frontier could be constructed with the Y-axis indicating the total production of non-essential consumer goods and the X-axis indicating the total production of essential and holistic goods, one is likely to find that all these countries will be inside the frontier at sub-optimal points. For China, the sub-optimal point is likely to be located more towards the Y-axis; and for India, the point is likely to be located closer to the X-axis. For other countries, those points should be somewhere between those of China and India.

SOCIETY, THE STATE AND MARKET RELATIONSHIP

A country's success in achieving the alleviation of extreme poverty, empowerment, human development and human happiness for its populace depends on the presence in the country of a virtuous relationship between the society, the state and the market. The society creates the state and hands over a part of its sovereignty to the state to enable the governance group to implement programmes promoting the political, economic, social and human development of its citizens.

The society, therefore, is ipso facto required to support the state's actions by modifying its old customs, traditions and taboos which have hampered economic and social progress. Employment generation which is crucial to realizing the state's developmental objectives requires the operation of a free market and of an outward-oriented economy. Society is required to support free market rules which include a completely deregulated labour market. Only then can this relationship become harmonious and capable of achieving the state's developmental goals. Such a virtuous relationship existed in Taiwan and Hong Kong in the past. It does exist in certain perceptible measure in the other five countries, except in India.

Karl Polanyi's (1957) assertion that historically the market that has been kept open by an enormous increase in a continuous as well as centrally organized and controlled intervention in the economy by the state has also been deeply introduced with all kinds of social ties and changing forms and policies of regimes capturing state power (Fukuda-Parr and Shiv Kumar, 2003). The forms of the regime change have contributed to Polanyi's pendulum of policy change to swing to state regulation and from state regulation to markets.

However, the possibility of the capture of power by a regime in pursuing its vested interests in a Northian state (North, 1981, 1987, 1990) has led to Olson's (1982) theory that a coalition of self-interested groups tries to redistribute income and other attendant benefits toward the coalition, instead of working to increase productive efficiency. In this scenario, which is most widely prevalent in India, but is also present in China, Korea and Malaysia, the effectiveness of the Keynesian interventionist-state policy in achieving developmental goals is considerably weakened. Hence, the virtuous relationship between society, the state and the market is only partially present in these Asian countries.

For India, Polanyi's pendulum, which shifted to the left more than half a century ago, has been slowly shifting to the market. But the major problem that confronts India is that it is not a federal state. It is, by all measures, a confederation as the provinces are virtually sovereign states. Hence, Polanyi's pendulum of policy may change in one sovereign province due to regime change towards the market but may change in another sovereign province towards the left to controls and restrictions. Hence, the confederate government's policies cannot be effectively implemented throughout the confederation. The problem is that implementing programmes for human development becomes more difficult for the confederate government because the control over land is vested in sovereign provinces, not in the confederation.

NOTES

1. In a village in Bihar Province in India, a self-styled caste council recently banned girls from wearing jeans, blaming the attire for incidents of teasing and young couples eloping.
2. On 7 January 2011, armed cadres and hired gunmen of CPM killed seven people and grievously injured 21 innocent people in a village in West Bengal in broad daylight, because these villagers were expressing their opposition to the presence of such gunmen in the house of a local CPM leader. The members of the local police force who were also members of the CPM party took no action to arrest these gunmen.
3. Based on one of the authors' (Roy) calculations from data in World Bank (2010:62–64).
4. This information was obtained by one of the present authors (Roy) through interviews with mothers and girls in a *bustee* located close to his house in Calcutta during January 2011.
5. For a much more detailed discussion of such unfreedom and discrimination against women, see Roy et al. (2008).
6. Such practices occur in rural areas in Bihar, UP (Upper Province) and Rajasthan, which are India's socially and economically backward provinces.

7. Managing development in the Asian states

As discussed in detail in Chapters 1 and 2, the state almost inevitably plays a role, positive or negative, in a nation's development efforts. In this chapter, we discuss how the Asian countries in our analysis managed their development programmes. It covers the historical background for these nations, their strategies for maintaining governmental legitimacy, the policies for promoting agricultural and industrial development that they adopted, and the necessity for focusing upon a broader conception of 'human development'.

HISTORICAL BACKGROUND

As discussed in Chapters 2 and 3, the primary goal of development management in the Asian states since the early 1950s has been to maintain the legitimacy of governance regimes whose assumption of power involved considerable upheaval in all Asian societies. The promotion of development and industrialization came to be one of the central strategies for establishing and maintaining legitimacy in these countries.

China and India

In China, the People's Liberation Army (PLA) and Mao Zedong led a communist revolution that threw the nationalist government out of power and installed a communist party-led government in 1949. The revolution contributed to the loss of human lives and enormous disruption to social and economic order. In 1949, the income inequality was modest in the rural areas in China (Myers, 1970; Brandt, 1997; Brandt and Sands, 1992). Thus, the revolution was a product of poverty and peasant nationalism rather than an outcome of income inequality (Bramall, 2009; Buck, 1937; Tawney, 1932).

The breakup of India into three parts by the British Raj in 1947, the loss of human lives due to Hindu-Muslim religion-based riots in 1946, the mass transfer of population (one of the largest in human history) between India and Pakistan in 1947, and the installation in 1951 of a democratically elected governance regime led by Jawaharlal Nehru in New Delhi also contributed to a great upheaval in Indian society. The partition of India, by sowing the seeds of a further breakup of India into many parts promoted by ethnicity and the lust of self-styled leaders of ethnic, religious and political groups for gaining political power, heralded the beginning of the end of India as a unified country.

Nehru's (1954) professed goal was to eliminate differences between people on the basis of differences in caste, religion and provincial culture so as to bring about a more unified society by adopting economic democracy to achieve national development goals. However, the means adopted to achieve his professed goal was the adoption of the centralized planning of the Soviet type to which economic democracy was anathema. Indian economic policies, particularly since the occurrence of the foreign exchange crisis in 1957, degenerated into an extravagant display of bureaucratic controls and restrictions which ultimately became the end product of economic planning and were not conducive to economic development (Bhagwati and Desai, 1971; Chakraborty, 1987; Chai and Roy, 2006).

The mistaken belief of Nehru and his ministers that the departure of the British Raj from India would be replaced by the control of the Indian economy by the Western powers led them to adopt a policy of total autarky rather than a policy of the adoption of free market, outward-oriented economic principles. Although an important objective of the adoption of a policy of autarky might have been the preservation of national unity, the low level of economic growth, almost total absence of freedom of private enterprise and capital to apply the free market principle in investment and production decisions, systematic decapitation of the formal institutions of governance which began during Indira Gandhi's regime and the fragmentation of provinces which began under Nehru's rule made it impossible for this goal of national unity to be realized.

Since in the early years of India's independence, Nehru's government did not face any external threat to the country's independence, which would have forced it to adopt policies to improve the economic welfare of the masses and to enhance the strength of the military, its dedication to the goal of achieving genuine economic democracy in the country was weak.

The absence of external threat to the country's independence, combined with the tragic effect of the partition of the country, the incorporation into India of princely states and the presence of centrifugal forces of diverse language, culture and ethnic groups (Mellor, 1976) prevented the rise of the spirit of nationalism and the formation of a spontaneous social opinion supporting the legitimacy of the post-independence governance regime. In fact, only two provinces – Punjab and Bengal – had to bear the tragic effects of partition, not the rest of India. All kinds of non-violent movements against the British rule promoted by Gandhi were sporadic and not continuous. Thus the theory that agitation is produced by agitators and not agitators by agitation seems to be quite valid in pre-independence India as the Congress party which was formed with the primary objective of gaining India's independence from the British rule was led by a handful of elites who had the ultimate objective of capturing state power (North, 1987, 1990).

One may also argue that such a capture of the state would have enabled those elites to organize politics to satisfy their interests rather than those of the masses (Olson, 1982). Paying attention to collective interests by the leaders of the state was more difficult in India than in China because the heterogeneous society embodying social and economic inequalities and conflicts posed a serious obstacle to any long-term investment for economic development (Bardhan, 2010). On the other hand, in China the communist revolution had received strong support from peasants and the middle-class population due to the economic collapse that occurred under the Nationalists. After the communist takeover, however, Maoist policies such as the Great Leap Forward and Cultural Revolution resulted in millions of deaths (MacFarquhar et al., 1989). Hence popular support of Mao's government did exist in China, although it later dropped due to his radical policies.

East Asia

Japan remained a feudal society that cut itself off from the external world for most of the eighteenth and nineteenth centuries. Growing pressures from Western imperialism, however, sparked the Meiji Restoration of 1868, in which a regime of military technocrats restored sole power to the Japanese Emperor. The Meiji regime ended feudalism and quickly implemented a programme of industrial development and increasing military power, which proved to be spectacularly successful. In particular, Japan radically restructured its economic, social and political systems based on appropriating experience and ideas from the world's industrial leaders and applying them to the Japanese context. By the early twentieth century, Japan was a regional military power, had industrialized and created a prosperous society, and was evolving toward a democratic polity. Economic problems after World War I, however, resulted in growing popular discontent that allowed the development of a militaristic and highly nationalistic dictatorship, culminating in World War II which ended in total defeat and occupation by the victorious Allied Powers. Following the end of the Occupation in 1952, Japan became a democracy whose government was dominated by the economic technocracy that had been established before the war. Politically, the Liberal Democratic Party (LDP) has dominated Japan for almost all the post-war era; and the state technocracy led a very rapid reindustrialization drive that lasted four decades (the 1950s through to the 1980s) before falling into economic stagnation in about 1990 (Alexander, 2003; Johnson, 1982; Pye, 1985; Reischauer, 1988).

Unlike Japan, which had become an industrial power by the early twentieth century, Taiwan remained poor and agricultural at the dawning of the post-war era. After 50 years of colonial administration by Japan, Taiwan reverted to China at the end of World War II. When Chiang Kai-shek and his Nationalist or Kuomintang (KMT) Party lost the Civil War in China, they evacuated to Taiwan in 1949. Despite a democratic constitution, the KMT instituted fairly harsh authoritarian rule in Taiwan, generating significant antagonisms between the Mainlanders who had come from China with Chiang (15 per cent of the population) and the large majority of long-time residents or Islanders (who also were overwhelmingly Han Chinese). While the economic development strategy that evolved was much different from Japan's and Korea's, Taiwan also created a strong economic technocracy that led the country through a series of economic transformations (Clark and Tan, 2011; Copper, 2009; Gold, 1986).

South Korea was in an even more dire situation than Taiwan during the early post-war period. Like Taiwan, it was a colonial possession of Japan's before World War II and was fairly poor and agricultural at the end of its colonial era. Furthermore, the end of World War II brought even greater political problems to Korea than Taiwan had as the United States and the Soviet Union divided the country into a communist North and American-supported South. Cold War tensions grew, culminating in the Korean War of 1950–53 that devastated much of the South. Politically, the repressive Syngman Rhee served as President from 1948 until 1960 when he was forced to resign because of student demonstrations. The next year General Park Chung Hee took power in a bloodless coup and soon implemented an aggressive programme of state-led industrialization (Amsden, 1989).

Malaysia was created in 1963 through a merger of newly independent (1957) Malaya, Singapore and the British-ruled provinces of Sarawak and Sabah on Borneo. However, Singapore left the federation in 1965. At independence Singapore was in a very difficult situation, having lost its natural hinterland and having little industry and a largely uneducated labour force. To make things worse, the British announced their impending abandonment of their military bases, which were very important employers of labour. The country then embarked on a strategy of outward-oriented development, based on a combination of foreign direct investments in manufacturing and so-called government-linked companies (GLCs), many of which utilized infrastructure and installations left behind by the British military, such as shipyards and harbour facilities. The strategy proved to be a success and Singapore is today one of the wealthiest countries in the world.

In Malaysia the situation was less acute even if the country's industrial sector was small and uncompetitive, and the rapidly increasing population posed a challenge as to providing employment to the labour force. The early development of the Malaysian economy was mainly based on market forces, however, but with protection of selected industries, with some distortions of the manufacturing sector as an inevitable consequence (Ariff, 1991:20). Increasing interracial tensions towards the late 1960s led to a more interventionist approach on the part of the state. The core problem was that the majority of the population, the Malays, had less economic clout than the minority races (mainly Chinese and Indian). With proactive policies the government wanted to rectify the situation, intervening in the labour market and education system and establishing a state-owned manufacturing industry where indigenous people were favoured in various ways (Rasiah, 1997).

MAINTAINING THE LEGITIMACY OF GOVERNMENT

China and India

Maintaining the legitimacy of the government involves securing from the domestic society and global society the recognition of its customary right to govern the country on a continuous basis. With the help of the military force and the network of paraformal agents, the government by intimidation and elimination of opponents can secure the obedience of the domestic society to its rule for many years even in a country with a large population. But such obedience cannot be taken for granted for an indefinite period of time. The society's support of the legitimacy of the government can only be available if the country remains economically strong and its social and economic openness to the global society is rising.

The 'certificate of legitimacy' can, therefore, be said to be a product of an informal contractual agreement between the domestic civil society and the state's governance regime as well as between the global society and the governance regime of the state. This informal agreement seems to contain certain elements of Hobbes Contract (1651) and Locke's Treatise (1690), in that the state takes away from the society its political freedom in return for granting it economic freedom and security of livelihood. Alternatively, the informal agreement allows democratic state authorities to repress the economic freedom of the society significantly in return for granting it political freedom. Of these two conditions, the first condition was met by one-party autocratic China after the death of Mao, and the second condition was met by multi-party democratic India.

Because state power was captured by China's communist leaders by undemocratic means, all government policies and actions were driven by the paramount need to maintain a high level of economic growth consistently over a long period of time to enable the state to make provision for health, education, communications, housing, employment and other social services for the vast majority of the population. Rising economic power has increased the country's political and military power, and earned global acceptance of China's emergence as an economic and political superpower (Roy, 2010; Bramall, 2009; Meier and Rauch, 2005; Cypher and Dietz, 2009; Roy, 1991; Bardhan, 1984).

Deng Xiaoping, who gained power in the late 1970s, pioneered the model of basing the government's legitimacy upon a strong economic performance. Deng and the Chinese leadership feared political change and reform, especially after the collapse of the Soviet Union and the Eastern European states in the late 1980s and early 1990s. In contrast to continued authoritarian rule, they enacted increasingly radical economic reforms that proved phenomenally successful in stimulating rapid growth and a rising standard of living. Thus, there was an informal 'contract' that the regime would provide sustained economic growth in return for the society's informal permission for Deng's government to rule the country (EIU, 2009). In recent years, government leaders have felt the need to respond and react to public opinion on social and economic issues. This has been making the government accountable even in a mild way to domestic and global society. One could therefore argue that the important transformation of the Beijing model from the perspective of boosting prosperity has involved loosening of a little control over the society (Junning, 2011). This mild accountability of the government to public opinion does not mean that China is becoming more tolerant to mild opposition to the state's political agenda. On the contrary, the phenomenal rise in its economic and military might may have forced the global society to endorse China's suppression of human freedom.

In India, on the other hand, the task of forming governments by elite groups through winning democratically held elections, even if they involved cash payments to voters, vote rigging and the intimidation of voters, was enough to satisfy the requirement for the establishment and maintenance of the legitimacy of the state. Hence, the urge to achieve and maintain a high rate of economic growth to achieve legitimacy was clearly absent, as evidenced in the Second Five Year Plan document (GOI, 1957).

P.C. Mahalanobis (1969) modified the Feldman model for Indian use, which came to be known as the Feldman-Mahalanobis two-sector growth model and which was implemented in 1956–57 (Bhagwati and Desai, 1971; Roy et al., 1992; Chai and Roy, 2006) with a strong emphasis on the growth of capital goods industries and other types of heavy industries. The differences between the Indian and Chinese development strategies were that (i) Indian planners left agriculture- and labour-intensive rural industries in utter neglect and did not adopt the Chinese and Russian system of the collectivization of agriculture and (ii) China has continued its economic liberalization measures, albeit partially, for the three decades since 1980, whereas India's economic liberalization began and also virtually ended in 1991.

In the Second Five Year Plan document, there was no mention of a particular rate of economic growth that the government wanted to achieve among the three principal objectives listed. A motion was made for a sizeable increase in national income. This could refer to any percentage of growth rate. Also, the objectives of industrialization with particular emphasis on heavy industries and a large expansion of employment opportunities were contradictory. Then finally, the increase in national income of whatever size was to be accompanied by a simultaneous reduction in the concentration of economic wealth and inequalities in income. However, the need for improving the growth of the agricultural sector to generate savings from the sector and to absorb an increasing proportion of the rural labour force was not clearly expressed in the objectives. Hence, none of the important traditional theories of economic development such as Lewis's labour surplus model (1954) or Rosenstein-Rodan's (1951, 1943) Big Push or the Korean-Taiwanese model can be fitted into India's development paradigm. Hirschman's (1978) unbalanced development strategy had some relevance to India's development strategy. On the other hand, some essential elements of all these models, including those of the Harris-Todaro model (1970), seem to have played a part in China's development paradigm.

Although both China and India adopted Soviet Russia's style of development based on Feldman's development model to suit their respective development needs, the Feldman model which was appropriate for Russia in the 1920s could not suit China in the 1950s. Hence, in the early 1950s, the central elements of the model such as comprehensive central planning, collectivized agriculture, price supports to extract agricultural surplus to finance the growth of heavy industries, and autarky in international trade, as well as the emerging tension and conflicts among rural peasantry due primarily to the collectivization of agriculture, created problems for the government which forced Mao to modify his development strategy to place greater emphasis on agriculture and small rural industries (Chai and Roy, 2006).

East Asia

The legitimacy strategies of the East Asian nations differed somewhat both among themselves and from China and India. Japan entered the post-war era with a functioning democracy and a fairly advanced (though grievously war-damaged) economy and quickly commenced a spurt of rapid industrialization that challenged the United States for world economic leadership in the 1980s. Thus, it had both political and economic legitimacy. Taiwan and South Korea followed the Chinese pattern of authoritarian regimes that sought to maintain their legitimacy through strong economic performance. Unlike China, though, their populations had become increasingly dissatisfied with authoritarianism by the 1980s, leading to rapid democratic transitions in the early 1990s. Finally, varying combinations of political gridlock and growing economic stress are producing growing unhappiness about all three governments in the early twenty-first century.

Japan started the post-war era with both advantages and disadvantages. On the one hand, it was a disgraced loser in World War II, whose economy and cities were devastated at the end of the war and who had a US Occupation imposed upon it. On the other, it had been an industrial power before the war; its economic technocracy was largely spared; and under American pressure, it established a full democracy when the Occupation ended. Its democracy soon became well established and stable, as voters have kept the Liberal Democratic Party in power throughout almost the entire post-war era. The government also earned legitimacy through its economic success. Specific industries were targeted; and the large conglomerates (keiretsu) of the pre-war period re-emerged as globally competitive innovators in one industry after another from textiles to automobiles to high tech industries (Johnson, 1982; Okimoto, 1989; Reischauer, 1988). In 1989, however, property and stock market bubbles burst; and the country has never really recovered its economic dynamism since (Alexander, 2003), leading to growing popular discontent and much more competitive politics (Rosenbluth, 2011).

Chiang Kai-shek's Kuomintang regime, which took over Taiwan following World War II and then moved to Taiwan when it lost the Chinese Civil War in 1949, imposed repressive authoritarian rule despite a seemingly democratic constitution. In particular, as noted above, the national government was dominated by Mainlanders who came with Chiang from China and in many ways treated the large majority of Islanders as second-class citizens. The KMT tried to build legitimacy in two ways, though, both of which were at least partially successful. First, like China, it supported an aggressive industrialization drive which brought growing prosperity to the country within a couple of decades. Second, unlike China, it did not try to destroy all the pre-existing political groups but integrated local Islander factions into the regime by using local elections to play them off against each other. This approach worked for several decades, but growing popular pressure for political reform led to a fairly smooth democratic transition in the late 1980s and early 1990s, culminating in the former opposition Democratic Progressive Party (DPP) winning the presidency in the 2000 elections. For the last decade, the even balance between the DPP and KMT has led to polarization and gridlock, which has produced some frustration in the citizenry (Clark and Tan, 2011).

Korea probably faced even more legitimacy problems than Taiwan. The partition of the country after World War II and the bloody Korean War (1950–53) not only reflected the division between North and South but also created severe political cleavages within South Korea as well that were generally repressed by authoritarian governments. The military coup of Park Chung Hee in 1961 continued the authoritarian tradition, but also created a regime committed to rapid growth and economic nationalism. Like Taiwan, Korea then experienced very successful industrialization and growing prosperity, but discontent by students and labour remained high (Amsden, 1989). Finally, in the 1990s democratic elections for President were institutionalized; and two opposition leaders from the authoritarian era won successive presidential elections (Hahm and Plein, 1997). More recently, as in Japan and Taiwan, conservative and liberal governments have alternated power with neither side seeming to win much popular affection (Moon, 2010).

Both in Singapore and Malaysia the legitimacy of the government was to a great extent based on a strong economic performance, like in other East Asian countries. In Singapore, the People's Action Party (PAP) has led a technocratic and 'meritocratic' government ever since independence, with great economic success and political stability as a result. In Malaysia the situation is similar in the sense that more or less the same political parties have been in charge for the whole period of independence. But it is also more complicated because the political parties are mostly ethnically based, which means that ethnic tensions are reflected directly in politics. Since the biggest group, the Malays, dominates the federal government, it means that the other groups have to struggle to make their voice heard. The aim of the so-called New Economic Policy (NEP), introduced in 1970, was to relieve ethnic tensions through a programme aiming at redistribution of wealth (for details, see Rasiah, 1997). In practice this meant favouring the Malay part of the population through granting members of this group privileges not available to members of other races. The main features of the NEP became a permanent feature in Malaysian economic policy, even though the programme itself expired in 1990. The legitimacy problem caused by this type of policy is serious, especially as economic efficiency has clearly suffered as a result, even if resentment has mostly remained under the surface. The discontent has in recent years led to the emergence of new opposition movements that have challenged the ruling coalition (Blomqvist, 2011).

MANAGEMENT OF AGRICULTURE

China and India

The growth in China's agricultural sector, which began to accelerate due to the reform of the sector in the late 1970s, was needed (i) to improve the living conditions of the rural population which accounted for about 60 per cent of the total population and (ii) to pacify the peasant community which was the principal support base of the communist revolution. Higher-than-market prices were paid by the government to growers for their agricultural produce to increase the domestic production of and demand for agricultural produce. In addition, there was a relaxation of government regulations forcing farmers only to produce grain, leading to a diversification of the production of agricultural goods such as sugar, vegetables and fruits in the non-grain growing regions.

Although land reforms and other types of asset redistribution attract less popular and state support today because of (i) the political difficulty in implementing programmes of land redistribution (Perkins et al., 2006), (ii) the lack of finance capital of new owners of land even to buy agricultural inputs as was experienced in Bengal in India during the late 1960s and early 1990s, and (iii) the brutal means used to carry out reforms, such measures did produce spectacular results in East Asia and China. While before the first reform of the communists, about 40 per cent of cultivable land was used by tenant farmers who had to pay 50 per cent of their produce to landlords who contributed nothing to improve the quality of land, in the immediate aftermath of the reform many of these landlords were executed; and the ownership of land was forcibly transferred to tenant farmers from landlords.

The conversion of tenant farmers to landholders by the government provided them with the security of land tenure and incentive to invest in land in all East Asian countries. This, however, did not happen in India. One of the reasons may be that in East Asian culture the average propensity to save in rural households in China is higher than that in India. In India, the number of landlords and the tenant farming system that still operate are small and confined to Bihar, Uttar Pradesh and Madhya Pradesh. The agricultural sector in the rest of India consists of small peasant farms with a few acres of land and also of large farms in Punjab and Haryana. It is only since the last decade of the past century that the prices of all agricultural commodities began to rise and the savings of farming households also began to rise. Furthermore, the administrative mechanism through which many agricultural products are brought to the retail market is managed by a corrupt middle layer of traders who offers very low prices to retailers but makes households pay higher prices for such produce at the retail market. The critical shortage created by wholesalers to increase prices significantly raises the inflation rate. Also, a few provincial governments, such as the government of West Bengal, a few years ago set an off-take price of potatoes per quintal at a level considerably higher than its prevailing market price, thereby incentivizing the production of potatoes. However, since the bankrupt government failed to fulfil its commitment, the market was flooded with potatoes and the market price dropped to near zero per kilogram, forcing many farmers to throw away large quantity of potatoes on the street.[1] On the other hand, in China, the government guarantee of a high price of agricultural produce acted as a powerful incentive to Chinese growers to increase output (Chai and Roy, 2006).

In India, due to the almost total absence in rural towns of small-scale storage facilities at a low cost to farmers, almost 33 per cent of all vegetables and fruits get rotten before they reach the market and only 2 per cent of farm output is directed to refining and processing (Ghosh, 2004; Luce, 2007). The absence of an adequate organized marketing network for exports of such products as fruits, vegetables and flowers also has hampered the growth of the agricultural sector in India.

In China, although the primary sector accounted for 11.3 per cent of GDP in late 2010, it provided 41 per cent of total national employment and the livelihood of around 314 million people from farming, forestry, animal husbandry and fisheries. But the actual share of the primary sector in total employment was only 32 per cent in 2004 because many villagers although officially residents in villages moved to cities (Bardhan, 2010). The reintroduction since 1978 of individual economic incentives in the countryside, allowing farmers certain freedom to choose the type of crop they liked to plant, led to a fivefold increase in real net per capita rural income up through 2000 and to a further increase in real net per capita income throughout the first decade of the 2000s (EIU, 2009).

In India also, the agricultural sector provides employment to 60 per cent of the country's workforce but contributes less than 20 per cent to the country's GDP. In the early part of the post-reform period (1992–97) the sector recorded an average annual growth rate of 4.7 per cent which pushed India's real GDP growth to more than 9 per cent, but the agricultural sector's growth in the 2000s averaged around only 2 per cent, which pulled the average real GDP growth of India down below 9 per cent (EIU, 2008b).

Since around only 40 per cent of cultivable land is irrigated, the scope and the incentive for migration to urban centres are still limited. The overwhelming majority of the country's population is tied to the land. Due to the inability of the state, resulting from bureaucratic regulations and rigid labour laws in both rural and urban sectors (GOI, 2010), to facilitate the expansion of employment opportunities in the urban formal sector, temporary migrants to the cities have been forced to survive on informal sector employment as vendors, cooks, rickshaw pullers, day labourers and so on. In China, the enormous expansion of formal sector employment in urban centres absorbed a large proportion of surplus rural labour (Chai and Roy, 2006).

Although productivity measured in agricultural value-added per worker at 2000 US dollar value was $US269 for China and $US359 for India during 1990–92, those amounts during 2005–07 for both countries were virtually equal at $US459 and $US460. The total factor productivity (TFP) growth in agriculture in China did not differ greatly from that in India during the 1970s and 1980s (Fan and Zhang, 2002; Mukherjee and Kuroda, 2003; Chai and Roy, 2006). But Bardhan (2010) estimated that the TFP growth in agriculture in

China and India from 1978 to 2004 to be 1.8 per cent and 0.8 per cent respectively. The marginal contribution of TFP to growth in agricultural output in India can be accounted for by the failure of the federal government and provincial governments to facilitate the full application of the Green Revolution technology in the rain-fed agricultural regions in India. The Indian government was also unable to improve rural production infrastructure and failed to develop appropriate technology for increasing output per acre and for use by the large number of female labourers traditionally used in rain-fed agriculture during the rice planting and harvesting seasons. In China, local governments took care of the management of agriculture with finance and other resources raised from the locality. In India, the agricultural sector is under the jurisdiction of provincial governments, some of which may have deliberately not taken action to lift the state of agriculture above subsistence level and to reduce illiteracy and poverty among the population because it is easier for the government to retain power by almost forcibly securing the votes of poverty-stricken rural masses in the next provincial election.[2] Overall, since agriculture has provided the principal vote bank for provincial governments, the diverse political interests of these governments have prevented them from being active participants in the composite and inclusive agricultural growth management strategy of the federal government.

Even with the country's population currently in excess of 1.2 billion, India's food production index, cereal yield in kilograms per hectare and the share of irrigated land in total arable land are considerably lower than those of China, which with a population in excess of 1.3 billion managed its agriculture so well that its food output per capita rose by 96 per cent between 1979 and 2005 (Cypher and Dietz, 2009).

In China, although land is still formally owned by village organizations, in 1998 the central government formalized an agreement for granting to farmers land tenure up to 30 years. In 2001, under the property law, farmers' land tenure rights were transformed into more formal property rights. In spite of this, local officials from time to time have been known to forcibly confiscate land from farmers by paying extremely inadequate compensation in violation of farmers' land rights, primarily for use of such land for commercial purposes (Bardhan, 2010).

Significant productivity increases in agriculture in the 1980s were achieved primarily due to (i) the change in the mode of cultivation and land user rights from collective farming to the household responsibility system, (ii) payment by the government of high procurement prices for agricultural output, and (iii) the transfer of some land from cereal production to the production of fruits, vegetables and sugar (CIA, 2002). But since the late 1990s China has been liberalizing its agricultural market and agricultural trade by abolishing the compulsory procurement of agricultural products as well as domestic and border taxes, significantly lowering import tariffs on agricultural goods, and instead subsidizing grain producers.

Despite the government's policy of maintaining national food security, China's agricultural sector will become increasingly export-oriented. The significant rise in the production of vegetables has been promoted by the rise in not only domestic demand but also foreign demand for packaged frozen vegetables. For example, Australia's large supermarket chains, such as Woolworths and Coles, are importing from China packages of such frozen vegetables as peas, beans, snow peas, baby carrots, broccoli, cauliflower and so on.

India's primary concern for maintaining national self-sufficiency in food staples has forced the government to maintain the system of procurement by the government of staple dietary items such as rice and wheat from growers. Apart from rice and wheat, onions and potatoes can be considered as semi-staple food items. There are restrictions on the export of these items. In India's subsistence agricultural sector, most emphasis is placed on the production of paddy wheat, onions and some pulses (legumes) such as lentils, mung beans, chick peas, peas and tur. By and large, Indians in the rice belt (consisting of Assam and the six hill provinces of Bengal, Orissa, Andhra Pradesh, Tamil Nadu, Karnataka and Kerala) eat mostly rice and a small quantity of pulses and vegetables per head, whereas in the wheat producing regions in Central, Western and Northern India, chapatti (made from wheat flour dough) is eaten with a small quantity of pulses and vegetables since in both rice and wheat the carbohydrate content is very high. Hence, the emphasis has always been on cereal production even when the land is fertile enough to be used for multiple cropping.

Between 1951 and 2008, while the per capita consumption of cereal in India increased by 12.10 per cent, the per capita consumption of pulse declined by 31.13 per cent (GOI, 2010). The decline in per capita pulse consumption and the lack of an adequate consumption of vegetables affect people's health. In China, cereal consumption is combined with the consumption of an adequate quantity of vegetables. This may have helped the Chinese labour force to maintain better health than India's poor labourers.

A lack of appropriate storage facilities, marketing networks and investment in the production and packaging of vegetables has prevented the growth of an export-oriented packaged vegetable and fruit industry in India. Also, since the agricultural sector is under the jurisdiction of provincial governments, the ability of the federal government to promote the growth of fruits and vegetables and the packaged agricultural products industry has been greatly curtailed.

Economists (Bardhan, 2010; Berry and Cline, 1979; Rosenzweig and Binswanger, 1993) have argued that there is evidence to suggest that the redistribution of land increases productivity in agriculture. Others (Gaylor and Zeira, 1993; Banerjee and Newman, 1993) have commented that a more equitable distribution of land can promote efficiency. But land reform involving a more equitable distribution of land requires compensation to be paid to large landholders for the loss of their land. Since landless and land-poor families are unable to pay this compensation, then the state has to transfer a substantial amount of money to those who will be losing their land. Also, an efficient and honest bureaucracy is required to carry out a land reform programme. Land redistribution in Bengal by the forcible confiscation of land even from small landholder families by the communist government in the late 1970s and early 1980s without any payment of compensation had a deleterious effect on the morale of landholder families and on productivity in the agricultural sector.

China stood for greater equality in the distribution of land as evidenced in the Gini coefficient of distribution of land, which was 0.62 in 2002 for India and 0.49 in 2002 for China (Bardhan, 2010; Khar, 2004). This combined with the spread of education in rural China to reduce the level of rural poverty there significantly. At the same time, local governments and communes developed rural agricultural infrastructure such as roads, electricity supply and so on without relying on assistance from the government in Beijing. In the Indian rural sector, the education level of members of landless families remains very poor. This lack of education has prevented youths from landless families and the poor from migrating to towns for employment. In China, village enterprises were able to absorb the surplus labour from the rural sector. Since significant restrictions still exist on the ability of rural households to buy or sell land, the savings generated from the rural sector could fuel China's industrialization. In India, a part of the savings is used by landholder families to purchase additional plots of agricultural land or other assets in their localities. Furthermore, adequate banking facilities are still not available in the rural sector in India. Landless and land-poor families do not have the capacity to save much, so the contribution of rural savings to India's industrialization cannot be as high as in China.

These factors relate to the countrywide management of agricultural development in China and India, but in both countries there are regional variations in income inequality and poverty level. For example, in China the income inequality in rural sectors in the southern and western provinces such as Sichuan and Guangdong is considerably higher than in rural sectors of other provinces. Similarly, inequality in land holdings and in income and the pervasiveness of economic poverty is more pronounced in the rice producing regions of Eastern and South Eastern India than the wheat producing regions of Punjab and Haryana. We believe that for India more permanent and better reformed tenancy arrangements, one for land-poor households and another for landless households, is the best way to manage inequality in rural poverty and agricultural growth. The tenancy arrangement for landless labour or farmers

would require the landlord to pay for all expenses to be incurred for cultivation; and the landless farmer or household would provide free labour and
take the overall responsibility of effectively managing these plots of land. The
produce would be distributed in accordance with the respective contribution of
the landlord and tenants.[3]

Urban sprawl has been spreading in China at a considerably faster rate than
in India. As industrialization and urbanization penetrate the inland territories
of China, less arable land becomes available for growing food products to
feed the country's population. Meanwhile, with rising per capita income, the
community's demand for greater varieties and more expensive types of food
such as meat has been rising. Hence, to ensure food security for future generations, China has entered into joint venture agreements with companies in
Argentina and Brazil to grow soy beans for feeding China's livestock and food
products for its population (*The Australian*, 2011). These countries are also
important exporters to China of mineral products which are needed to maintain
China's export-oriented industrial production. During the 12 months from June
2010 to the end of May 2011, China's total investment in Latin America, which
currently is mostly concentrated in Argentina and Brazil, amounted to nearly
US$16 billion. The expansion of China's investment and trade in Africa, Latin
America, East Asia and South Asia, which has also enabled China to exercise
some form of political hegemony over these countries, has been made possible
by China's accumulation of a massive amount of foreign exchange resource of
over US$3 trillion.

Urban sprawl has been spreading at a snail's pace in India primarily because
India's industrial sector has been expanding at a very slow rate. It is the expansion of the industrial sector which promotes the expansion of urbanization.
For example, at the time of India's independence from British Rule in 1947,
88 per cent of the country's total population lived in rural areas and only 12
per cent of the country's population lived in urban areas. In 2012, about 70
per cent of the total population lives in rural areas. Therefore in 66 years, the
total urban population has increased by only 18 percentage points. This is an
indication of the slower rate of expansion of urbanization in India. The forcible
acquisition of fertile agricultural land at a price well below the market price
per acre of land and against the wishes of the landholders by the Marxist-led
coalition government acted as a catalyst for the overthrow of this government
from power after 34 years of its rule in Bengal at the provincial election held
in May 2011. Consequently, the federal government is coming round to accept
the view that arable land can be used for industrial development if entrepreneurs can successfully negotiate directly with landholders for the sale of the
land. This means that industrial expansion into rural areas can only proceed at
a considerably slower rate than in China. It also implies that arable land will
be available for securing an adequate supply of food for future generations

in India. Furthermore, India with a little over only US$300 billion of foreign exchange reserves does not have the same capability to undertake a sizeable amount of investment in Latin America to ensure the supply of food items for its domestic consumption as China is doing. The extremely low value of India's trade with Brazil and other Latin American countries has also meant that India's political influence in those countries is minimal.

East Asia

Because of Japan's advanced industrial status, agriculture has not played a major role in the economy during the post-war era. However, due to political considerations, agricultural policy has had some important effects. Rural areas traditionally were an important part of the coalition that kept the Liberal Democratic Party in power, in part because they were overrepresented in the national parliament (the Diet). Thus, the dominant party was very solicitous of the economic interests of farmers and rural areas. Substantial subsidies were provided for agriculture; social policy provided aid to rural areas; and substantial protection was afforded to many agricultural products, which by the 1980s was generating substantial trade frictions with several of Japan's trade partners, in particular the United States. The result was a productive agricultural sector that was too expensive to be internationally competitive. More broadly, it shows the strengths and weaknesses of Japan's post-war development strategy. The government targeted specific industries and helped them become the best and most competitive in the world. However, in other sectors such as agriculture and retail trade, low levels of productivity were tolerated to gain the political support of the beneficiaries (Calder, 1988). For several decades this system worked quite well, but it unfortunately created a major barrier that prevented Japan from responding effectively to the economic crisis of the 1990s.

When Chiang Kai-shek and his Kuomintang (KMT) regime evacuated to Taiwan after losing the Chinese Civil War in 1949, they faced a poor and war-ravaged economy that was primarily agricultural in nature. To promote economic development and reconstruction, the KMT administration developed a radical land reform programme to spur agricultural growth and reduce rural poverty and inequality. Implicitly, in addition, the Mainlander regime was also striking at the economic base of the Islander rural gentry who formed a potential rival for power on the island.

The land reform had three components: a rent reduction of 37.5 per cent in 1949, a series of sales of public farmlands targeted at their current cultivators between 1948 and 1958, and the capstone 1953 Land-to-the-Tiller Act which forced landlords to sell their agricultural land over about three hectares to the government, who then resold it back to the tenants. The radical change in land tenure was complemented and supported by an aggressive programme of agricultural extension directed by the Sino-American Joint Commission on Rural Reconstruction (JCRR). The JCRR created an extensive set of Farmers Associations that promoted new technologies, created marketing and credit cooperatives, and participated in agricultural planning. The government also made a substantial financial commitment to agricultural modernization as during the 1950s agricultural investment accounted for about a fifth of total national investment and averaged a real (i.e. inflation-adjusted) growth rate of 14 per cent a year (Ho, 1978).

Overall, therefore, land reform created a nation of smallholders with greater individual incentive to innovate and produce; and government programmes generated more investment, local involvement and technological innovation. It is impossible to separate the effects of these two factors on agriculture since they were interrelated and complementary. Together, though, they affected rural life and Taiwan's economy considerably. Land reform produced major income gains for the former tenants which equalled 44 per cent of their total income in 1959 (Ho, 1978); agricultural production grew by 4.6 per cent annually during the 1950s; and agriculture supplied the bulk of Taiwan's exports for most of the 1950s (Ho, 1978; Thorbecke, 1979). Subsequently, however, Taiwan's rapid industrialization marginalized agriculture (e.g. by 1987 it only constituted 17 per cent of employment and 5 per cent of GDP); and by the 1980s, the agricultural and rural economies had clearly become a lagging sector (Clark, 1989).

More broadly and indirectly, agriculture generated a considerable surplus that was used to finance industrialization. The principle outflow from agriculture was caused by the 'hidden rice tax' that resulted from the government's acquiring a large share of the rice crop at depressed prices while selling fertilizer to the farmers at inflated ones. Ironically, it was fairly similar to the policies pursued by colonial Japan (1895–1945), with the one fundamental difference being that Japan siphoned these resources off to its colonial centre, while they became a major source of financing Taiwan's early industrialization (Kuo, 1983; Lee, 1971).

Korea's agricultural policies paralleled Taiwan's in that land reform and government support for agriculture were critical components. Also, rapid industrialization resulted in the growing marginalization of agriculture in the total economy as its share of GNP fell steadily from 46 per cent in 1956 to 28 per cent in 1970 to 16 per cent in 1980 (Kim, 1992:75). The major motivation was somewhat different, though. In the South, the US occupation forces provided the major push for land reform to reduce the attractiveness of communism to the poor peasantry. It did create smallholder agriculture; and the effects were fairly pronounced even if they were not as extensive as in Taiwan's land reform:

Although land-to-the-tiller in Korea never enriched the peasantry or overflowed the state tax coffers, its long-run effects were major. Reform redirected idle capital away from land speculation to manufacturing and uprooted a class that had not proved itself progressive. It relieved the bottleneck in food supply, which in turn dampened inflationary pressures. It created a far more equitable income distribution. Finally, it cleared the field for strong centralized state power.

(Amsden, 1989:37)

While agriculture never played a significant role in land-strapped Singapore, the primary sector has remained important in Malaysia, where its share of GDP was bigger than that of industry well into the 1980s. It is still bigger than usual in a country at this level of development, mainly because of the increasing importance of palm oil (Blomqvist, 2011). The country's agricultural sector is strongly dualistic and dominated by large-scale plantation-based cultivation of palm oil, rubber and cocoa (Faridah, 2001). Especially in the palm oil and rubber sectors there is also an important downstream industrial sector, refining the produce for exports. The production of foodstuff, e.g. rice, fruits and vegetables, is left to the much less productive smallholder sector, which holds only some 30 per cent of the cultivable land. In fact, despite its very fertile soil, Malaysia is dependent on imports of basic foodstuffs, especially rice. Much of the poverty problem of the Malays, mentioned earlier, originates in the fact that they comprise the overwhelming part of the rural population. Fierce competition from imported foodstuff and high input costs make it difficult for farmers to make ends meet, which is reflected in an aging workforce in the smallholder sector.

MANAGING INDUSTRIAL DEVELOPMENT

China and India

The primary objective of Beijing's management of industrial development in China after the late 1970s has been to turn the country into a giant export-oriented industrial hub for the manufacture and exports of consumer and capital goods to the rest of the world. The earnings from exports of goods and services and a large inflow of FDI from Taiwan, Hong Kong and Macao pushed China's foreign exchange reserves to 3.5 trillion US dollars. Such large and continuously rising foreign exchange reserves have also been helping China to extend its economic and political hegemony to Asia, Africa, Central Europe and later America. Foreign companies have brought to China their marketing networks, technology and management knowledge which have been used by both domestic private companies and state-operated enterprises (SOEs) to promote China's economic development.

Foreign companies established production facilities in China in the expectation that the rate of return from their investment in China would be higher than the return they would have received from the same investment in their home countries (Salvatore, 2001). China for its part also provided these companies with a business-friendly environment by deregulating labour markets and factory hours and by creating adequate road and rail networks, port facilities and so on. China's industrial management policy involved a combination of state intervention and control on the one hand and economic liberalization on the other closely in line with the policy that Japan and the East Asian countries followed (Clark and Roy, 1997).

Town and village enterprises
The operation of modern small and medium-sized town and village enterprises (TVEs) since 1978 in the coastal regions close to cities that produced agricultural inputs for rural peasants and wide-ranging consumer goods for both rural and urban centres, as well as producing for export markets, was allowed to continue independently of the central government's control. While this case of TVEs can be cited as an example of China's economic liberalism, the primary reasons for non-interference by the central government in the operation of TVEs were that (i) these enterprises being small and medium-sized could not obtain subsidized credit from state-owned banks to cover the losses they incurred routinely, (ii) the failure of these loss-making enterprises was quite acceptable politically and (iii) by leaving TVEs to local authorities, the central government could utilize the TVEs' adoption of modern technology and organization of factories to promote the industrial development effort in Southern China and in special economic zones or SEZs (Perkins et al., 2006).

However, since local governments had very little resources to cover their losses, these enterprises had to put in extra effort to ensure that they remained profitable to be able to survive. However since the late 1990s, the privatization of TVEs which were China's growth engine up to the mid-1990s and the rise in the share of the private sector in the economy led to the recognition by the state of the legitimacy of the private sector in the economy. The Chinese state allowed the township and village governments to retain the entire revenue collected from privatization and to continue the practice of levying on each local private firm a tax of 1.5 per cent of total sales revenues per year (Meier and Rauch, 2005). The revenue was used by local governments to improve local social conditions, thereby lessening their dependence on the central government for public transfers to undertake public works activities.

In India, hardly any such enterprises have been built in rural areas by local governments. Provincial governments own a large number of small and medium-sized public sector enterprises (PSEs). Pilot infrastructure projects under the Public-Private Partnership (PPP) have been taken up for the expansion and redevelopment of airports, energy posts, roads and other areas in urban development in the provinces. However, the total value of such contracts in 2009–10 stood at only 50 billion US dollars (GOI, 2010). Amongst the provinces, for example, West Bengal Province ruled by the Marxist Communist Party had the misfortune of securing contracts worth only about 0.45 billion US dollars. The primary reason for such a low interest by the private sector in a PPP arrangement in Bengal was that the operation of Bengal's industrial structure with the exception of information technology had been interfered with by the Marxist Communist Party affiliated trade union. Out of the total of 450 projects under the PPP scheme in India only 5 were in West Bengal compared with 97 in Karnataka and 63 in Andhra Pradesh. Therefore, the private sector's involvement in enterprises in local government areas has been marginal.

The manufacturing sector

It is estimated that since the mid-1990s local private entrepreneurs along with foreign investors in the form of wholly foreign-owned subsidiaries or of joint ventures with Chinese interests were the major propellers of the rapid growth of China's export-oriented manufacturing sector. The rate of growth of foreign invested enterprises (FIEs), which began in 1980 in the SEZ of Shenzhen, accelerated after 1997 to such an extent that in 2006 the FIEs accounted for about 32 per cent of gross industrial output, compared to just over 21 per cent from domestic private firms in China. In the 1980s and early 1990s, to attract foreign investment to Shenzhen and other SEZs in Guangdong and Fujian province and in Hainan Island, the Chinese government offered to foreign investors a lower rate of tax on business income, an abundant supply of least expensive labour, deregulated factory hours, security of industrial property, absence of trade unions, and a stable and autocratic government capable of minimizing delays in the implementation of the government's industrial reform policy caused by bureaucratic red tape. By concentrating the application of the economic liberalization policy only to FDI in SEZs, China was able to receive a very large amount of foreign direct investment. That foreign invested enterprises dominated China's industrial and trade sectors is supported by the fact that in 2007 the FIEs contributed nearly 60 per cent of China's total export income (*Business Times*, 2010). The size of the inflow of FDI in US dollars to China has been discussed in Chapter 4. China's eagerness to join the World Trade Organization (WTO) with a view to securing access to the global market for its manufactured goods played an important part in China's decision to reform its SOEs which had generally been inefficient, running at a loss over the years and had been overstaffed with employees who survived in their employment with state subsidies.

Despite being faced with strong opposition from SOE employees in the form of strikes and civil unrest, the government restructured and closed down many enterprises, resulting in the lay-off of millions of SOE employees. One estimate suggests that if the reform of SOEs was properly carried out, it would have led to the retrenchment of 35 million SOE employees. The full reform of SOEs could not be carried out, however. Many SOEs, which still survive and have been able to increase their production level significantly, have been corporatized in their operation. The practice of the Communist Party to appoint important members to top managerial positions has been a major obstacle preventing the proper reform of SOEs (Meier and Rauch, 2005). Many studies on the Chinese economy have also underplayed the role of the state whose influence in firms could be strong even when it is not officially the controlling shareholder in a company. However, those SOEs which in the late 1970s accounted for about 80 per cent of manufacturing output contributed just above 30 per cent to the total manufacturing output in 2007 (EIU, 2009). Hence, the role of SOEs in the Chinese economy is diminishing.

The next important aspect of industrial sector management was foreign trade reform in the 1980s which involved taking actions to break up the monopoly power of 12 foreign trading corporations by granting hundreds of licences to new foreign trade corporations by local governments. The objective of this exercise was to lower the cost to foreign consumers of China's exportable items. This action also enabled China to undertake a gradualist approach in the reduction of mean and peak import tariff rates. The mean tariff rate has come down quite substantially to below 10 per cent in 2008–09, as discussed in Chapter 4.

In the early days of China's industrialization, there was no insistence by the Chinese state on the transfer of technology by foreign companies to their Chinese joint venture partners. However, now that China is recognized as the world's factory for the manufacture of essential and non-essential consumer goods, the state's indirect pressure on foreign companies to transfer technology to local partners has been rising. It is posing a serious concern for European companies. In recent years, China has prevented foreign investment in certain sectors considered to be important to national security. Nevertheless, foreign direct investment played a profoundly important role in China's successful management of industrial development.

There is very little to comment on India's management of industrial development. In 2008, their respective shares at 24 and 16 per cent of GDP, India's total industrial sector and manufacturing industrial sector were considerably smaller than China's industrial and manufacturing industrial sectors with their respective shares at 49 and 34 per cent of GDP. Without fuelling inflationary pressure, the expansion of this still small manufacturing sector to account for 25 per cent of the country's GDP and to create enough job opportunities to absorb 10 million people entering the workforce every year can only be achieved if the sector can grow at 15 to 17 per cent a year (EIU, 2008b). However, such high growth rates are unlikely to be achieved because (i) this sector is not reformed to become export-oriented, (ii) it is not open to large amounts of foreign direct investment, (iii) the labour market is not deregulated and trade union interference in the operation of enterprises has never stopped, and (iv) measures have not been taken to revive viable small and medium-sized sick and closed-down industrial units.

The government of India's (GOI, 2010) estimate of the share of different industries in total FDI shows that apart from the automobile industry, which received 6 per cent of total FDI inflow, no other manufacturing industry in the private sector that has the capacity to create a large number of jobs did attract FDI. But the manufacturing industry in the public sector received a little more than 18 per cent of total investment much of which was financed from internal sources. The continued restriction on the entry of FDI in banking, insurance and the retail trade sector, including the involvement in India in comprehensive retail trade by Wal-Mart which can also be regarded as a giant manufacturing industry, has prevented the creation of millions of new jobs which in turn has prevented the realization of the government's objective of achieving 10 per cent economic growth.

Although by the government's own admission (GOI, 2010), India's antiquated trade unions and labour laws, such as the Industrial Disputes Act 1948 created primarily to protect trade unions and perceived workers' interests, are required to be changed, no government since 1951 has made any genuine attempt to reform trade unions and the labour laws enacted in the 1940s. Overstaffing created losses for 2007–08 and 2008–09 amounting to Rs102.6 billion and Rs144.2 billion, accounting for 1.4 per cent and 1.8 per cent of total invested capital as well as 0.9 per cent and 1.1 per cent of total turnover (GOI, 2010). The firms have not been privatized, though, due to the failure of the federal government to pass an 'exit law' for loss-making enterprises that are declared sick units. The total number of sick units in India in both the public and private sectors currently stands at 244,304, of which 113,846 units (46 per cent of the total) are located in Bengal alone.

Also in Bengal, 60,000 factories, mainly in the private sector, have been closed down (Ray, 2011) during the last four decades since the communist movement gained momentum there. Lack of education and training of workers in small and medium-sized enterprises kept labour productivity at a low level. The rise in labour wages and fixed and other variable costs combined with man days lost in factories due to frequent strikes and *bandhs* (shutdowns of all economic activities) pushed the average cost of production per unit of output to a level at which these enterprises were unable to break even at the market price of their manufactured items.[4] On the other hand, in the management of public sector enterprises (PSEs), the autonomy of managers was curtailed from above by the interventionist Indian Administrative Services (IAS) bureaucrats in the relevant ministries as well as from below by militant trade unions affiliated with political parties (Bardhan, 2010). The problems of managers of PSEs have been further compounded by the fact that many of these IAS officers with generalist degrees tend to interfere with the administration of an engineering enterprise such as a steel plant (Bhagwati and Desai, 1971). Such bureaucratic action, which causes delay in the completion of production schedules, increases the overall cost of the operation of the enterprises and the delivery of projects and is part of the administrative delays caused by bureaucrats in governments' hierarchical administrative structure of decision making. A recent study conducted by Singh (2010), with data from the Ministry of Statistics and Programme Implementation, found that of 894 infrastructure projects completed between April 1992 and March 2009, the percentage of projects with positive time overruns stood at 60.8 per cent in the power sector, 79.7 per cent in the petroleum sector, 95.1 per cent in shipping and ports, 98.4 per cent in railways and 100 per cent in health and family welfare. In most projects, time overruns have also inevitably been associated with cost overruns. The bureaucratic delays spanning several years in granting approval to FDI projects have acted to strengthen the negative image that persists among the global business community of an institutional environment in India not suited for attracting foreign investment. For example, it took five years for the government of India to approve an investment proposal of Korea's Posco for a steel plant worth $US12 billion (Joshi, 2011).

In contrast to the highly creative role played in the expansion and management of industries by bureaucrats in East Asia, the apparent disdain of Indian bureaucratic elites for the growth of business and industry can be partly due to the facts that the Indian bureaucrats by and large developed an almost innate empathy for socialist ideology since the Nehruvian era and that IAS personnel in the past usually came from uppe-caste families whereas the business community came from the mercantilist caste (Bardhan, 2010) and partly to the fact that bureaucrats are sometimes also forced to follow their political masters' dictates, which may not promote the development and management of industry and business in the country. Unfortunately, however, bureaucrats' actions also affect the growth of enterprises in the organized private sector, which accounted for 71.3 per cent of the total share of gross fixed capital formation in the country during 2008–09 (GOI, 2010).

However, some bureaucrats also appear to have taken up the role of policy formulators for corporate industrial enterprises and have tried to help enterprises achieve their developmental goals by using informal channels of communication (Pingle, 1999). Furthermore, these bureaucrats aided by their informal relationships with other bureaucrats also seem to have provided relief to some entrepreneurs from intervention by relevant state agencies in the operation and management of their enterprises. Inevitably one has to admit that India's private sector corporations are significantly less controlled by the state, are considerably more autonomous and are able to operate in a more uncertain political and business environment than their Chinese counterparts who are required to trade away to the state some of their operational autonomy in exchange for the guarantee of property rights, access to resources of the state, and a predictable political and business environment.

Apart from the private corporate enterprises, India's industrial economy also consists of hundreds of thousands of micro and small manufacturing firms spread throughout the country in the informal sector, which contributes 94 per cent of the total employment in the country and is characterized by mostly non-unionized casual labour, deregulated wage and factory hours, extremely low amounts of capital, low mark-up costs of production per unit of output, the presence of other elements of monopolistically competitive firms, and the absence of state control over the activities of the informal economy. It is estimated that production activities in the informal economy contribute 60 per cent to the net domestic product, 68 per cent to the country's income, 60 per cent to the country's savings, 31 per cent to agricultural exports and 41 per cent of total manufactured exports of the country (Harris-White, 2004). The operation of production units in the informal economy is regulated by social norms and customs, and receive virtually no financial help from the formal institutions of the state.

State intervention in the economy

Despite China's efforts to achieve its successful transition to a market economy from a command economy, some commentators (Callick, 2011) believe that China remains Soviet-inspired – an empire set apart from the world. The intervention of the state in the operation of the free market has been quite pervasive. The major areas in which the state has intervened are exchange rates, subsidies to producers, technology transfer, export and import trade, and the financial market. In the following paragraphs brief comments are made on the nature of intervention that has taken place in these areas.

A devaluation of China's currency in real terms took place during the 1980s and early 1990s. Restrictions on foreign currency were then gradually lifted. A developing country under GATT (General Agreement on Tariffs and Trade) and WTO rules can undertake a devaluation of its currency if it suffers from a large balance of payment deficit and if it is implementing an IMF directed economic stabilization policy. In recent years China has recorded consistently twin surpluses in its trade account and current account as well as a very large inflow of money to its capital account. In line with what economic theory states, China's currency would have appreciated if China had adopted a flexible exchange rate policy. Several commentators (Garson, 2011) have argued that the maintenance of a depreciated Chinese currency has provided China's export-oriented industrial goods with considerable advantage in countries importing Chinese made products. But the maintenance of a depreciated Chinese currency and other restrictions on imported goods to China have made it difficult for both developed and developing non-resource exporting countries to export their manufactured goods to China.

Since the euro was not depreciated in any perceptible way after its introduction as the single currency for the European Union and since the US dollar has been depreciating consistently from 2003, estimates show that between 1998 and 2009 the percentage of depreciation of the US dollar, the Indian rupee and the Chinese yuan against the euro stood at 31.33 per cent, 46.44 per cent and 8.96 per cent (IMF, 2010). The substantial depreciation of the US dollar and Indian rupees can be justified in the context of their respective current account deficits. For the US, this increased from 215.04 billion US dollars in 1998 to 803.55 billion US dollars in 2006 representing an increase of 273.7 per cent before declining to 706.07 billion US dollars in 2008. For India, it increased from 6.90 billion US dollars in 1998 to 9.30 billion US dollars in 2006, representing an increase of 34.8 per cent; and it further increased to 36.08 billion dollars in 2008, representing an increase in current account deficit between 1998 and 2008 of 422.8 per cent.

For China, in contrast, the current account surplus increased from 31.47 billion US dollars in 1998 to 253.30 billion US dollars in 2006 representing an increase in the current account surplus of 704.7 per cent; and it further increased to 426.10 billion US dollars in 2008 representing an increase in current account surplus between 1998 and 2008 of 1,253.9 per cent. China still has not adopted full capital account convertibility, in the absence of which a freely floating exchange rate system cannot be implemented. Hence the pressure is mounting on China to take action to allow the renminbi to appreciate as the first step in its financial reform (Murdoch, 2011). However, it should be noted here that since China is currently the second largest economy in the world and the economy continues to grow at a high rate, it has become difficult for even the WTO to make China agree to appreciate its currency against its wishes. India also has not yet adopted full convertibility in the capital account of the country's balance of payments. Nevertheless, the control of the Reserve of India over the Indian rupee's exchange rate is marginal as evidenced in its relatively free movement in the international currency market.

There have also been criticisms (Howe, 2011) of China's practice of supporting its producers of certain products to enter and capture new export markets such as Australia, particularly in green technology-based products such as solar energy, windmills, advanced batteries and energy-efficient vehicles by subsidizing the domestic average cost of production per unit of such a product in a way that the total cost per unit of the imported product in the new market is considerably lower than the average cost per unit of the domestically produced import-competing products. The systematic penetration of the Eastern European market by Chinese goods and investments supported by state subsidies has been a cause of major concern for Western European industries (Dempsey, 2011). However, the use of state subsidies to help a new industry to capture export markets for its products has been an important tool in the past in Japan's strategic trade policy and also has been a common practice in other countries in East Asia.

The government of India primarily provides support to domestic private sector industries in the form of the availability of credit, particularly to export-oriented industries and by fiscal measures in the form of tax relief. These schemes become more prominent during a recessionary phase of the business cycle. The use of subsidies to help domestic companies to sell their products on export markets at prices below the price of import-competing domestically produced goods in foreign markets has not been used in India in any perceptible way.

Tariff and nontariff barriers have been extensively used by both China and India to manage their foreign trade outcome. While mean tariff rates in China and India have declined to very low levels, nontariff barriers provide specific restrictions on individual items of imports such as an average real agricultural tariff rate of 34 per cent (Roy Chowdhury, 2009), which can under WTO rules be raised to 114 per cent if a sudden surge in a particular agricultural import is likely to undermine the livelihood of local farmers. This, of course, is a kind of countervailing measure to prevent the dumping of heavily subsidized grain and other food products on the Indian market by US producers. Import restrictions in some form prevent other countries such as Brazil and India from exporting manufactured goods to China (Prada, 2011).

China's restrictions on the export of rare earth materials, which are used as vital inputs for the manufacture of durable consumer goods, under the pretext of maintaining national security and preserving the environment, impose an important constraint on China's export trade. Since China manufactures and exports to the rest of the world just about everything that a human being requires in one's daily life from toothpastes to pillowcases, the restriction on the export of rare earth materials can raise the possibility of China's giant companies becoming monopsonists and monopolists.

While the Chinese state continues to accept the voluntary status as to transfer of technology from foreign companies to China's SOEs and also private joint venture partners, in most cases foreign companies do seem to have no other choice than to transfer the technology to local state-owned and private companies if they want to operate in China (Dempsey, 2011). Foreign companies are also required to obtain a certain proportion of total factor inputs used in the production process from domestic sources. The technology transfer refers to the transfer of knowledge from one company to another and, therefore, is to be treated as a private good. But it is not a pure private good, as it has a public good component. Accordingly, in a purely competitive market, if one firm acquires new technological knowledge due to the freedom of information prevailing in this market, all other firms will acquire this knowledge and consequently all of them will in the long run enjoy the benefit of a Marshallian real externality in the form of a continuously declining long run supply curve for the industry as a whole (Romer, 1994; Roy and Ali, 2011).

However, what has happened in China is that the state has made it possible for the benefit of a Marshallian real externality to be felt by all firms in the imperfectly competitive industry by transforming knowledge from a pure private good to a substantially public good. So the question is why foreign companies continue to shut down their domestic factories and shift production units to China. Apart from standard economic incentives provided by China to foreign companies, certain elements of a favourable herd mentality and bandwagon effect also seem to drive foreign capital and companies to China. Here again, the public good characteristics of knowledge make the knowledge gained by the first entrant to start production facilities in China spread to others in the herd. Consequently, foreign companies seem to come into China in droves.

In India too, the transfer of technology to local joint-venture firms is an important semi-voluntary condition for the entry of foreign companies to the Indian market. But the role of foreign capital in India's industrial and service sector has been significantly smaller than its role in China's industrial and service sector primarily because, as already discussed in Chapter 4, India's industries are mostly inward-oriented; and consequently the limited amount of FDI that enters into India's manufacturing industrial sector is utilized to produce goods to satisfy domestic consumption.

Some technology transfer has been taking place in the manufacture of pharmaceutical products, information technology and in the manufacture of highly sophisticated products such as military artefacts at public sector enterprises. In the export-oriented automobile industry, particularly in the manufacture of cars, motorbikes and scooters, technology has been transferred to the Suzuki-Maruti Company, Bajaj Auto and so on.

Access to resources

China's measures to secure access to resources to feed its giant industries have involved the acquisition of mines for extracting minerals, including metals such as copper, bauxite and so on, as well as the imposition of restrictions on the export of valuable domestic resources and importing resources even when the demand for inputs from China's factories has slackened with the aim of building up inventories when prices for resources in the global market still remain low. The principal economic reason behind this strategy is that in China's manufacturing industries the cost of production per unit of output would be considerably lower when prices of all kinds of resources used in the manufacturing industries begin to rise. The other reason for imposing restrictions on the exports of many rare earth materials, including zinc, to many new foreign companies is to entice these companies to locate their operations in China (Miller and Areddy, 2011).

China's objective is to secure a substantial proportion of its total resource requirement from its own mines in other countries in the world (Sainsbury, 2011c, 2011e). With this objective in view, the first Africa-China summit held in October 2006 in Beijing has been able to extract significant access to mines in Africa from African heads of states. China's aid and loans to African governments contain features of 100 per cent source-tied aid (*The Statesman Weekly*, 2011). The state's management of access to resources has also been directed to ensure that China's state-owned companies and private companies receive from foreign governments the same treatment for undertaking investment in foreign mines and in such other areas as finance, agriculture, telecommunication, civil aviation and so on (Puddy, 2011). In pursuance of the same policy of conserving domestic resources, the interventionist state may terminate any foreign investment contract if it is found to be threatening national security, particularly in such areas as defence, energy, resources, infrastructure, transport, technology, equipment and manufacturing (Sainsbury, 2011e).

Overall, the management process of China's mining industry, which had been plagued by an unfair pricing system and enormous safety problems, has been rationalized, but China's local mines, which are regarded as death traps, continue to create problems for the government, although state-managed mines are considered to be safer than the thousands of privately managed mines. With the rise in China's economic might and the phenomenal rise in China's foreign exchange resources, the new investment in the resource sector which has boomed since mid-2005 (EIU, 2009) was directed to coal, petroleum, natural gas, and most non-ferrous and ferrous metals such as manganese, bauxite, magnetite ore and potassium.

India's major reserves primarily consist of coal, iron ore and bauxite. Although it produces considerable quantities of mica, manganese, dolomite, chromite and magnetite, apatite and phosphate, the country's oil and gas requirements are met from imports. However, the weak political strength of the government, limited foreign exchange reserves at its disposal and strict licensing rules have severely limited the exploration and production of minerals. In contrast, the liberalization in 2006 of the Mines and Minerals Act of 1957 allowed 100 per cent foreign investment in the mining of titanium, a metal which is available in abundance (30 per cent of total global reserves) in India (EIU, 2008b).

The size of India's industrial sector and manufacturing sectors, accounting for 29 per cent and 16 per cent of GDP in 2008, compare very unfavourably with the size in China of those sectors, which are 49 per cent and 34 per cent of China's GDP (World Bank, 2010). Thus, since India's industrial sector is smaller and much less export-oriented than China's, India's need for a global search for access to resources appears limited. Hence, India's private sector companies have taken the lead in securing access to mineral resources in Australia and Africa. However, India held its second Indo-African summit in 2011 to secure mining rights, while China had already held four such summits with African countries (*The Statesman Weekly*, 2011).

Nevertheless, exploration activities with the initiative from the Indian state to find and mine gas, oil and coal from domestic reserves and from India's foreign assets in Sweden, Vietnam, Venezuela, Russia, Syria and Columbia have been taking place. However, with a smaller reserve of foreign exchange (over $US300 billion) at its disposal, India's capacity to buy political favours in order to secure mining rights in Africa is very limited. Furthermore, the state enterprise, the Oil and Natural Gas Corporation Videsh Limited, has acquired a number of oil blocks in Brazil, Columbia, Myanmar, Venezuela and Trinidad and Tobago as well as acquiring a foreign energy company, the Imperial Energy of the UK, in 2008–09 (GOI, 2010).

In the overall management of the production and use of energy resources, China recorded a 104.7 per cent increase between 1990 and 2007 compared with only a 54.7 per cent increase in India's total energy production. But in total energy use, China recorded a 126.6 per cent increase whereas India only had an 87 per cent increase during the same period. The same trend can also be seen in the greater rise in per capita energy consumption in China than the rise in India between 1990 and 2007. The respective rates of increase were 95.3 per cent for China and 41.1 per cent for India. However, China's effort to meet an increasing proportion of its energy demand from domestic production has been more successful than India's efforts, as in 2007 China and India's energy consumption accounted for 107.8 and 131.9 per cent of domestic production respectively.

Other important trends in energy use in China and India which are common to both countries are that while the share of nuclear energy in total energy production is very low and the share of renewable resources and waste in total energy use has fallen in both countries substantially from 23.2 per cent and 41.9 per cent in 1990 to only 9.9 per cent and 27.2 per cent in 2007, the share of fossil fuel in total energy use in both countries increased from 75.5 per cent and 55.6 per cent in 1990 to 86.9 per cent and 70.0 per cent in 2007. While these trends indicate that fossil fuel will remain the predominant source of the energy supply in both countries (World Bank, 2010), China with a known petroleum reserve of 2.8 billion tonnes and natural gas reserves of 3.2 trillion cubic metres has a greater scope of increasing the fossil supply from domestic sources than India with considerably less known reserves of fossil fuel and natural gas (EIU, 2009).

Infrastructure

The improvement in infrastructure in China received a strong boost under the large-scale public works expenditure programme undertaken by the government during the financial crisis of 2007 to 2009. While the infrastructure in cities along the eastern coastline is generally in good condition, it is not so good in the vast interior of China. Occasional oversupply and shortages of power have badly affected economic activities in Guangdong Province and in other nearby areas. Among the BRIC (Brazil, Russia, India and China) countries, India's infrastructure is in the poorest condition. The number of dual carriageways (four-lane roads) is small, and most of the single carriageways (two-lane roads) are full of potholes and clogged up with heavy traffic, contributing to considerable delays in the transportation of goods and humans to their destinations. Frequent breakdowns on the road of trucks overloaded with perishable food products contribute to the rise in price level in the country. Most of the 3.3 million kilometres of Indian roads, which carry almost 70 per cent of total freight and 85 per cent of passenger traffic, are in rather bad shape.

Road management programmes have been implemented quite successfully in China with 53,900 kilometres of expressways built by 2007, while before 2000 there were hardly any highways linking the capital city and other cities and towns to distant provinces. During the Eleventh Five Year Plan from 2006 to 2010, the government built nearly 1 million kilometres of new rural roads. Despite such improvements, the problem of congestion in roads in China has not been redressed properly.

In India in 2002 under the National Highway Development Programme, the Indian government aimed to improve the condition of 65,000 kilometres of national highways in seven phases, but very few projects have ever been completed in full on time and without cost overruns, resulting from repeated stoppage of work by labourers and from problems with land acquisition (EIU, 2008b). Under the National Highways Development Projects, in November 2009 out of a total length of 33,642 kilometres of the national highways which had been expected to be built, only 12,531 kilometres of four-lane highways had been constructed and 5,595 kilometres of highway were under construction.

Although China's rail network is the third largest in the world and the state-owned railways are heavily debt ridden, large amounts of money have been spent to upgrade the rail network. In 2007 the total length of track in operation, which stood at 78,000 kilometres and had expanded to more than 100,000 kilometres in 2008, carried about 25 per cent of total freight (2,379.7 billion tonnes) and about 33 per cent of total passengers (721.6 billion) (EIU, 2009). In contrast, in India in 2006–07, the total length of track in operation, which totalled 63,300 kilometres, carried 483.4 million tonnes of freight and 6.2 billion passengers. Such differences in achievements of the Chinese and Indian railways can be explained by the differences in the sizes of the two economies and in geographical areas. The Indian Railways, which also is entirely publicly owned, has suffered from underinvestment, under-pricing of fares and cross-subsidization of passenger traffic cost by higher freight charges (EIU, 2008b). In recent years the Railway has been able to recover its operating costs from total revenues. Furthermore, the demand for rail travel has declined with cheaper air fares made available to the commuting public after the implementation of the 'open sky' policy and the liberalization of freight sector management. Just as in China, where many high-speed rail links have been opened to connect major cities such as Beijing and Shanghai, Beijing and Tianjin, and so on, in India too many high-speed (by Indian standards) rail links have been opened in recent years to connect metro cities such as Calcutta and Delhi, Delhi and Mumbai, Calcutta and Mumbai, Calcutta and Chennai, Calcutta and Bangalore, and so on.

East Asia

Rapid industrialization in the East Asian nations is widely credited to the policy leadership of their developmental states which, at least until the bursting of Japan's 'bubble economy' in the early 1990s, were generally seen as quite successful. These developmental states followed three very distinct patterns or strategies, though. In Japan and Korea, the government played a leading role in targeting huge corporate conglomerates as national champions with subsidies and protection from international competition. The role of the state in Taiwan, in contrast, focused more on creating a conducive economic environment in which small and medium enterprises could thrive. In South-east Asia the emphasis of industrial policy was much more on attracting FDI, while there was less intervention in markets.

Japan

From the 1950s through to the 1980s, Japan's rapid economic growth and transformation clearly constituted the best economic performance among the developed capitalist nations. Yet, a leading MITI official's (Naohiro Amaya) reflections on the 'Japanese miracle' suggest that Japan pursued its own development model (Prestowitz, 1988, p. 128): 'We did the opposite of what American economists said. We violated all the normal concepts.'

In particular, Japan embarked on a state-led reindustrialization project at the beginning of the post-war era that flouted a strictly market-based logic.

Japan had been an industrial power before World War II, but wartime destruction resulted in a poor country with not much functioning industry but with a potentially educated and very cheap workforce. This suggested a comparative advantage in labour-intensive light industry. Indeed, such light industries as textiles played a crucial role in Japan's post-war industrial recovery and dominated her early exports. However, the Japanese government was not content to let international comparative advantage limit it to what was perceived as too gradual a climb up the international product cycle. Rather, it decided to target more advanced sectors almost immediately, as Nester (1991:79) neatly summarizes:

> Japan is [now] the world's leading producer of steel, machine-tools, and automobiles. By the early 1950s, Tokyo had targeted all three for development as strategic industries, and over the next four decades nurtured them with a range of subsidies, cartels, technology incentives, cheap loans, import barriers, and export incentives. None of these industries would have survived had they been exposed to free-market forces – American and European producers held a comparative advantage in all three industries up through the mid-1960s and would have wiped out their struggling Japanese rivals. However, the success of these industrial policies varied widely, with those targeting steel and automobiles being remarkable successes while those promoting the machine-tool industry had a more limited effect – machine-tools is one of Japan's few industries whose success depended as much upon entrepreneurship as cartels, government handouts, and import barriers.

One reason for Japan's success, as indicated by Nester's (1991) preceding summary, clearly has been the assistance that the state has rendered to specific industries and firms in myriad forms of subsidized finance, R&D support, market cartelization, protection against imports and extremely hard-nosed trade bargaining. The government, moreover, targeted specific industries and even firms for such support, positioning the nation to move into increasingly sophisticated and higher value-added production. In particular, Japan's initial import-substitution policies, which were adopted with American approval to revive the economy in the 1950s, have continued, even as the nation has benefited from booming exports over the past three decades. Controls on foreign capital were quite stringent up through the early 1980s (e.g. licensing of technology to Japanese firms was made a condition for doing business there), and, while formal trade barriers were cut, many informal nontariff barriers (NTBs) remained. Japan, therefore, has clearly benefited from a developmental state (Johnson, 1982; Prestowitz, 1988).

More than just governmental activism was involved in the Japanese success story, though. Indeed, Japanese management practices have been given considerable credit for the strong performance of its enterprises. One important characteristic was the concentration upon the quality of products and the continuous upgrading of process technology in a system of 'total quality management' or TQM and 'flexible production' – both of which contrast greatly with the Western traditional mass production ethic of winning markets through low-cost, medium-quality goods. The ability of Japanese firms to pursue TQM and flexible production (which, ironically, were brought to Japan by the American engineer Edwards Deming during the Occupation) in turn rested upon a paternalistic management system which built strong bonds of employee loyalty through such practices as lifetime employment (which was confined to approximately one-third of the workforce in large corporations) and quality circles which involved workers in key production decisions. In addition, because of the strong company-worker ties, Japanese corporations invested far more than American ones in the training that their well educated workers needed to be 'flexible' without the fear that they would leave for better jobs (Hofheinz and Calder, 1982; Okimoto, 1989; Prestowitz, 1988; Reischauer, 1988).

Japanese firms operated within an economy that is structured quite distinctively, and the nature of its firms and markets, in turn, explain why its business strategies were so competitive. The economy was organized around huge conglomerates called keiretsu, which included firms in major industries (electronics, chemicals, construction, machinery, etc.), a large bank, and one of Japan's famous foreign trading companies. These companies owned stock in each other and gave each other preference in doing business. In addition, there were 'supply' keiretsu in industries involving multiple stages of production, such as electronics and automobiles. The parent firm diffused technology and quality-control techniques to its suppliers, creating a reciprocal relationship. The parent was assured of high-quality components, while the assured sales permitted the suppliers to invest in retooling and technological upgrading (Gerlach, 1992; Harrison, 1994; Hofheinz and Calder, 1982; Okimoto, 1989; Womack et al., 1990).

The nature of the keiretsu system, in turn, explains several features of firm behaviour which contributed to international competitiveness. First, the internal market was extremely competitive. Major corporations with huge resources behind them fought for almost every market segment, keeping the pressure up for continuous improvement in quality and cost – that is, for flexible production rather than mass production. Accordingly, corporate strategy focused upon market share, rather than short-term profits. Japan's corporations were able to take a more long-term or strategic perspective, furthermore, because of the nature of corporate financing. Unlike the equity-based financing in the United States, Japan's corporate finance is much more debt-based – which is where the keiretsu banks came to play a key role. While American executives must look at how the quarterly bottom line will play on the stock markets, keiretsu banks formed a 'deep-pockets' partner for other conglomerate members. Moreover, capital was significantly cheaper in Japan than in the

US, providing another incentive for high levels of investment (Gerlach, 1992; Hofheinz and Calder, 1982; Okimoto, 1989; Prestowitz, 1988; Zysman, 1983).

At least until the early 1990s, this economic system also dovetailed well with the organization of the polity, creating a highly effective political economy. Industrial policy was set by consensus between business leaders and permanent technocrats in Japan's leading ministries (such as the Ministry of International Trade and Industry or MITI, the Ministry of Post and Communications or MPT, and the Ministry of Finance or MOF). Because these relationships were reciprocal and consensual, the technocrats were able to keep corporate Japan honest, while the business community was able to keep government officials from making egregious errors of judgment. Such benign industrial or strategic trade policy was possible, furthermore, because it was generally isolated from the hurly-burly of Japan's electoral politics (Calder, 1988; Johnson, 1982; Okimoto, 1989; Prestowitz, 1988).

Technocrats and their big business allies were able to rule because of the strategy used by the Liberal Democratic Party (LDP) to maintain power throughout almost the entire post-war period. Despite its name, the LDP is a conservative, pro-business party; however, it retained power by periodically reaching out to new constituencies with what appeared to be liberal policies of assistance in what Kent Calder (1988) has insightfully called a pattern of 'crisis and compensation'. That is, economic (or political) crisis would erode the electoral base of the LDP, which would respond by extending benefits to a new constituency which was viewed as an acceptable cost for maintaining political stability. This obviously is the classic model of patronage politics which is usually considered antithetical to promoting economic efficiency. In Japan, however, an ingenious system evolved in which the patronage politics and the artificially high prices or rents that it generated were limited to sectors not involved in international trade (e.g. agriculture, construction, domestic retailing), while technocratic control over major export industries based on business-bureaucracy consultative ties was preserved (Calder, 1988; Okimoto, 1989).

Japan's economic difficulties over the last two decades (Alexander, 2003) can also be explained by a complex interaction among market, state and society set off, ironically, by the past successes of the Japanese political economy. A wide range of Japanese industries had become highly competitive by the early 1980s as they used infant industry protection, both direct and more informal, to get started, then applied Japanese management strategies, such as TQM and capturing market share, to outpace their foreign rivals (Prestowitz, 1988; Tyson, 1992). The combination of rapid export growth and continued import restrictions, which both the benefiting industries and sponsoring ministries were loath to surrender, created huge and continuing trade surpluses. The result was a tremendous accumulation of financial assets that created a 'bubble economy' by the late 1980s that, much like the Wall Street frenzy a few years earlier, provided inexorable incentives for corporate speculation and asset acquisition. When the bubble burst, the tremendous loss of assets for the financial system then seriously eroded the ability of Japanese companies to continue the high investment rates necessary to stay competitive in leading technology- and capital-intensive industries. Obviously, the bursting of the Japanese bubble had many economic antecedents, both domestic and foreign. A primary reason for the catastrophe of the early 1990s, though, very probably lay in the failure to act decisively to first economic (the 'bubble') and then political (voter rejection of the LDP for the first time in the post-war period) threats (Noble, 1994). This inaction, in turn, seemingly resulted from the institutional sclerosis of the political economy that had been created over the previous decades. In particular, both the state (politicians and bureaucrats) and business had developed so many vested interests that they became paralysed in the face of crisis (Krauss and Pekkanen, 2011).

Taiwan

Unlike Japan which had been an industrial power before World War II, Taiwan entered the post-war era as a poor agricultural society with much dimmer economic prospects. Thus, its subsequent rapid industrialization is, if anything, more impressive than Japan's. Given the difficulties in achieving structural transformations of an economy, perhaps the most impressive facet of Taiwan's economic miracle has been that the country has successfully negotiated several sharp structural transformations with what, in retrospect, appears to be surprisingly few problems.

In particular, five periods of major structural transformation can be discerned. The first occurred during the 1950s when the transformation away from an agricultural economy was consolidated, as domestic light industry developed rapidly. Second, the 1960s and early 1970s witnessed an impressive export boom for light industry and assembly products that revolutionized the economy and set off significant social changes as well. From the mid-1970s to the mid-1980s another substantial economic upgrading into the heavy and high-tech industries occurred that was accompanied by the emergence of a middle-class society and a significant political liberalization in a third structural transformation. A fourth transformation occurred over the next decade with the most important component probably being democratization in the political sphere, although there was very significant change economically as well in the form of the 'Mainland revolution' in the country's economic orientation as its mature industries increasingly had to move offshore. Finally, in the period since the mid-1990s, the loss of mature industries has, if anything, accelerated; and Taiwan has responded by trying to break into the most advanced industrial sectors, such as bio-technology.

During the first stage in the 1950s, there were two major economic changes which brought very significant progress to the country. First, as discussed above, a dramatic land reform led to greatly increased productivity in agriculture, which both helped to alleviate poverty in the rural sector and created resources that were used to finance industrialization. Second, the government introduced import-substitution policies (import controls and protection) to stimulate the rapid growth of light industry. State policy also greatly enhanced the resources that could be devoted to Taiwan's development. Most importantly, mass education created human capital, and the government substantially increased its economic leadership capability by bringing skilled technocrats into the top levels of the regime (Galenson, 1979; Ho, 1978).

Despite the initial success of the first transformation, import-substitution soon reached its inevitable high point with the saturation of the local market for light industrial goods, setting off a new challenge for Taiwan. It responded by making a fateful decision to promote exports in the hope that its products could become competitive on world markets, especially in the developed world. There were two prongs to this strategy: attracting foreign investment for assembly operations in export processing zones and getting domestic businesses to export. The resulting export boom succeeded probably well beyond the expectations of even its proponents. Taiwan's economy boomed, promoting both rising prosperity and a comparatively low level of income inequality. The resources accumulated during the first stage formed a vital foundation for this new transformation during the 1960s and early 1970s. The technocrats conceived and implemented the major policy changes which made this transformation possible, while its success rested on the human capital that had been developed in the workforce and business community. For example, many managers would go to work in foreign companies, learn the business and production techniques, and then start their own businesses. Just as during the first period, in addition, small and medium enterprises played the leading role in the new and expanding industrial sectors (Galenson, 1979; Gold, 1986; Wade, 1990).

Just as with import-substitution, the success of Taiwan's export-led strategy contained the 'seeds of its own destruction' in the sense that the island's rising prosperity and wages began to price it out of the niche of low-cost manufactured products in the world economy. Economically, the country responded to this new challenge with two somewhat disparate transformations from the mid-1970s through the mid-1980s. First, there was a state-led push into heavy industry (e.g. steel and petrochemicals); second, the small-scale business sector began to upgrade its production techniques into such fields as advanced electronics (Fields, 1995; Gold, 1986; Kuo, 1995; Noble, 1998; Wade, 1990). Considerable change occurred in the political and social realms as well with the emergence of a strong middle class (Cheng, 1990) and a growing role for 'electoral politicians' and for social movements, and an emerging opposition to the ruling Kuomintang who pushed for further liberalization (Clark, 1989; Copper, 1988; Tien, 1989).

The fourth structural transformation commenced in the mid-to-late 1980s. Economically, Taiwan emerged as a major player in the global high-tech industry (e.g. ranking third in semiconductor production as the new millennium opened) and, correspondingly, saw a massive movement to offshore production in its traditional labour-intensive industries, primarily to the PRC (Leng, 1996; Naughton, 1997). Unlike earlier eras, though, economic change was probably dwarfed by the transformation of the polity, as Taiwan went through a very successful democratic transition (Chao and Myers, 1998; Rigger, 1999; Tien, 1989, 1996; Wu, 1995). Again, there were several important facets of resource creation. Economically, Taiwan's surprisingly strong development of its high-tech industry and the increasing integration of its businesses into international production networks represented a substantial improvement in economic capacity. Politically, democratization led to a more open society and direct political representation for the general population.

Probably unfortunately for Taiwan, economic and political change did not end in the mid-1990s. Its basic industries, even high-tech ones, continued to be squeezed by new competitors, such as China. Consequently, the nation is now being forced into a new transformation to a much more information-age economy with a growing emphasis on innovation and competition with the most advanced economies in the world, where the competitiveness of its political economy is much more problematic (Wong, 2010). Politically, Taiwan's democracy has certainly become consolidated in the sense that election results and transfers of power are accepted and considered legitimate. However, its politics are now marked by vicious partisan polarization and by policy gridlock that results from the fairly close division in party strength (Clark and Tan, 2011), which certainly inhibits responding effectively to the challenges presented by the new economic transformation. Perhaps because this final structural transformation is not yet complete, it appears more problematic than the first four.

In contrast to Japan, therefore, Taiwan pursued a strategy that was more focused on the traditional climb up the international product cycle; and Taiwan's economic structure was different as it was dominated by small and medium enterprises rather than huge conglomerates like the Japanese keiretsu (Clark and Roy, 1997; Fields, 1995). More broadly, the role assumed by Taiwan's state was quite significantly different as well. During the first two periods, the government created a conducive environment for first import-substitution light industry and then the switch to exporting these products rather than supporting specific national champions. The third stage did see the emergence of a more traditional role for a developmental state. State corporations played the leading role in Taiwan's push into heavy industry, and government research institutes developed and commercialized new technologies (e.g. advanced electronics like semiconductors) that were then transferred to private firms in the emerging high-tech industries (Clark, 1989; Greene, 2008). State economic leadership, if anything, declined over the last two periods for two reasons, however. First, Taiwan was pushed to compete in the most advanced industries and technologies in the world, such as bio-technology, where basic research, development and commercialization have such long and uncertain gestation periods that it is very hard to devise government policies to promote industrial upgrading (Wong, 2010). Second, Taiwan's very successful democratization increasingly led to the politicization of economic policy-making (Clark and Tan, 2011).

South Korea
South Korea followed a strategy that was quite similar to Taiwan's until the 1970s but then switched to a model that was similar to Japan's. In the 1950s, it used protectionism to encourage import-substitution in light industry, similarly to Taiwan, and in the mid-1960s (a couple of years later than Taiwan), it engaged in a major transformation to exporting its labour-intensive manufactures. As the 1970s opened, then, South Korea and Taiwan had fairly similar export-based economies. In the 1970s, though, both countries decided to upgrade their economies by engaging in 'secondary import-substitution' – that is, the state-sponsored development of the heavy, chemical and high-tech industries (Gereffi, 1990). The data in Chapter 2 demonstrated that both were successful in leapfrogging into more advanced industrial sectors. However, South Korea was able to change its industrial structure more radically than Taiwan for two reasons. First, its domestic market was much larger, so it could pursue industrial deepening with an emphasis on the heavy and chemical industries to a much greater extent than Taiwan, where internal demand was much more limited. Second, the powers of the state were much stronger, so that it could forge new industries much more quickly (Amsden, 1989).

Turning to the effects of this policy, the rapidity with which Korea became internationally competitive in these industries is almost breathtaking. In almost a decade and a half between 1971 and 1984, heavy industry's share of total industrial production rose by a half, from 40 to 62 per cent. What is much more impressive, though, is the tremendous transformation of South Korea's export mix that occurred. In 1971, heavy industrial products constituted just 13 per cent of all industrial exports, demonstrating that the heavy industries were primarily import-substitution ones. In 1984, in very sharp contrast, they formed 60 per cent of industrial exports, almost exactly the same as their proportion of industrial output (Amsden, 1989; Haggard and Moon, 1983; Jones and Sakong, 1980; Kang, 1989; Woo, 1991).

To promote rapid industrialization, the government resorted to a battery of policy instruments, including the allocation of financial credit, production subsidies, tariff protection, export quotas and tax rebates to influence entrepreneurial incentives. The financial system was probably by far the most important and distinctive policy instrument in the state arsenal. South Korea had extreme governmental control of its financial system, including the large amounts of funds borrowed abroad. This allowed the government both to funnel these funds to enterprises selected as national champions in a specific industry and to enforce 'performance standards' by threatening to withdraw credit if production, export or quality goals were not met (Amsden, 1989; Fields, 1995; Woo, 1991).

Such a strategy of financial control could only work, though, when there are a relatively limited number of economic players – which is the case in South Korea where large business groups (chaebol) were even more dominant than the keiretsu in Japan. In just the decade between 1974 and 1984, for example, the sales of the top five chaebol skyrocketed almost fivefold from 12 to 52 per cent of gross national product (GNP). Until the early 1980s, the state essentially dictated to the business community, even the large chaebol. However, the success of the state-led national development project ironically made the chaebol so rich and powerful that the balance of power began to tip in their direction (Amsden, 1989; Hahm and Plein, 1997; Kang, 1989).

The heavy industry programme is also quite instructive for testing the neoclassical and developmental state models in the Korean context. South Korea instituted this programme as a reaction to the same pressures on its labour-intensive exports that Taiwan faced in the early 1970s. Because the state's links with and control over private industry were much tighter in Korea than in Taiwan, it was able to take a much more aggressive strategy which ultimately proved far more successful in upgrading into such heavy industries as automobiles, steel and petrochemicals (Amsden, 1989; Mardon and Paik, 1992; Wade, 1990). The ability to defy the short-term logic of the market by launching such a 'big push' is certainly consistent with the statist critique of neoclassicalism, but more than a developmental state was in operation within South Korea's political economy. First, most of these heavy industries were in private hands. Thus, their ultimate success rested on the efficacy of the chaebol, not the developmental state. For example, the upgrading in semiconductors primarily was the result of private initiative in an area that state policy-makers relatively ignored (Hong, 1992). Second, while the heavy industry strategy ultimately succeeded, it did so only after a decade of economic imbalances which caused considerable criticism and political upheavals that significantly altered the nature of the regime (Haggard and Moon, 1983, 1990; Hahm and Plein, 1997).

South Korea also stood out for its statist practice of placing stringent limits on direct investment in Korea by foreign MNCs. However, these restrictions on foreign capital were not aimed at simple exclusion. Rather the regime acted to channel MNCs into a few high-priority sectors and to regulate them to maximize their contribution to the development of Korean national champions. According to this strategy, foreign investment in an industry would first be solicited but would only be allowed in the form of joint ventures with domestic firms. Once the domestic partner learned the business and the technology and was strong enough to carry on operations on its own, the MNC would be forced to divest itself (under the terms of the original contract), thereby leaving a new industry in local hands (Amsden, 1989; Haggard and Moon, 1983, 1990; Mardon and Paik, 1992).

Malaysia
Although Malaysia is rich in terms of natural resources, its outlook appeared to be rather bleak at independence. The economy almost totally lacked an industrial tradition, and political stability was in danger because of ethnic fragmentation (Lim and Nesadurai, 1997) as well as external threats. Not until the mid-1980s did the manufacturing sector's share of GDP become larger than that of agriculture. In hindsight, however, the economic development of Malaysia was a success story, even if it has been turbulent at times.

The characteristic trait of the Malaysian developmental state almost from the outset was its double targets of nurturing various industries and changing the prevailing income distribution in favour of the majority race, the Malays, who were seen as disadvantaged. While the latter policy certainly led to a less confrontational political climate, it also created resentment under the surface, and was a fertile ground for rent seeking and outright corruption.

After independence, Malaysia embarked on a mildly import-substituting industrial policy with an emphasis on consumer goods (Ariff, 1991:10). But because the domestic market was limited and because exports proved difficult, the industrial sector could not contribute much to relieving the excess supply of labour. Hence, the country switched to a generally export-oriented policy stance based mainly on FDIs and export processing zones (EPZs), while retaining import-substitution in selected industries, such as automobiles (Jomo et al., 1997:94).

The Investment Incentives Act of 1968 entailed several measures geared mainly towards the export industries, such as accelerated depreciation, tax holidays, etc. (Ariff, 1991:10). The EPZs established in 1971 especially favoured export-oriented manufacturing because of duty free access to imported inputs in excess of other investment incentives. A condition was, however, that most of the production had to be exported. This system prevails, by and large, up to this day. The incentives for investors have remained as well, although their generosity has varied over the years and in response to the general economic situation. The firms taking advantage of the incentives were mostly foreign affiliates. The EPZs seem to have been important as employers of non-skilled labour, not least women. However, most of the manufacturing was simple assembling operations to begin with, activities that were easily relocated if productions costs threatened to increase compared to alternative locations. Due to high import content and very limited domestic linkages, the foreign exchange earnings from these industries were not impressive in the beginning, and real wages did not develop favourably (Kanapathy, 2001). More seriously, they were of limited value as a source of technology transfer. Another reason for problems in the upgrading process in high-tech industries appears to be a relative lack of supporting institutions, such as incentives to venture into risky activities, promotion of international standards, intellectual property rights, etc. The supply of highly-skilled labour has been a bottleneck too (Rasiah, 2006). This is still the case, to some extent.

Although the protection of manufacturing was not that pervasive compared to other developing countries, it has been quite far-reaching, especially in some targeted industries. In a 'second round of import substitution' (Kanapathy, 2001) in the early 1980s, the government launched a programme, modelled on South Korea (Jomo et al., 1997:101), aimed at setting up a number of heavy industries, such as steel, petrochemicals and automobiles. The goal was to create a domestic capital goods sector with strong domestic linkages, especially to *bumiputera* (Malay) enterprises (Jomo et al., 1997:101). The Heavy Industries Corporation of Malaysia (HICOM) was established in 1980 as a state-owned company (SOE) (Ariff, 1991:10–11) and invested in capital goods industries, such as automobiles, steel, cement, etc. Another important task for the organization was training *bumiputera* managers and technicians and to promote the emergence of *bumiputera*-led SMEs that could function as subcontractors to the large companies (Rasiah, 1997). The idea was that the shares would gradually be transferred to individual Malay holders. Thus the programme was a very important part of the affirmative measures in favour of the *bumiputera*. Today the state retains a minority share in the company (now DRB-HICOM).

Unfortunately, the heavy industries programme was not successful (Ariff, 1991:11; Jomo et al., 1997:102). The new industries were established in sectors where Malaysia did not necessarily have comparative advantages. Production and administration costs were relatively high, and the rate of capacity utilization was insufficient (Jomo et al., 1997:102). Even when competitiveness could well have been achieved, such as in the 'national car' project, well-meaning but excessive protection effectively prevented the industries from maturing.

Coming out of a severe recession in 1987, Malaysia embarked on a policy of further deregulation and encouragement of FDI with new incentives for investors, while the ambition to redistribute wealth remained. This policy was fortuitously but strongly supported by the appreciating yen, which prompted

Japanese companies, but also companies from the Asian NIEs, to outsource or relocate simpler parts of their value chain. Moreover, the value of the ringgit depreciated compared to the US dollar and most other East Asian currencies (Jomo et al., 1997:103).

The first Industrial Master Plan (IMP) of 1986–1995 envisaged industrial development on two dimensions: resource-based and non-resource-based industries (Lim and Nesadurai, 1997). Another way of supporting industrialization was heavy investment in infrastructure, such as roads, ports and airports as well as in industrial parks and later in ITC infrastructure (Lim and Nesadurai, 1997). As a consequence of these measures, the Malaysian economy grew rapidly in the early and mid-1990s.

A particular characteristic of the Malaysian model that remained, however, was the restriction of ownership, as well as structure of employment, of foreign subsidiaries, aimed at granting the *bumiputera* a certain share. As the *bumiputera* partners often had little to contribute to the firm, this was seen as a problem by foreign investors and non-Malay entrepreneurs. The Chinese businesses suffered in particular, since they already had to face competition from foreign firms with superior resources (Jomo and Gomez, 2000). Also, the fact that only part of the policy of favouring *bumiputeras* is explicit leaves a good deal of discretion to individual officials and adds to the uncertainty for investors (cf. World Bank, 2009a). The strict limitations on the number of expatriates that a company was allowed to employ also served the purpose of empowering the Malay part of the population, especially as the composition of the workforce was expected to reflect the ethnic composition of the country. Although the favouring of Malay interests has been more subdued during the last couple of decades, these problems largely remain. When competition for FDI hardens, this type of requirement is likely to create negative incentives for the investors. Moreover, rising wage costs have rendered Malaysia less attractive as a production base for low-tech goods. The government has deliberately gone for encouraging more advanced industries in its policy towards foreign investors.

The resource-based industries developed well, volume-wise, but the problem has been that they have not been able to develop very much in terms of value-added. Other industries have done better in this respect, especially in cases where FDI has been prominent. Especially electronics and electrical products have been reasonably successful at achieving more value-added (Lim and Nesadurai, 1997). The government tried to put increasing emphasis on exports and technological deepening from the late 1980s onwards by tying incentives to these matters (Jomo et al., 1997:108). The so-called Multimedia Super Corridor (MSC), perhaps the best example of this approach, was established during this period. The MSC is a special zone established for developing the ITC cluster, offering generous incentives to foreign investors.

However, the increasing emphasis on advanced production processes creates a problem on the labour market, because of the short supply of skilled labour and professionals. This is arguably the most important constraint to the country's further development (see Department of Commerce, 2008). Due to this, the ability to absorb new technologies is limited which also limits the prospects of technology spillovers (Jomo et al., 1997:113). Moreover, the quota system in education also backfires in the sense that many students from minority races have to go overseas to study and may not return to Malaysia after graduating.

Singapore

At independence, the government of Singapore was desperate to create jobs for its workforce. Since import-substitution was out of the question in this then tiny economy, the country went for a strongly export-oriented strategy, based on FDI and a number of state-owned companies. While tax incentives were offered to new industries, the more important thing may have been the availability of infrastructure, a minimum of bureaucracy and perhaps also the strong position of the English language. The country's geographical position alone is a distinct advantage from a logistic point of view. In any case, the policy was very successful, not only in terms of luring in foreign subsidiaries but also in terms of industrial upgrading. While the bulk of the investment has been in electronics, the industrial structure has recently moved towards more sophisticated activities, such as life sciences, information technology, etc. The backside of all this is, however, a strong dependence on foreign companies, which may be able to put pressure on the government in such matters as taxation.

Despite the fact that the Singapore government is very market-oriented, it has never shied away from establishing so-called government-linked companies (GLCs). Originally the reason for setting up GLCs was the lack of domestic capital, but even now these companies are not seen as a problem as long as they function in a business-like manner and do not enjoy special privileges. However, there are also the statutory boards, which are a type of semi-governmental organizations in charge of producing mainly public utilities and the operation of infrastructure. There are a large number of these units, big and small, and they have a monopoly position. They are supposed to follow economic principles, though, and are required to make a profit. Still, the private sector often sees the statutory boards as unfair competitors, encroaching on their turf.

Originally, Singapore had few domestic entrepreneurs in manufacturing. Those that did exist tended to flee the competition from foreign firms and GLCs to the service sector. Many of them felt that the government neglected them and, at the same time, they were suspicious of government involvement, fearing excessive control by the authorities. Furthermore, there was no pressing need to become an entrepreneur for a well-educated Singaporean, as foreign subsidiaries and the public sector offered an abundance of well-paid jobs for them. Thus the propensity for risk-taking was rather low.

Gradually, however, things have begun to change. The foreign companies have been a hotbed for technology transfer and have created a basis for a domestic industry of subcontractors, assemblers and service providers. The government has also recently taken a more proactive role towards the SME sector. The incentives offered during the first decades of independence in practice tended to favour large foreign companies, since they targeted big investments in high-priority sectors and could not be taken advantage of by SMEs. Measures to help small domestic companies were developed much later, for example, in the form of funding schemes and technical assistance programmes. All in all, the domestic industrial sector has started to develop during the last couple of decades, catering partly to the larger mainly foreign-owned manufacturing sector and partly developing their own brands and technology.[5]

INCLUSIVE DEVELOPMENT

Inclusive development refers to a kind of development in which citizens' voices are taken into consideration and given due regard by leaders of the government and its administrative apparatus in framing and implementing development programmes which affect those citizens' livelihoods and lives. Thus, inclusive development should be necessary to promote a pattern of development that benefits the general population.

The important enabling prerequisites for such a development to occur are that: (i) citizens enjoy unrestricted freedom to express their opinions openly on any issue which affects their lives; (ii) the state guarantees to its citizens the protection of their private properties including non-intrusion by the state's agents in their private lives as well as in economic and social interactions; (iii) bureaucrats and technocrats remain apolitical; (iv) the rule of law is strictly adhered to by the state by making the judiciary and police force completely independent of the executive branch; and (v) economic and social disparities between labour and capital, rich and poor are reduced.

China and India

In China, none of these five prerequisites is observed fully. The state does not yet allow its citizens the security of private property, the unrestricted freedom of speech and assembly, or freedom of the press. This view is confirmed by the announcement, in 2011, by the government in the wake of popular uprising in Africa and the Middle East of an increase in the public security budget of 13.9 per cent to 93.7 billion US dollar in 2011 from 83.5 billion US dollar in

2010 to be spent on police, state security, armed civil militia, law courts and jails (Sainsbury, 2011a, 2011b). Violence against reporters of the foreign press and hacking of foreign journalists' emails do occur from time to time. Also the recent deployment of thousands of riot police to quench the violent protest in Xintang by migrant workers from Sichuan over the low wages they receive at the Jeans Manufacturing Centre bears testimony to the fact that freedom of speech, assembly and the press do not seem to exist in China.

Despite its many deficiencies, India still has a fully-functioning democracy. For example, the provincial election held in April–May 2011 in Bengal threw out of power the communists who had ruled the Province for 34 years. In the absence of freedom of speech, assembly and the press, the people of Bengal and of India could not have exercised their democratic rights.

The Chinese state has given some recognition to the right of Chinese citizens to own property. However, local governments with the help of local police do allocate lands to investors for the establishment of factories and other business ventures against the wishes of the owners, even though they receive some compensation. In India, it is more difficult for provincial governments to acquire land forcibly from unwilling landholders to allocate to an investor to establish factories. The government of India is planning to pass a law which would make it illegal for any forcible seizure of fertile agricultural land for its use for new industrial ventures.

In both China and India, bureaucrats and technocrats form an unholy alliance with their political masters and consequently carry out the politicians' wishes even if these wishes contradict national interests (Evans, 1995). In India, the politicians and the bureaucrats, perhaps under the influence of 'crony socialism' are generally not interested in starting new programmes for inclusive development (Dhume, 2011). Since police, prosecutors and courts fall under the control of the political and legal committee of the Chinese communist party and have little legal education and practical experience; independence of the judiciary and police force do not seem to exist in China (Sainsbury, 2011a, 2011b). In India, the judiciary is by and large independent at both the centre and in the provinces. The Indian judiciary has proven to be a very activist one. However, there are examples of police forces in some provinces losing their independence under the pressure of the ruling political party.

In Chapter 5, we commented on the income distribution in China and India. Between 1990 and 2007, the fact that the share of the poorest quintile in national consumption in China and India stood at 5.7 per cent and 8.1 per cent respectively (World Bank, 2010) implies that there has been a massive transfer of income from politically weak households to politically powerful ones in China during the last few decades (Wessel, 2011). Also, the bank sector credit which includes bank loans and holdings of bonds as a proportion of GDP increased from 121 per cent in 2008 to close to 150 per cent in 2010 in China

(Smith, 2011). What these income distribution statistics and the massive transfer of funds to the politically powerful and rich class mean is that for decades the respective shares of poor labour and the share of the rich and capitalists in the value-added component in the average cost of production per unit of output have been falling and rising at faster rates in China than in India.

The widening gap between the rich and the poor as well as between the urban and the rural sectors in China can also be attributed to the integration of the Chinese economy into the global economy more extensively and deeply than the Indian economy, as Williamson's (2011) study of the relationship between trade and poverty found a close association between these two under globalization. Pervasive graft and rent seeking behaviour which is endemic in the Chinese society may also have contributed to the widening of the rich-and-poor divide. To pursue inclusive development, however, the government plans to improve the economic condition of labour under the Twelfth Five Year Plan by significantly raising the minimum wage and constructing 35 million apartments for the poor (Smith, 2011). Beyond this, China needs to relax its restrictions on the basic political freedoms of the people and also reduce the state's intimate involvement in every facet of the Chinese society and the economy. For example, China seems to have performed the best when it pursued liberalizing market-oriented economic reforms and moved away from statist policies (Junning, 2011).

In India, as Bardhan (2010) observes, despite the long tradition of the maintenance of a democratic governance structure, the large number of the poor in an assertive electorate has not always succeeded in focusing the attention of politicians on the sustained implementation of programmes to alleviate mass poverty or to extend facilities of education and healthcare to the masses. In comparison with Chinese society, the heterogeneity of Indian society along with its socio-economic inequalities and conflicts has made it difficult for the Indian state to make long-term changes in the socio-economic condition of the masses (Bardhan, 2010; Olson, 1982). Accordingly, populist obstacles to long-term investment in infrastructure and social services have prevented the principal goal of inclusive development from being met fully in India.

Since the first economic reforms were implemented in 1991, no other reform measures have been implemented in India. The only major reforms undertaken by the Indian government were the abolition of industrial licensing and the import control regime in July 1991. These two reforms have unleashed the dynamism of India's entrepreneurs in the private sector, which has contributed greatly to the growth and development of the Indian economy. One has to realize that in India's democracy, any kind of economic reform and management can only be implemented if it is politically acceptable in a coalition government to partners with diverse political interests. In India, too, elements of economic liberalization and state control are present in the management of industrial development.

East Asia

In contrast to China and India, Japan has a fairly good record on most of the criteria for inclusive development. It has been a democracy throughout the post-war era; economic and property rights were generally respected; the economic technocrats were very highly respected; the rule of law was generally maintained; and the nation was one of the world leaders in reducing income inequality. Thus, in the early 1990s, Japan would have appeared to be a major success story for inclusive development. The country's stagnation over the last two decades indicates that there is more to sustaining economic success than inclusive development, however, because these five basic parameters really did not change very much.

South Korea and Taiwan have profiles for inclusive development that are quite similar despite their different economic strategies. For most of the post-war era, both were ruled by authoritarian states that limited democratic freedoms quite significantly and subordinated the rule of law to political considerations. In contrast, both had well-regarded technocratic bureaucracies that shaped very successful economic policies and generally respected economic and property rights. Finally, as demonstrated by the data in Chapter 5, industrialization in both countries reduced income inequality to comparatively low levels.

Malaysia and Singapore both have democratic constitutions; however, in practice there are some limitations. Since much of the political process in Malaysia revolves around balancing the interests of the various ethnic groups, a coalition of racially-based political parties has been in power for the whole period of independence. While this coalition has been ready to co-opt other parties into government, it has tried (sometimes heavy-handedly) to circumscribe the opportunities for the 'real' opposition (i.e. those parties that do not want to be co-opted). Also, the autonomy of the bureaucracy and judiciary are doubtful. However, in economic and business matters, legislation is of high quality and largely fairly implemented, which no doubt is one of the reasons for the country's relative economic success. Because of the positive discrimination of the Malay part of the population and side effects following from this, there is a good deal of discontent under the surface, as mentioned earlier, and the minority groups often feel that they are treated like second-class citizens. An almost automatic consequence of these conflicts – while rather invisible in daily life – is that the government controls the media rather tightly but in the era of the internet this is not very effective. The pro-Malay policy has been moderately successful at a macro level, but has tended to create increasing income differences within the Malay group.

Singapore is a multi-ethnic country like Malaysia, but at independence it adopted a 'meritocratic' system where politicking on racial or religious grounds is strictly not tolerated. Despite this the Malays (some 15 per cent of the population) were rather unhappy with the separation from Malaysia and have often kept their distance from the mainstream society, sometimes with marginalization as a result.

The country has been ruled by the People's Action Party (PAP) ever since independence, which gradually blurred the distinctions among 'party', 'state' and 'government'. The opposition parties have been weak and easily repressed by the PAP (Blomqvist, 2005:60–66). The media are operated by GLCs and are thus indirectly under government control. However, the share of the vote of the PAP has been slowly shrinking, being about 60 per cent in the general election in 2011. This has not been fully reflected in terms of seats in parliament, though, because of the election system. Thus the political situation is unlikely to change drastically in the near future at least, and there is little doubt that the government enjoys genuine support among many Singaporeans because of its stellar economic performance. Although the income distribution in Singapore is far from equal, the government does try hard to help the more disadvantaged parts of the population though various programmes. The civil service and judiciary are of a high quality, and property rights and other economic rights are well protected.

NOTES

1. One of the authors' (Roy) personal experience in the Calcutta market in December 2008 and January 2009.
2. The Indian Province of West Bengal was under the rule of the Marxist Communist Party for 34 years.
3. This opinion was expressed by many landless and land-poor family members to one of the authors, Roy, during his conversations with them in rural Bengal, Bihar and Jharkand during January 2009 and 2010.
4. A remarkably similar cost condition is affecting many privately run enterprises in China. After paying for all fixed and variable costs excluding normal profit, an entrepreneur can get a mark-up profit of about 3 per cent of total costs from the export of clothing and apparel manufactures because there is a high level of competition in the industry. Since companies from importing countries determine the price they will pay for their imports from their respective exporting firms under some forms of contractual agreements, the failure of a firm to fulfil its export contract can lead to the cancellation of the contract; and another firm can fulfil that export contract even if that price does not cover that firm's average cost of production per unit of output with mark-up. The export instability which affects firms in the agricultural sector also affects firms in the low-valued manufacturing industrial sector. A sudden surge in import orders from foreign companies forces firms to hire more labour and to obtain more raw materials to increase output to meet the foreign demand, but when the demand slackens, these firms are left with surplus labour and output. The maintenance of this surplus forces the firm to hope to receive similar orders in the foreseeable future and to increase the average production cost of the output. The surplus output is disposed of at a price which is well below the average cost of production per unit of output. The average cost of production per unit of output also rises, because the interest rate that the entrepreneur pays to the bank on borrowed money is generally about 30 per cent higher than the central bank's

discount rate. The cost of insurance and the payment for annual lease of the factory premises to the government also rise. The mark-up profit per unit of output in higher valued-added manufacturing units ranges between 5 and 7 per cent (information collected by one of the authors, Roy, from interviews with several entrepreneurs in Jiangsu Province on the eastern China coastline north of Shanghai in 2011).

5.   The above section draws on Blomqvist (2005, Chapter 3).

8. Should political openness precede economic openness?
The Asian experience

Many analyses of the 'Third Wave' of democratization that commenced in the 1980s presumed that the political freedom and openness of democracy went hand-in-hand with the economic freedom and openness of laissez-faire economics. Both, for instance, placed their prime emphasis on individual freedom and choice. Thus, there were predictions that the expansion of political freedom in the Third Wave would fuel greater economic openness, thereby producing faster growth and human development (Dawson, 1998; Friedman, 1962; Huntington, 1991). Yet, a moment's thought would suggest that this virtuous cycle might be more than a little questionable. On the one hand, greater economic openness could concentrate resources in the hands of groups who could use them to distort the political processes; on the other, newly empowered groups could seek to enrich themselves through political rather than economic activities. Furthermore, as we demonstrated in Chapter 7, even the very successful export-led development of many Asian nations, which might appear to be quintessential 'economic openness', relied upon an important state role in the economy.

This chapter, hence, explores the question raised by the Third Wave of whether political openness should precede economic openness. The first section discusses the relationship between economic and political openness, which serves as the theoretical foundation for the three cases studies considered here. The next section examines how India's immediate political openness created significant problems; then it is shown that authoritarian China was able to pursue economic openness but also that the lack of political openness in the PRC still allows significant economic distortions; and the following section examines economic development in East Asia to demonstrate that a good deal of complexity exists in the relationship between political openness and economic openness. Overall, therefore, these three analyses suggest that a nuanced approach to evaluating the role of political and economic openness in development is necessary and that a significant amount of 'balance' is necessary in the pursuit of these objectives.

ECONOMIC OPENNESS AND POLITICAL OPENNESS

In this chapter we use democratic political governance as the proxy for political openness. The characteristics of democratic political governance are that a country would consist of a legislative (parliament), an executive and a judiciary completely independent of the executive branch of the government. Members of the legislature are elected as representatives of individual political parties through a democratic election process. The leaders of the party winning the largest number of seats form the government in a parliamentary system; or the chief executive is elected directly in a presidential one. Before the election of representatives takes place, each political party presents to the electorate its agenda for action if it forms the government and tries to persuade the electorate to vote for its candidates at the forthcoming election. However, if there are too many political parties and too many agendas are put forward to the electorate in the pre-election period, people fail to make a clear differentiation between the objectives of different political parties and, hence, may fail to cast their votes for their respective candidates on the basis of an informed choice. However, the task of making an informed choice by a voter becomes more difficult if that voter does not have at least some elementary education (e.g. primary education) and is not engaged in income earning employment. This engagement in income earning employment assumes crucial importance because it provides the voter with the economic strength to refuse to be pressured and intimidated by paraformal agents of some political parties seeking the voter's support for the party's candidate at the election.

John Stuart Mill (1947) in his classic essay on *Representative Government* placed the strongest emphasis on the education of the electorate as the principal catalyst for enabling a voter to make an informed choice about the candidates. However, he also observed that it may take many years for political openness under a representative democracy to bring about a perceptible improvement in the economic and social conditions of an individual. But the representative government that in Mill's opinion was the best form of government could function effectively only if there were two political parties so that the difference between the majority and minority party in terms of number of representatives is quite small. Hence, the opposition political party remains almost as strong as the party in political power and is ready to take over the reins of the government, if the majority political party fails to discharge the tasks it was entrusted with before the election.

Apart from this requirement, there is the need for the state to ensure that citizens enjoy freedom of speech and assembly, as well as that the judiciary and police force remain non-aligned with the political party in power and strictly uphold and enforce the rule of law. Furthermore, it is necessary for the press and the media to enjoy complete freedom in pursuing their activities. Also in a country where many elections are held to form different levels of government, the chances of vote rigging and the adoption of other unfair means by all the political parties to win elections increase greatly. The number of political parties as well as of their affiliated trade unions and informal agents also increases. In such a situation, political openness, instead of creating the enabling environment for leaders to be responsive to the needs of the population, creates the state's vested interest groups which engage in rent seeking activities and fight to maintain their hold on the state power by winning the next election. Almost all developing countries adopt a formal structure of political openness under which the legitimacy of a government can easily be established and maintained, enabling leaders to make substantial gains by pursuing extensive unproductive and profit seeking activities instead of making efforts to create a genuine and well-functioning state which promotes democratic institutions and economic progress (North, 1987; Varyrynen, 2000; Keen, 1998, 2000; Roy and Sidenko, 2007a). This kind of predatory behaviour of the government can be found in several African countries which possess mineral resources. But such behaviour is present in the governments of almost all developing countries, although on a smaller scale in countries such as India which does not possess abundant reserves of mineral resources (Varyrynen, 2000).

Even in developed countries such as the United States where there is genuine political openness, rent seeking behaviour of politically powerful vested interest groups can also be found to be present (Greider, 1992; Olson, 1982). Consequently, the electorate tends to lose interest in its leaders and in the governance of the country because either it fails to make a distinction between the agenda of the political party in power and that of the party in opposition or it is too ignorant to be able to understand the contents of the agendas. Hence, even without making any progress in achieving improvements in people's living conditions, the leaders can continue to maintain the legitimacy of their existence in power in both developed and developing countries. For example, India's Marxist Communist Party that ruled the provinces of Bengal, Kerala and Tripura developed a paraformal army of thugs and maintained a parallel administrative structure alongside the formal structure of political governance under which the patrimonalism formed the dominant pattern of relationship between the Party as patron and civil society, business and industry groups; even the executive branch of the government consisting of ministers and bureaucrats became clients. The entire province of Bengal became the private fiefdom of the political party which made the political administration (ministers and bureaucrats) treat all public affairs as personal affairs and political power as the private property of the political party in power (Weber, 1968).

This kind of affair develops because natural asymmetries of information do exist between governing elites and their citizens (Stiglitz, 2002). Hence, checks against the predatory behaviour of government and the political party in power are exercised by the presence of a free and competitive press and media. However, paraformal agents (thugs) of the ruling political party may take away that freedom of the media and also may impose restriction on people's right to choose the newspaper that they want to purchase and read. Media freedom does appear to be highly correlated with political openness, economic efficiency and development (Stiglitz, 2002; Islam, 2002a).

Political openness in a country after many years of foreign rule or the suppression of political freedom may unleash a previously pent-up demand for autonomy of various groups on the basis of ethnicity, religion, caste and so on through the creation of their separate political identities. As Huntington (1968) observed, such demands by ethnic groups can contribute to a political instability and seriously undermine the existence of the country as a unified and organic whole. Dawson's (1998) study which found that economic openness by promoting the role of the free market in a country and protection of property rights leads to progress and political openness also lends a strong support to Friedman's (1962) assertion that one kind of openness tends to promote the other. Unfortunately however, as Barro (1997) suggests and as we find it in India too, a high level of political openness in the early stage of a country's development process significantly retards its economic growth because so much political openness makes different income and social groups and other vested interest groups exert pressure on the government to undertake measures to redistribute income rather than to promote economic growth. This income redistribution is exactly what Nehru embarked on achieving in the very early stage of India's economic development in the Second Five Year Plan (GOI, 1957), instead of putting in place measures to achieve a high rate of economic growth. The other interesting result of Barro's study, which also demonstrated the presence of a positive relationship between political openness and prior levels of national income, implies that if the country has a record of achieving higher levels of economic growth and prosperity, then this record tends to promote political openness. The implication of Barro's study is not valid for India, which had an extremely poor record of a low level of economic growth throughout the Nehru and Indira Gandhi regimes but a high level of political openness during Nehru's era, which lasted for 14 years. In contrast, the results of Barro's study do seem to have some validity for China, which maintained a very high rate of economic growth since the early 1980s; subsequently it would appear that China has marginally lifted the restrictions on political openness.

Political Openness's Relationship with Per Capita Income Growth and Human Development

It is generally contended that while political openness tends to be increased by democratic governance and curtailed by autocratic governance, no definite answer from empirical studies seems to emerge to the question: Do political openness and democracy promote or hinder economic growth? On the other hand, on the issue of the impact of a high level of ethnic diversity as found in India on economic growth, one study (Easterly and Levine, 1987) found that the most important reason for very slow rate of economic growth was a high level of ethnic diversity, but Collier and Hoeffler (1999) suggest that while the growth-reducing effect of ethnic diversity tends to depend on the political system, the autocratic or repressive governance regime may not necessarily generate a higher rate of economic growth than the political openness and democratic governance regime, although democracies may not always seem to have a positive influence on growth.

However, the underground economy, graft, the largesse of the government to its vested interest groups, transfer activities and many forms of corrupt practices which undermine a country's capacity to achieve a high rate of growth seem to be more pervasive in a country with full political openness and democratic governance than in a politically closed country with an autocratic governance. The fact that in an autocracy with one centre of power, important economic decisions can be made and implemented far more rapidly than in a politically open and democratically governed country with many political parties, many provinces and many centres of power can be testified by the experiences of China and of countries in East Asia which achieved consistently high rates of growth in per capita income under politically repressive, authoritarian governance regimes as well as semi-politically repressive, partially democratic governance regimes. These governments completely dismantled all forms of labour market rigidities and introduced economic openness in their countries on a scale not attempted by the politically open and highly decentralized democratic governance regimes in India. Although in recent years considerable restrictions have been placed on economic openness in China, the scale of economic openness is still far greater in China than in India. This has driven the Chinese state, market and society to engage more in wealth creation than in transfer activities. In South Korea, Taiwan and China, economic progress and wealth creation under repressive political regimes and one party rule were achieved primarily by investment expenditures in the production of physical goods.

Gandhi placed strong emphasis on the production of physical goods as the most important means of making progress in India's development (Narayan, 1962; Roy, 1986). In China, although black market activities are present, wealth creation activities take precedence over transfer activities. On the other hand, in India political openness and the democratic governance regime have invited political turmoil, corruption, labour unrest, trade union militancy, and a rise in black market income comprising in the early 1990s 18 to 21 per cent of GDP and in 2010 amounting to US$1.6 trillion (Venkateswara, 2010). These problems have encouraged consumption expenditures taking precedence over investment expenditures for the production of physical goods and other wealth-creation activities (Nelson and Singh, 1998).

Although the rate of growth in per capita income is influenced by growth-promoting economic policies and a conducive institutional environment, the size of the per capita income is influenced by the size of the country's population. China and the countries in East Asia have been able to achieve success in all the above areas under autocratic regimes and one-party rule, whereas India's failure to implement adequate growth-promoting measures and measures to reduce population growth due to its institutional rigidities prevented the country from achieving a higher rate of growth in per capita income.

In Table 8.1 we present the growth in per capita income of China, India and the East Asian countries since 1999–2000. As the table shows, the growth in per capita income in India was considerably lower than in China and in other East Asian countries except Japan and Taiwan in 1999–2000. But since 2002–03 the rate of growth in per capita income began to increase in India although this rate was lower than that in China. The other interesting points to be noted here are that from 2000–01 onwards, the other fairly democratic countries (Japan, Korea, Malaysia and Taiwan) have generally recorded lower growth rates than Singapore and China and that India has consistently achieved a higher rate of growth than Korea, Malaysia, Japan, Singapore and Taiwan.

Table 8.1 Average annual growth rate in income per capita

	China	India	Japan	Korea	Malaysia	Singapore	Taiwan
1999–2000	7.3	3.9	1.7	7.8	6.0	8.1	2.1
2000–01	6.5	2.7	−0.6	2.3	−1.8	n.a.	−3.4
2002–03	8.4	6.4	2.7	2.4	3.2	−1.0	2.4
2003–04	8.8	5.4	2.5	4.1	5.2	6.3	3.3
2004–05	9.2	7.1	2.6	3.5	3.4	3.7	1.2
2005–06	10.1	7.7	2.4	4.7	4.2	6.6	3.0
2007–08	8.4	5.7	−0.7	1.9	2.9	−4.1	−6.4
2008–09	8.5	6.2	−5.1	−0.1	−3.3	−4.2	n.a.

Sources:
World Bank (2002), *World Development Report*, Washington, DC: World Bank, pp. 232–233.
World Bank (2003), *World Development Report*, Washington, DC: World Bank, pp. 234–235.
World Bank (2005), *World Development Report*, Washington, DC: World Bank, pp. 256–257.
World Bank (2006), *World Development Report*, Washington, DC: World Bank, pp. 292–293.
World Bank (2007), *World Development Report*, Washington, DC: World Bank, pp. 288–289.
World Bank (2008), *World Development Report*, Washington, DC: World Bank, pp. 334–335.
World Bank (2010), *World Development Report*, Washington, DC: World Bank, pp. 378–379.
World Bank (2011), *World Development Indicators*, Washington, DC: World Bank, pp. 344–345.
CEPD (2009), *Taiwan Statistical Data Book 2009*, Taipei: CEPD, p. 56.

The spirit of nationalism which helped the Chinese people to devote their time to wealth-creating activities rather than in other kinds of non-economic pursuits was able to be inculcated in people's minds more easily than in India because: (i) the authoritarian regime suppressed all kinds of political openness in the unitary state and glorified the pursuit of wealth creation for citizens to become wealthy; (ii) the Chinese people had also been under the imperial rule for 2,100 years without any significant political openness; and (iii) the homogeneity of language, low level of ethnic diversity and cultural conditioning promoted savings and investment expenditures well above consumption expenditures at the household and national levels.

While the current literature on the impact of political openness on the economy has concentrated mostly on the impact of political openness on economic growth, growth must translate to economic development, which must also translate to human development, which must be the end product of economic growth. However, since the most fundamental requirement for achieving human development, as Gandhi observed (Narayan, 1962; Schumacher, 1962; Roy, 1986), is to keep a country's labour force fully employed by paying decent wages, it can be said by following Gandhi that in a country such as China which has been able to achieve the status of the world's largest manufacturing goods' exporting country by keeping the labour cost per dollar worth of output at the lowest possible level, the economic growth has not been able to be translated to human development as the labour force has to bear the inordinate burden of reduction of the average cost of production per unit of output. To Gandhi, the value of an industry should be gauged less by the dividends it pays to its sleeping shareholders than by its effect on the bodies, souls and spirits of people employed in it.

In accordance with the dictum of Western economics, if a low-cost producer replaces a high-cost producer, that replacement becomes beneficial to the consumer as consumers of this output produced at a lower cost and consequently at a lower price enjoy a higher consumer surplus. However, if we accept the concept of opportunity cost as the socially relevant cost, then for the 'high-cost' producer with no opportunity to engage in alternative production, the opportunity cost of this producer's labour is zero. Hence, by accepting the Gandhian view that for achieving human development, it is essential for producers to pay a decent wage to labourers, the production of goods in a low-cost production unit can be justified then only if non-labour costs of the low-cost producer appear to be lower than non-labour costs of the high-cost producer who is being sought to be displaced (Schumacher, 1962). Such an ideology of Gandhi and Schumacher has far-reaching implications for the regeneration of the manufacturing sectors in most developed and developing countries which have witnessed the decimation of that industrial sector and the unemployment of labour continuously ballooning to higher levels in absolute numbers and in percentage terms under globalization.

For this ideology to work, therefore, domestic consumers will have to buy consumer goods produced by domestic industries at a per unit cost of an output higher than that of an imported product from countries which have kept the per unit price of their product very low. Furthermore, some form of protection needs to be provided to domestically produced import substitutes.

In countries exporting consumer goods successfully to the rest of the world, not only do employed workers receiving very low rate of wage fail to achieve the level of development that they deserve, but also the rate of unemployment of labourers may continue to rise. Political openness is necessary to make the state and industry leaders listen to and work on people's demands for better wages and full employment. Hence, for economic growth to be able to contribute significantly to economic and human development in a country, economic openness has to be combined with political openness in a robust way.

Under economic openness, the state intervention in the free market has to be justified by an economic rationale such as the need for provision of neutral incentives to trade regimes and for the correction of market failure resulting from the presence of imported capital market, problems of appropriability and the presence of favourable externalities.

INDIA: THE CHALLENGES OF POLITICAL OPENNESS TO ECONOMIC OPENNESS

During British rule, while political openness did not exist, economic openness did exist in India, although in a contrived form to further the economic interests of Britain more than those of India (Roy, 1988). Nevertheless, throughout British rule, laissez-faire economic policies in general were present in India. However, economic openness continued to be present in India up to the end of the First Five Year Plan on 31 March 1956. The political freedom or 'Swaraj', which along with the productive employment of millions of poor labourers at a decent wage formed Gandhi's quintessential preconditions to human development, was granted to Indians on 15 August 1947. Nehru's adoption in India of the centralized planning of the Soviet type for India's economic development in the Second Five Year Plan which commenced on 1 April 1957 heralded the beginning of a long period of state intervention in economic openness by the imposition of a comprehensive Quantitative Restriction (QR) regime consisting of industrial licensing, a high level of tariffs on the import of goods and services, import quotas on certain items of goods, the outright ban of the import of certain goods, controls on the use of foreign exchange and the maintenance of an overvalued exchange rate to enforce detailed controls over manufactured goods and also to enable the state to produce all kinds of manufactured goods under the Import-Substituting Industrialization

(ISI) strategy, thereby raising the share of the public sector in total investment significantly above that of the private sector and severely restricting India's openness to the rest of the world in trade, foreign direct investment inflow, technology acquisition and so on (Bhagwati and Desai, 1971; Lal, 1988; Bardhan, 1984; Rudolph and Rudolph, 1987; Encarnation, 1990; Kohli, 2004; Meier and Rauch, 2005; Cypher and Dietz, 2009; Chai and Roy, 2006; Clark and Roy, 1997).

These restrictions imposed on economic openness in 1957 under Nehru's leadership led to a continuous rise in the size of the bureaucracy to oversee the operation of industrial licensing, the import control and foreign exchange control regimes, and the concomitant rise in contacts among industrialists, bureaucrats and ministers in charge of various government departments. This led to growing corruption, bribery and the payment of government largesse to favoured companies. Since the suppression of economic freedom in India could only have been instituted with Nehru's permission, it would be wrong to support Rudolph and Rudolph's (1987) view that the erosion of state institutions began after the death of Nehru.

In contrast, we tend to agree with the view of Cypher and Dietz (2009) that it was the nature of the political process and the privileged access that some groups (North's vested interests) have had on the Indian state's decision making that created a barrier to the desired reduction in intervention in economic openness in the country. During Indira Gandhi's regime, the suppression of economic freedom continued also with the suppression of political freedom during the 1975–76 national emergency. Although during Rajib Gandhi's tenure as the Prime Minister of the country, restrictions on economic openness began to be slowly relaxed, it was Narashima Rao who with the help of his Finance Minister Manmohan Singh lifted major restrictions on economic openness and implemented broad measures of economic reform in July 1991. The Bajpayee government undertook some measures to lift further restrictions on economic openness, but uncontrolled political freedom and ineffective governments (at the federal and provincial levels) captured by elites (vested interest groups) from the powerful landowning and industrialist classes failed to direct economic policies towards creating greater wealth for the country and protecting consumers' interests (Bardhan, 1984; Colander, 1984; Evans, 1995).

The following questions need to be answered here:

1. Why did the economic openness in India fail to match economic openness in China and East Asia?
2. What institutional advantages made it possible for the economic reform measures to be implemented by Rajib Gandhi in the 1980s, Narashima Rao in late 1991 and Bajpayee in the late 1990s?

3. Can political and economic openness in full measure co-exist in a virtuous relationship to deliver a high rate of economic growth and human development in India?

It has to be noted here that very rarely has a sound economic policy been implemented in India unless that policy favoured the political interests of the party in power at the federal level. In a multi-party coalition government, even if a good economic policy may achieve in the long run political gains for most parties in the coalition, it may still not be implemented if in the short term the implementation of the policy may have a chance of creating a backlash against the regional political parties in the coalition. Hence, the maintenance of the status quo in improving economic openness has been the objective that governments at the federal level and even at the provincial levels have followed.

Institutional Barriers to Economic Openness

The reasons as to why India failed to undertake any more substantive measures of economic openness by the relaxation of rules to allow foreign investment in the banking and financial sector, agricultural sector, infrastructure development, tourism, civil aviation, manufacturing and education sectors are mostly political and can be found in the adverse institutional environmentalities that have accompanied India at the time and in the aftermath of her independence from the British rule. In particular, four important adverse institutional factors are:

1. the partition of the country;
2. the Indian Constitution;
3. the rise of the 'Nehru Dynasty'; and
4. the weakness of Indian nationalism.

The partition of the country
The first adverse institutional factor was the partition of India and the breakup of a unified subcontinent into three parts – which would not have happened if Nehru refused to accept it. Then in 1971, Indira Gandhi's government in a military engagement against Pakistan drove the Pakistan government out of East Pakistan (the former eastern part of undivided Bengal Province) and contributed to the birth of a new nation called Bangladesh. While Bangladesh received enormous financial and political help from the rest of the world, West Bengal Province, which suffered twice from two partitions (1947, 1971), received very little financial help from the Indian government and from the rest of the world to recover from the after-effects of the two partitions. This kind of discriminatory treatment meted out by the federal government to

Bengal and other provinces made their allegiance to the federal government very weak indeed.

An economically, politically and militarily strong unified country would have been able to create a supply chain of dedicated, effective and young leaders ready to take on the reins of the government. Consequently, the partition undermined the opportunity for the development of effective leadership for the nation.

Furthermore, if the partition had not occurred, there would have been two major political parties in the country – the Congress and the Muslim League. All other political parties excluding the Bharatiya Janata Party (BJP) but including the Communist Party would not have been able to gain political strength in the country. In this two-party system of parliamentary democracy, both parties would have been politically strong, and the government would have been forced to undertake measures to improve the economic and social condition of the country's population. Also, such a representative government would have been able to draw valuable lessons from the British democracy.

The Indian Constitution

The Indian Constitution is an exhaustively written Constitution (Majumdar et al., 2009). Any amendment to the Constitutions as specified by the Eighth Amendment of Indian Constitution Act of 1966 requires a bill to that effect to be passed by a majority vote in both houses of the Parliament and also by a majority of legislatures of provinces. However, as the existing provinces are being broken up to create more provinces by the Indian Parliament, getting the required majority of provincial legislatures to ratify the bill for an amendment of the Constitution is becoming increasingly difficult to achieve.

While the Sixth Constitutional Amendment Act of 1963 authorized provinces to impose restrictions on the exercise of fundamental rights to preserve the integrity of the country, such restrictions have rarely been imposed by the provincial governments, although the uncontrolled exercise of freedom of expression and action caused significant hardship to the civil society and damage to state-owned and privately-owned properties.

Since the power to create and exercise control over police forces and to create an unlimited number of trade unions has been bestowed on provincial governments, the neutrality of the police force has been lost and its capacity to implement the decisions of the judiciary has been greatly impaired. The rampant growth of trade unions and of political parties to which these unions belong has caused enormous disruption to industrial and business activities because of their support for strikes, *bandhs* and so on. Furthermore, the judiciary has been made subservient to the dictates of the Parliament. Also the Constitution did not specify the maximum number of terms a person can be elected to the federal parliament and provincial legislatures as well as the maximum number of terms an elected person can hold the position of a minister. The lack of a clear provision on these matters has enabled the same person to be elected and even to be a minister until their death. Consequently, the supply of new leaders has been extremely limited.

The 'Nehru Dynasty'

The rule of Nehru's Dynasty began in 1951 and has continued in both politically visible and invisible ways up to the current (2009–14) government of Manmohan Singh with the exception of the Janata government and BJP-led government lasting for a period of seven years. However, it was Indira Gandhi who, after assuming power, entertained the growth of rapacious sycophants who formed her vested interest group which helped her to break up the original Congress party into two groups, thereby weakening the inner strength of the party. Moreover, with the help of these followers, she began to incapacitate the formal institutions of good governance. The primary job of these sycophants, who hold responsible positions in the Congress party's administrative body and in ministries, is to keep the dynasty in power by propping up a new leader of the dynasty even before the current dynastic head contemplates making such a move and by actively canvassing for the proposed leader so that, when the new leader leads the government, their sycophancy will be rewarded.

The presence of such a dynastic rule, which is anathema in a parliamentary democracy, has prevented the growth of young, intelligent and vibrant leaders outside the dynasty to take on the reins of government. Also in the current situation since the paramount leader of the Congress party as well as the current dynastic leader of the family does not hold the position of the Prime Minister, the current Prime Minister does not possess effective power to implement new measures of economic openness.

A limited spirit of nationalism

The spirit of nationalism which can be invoked relatively easily to unite people to work for achieving the country's developmental goals is promoted by the presence of a homogenous language. In India, except for English, which was disbanded as the official language after 15 years of the adoption of the Indian Constitution, there is no other language which is accepted in all provinces as the national language. Hindi, which was accepted as the official language with the support of a President who hailed from Hindi-speaking Bihar Province, is still not customarily accepted in Southern and Eastern India as the official language.

The repeated failure of the federal government to deal effectively with the activities of foreign terrorists on Indian soil has certainly dented people's faith in the capability of successive governments to govern the country and also has weakened the capability of the federal government to increase the level of economic openness in the country by making provinces with considerable sovereign status accept economic openness to accelerate the rate of economic growth and development.

Reforms Promoting Economic Openness

Beginning in the 1980s, India moved toward greater economic openness, although often reform attempts were not particularly successful. Here, we briefly describe three such reform efforts: Rajib Gandhi's reforms in the mid-1980s; P.V. Narasimha Rao's major reorientation of India's economic policy in the early 1990s; and Manmohan Singh's inability to continue the reform process after becoming Prime Minister in 2004.

Rajib Gandhi's reforms for economic openness

The important political advantages that Rajib had became apparent after he won the national election in 1984 following the assassination of his mother in a landslide. He was young and was attached more to his friends and other young advisers than to those sycophants who also surrounded him, but failed to exercise the same baneful influence on him as they did on his mother's decision making process (Meier and Rauch, 2005; Varshney, 1999; Haggard and Web, 1994).

The other political advantages for Rajib (of which most commentators fail to take note) were that the Marxist Communist Party, while engaged in the methodical destruction of Bengal's and Kerala's economy, had no influence on national policies; and the breakup of existing provinces with the attendant rise of new political parties and trade unions was absent. Measures of Rajib's economic openness which were pro-growth, pro-business and pro-export included: (i) the abolition of restrictions on the import of capital and intermediate goods at a substantially diminished rate of tariff; (ii) the reduction in taxes on the income of exporters; (iii) the reduction in the number of industries requiring capacity expansion licences from the government; (iv) the elimination of price controls on industrial inputs; and (v) the reduction in subsidies and taxes on the supply of food, fertilizer and fuels such as kerosene.

Rao's promotion of economic openness

The relaxation of restrictions on capital goods imports would have been a factor which contributed to a significant rise in the payment in foreign exchange for the import of capital goods accounting for 3 per cent of GDP and more than 25 per cent of export income by the end of the 1980s (Meier and Rauch, 2005). Those compelling economic circumstances for carrying forward the policy of Rajib's economic openness included the following:

1.   the decline in export income and rise in adverse balance of payment;

2. the decline in remittance of Indian workers from the Middle East due to the Gulf War of 1990;
3. the rise in India's oil import bill resulting from a rise in the price of oil;
4. the unforeseen and non-budget foreign exchange cost of repatriation of workers from the Middle East; and
5. the alarming decline in foreign exchange reserves resulting also from importers bringing forward their import payments and exporters keeping their earnings overseas until the rupee was devalued (Teja, 1992; Chai and Roy, 2006).

Apart from the removal of the industrial licensing and the quantitative restriction regime, Rao's major economic openness reforms included: attempts to limit the growth of money supply; reduction in budget deficit; reduction in subsidies to limit claims on resources for social expenditures in excess of the government's revenue; automatic approval for foreign direct investment as joint ventures for allowing foreign companies to hold 51 per cent of the equity; automatic approval of licensing for acquiring foreign technology; and reduction in the scope of state monopolies and the privatization of loss-making PSEs.

But how could his minority government implement such major economic reform measures? Here, Echeverri-Gent's (1998) observation that because Rao's government was so weak, it could become very strong, tends to explain only one of those political factors encouraging Rao's government to implement some important reform measures. Indeed, several other factors seem to be important as well. Rao's relationship with the head of the Gandhi Dynasty was quite tenuous. Hence, his chances of becoming Prime Minister again after the next national election were bleak, and he did not want to be involved in politics again. Furthermore, Manmohan Singh joined Rao's ministry as a nominated member from the upper house of the Parliament. So, Singh did not have to face the electorate in the next election. Therefore Rao and Singh had very little to lose, if these reform measures were not well accepted by the Indian society.

Subsequently, since Bajpayee's BJP-led coalition government, which assured political power in the next national election, was also in a politically weak position and its chance of returning to the seat of power again was bleak, it could continue to implement such new measures of economic openness as the removal of licensing restrictions for capacity expansion in fossil-fuel, pharmaceutical and other industries, as well as support for the expansion of the information technology industry and the introduction of competition into telecommunication and other state run semi-monopolies and so on.

Singh's failure to push economic openness forward
However, Manmohan Singh's Congress-led united front government of 2004–09 and his current Congress-led united progressive alliance government have

not been able to achieve any major success in economic openness, although Manmohan Singh is well supported by the head of the Gandhi Dynasty. He would be quite aware of the facts that after the next national election in 2014 he is most likely to be replaced by Rajib's son, the Dynasty's youngest member, and that sycophants are already working towards making this a reality. Singh also would be well over 80 years old at that time.

However, his current regime has been good at making announcements of large investments in infrastructure, particularly on roads, transport and other communications facilitating the entry of FDI in multi-brand retail trade, and so on without following through on such announcements (Panagariya, 2008). The FDI flow to India, an indication of India's economic openness, which increased from US$17.5 billion in 2006 to US$41.2 billion in 2008, declined to US$34.6 billion in 2009 (World Bank 2008, 2010, 2011). The FDI and foreign exchange inflow to the country have not exhibited any robust trend in 2010 and 2011. Commentators do believe that Singh's problem lies within his government in which ministers follow their own agenda; the bureaucracy is not cohesive; and his decisions seem to be made for him by others. Nevertheless, India has always been and will always be a socially regulated economy. Accordingly, Indian society and private entrepreneurship will determine its growth and development-promoting efforts.

In contrast, economic openness does exist in India's informal economy consisting of the agricultural sector, the micro- and small-scale manufacturing sector and the micro service trade sector. There is imperfect competition in micro and small manufacturing firms in the informal economy, and the owner manager's profit can even be lower than their opportunity cost of employment; the employees' wages also might not even be higher than the wage of rural labour. This would imply that the exploitation of labour by employers may not be present in the informal sector. In the service trade sector, particularly for clothes, washing and ironing, house cleaning, cooking and discharging other household chores, the demand for labour has been continuously rising as the number of households in the middle income group continues to rise. Migrants from India's rural sector and illegal migrants from neighbouring countries fill vacancies in the informal sector job market. Since this informal sector accounts for the largest proportion of India's total population, the nature of economic openness in India does tend to differ from the nature of economic openness in China and East Asia.

Political Freedom and Its Effects In India

In India, political openness has preceded economic openness. The level of political freedom that Indian citizens enjoy is probably the highest among all developing countries as no restriction has been placed on political freedom.

This has led to the misuse of political freedom by different sections of the community resulting in the loss of political freedom of other sections of the community. For example, in India rallies and processions, strikes and *bandhs* (total shutdowns), organized by political parties and their affiliated trade unions to uphold workers' freedom to protest against any issue, have also led to disruption to business and industrial activities, disruption to traffic and destruction of private property, all of which have contributed significantly to the loss of political freedom for a vast proportion of citizens of India. Political freedom in India, therefore, has been treated as a pure public good possessing these two features: non-rival and non-exclusive in consumption. Currently, because it is available for free, it is overused and misused.

Hence, if one wants to demonstrate this situation in a diagram, the supply curve of political openness would be horizontal and be represented by the X-axis. The social demand for political openness and political freedom can be represented by a downward-sloping curve which would intersect the supply curve at the X-axis at the point of the potential supply of political openness and freedom. Hence, the equilibrium price for each individual for the consumption of political openness and freedom would be zero. Therefore, the supply curve for political openness and freedom is needed to be made at least marginally inelastic so that Indians would still enjoy a high level of political openness and freedom by paying a price which consists of strict enforcement of rules governing the use of political openness including measures to make the mis-user of the political openness pay for the damage if they have caused damage to the victim's fundamental rights as a free individual. Since Indians will never give up their political freedom, some restraint will have to be placed on the uncontrolled use of political freedom which has hampered India's growth and development outcomes. For this objective to be realized, the current Constitution will have to be scrapped; a new Constitution will have to be adopted and a two-party system of parliamentary democracy with two unions to be installed. This can be made possible by a bold president declaring emergency rule with the help of the military in the country for a limited period of time. But this is unlikely to happen in confederate India.

The level of political freedom that Indians enjoy can be seen from Table 8.2 which presents the indices of democracy in China and India. As columns 7 and 3 of the table show, in civil liberties and electoral process, India's score is just below the perfect score of 10. Although in political culture, both countries recorded the same score of 6.25, India's score after the completion of electoral process in five provinces in 2011 would have gone up considerably due to people's determination to cast their votes freely irrespective of the possibility of being subjected to physical violence by cadres of the ruling political party in several of these provinces. Among 167 countries, India's rank of 35 in level of democracy is well above the ranks of almost all developing countries and

Table 8.2   Indices of democracy in China and India

	Overall score	Overall rank	Electoral process	Government functioning	Political participation	Political culture	Civil liberties	Regime type
	1	**2**	**3**	**4**	**5**	**6**	**7**	**8**
China, 2009	3.04	136	0.00	5.00	2.78	6.25	1.18	Authoritarian
India, 2008	7.8	35	9.58	8.21	5.56	6.25	9.41	Flawed Democracy

Notes:
Overall and component scores are on a scale of 0 to 10;
Overall rank is out of 167 countries.

Sources:
Economic Intelligence Unit (2008b), *Country Profile*, India, London: EIU, p. 8.
Economic Intelligence Unit (2009), *Country Profile*, China, London: EIU, p. 9.

is better than the ranks recorded by the East European countries. This rank would place India among the Western European and North American developed countries.

CHINA: PROMOTING ECONOMIC OPENNESS BY AN AUTHORITARIAN REGIME, BUT STILL CONTINUED PROBLEMS WITH AUTHORITARIAN RENT SEEKING

China in many ways presents a direct contrast to India. It has remained a highly authoritarian governance regime, while being very successful at promoting economic openness over the last three decades. The China–India comparison, therefore, provides some support for the argument dating back to Samuel Huntington's classic *Political Order in Changing Societies* (1968) that too much political openness can overwhelm a nation, thereby undermining attempts to pursue such goals as economic development and openness. In addition, despite its progress on economic openness, China clearly has had a successful development state, but the authoritarian government has also promoted serious rent seeking activities, suggesting that more political openness might be desirable to limit the abuse of power by the government.

The Success of Pursuing Economic Openness Before Political Openness

The Chinese state after the communist revolution in 1949 began to function as a totalitarian state which had the following four fundamental features:

1. one-party government;
2. complete subservience of citizens to the state;
3. total absence of political openness which consisted of freedom of speech, movement, assembly of citizens and freedom of media and the press; and
4. closure to the outside world economically and politically.

The state since the economic reform began in 1978 has gradually discarded its totalitarian characteristics and has functioned as an autocratic state still favouring strict obedience of citizens to the government. However, the economic openness since 1978, by increasing the inward flow of foreign direct investment and China's trade with the rest of the world, pushed up China's rate of economic growth and increased the interaction of the Chinese state and the society with the outside world. This interaction and the internet revolution have weakened to some extent the capacity of the government to maintain the total repression of political openness in China. Most certainly, by adopting the policy of economic openness first and keeping political openness suppressed, the Chinese government has been able to achieve a phenomenal rate of economic growth for a period of three decades since 1980 and to greatly enhance China's economic as well as political and military power.

The authoritarian regime with one-party rule has been able to remove without any opposition all institutional hindrances such as trade union militancy, limitations on factory hours, regulated labour wage and labour hours, infrastructure bottlenecks and so on to achieve a high rate of economic growth. Investment decisions on any project have been taken without any delay; and once a decision is made, the time lag between the finalization of the decision and the commencement of the work on the project is generally short. Since the Chinese state is a unitary state, any law, policy and measure formulated by the government in Beijing to deal with economic, social and environmental development or a disaster such as an earthquake, flood, rail accident and so on can be implemented immediately throughout the country. This cannot happen in confederate India. Since top leaders such as the President and Prime Minister can hold their respective positions for a maximum of two terms, such fixed terms allow top leaders to utilize their terms in office to serve their country best. Furthermore, the top positions of government are regularly filled with new and younger leaders with new ideas. However, the success of the government in achieving such a high rate of economic growth has also been made possible by the presence of efficient and agile bureaucrats and technocrats. If China had allowed political openness first, there would have been more than one political party, democratic government, free press and public action against the government on any issue or project which the society felt did not serve its interest. Also an opposition party could oppose any action of the government even if it were good for the country, just to discredit the government.

An effective developmental state

Despite its very wide-ranging reforms for economic openness, China also developed an effective developmental state. The state played a major role in guiding the country's process of industrialization. Chinese SOEs producing and exporting all kinds of manufactured goods received preferential treatment in the allocation of bank credit at subsidized interest rates in the acquisition of foreign technology, the payment of subsidies to keep the price of products on export markets well below the per unit cost of production and so on. The enforcement of a domestic content requirement rule on foreign firms entering the Chinese market to produce and export their products to their home country markets and to sell their products at local markets has increased the domestic production of components of final goods and prevented these firms from sourcing components of the best quality from the international markets.

The Central Bank of China manages the bank rate and also exercises its control over the fluctuation in the price of yuan in international markets. Restrictions on the import trade continue to be maintained by the state.

Nature has endowed China with 28 of the 52 most valuable mineral elements which are necessary for maintaining robust economic growth and development in both developed and emerging developing countries. Compared with China, the size and diversity of mineral resources in India is quite small. While the autocratic government in China can undertake exploration activities any time, anywhere in the country, the government of India is unable to take such action because there are multi-party democratic governments at the federal and provincial levels.

Authoritarian support for rent seeking

While the authoritarian government very probably benefited from a lack of political openness when it implemented its economic openness reforms, it also used the lack of the 'checks-and-balances' normally supplied by political openness to engage in a variety of rent seeking activities. For example, the provision of incentives to state-owned industries by the autocratic government was not neutral in its effect, as such incentives were not accorded to private sector enterprises; also it is doubtful that such interventions to support SOEs could be justified by the presence of market failure, coordination failure or the emergence of pecuniary external economies.

Frequent and arbitrary changes to rules and regulations by local governments concerning business transactions involving both domestic and foreign firms have been making business rules and regulations more and more opaque. For every kind of transaction, money has to be paid to several layers of bureaucracy. For example, if a person residing outside Shanghai wants to travel to Shanghai by car to visit a relative, that person has to buy an entry permit and an exit permit for that visit because they are not a citizen of Shanghai. On the other hand, payments made by a person making frequent visits to Shanghai by car on business matters add to the total cost of operation of that business which increases the price of the product or service that business is making or delivering. Even in India such kind of transaction cost does not exist, although for the transportation of goods from one province to another at various checkpoints money is paid to checkpoint managers.

Some owners of small and medium-sized private companies, who due to a lack of credit from state-controlled banks at a low interest rate were forced to borrow at interest rates ranging between 60 and 70 per cent per annum from shadow financing institutions which operate outside normal banking channels, have committed suicide; others have left the country, keeping their companies heavily indebted (Lewis, 2011; Wei, 2011). The failure of the central government to control such unscrupulous practices of shadow lenders can greatly undermine the long-term sustainability of China's financial system. Such state intervention in economic openness based on political consideration cannot be justified by economic rationales.

The forcible seizure of land and homes to make way for the expansion of urban sprawl, industrial parks and housing complexes with virtually no compensation to landowners and homeowners, who overnight became homeless and destitute, and the selling of those lands to developers and industrial firms at a very high price by local governments in collusion with local police and real estate companies have led to violent protests by angry people in different parts of the country. The central government's attempts to standardize land acquisition laws have been routinely flouted by local authorities (Spegele, 2011; Jacobs, 2011).

The total number of homeless and landless people migrating to the outskirts of major cities may exceed 100 million by 2020. Without a resident permit for the respective cities, these families cannot access healthcare, low-cost education in good schools and pensions. Also, a large number (over 200 million) of China's floating workers without jobs would swell the number of people living as persona non grata at the outskirts of cities doing odd jobs. The wage rate of the internal migrant labour force varies between 500 and 1,000 yuan per month. These migrants live in extremely poor conditions and suffer from the deprivation of freedom to secure a decent income and from the deprivation of basic property rights (Sainsbury, 2011d). Since the informal economy in China is not as large and organized as in India, the condition of these migrants and homeless workers is worse than those who survive in India's informal economy operating within and outside all major cities.

Due to the absence of press freedom, civil liberty and judicial independence, public opinion and national awareness on these issues have not been able to be formed. Consequently, a genuine human development cannot be said to have been achieved in autocratic China. Furthermore, without political openness, the rate of innovation in China has remained considerably lower than in Japan and Western countries. This also is a factor which would have delayed the onset of China's industrialization (Chai, 2011). Although the contribution to India's export of high value-added manufactured goods is low, overall innovation is taking place in the industrial and service sector; and a high level of political openness is clearly a factor facilitating this drive of innovation. Without political openness, which provides citizens of a country with some basic human rights, economic openness alone cannot achieve genuine social and human development.

THE EAST ASIA EXPERIENCE: CONFIRMING THE NEED FOR 'BALANCE' IN EVALUATING POLITICAL AND ECONOMIC OPENNESS

The two detailed case studies of India and China that we have just presented suggest that the relationship between political openness and economic openness is far more complex than the view that they are mutually reinforcing elements of freedom and individualism. India's immediate democratization and a high level of political openness created considerable problems subsequently for implementing the reforms necessary to create the economic openness that was necessary for economic development. China, in sharp contrast, achieved economic openness under a strongly authoritarian regime. It would be premature, however, to conclude that political openness is necessarily bad or undesirable. In China, for example, the authoritarian government also used its power to harass some businesses and to allow the powerful to dispossess smallholders and the economically weak. This certainly reinforces the argument that we made in Chapter 6 that political openness is almost necessary if income growth is to be translated into real human development.

A second complexity concerns the very concept of economic openness itself, which is often associated with laissez-faire economics in general and export-led development strategies in particular. India's statist and inward-oriented economy is often used to explain why it long lacked the economic dynamism of China and the East Asian capitalist economies, and why its growth jumped noticeably after the reforms described above. Yet, despite its market-based reforms, the state in China continues to play a leading economic role. This re-emphasizes the points made in Chapter 7 that developmental states have been very important in Asian industrialization and that, indeed, almost all nations who have industrialized (including the self-proclaimed laissez-faire US) have needed supportive state policies to get new industries off the ground.

The capitalist East Asian nations certainly demonstrate that there is no single pattern of how economic and political openness are related, as discussed in Chapter 7. Japan has been a democracy (albeit one dominated by a single party) throughout the post-war era. It also had a highly skilled and powerful permanent technocracy with strong ties to the country's major business conglomerates (keiretsu) that was insulated from party politics and patronage. From the 1950s through to the 1980s, this system worked very well in designing and implementing effective economic policy (Calder, 1988; Johnson, 1982; Okimoto, 1989). Both the politicians and the technocrats failed, however, in responding to the economic crisis at the beginning of the 1990s (Alexander, 2003; Krauss and Pekkanen, 2011). Singapore also has one party that has dominated electoral politics since independence, although it scores substantially below Japan on many measures of political openness. It also has had an extremely successful developmental state that emphasized economic openness, especially to FDI, which has propelled it to one of the highest GDP per capitas in the world (Blomqvist, 2005; Rodan, 1989). Similarly, in Malaysia the same parties have generally run the government since independence. Because of ethnic issues in the country, the government has long pursued *both* economic development and redistributive policies to help the comparatively impoverished majority of Malays (Jomo et al., 1997; Rasiah, 1997).

South Korea and Taiwan followed a path that was different from Japan's and somewhat similar to China's, at least initially. Both had authoritarian regimes that persisted until the early 1990s and which proved quite successful in promoting industrialization and economic transformation under the leadership of a politically-insulated technocracy (Amsden, 1989; Clark and Tan, 2011; Wade, 1990; Woo, 1991). In addition, the two regimes were insulated from the business community in idiosyncratic ways that made them much less susceptible than normal to pressures to provide politically-sponsored rents. South Korea was ruled by a military regime for approximately 30 years (Hahm and Plein, 1997), and up until the early 1990s, Taiwan's government was dominated by Mainlanders who had come to the island with Chiang Kai-shek, while businesses were primarily run by Islanders who had come to Taiwan before the imposition of Japanese colonialism in 1895 (Wachman, 1994).

Taken together, the experiences of these seven Asian nations certainly indicate that the relationship between political and economic openness is quite complex. India shows a very unfortunate trade-off between the political openness required for human development and the economic openness necessary to increase the economic growth rate since the nation's high political openness has clearly limited its ability to implement economic reforms. Similarly, in Malaysia political openness has led to redistributive programmes that undercut economic performance. Looking at the other side of the coin, China, South Korea, Taiwan and Singapore all implemented developmental strategies based on economic openness in the sense of strong integration into the global economy that were facilitated by significant (Singapore) to extreme (China, South Korea and Taiwan) limits on political openness.

Still, it would be very rash to jump to the conclusion that political freedom and democracy should be limited to make economic progress possible for several reasons. First, Japan proved that democracy and a successful developmental state can go (and crash) together. Second, authoritarian China, South Korea and Taiwan, while having a decent record for respecting economic rights for extended periods of time, indulged in substantial violations of human rights. Third, economic development helped create social change and pressures leading to successful democratizations in South Korea and Taiwan as often occurs (Boix, 2011; Lipset, 1959), but rapid growth and industrialization have yet to have much of an impact on political openness in China. Finally, whatever the limitations on their economic reforms, the Malaysian and Indian economies have recorded substantial development and growth over sustained periods of time.

This certainly suggests that a balance needs to be maintained between political openness and economic openness. Furthermore, there also needs to be a balance between the various dimensions of economic openness. China and the other East Asian nations considered here have had remarkable success with export-led development strategies, which is often taken to denote economic openness. Yet economic openness also generally means laissez-faire economics, and, as detailed in Chapter 7, all of these nations had developmental states that explicitly rejected the laissez-faire philosophy. Such state intervention in economic openness was justified on the grounds of market failure which would have occurred due to the imperfection of capital markets, the problem of appropriability, the imperfect tradability of key inputs and pecuniary external economies which make the long run supply curve embodying Marshallian real externalities continue to fall. Such conditions which create coordination failure result in a rate of return to coordinated investments remaining high and that to non-coordinated single investments remaining low (Meier and Rauch, 2005). Hence, measures by the state appear to be well justified to remove distortions in the market created by particular economic policies and to coordinate and subsidize private investment via credit at a concessional rate of interest, the provision of a lower rate of tax on business profits and administrative guidance for investment by the public sector.

Hence, we have to conclude that since without political openness, genuine human development cannot be achieved, and since the ultimate objective of economic growth in a country is to enable its citizens to enjoy real happiness, some political freedom is necessary for economic openness to facilitate the realization of a country's economic growth and developmental goals. In addition, since China and these Asian countries have not adopted total economic openness and laissez-faire policy in the management of their economies, these nations will have to combine certain fundamental forms of political openness with economic openness to make their economic and social development sustainable.

9. Development and institutions in Asia: pertinent lessons

This book presents an analysis and interpretation of industrialization and development in Asia: in particular, India, China, Japan, Malaysia, Singapore, South Korea and Taiwan. These countries have been widely seen as economic success stories during the post-war era. Japan's 'economic miracle' commenced in the 1950s as it quickly regained its place among the developed nations after the devastation of World War II and challenged the United States for global economic leadership in the 1980s, although it has generally stagnated since its economic bubble burst in 1989. During the 1960s, Singapore, South Korea and Taiwan commenced rapid industrialization drives; China and Malaysia followed suit in the 1980s; and India has made considerable progress over the last two decades. An analysis of the Asian experience, therefore, should be quite instructive for understanding the dynamics of development in the contemporary world.

Most importantly, the rise of Asia strongly indicates that we need to look at development from a somewhat different perspective than the emphasis of traditional analyses. The 1980s witnessed the growth of a consensus among many development agencies and Western governments that development was best promoted by laissez-faire policies and limited government. This reflected the growing economic problems both in the communist command economies and in the many developing nations that had tried to promote import-substitution industrialization. This was ironic, however, because at the same time there was growing recognition of the rapid development that was occurring in many Asian countries with highly interventionist governments (Clark and Roy, 1997; World Bank, 1993).

This book has been organized around five themes that generally challenge the neoclassical orthodoxy. First, development does not occur within a purely economic laissez-faire vacuum. Rather, different economic fundamental structures or 'institutions' strongly shape economic activities and developmental outcomes (North, 1990). These economic institutions, in turn, are imbedded within a broader context of social and political institutions (Evans, 1995). This brings us to the second theme: that supportive governmental policies almost inevitably are necessary to promote development. Consequently, an important branch of political economy now emphasizes the 'developmental state' (Clark and Roy, 1997; Evans et al., 1985; Johnson, 1982). Third, the traditional emphasis on GDP growth and GDP per capita as the basic measures of development are overly simplistic as well. Rather, general quality of life and what has been called 'inclusive development' form the best criteria for evaluating developmental success.

The other two themes focus upon more specific questions than the overall nature of development. First, we put especial emphasis upon a comparison of India and China. Since these are the two countries in the analysis at the lowest levels of development, their current political economies involve the broadest range of development issues, including the all-important early stages of the developmental trajectory. Their economic strategies also differed quite markedly, giving rise to the question of why China's economic performance has generally surpassed India's over the last three decades. This leads us to the final question of the relationship between economic openness and political openness, on which India and China vary considerably. Theoretically, these two institutional characteristics should be compatible and even mutually reinforcing. Yet the contrasting cases of India and China show that this is not necessarily so in the 'real world', raising the question of what combination of economic openness and political openness is best for stimulating economic growth and human development.

Certainly, these Asian countries challenge the orthodoxy of laissez-faire economics that advocates reliance upon free markets, both domestically and internationally. While all except India have pursued export-led growth, all seven including India have had states that intervened aggressively in their economies. More broadly, this points to the importance of examining the 'institutions' that shape economic success. Why was statism successful in China and the East Asian capitalist nations, while it inhibited economic growth in India? Thus, we developed an institutionalist model based on governance regime, religion, culture and geography, and then applied it to explain the disparate economic strategies and outcomes among the Asian countries.

In contrast to laissez-faire economic models, government support for and promotion of industrialization and economic transformation have appeared necessary in almost all nations which have had much developmental success, including the self-proclaimed laissez-faire United States. This is because wide-ranging problems of 'market failure' inhibit the emergence of new industries. Yet, if state intervention is necessary for development, there is no guarantee that a government's economic policies will be successful. States may become 'predatory' by extracting resources from the economy and society, or may allow rent seeking activities by vested economic interests. Less maliciously, the state may target the wrong industries for development or rely upon ineffective incentives. Thus, paradoxically, many proponents of a developmental state argue that it should promote 'market conforming' industrial strategies (Clark and Roy, 1997; Evans, 1995; Wade, 1990).

This raises the question of what the institutional foundations of a successful developmental state are. This involves both the environment in which a state is embedded and the nature of the political governance regime itself. The external context for a regime includes the culture, especially religious practices, geography and its international situation, all of which can either support or hinder developmental activities. One key aspect of a nation's governance regime is whether it bases its legitimacy upon economic performance or the consent of the governed through democratic institutions. In terms of the structure or institutions of the government itself, a variety of factors appear to be crucial to creating and maintaining a successful developmental state. These include the commitment to development by the top political leadership, an independent and skilled bureaucracy and technocracy, government–business cooperation, policies that develop human capital, incentives for savings and investment, and land reform.

Our detailed analysis of development management in Asia is quite suggestive regarding the role of the state. For example, a clear distinction in agricultural policies is easy to discern. Japan, Taiwan, South Korea and post-Mao China all instituted fairly extensive land reforms. All these programmes proved to be quite successful, at least in the short term, for stimulating increased output, improving the rural standard of living, and generating resources to support these countries' industrialization drives. In contrast, the absence of reform and support for smallholder agriculture in India, Malaysia and Maoist China was associated with continuing economic problems.

The comparison between India and China in terms of industrial development is quite instructive as well. India and Maoist China pursued inward-looking strategies of import-substitution industrialization. While this produced significant industrial transformation, especially in China, the industries became increasingly inefficient and obsolete, and in India in particular rent seeking became pervasive. Under Deng Xiaoping, in stark contrast, China engaged in massive marketization reforms (although state corporations remained important in the economy), embarked on what turned out to be a hugely successful strategy of export-led growth and attracted massive amounts of foreign capital. Consequently, China has had considerably stronger growth over the last three decades, resulting in markedly lower poverty and better living conditions. Still, India has had good growth recently and (unlike China even today) has had a fully-functioning democracy since independence.

Another important question concerns whether China could have been so successful economically if it had had the same institutional context that India faced. In terms of political institutions, it is almost certain that China's economic performance would have suffered. The presence of those institutions in China would have created a highly decentralized, democratic governance system with a multi-party structure descending from the federal level right down to the village level. It would have made the process of decision making move very, very slowly. Many political parties in the name of expressing their freedom to demonstrate the will of the people probably would have contributed to the continuous disruption of economic activity. The objective of governance would have been simply to win elections and stay in power for the political party or the coalition of parties at the federal and the provincial level. Currently in India, there exist at least a dozen centrally controlled trade unions which are the apex organizations of many subordinate trade unions at the provincial levels. So, a significant restriction on labour wages would have been placed by these trade unions and also restrictions on factory hours. Once again, these would have significantly lowered the actual level of output that would have been achieved and also the prospect of increasing the level of employment in the country. Under these conditions, China's economic growth might have been even lower than India's growth rate, because apart from these institutional rigidities the greater political openness in China after a long period of political repression would have created the situation described by Huntington (1968). Many self-styled leaders would have created their own groups with the promise to help these people to satisfy their pent-up demand. Consequently, the country would have rapidly declined into a state of anarchy. In India's case, this anarchy has been absent because Indians have been exercising their political freedom for 62 years.

Rapid industrialization in the East Asian nations, furthermore, is widely credited to the policy leadership of their developmental states which, at least until the bursting of Japan's 'bubble economy' in the early 1990s, was generally seen as quite successful. These developmental states followed three very distinct patterns or strategies, though. In Japan and Korea, the government played a leading role in targeting huge corporate conglomerates as national champions with subsidies and protection from international competition. The role of the state in Taiwan, in contrast, focused more on creating a conducive economic environment in which small and medium-sized enterprises could thrive. In South-east Asia the emphasis of industrial policy was much more on attracting FDI, while there was less intervention in markets.

Another important factor is that first capitalist East Asia and then China were able to take advantage of the forces of globalization. In particular, starting in the 1960s, American and European industrialists extended the standardized production by the semi-skilled workers segment into the developing world in response to growing prosperity and rising wages in the West. Because of their traditional stress on education, the East Asian nations (including China) were very well positioned to enter the global manufacturing system and to climb up the product cycle quickly into increasingly sophisticated production activities (Clark and Roy, 1997). Furthermore, the increasing liberalization of the global financial system was vital to the expansion of both the corporate and consumer credit necessary for rapid economic growth. It is precisely these policies of the West and the United States that has enabled China to amass huge foreign exchange reserves which has greatly increased its global economic, political and military power.

In contrast to the generally good records of these Asian nations on growth over considerable periods of time, there are much more substantial variations among them in terms of poverty and inequality. 'Extreme poverty' is only a major problem in India and China with the situation being much worse in the former. In terms of 'multidimensional poverty' which includes deprivations suffered by individuals, households and larger groups in education, health, nutrition, liveable housing facilities, social inclusion and active participation in the political, social and economic decision making processes as well as income poverty, the situation is fairly similar as well. However, the ranking of the countries on income inequality is substantially different. Only Japan and Korea have fairly low levels of inequality. In contrast, Taiwan and India are at a medium level, while China, Malaysia and Singapore are fairly inequalitarian. Similar disparities exist with regard to education and empowerment, two key processes for promoting human development and reducing unfreedom. In terms of education, the records of the East Asian nations are generally good, especially after their development levels are taken into account, while India lags substantially behind. Two countries have poor records on empowerment in general: India because of its traditional customs and China because of its authoritarian governance regime. In contrast, only Japan and Singapore have decidedly low levels of corruption.

One key institutional feature of the Asian nations is their different sequences of promoting political openness and economic openness. Many analyses of the 'Third Wave' of democratization that commenced in the 1980s presumed that the political freedom and openness of the democracy went hand-in-hand with the economic freedom and openness of laissez-faire economics. Both, for instance, placed their prime emphasis on individual freedom and choice. Thus, there were predictions that the expansion of political freedom in the Third Wave would fuel greater economic openness, thereby producing faster growth and human development (Dawson, 1998; Friedman, 1962; Huntington, 1991). Yet a moment's thought would suggest that this virtuous cycle might be more than a little questionable. On the one hand, greater economic openness could concentrate resources in the hands of groups who could use them to distort the political processes; on the other, newly empowered groups could seek to enrich themselves through political rather than economic activities. Furthermore, even the very successful export-led development of many Asian nations, which might appear to be quintessential examples of 'economic openness', relied upon an important state role in the economy.

The two detailed case studies of India and China suggest that the relationship between political openness and economic openness is far more complex than the view that they are mutually reinforcing elements of freedom and individualism. India's immediate democratization and a high level of political openness created considerable problems subsequently for implementing the reforms necessary to create the economic openness that was necessary for economic development. China, in sharp contrast, achieved economic openness under a strongly authoritarian regime. It would be premature, however, to conclude that political openness is necessarily bad or undesirable. In China, for example, the authoritarian government also used its power to harass some businesses and to allow the powerful to dispossess smallholders and the economically weak. This certainly reinforces the argument that political openness is almost necessary if income growth is to be translated into real human development.

A second complexity concerns the very concept of economic openness itself, which is often associated with laissez-faire economics in general and export-led development strategies in particular. India's statist and inward-oriented economy is often used to explain why it long lacked the economic dynamism of China and the East Asian capitalist economies, and why its growth jumped noticeably after the reforms of the 1990s. Yet, despite its market-based reforms, the state in China continues to play a leading economic role.

The capitalist East Asian nations certainly demonstrate that there is no single pattern of how economic and political openness are related. Japan has been a democracy (albeit one dominated by a single party) throughout the post-war era. It also has had a highly skilled and powerful permanent technocracy with strong ties to the country's major business conglomerates (keiretsu) that was insulated from party politics and patronage. From the 1950s through to the 1980s, this system worked very well in designing and implementing effective economic policy (Calder, 1988; Johnson, 1982; Okimoto, 1989). Both the politicians and the technocrats failed, however, in responding to the economic crisis at the beginning of the 1990s (Alexander, 2003; Krauss and Pekkanen, 2011). Singapore also has one party that has dominated electoral politics since independence, although it scores substantially below Japan on many measures of political openness. It also has had an extremely successful developmental state that emphasized economic openness, especially to FDI, which has propelled it to one of the highest GDP per capitas in the world (Blomqvist, 2005; Rodan, 1989). Similarly, in Malaysia the same parties have generally run the government since independence. Because of ethnic issues in the country, the government has long pursued *both* economic development and redistributive policies to help the comparatively impoverished majority of Malays (Jomo et al., 1997; Rasiah, 1997).

South Korea and Taiwan followed a path that was different from Japan's and somewhat similar to China's, at least initially. Both had authoritarian regimes that persisted until the early 1990s and which proved quite successful in promoting industrialization and economic transformation under the leadership of a politically-insulated technocracy (Amsden, 1989; Clark and Tan, 2011; Wade, 1990; Woo, 1991). In addition, the two regimes were insulated from the business community in idiosyncratic ways that made them much less susceptible than normal to pressures to provide politically-sponsored rents. South Korea was ruled by a military regime for approximately 30 years (Hahm and Plein, 1997), and up until the early 1990s, Taiwan's government was dominated by Mainlanders who had come to the island with Chiang Kai-shek, while businesses were primarily run by Islanders who had come to Taiwan before the imposition of Japanese colonialism in 1895 (Wachman, 1994).

Taken together, the experiences of these seven Asian nations certainly indicate that the relationship between political and economic openness is quite complex. India shows a very unfortunate trade-off between the political openness required for human development and the economic openness necessary to increase the economic growth rate, since the nation's high political openness has clearly limited its ability to implement economic reforms. Similarly, in Malaysia political openness has led to redistributive programmes that undercut economic performance. Looking at the other side of the coin, China, South Korea, Taiwan and Singapore all implemented developmental strategies based on economic openness in the sense of strong integration into the global economy that were facilitated by significant (Singapore) to extreme (China, South Korea and Taiwan) limits on political openness.

Still, it would be very rash to jump to the conclusion that political freedom and democracy should be limited to make economic progress possible for several reasons. First, Japan proved that democracy and a successful developmental state can go (and crash) together. Second, authoritarian China, South Korea and Taiwan, while having a decent record for respecting economic rights for extended periods of time, indulged in substantial violations of human rights.

Third, economic development helped create social change and pressures leading to the successful democratizations in South Korea and Taiwan as often occurs (Boix, 2011; Lipset, 1959), but rapid growth and industrialization have yet to make much of an impact on political openness in China. Finally, whatever the limitations on their economic reforms, the Malaysian and Indian economies have recorded substantial development and growth over sustained periods of time.

This certainly suggests that a balance needs to be maintained between political openness and economic openness. Furthermore, there also needs to be a balance between the various dimensions of economic openness. China and the other East Asian nations considered here have had remarkable success with export-led development strategies, which is often taken to denote economic openness. Yet economic openness also generally means laissez-faire economics, and all of these nations had developmental states that explicitly rejected the laissez-faire philosophy. Such state intervention in economic openness was justified on the grounds of market failure which would have occurred due to the imperfection of capital markets, the problem of appropriability, the imperfect tradability of key inputs and pecuniary external economies which make the long run supply curve embodying Marshallian real externalities continue to fall. Such conditions which create coordination failure result in a rate of return to coordinated investments remaining high and that to non-coordinated single investments remaining low (Meier and Rauch, 2005). Hence, measures by the state appear to be well justified to remove distortions in the market created by particular economic policies and to coordinate and subsidize private investment via credit at a concessional rate of interest, the provision of a lower rate of tax on business profits and administrative guidance for investment by the public sector.

Hence, we have to conclude that since without political openness, genuine human development cannot be achieved, and since the ultimate objective of economic growth in a country is to enable its citizens to enjoy real happiness, some political freedom is necessary for economic openness to facilitate the realization of a country's economic growth and developmental goals. In addition, since China and these other Asian countries have not adopted total economic openness and laissez-faire policy in the management of their economies, these nations will have to combine certain fundamental forms of political openness with economic openness to make their economic and social development sustainable.

The problems involved here can be seen in intergovernmental relations in India. Currently, both centripetal and centrifugal forces seem to be gaining prominence in the centre-province relationship in India due to the habit of national octogenarian leaders making decisions without prior consultation with those provinces which are most likely to be affected adversely by such policies. Furthermore, the benefits of growth have not been directed in any perceptible way to most Eastern Indian provinces. In the federal American government, the national government consciously adopted a policy of distributing the gains of growth through the establishment of departments and industries (service and non-service) in all regions of the country for the creation of employment for the regional populations. In India, the benefits of the largesse of the confederate government have been directed mostly to the Northern, Western and Southern regions at the expense of the Eastern region. Consequently, the pervasive poverty and relative backwardness of the East has created a fertile ground for the growth of many splinter political parties including the Maoist Party and most importantly the Communist Party of India (Marxist). Thus on the one hand, the confederate government by its own action has been pushing provinces away from the centre; on the other hand, by varying the amount of government transfers to sovereign provinces and by many other ways, the government has been trying to pull the provinces towards the centre.

New investment and other growth-promoting and employment-generation activities tend to thrive in those regions which are already well developed. This has been found to be happening in India's Eastern region more prominently since 1991. Hence, the relatively underdeveloped provinces of confederate India are more forcefully exercising their sovereign rights to be consulted before the formulation and implementation of any policy which may not further their interests. In the UK, the USA and other Western democracies, considerable discussion and debate take place in public fora before the national government gets down to the task of formulating policies. This practice was disbanded in India after Nehru's death. Such frictions between the centre and provinces are a reflection of the relative immaturity of Indian democracy vis-à-vis the maturity of Western democracies. Proper education (almost universal) up to the higher secondary level for all citizens and employment generation for the vast majority of unemployed are the factors which can make India's democracy capable of achieving maturity and of catching up with China in the attainment of economic growth and developmental goals.

In contrast, the problem of a lack of political openness remains especially acute in China whose society has remained deprived of basic political freedom throughout the post-war era. But in such a country, citizens who have lived under unfreedom for decades will not be able to understand and appreciate the value of democracy and freedom, whereas those who enjoy freedom abundantly tend to misuse it as they will not know the value of it unless they lose it. This is the situation that prevails in India.

However, the movement for the removal of unfreedom which is gaining momentum in China will inevitably slow down the rate of economic growth. The independence movements in South Africa and in other African countries and the Arab Spring revolution which certainly drew inspiration from the resilience and vibrancy of Indian democracy also will inspire the Chinese citizens to demand their democratic rights and human freedom from the Chinese government. Therefore, in the twenty-first century, one would expect to see a perceptible change in China in the relationships among the state, society and the market which will continue to place greater emphasis on political openness and lesser emphasis on economic openness. This trend already began in South Korea and Taiwan during the 1990s. Similar change is also likely to occur in Singapore. One may in addition expect to see India becoming more integrated with East Asia in trade, investment, security and political alignments, and slowly gaining the strength to attain the status of the fourth economic super-power in the world. Surely, it will take a considerable time in India to finalize decisions on domestic and global matters involving economic, political and environmental issues because of the enormous interest of India's citizens in any national decision that is likely to affect their lives. But this is the reflection of the maturity and vibrancy of India's democracy.

References

Agarwal B. (1997), 'Bargaining and gender relations: Within and beyond the household', *Food Consumption and Nutrition Division, Discussion Paper, No. 27*, Washington, DC: Food Policy Research Institute.

Ahluwalia, M.S. (1974), 'Income inequality: Some dimensions of the problem', in H.B. Chenery, M.S. Ahluwalia, C.L.G. Bell, J.H. Duloy and R. Jolly (eds), *Redistribution with Growth*, London: Oxford University Press.

Ahluwalia, M.S., N.G. Carter and H.B. Chenery (1979), 'Growth and poverty in developing countries', *Journal of Development Economics*, 6, 299–341.

Akamatsu, K. (1961), 'A theory of unbalanced growth in the world economy', *Weltwirtschaftliches Archiv*, 86 (2), 196–215.

Akamatsu, K. (1962), 'A historical pattern of economic growth in developing countries', *The Developing Economies*, 1 (1), 3–25.

Ake, C. (1996), *Democracy and Development in Africa*, Washington, DC: Brookings Institution.

Alexander, A.J. (2003), *In the Shadow of the Miracle: The Japanese Economy Since the End of High-Speed Growth*, Lanham, MD: Lexington Books.

Amsden, A.H. (1989), *Asia's Next Giant: South Korea and Late Industrialization*, New York: Oxford University Press.

Ariff, M. (1991), *The Malaysian Economy: Pacific Connections*, Singapore: Oxford University Press.

Arrow, K.J. (1962), 'The economic implications of learning by doing', *Review of Economic Studies*, 29, 155–173.

Asian Development Bank (ADB) (1997), *Emerging Asia: Changes and Challenges*, Manila: Asian Development Bank.

Athukorala, P.-C. (2007), 'The rise of China and East Asian export performance: Is the crowding-out fear warranted?', Canberra: Australian National University, *Working Papers in Trade and Development*.

Athukorala, P.-C. and N. Yamashita (2005), 'Production fragmentation and trade integration: East Asia in a global context', Canberra: Australian National University, *Working Papers in Trade and Development*.

Ayyagari, M., A. Demirgiic-Kunt and V. Maksimovic (2006), 'Firm innovation in emerging markets: Role of governance and finance', Washington, DC: unpublished Working Paper, World Bank.

Backhouse, R. (1985), *A History of Modern Economic Analysis*, Oxford: Basil Blackwell.

Baker, K. and S. Jewitt (2007), 'Evaluating 35 years of Green Revolution technology in Indian villages of Bhulandshar District, Western UP, North India', *Journal of Development Studies*, 43, 312–329.

Balassa, B. (1971), 'Trade policies in developing countries', *American Economic Review*, Papers and Proceedings, 61, 178–187.

Balassa, B. (1981), *The Newly Industrializing Countries in the World Economy*, New York: Pergamon Press.

Balassa, B. (1991), *Economic Policies in the Pacific Area Developing Countries*, Basingstoke and London: Macmillan.

Banerjee, A. and A. Newman (1993), 'Occupational choice and the process of development', *Journal of Political Economy*, 101, 274–298.

Bank of International Settlements (2003), 'Fiscal issues and central banking in emerging economies', Basel: BIS, *BIS Papers*, No. 20.

Bardhan, P. (1984), *The Political Economy of Development in India*, Oxford: Basil Blackwell.

Bardhan, P.K. (1998), 'Corruption and development: A review of issues', *Journal of Economic Literature*, 36, 1320–1346.

Bardhan, P. (2010), *Awakening Giants – Feet of Clay; Assessing the Economic Rise of China and India*, Princeton: Princeton University Press.

Barkan, J.D. and N. N'gethe (1998), 'Kenya tries again', *Journal of Democracy*, 9 (2), 32–38.

Barro, R. (1997), *Determinants of Economic Growth*, Cambridge: MIT Press.

Basu, K. (2004), 'The Indian economy: Up to 1991 and since', in K. Basu (ed.), *India's Emerging Economy: Performance and Prospects in the 1990s and Beyond*, Cambridge: MIT Press.

Bates, R.H. (1981), *Markets and States in Tropical Africa: The Political Basis of Agricultural Policies*, Berkeley: University of California Press.

Bates, R.H. (1983), 'Governments and agricultural markets in Africa', in D.G. Johnson and D. Schuh (eds), *The Role of Markets in the World Food Economy*, Boulder, CO: Westview.

Batson, A. (2010), 'Inflation key to higher yuan', in *The Australian* (Brisbane), Nationwide News, p. 34.

Bauer, P.T. (1972), *Dissent on Development*, London: Weidenfeld and Nicholson.

Bauer, P.T. (1984), *Reality and Rhetoric: Studies in the Economies of Development*, London: Weidenfeld and Nicholson.

Becker, G.S. (1973), 'A theory of marriage: Part I', *Journal of Political Economy*, 81, 813–846.

Becker, G.S. (1974), 'A theory of marriage: Part 2', *Journal of Political Economy*, 82 (2), s11–26.

Becker, G.S. (1991), *A Treatise on Family*, Cambridge: Harvard University Press.

Berry, R.A. and W.R. Cline (1979), *Agrarian Structure and Productivity in Developing Countries*, Baltimore, MD: John Hopkins University Press.

Bhagwati, J. (1982), 'Directly unproductive profit seeking (DUP) activities', *Journal of Political Economy*, 90, 988–1002.

Bhagwati, J. (1993), *India in Transition: Freeing the Economy*, Oxford: Clarendon Press.

Bhagwati, J. and P. Desai (1971), *India: Planning for Industrialization*, New York: Oxford University Press.

Blomqvist, H.C. (1996), 'The flying geese model of regional development – A constructive interpretation', *Journal of the Asia Pacific Economy*, 1, 215–231.

Blomqvist, H.C. (2002), 'The endogenous state and economic development: A survey', *International Journal of Development Issues*, 1, 1–23.

Blomqvist, H.C. (2005), *Swimming with Sharks: Global and Regional Dimensions of the Singapore Economy*, Singapore: Marshall Cavendish.

Blomqvist, H.C. (2007), 'Political economy of development: A stylised Asian perspective', in K.C. Roy and S. Chatterjee (eds), *Growth, Development and Poverty Alleviation in the Asia-Pacific*, New York: Nova Science Publishers.

Blomqvist, H.C. (2011), 'The developmental state of Malaysia: Efficiency versus management of ethnicity', *Asian Profile*, 39, 138–153.

Blomqvist, H.C. and M. Lundahl (2002), *The Distorted Economy*, Basingstoke, UK: Palgrave Macmillan.

Boix, C. (2011), 'Democracy, development, and the international system', *American Political Science Review*, 105, 809–828.

Bradford, Jr., C.I. (1986), 'East Asian "models": Myths and lessons', in J.P. Lewis and V. Kallab (eds), *Development Strategies Reconsidered*, Washington, DC: Overseas Development Council.

Bramall, C. (2009), *Chinese Economic Development*, Abingdon, UK: Routledge.

Brandt, L.A. and A.M. Turner (2003), 'The usefulness of corruptible election', in *William Davidson Institution, WP 602*, Toronto: SSRN Electronic Paper Collection, University of Toronto.

Brandt, L.L. (1997), 'Reflections on China's late 19th and early 20th century economy', *China Quarterly*, 150, 282–308.

Brandt, L. and B. Sands (1992), 'Land concentration and income distribution in Republican China', in T.G. Rawski and L.M. Lim (eds), *Chinese History in Economic Perspective*, Berkeley: University of California Press.

Buchanan, J. (1980), 'Rent seeking and profit seeking', in J.M. Buchanan, R.D. Tollison and G. Tullock (eds), *Towards a Theory of the Rent-Seeking Society*, College Station: Texas A&M University Press.

Buck, J.L. (1937), *Land Utilization in China*, Oxford: Oxford University Press.

Burenstam Linder, S. (1986), *The Pacific Century: Economic and Political Consequences of Asian Pacific Dynamism*, Stanford: Stanford University Press.

Burton, H. (1989), 'Import substitution', in H.B. Chenery and T.N. Srinivasan (eds), *Handbook of Development Economics*, Vol. 2, Amsterdam: Elsevier Science Publishers.

Burton, H. (1998), 'A reconsideration of import substitution', *Journal of Economic Literature*, 36, 306–936.

Business Monitor International (BMI) (2010), *Asia Monitor: South Asia* 16, May, p. 2; June, p. 2.

Business Times (Singapore) (2010), September, p. 18.

Byrd, W. and Q. Lin (1990), *China's Rural Industry: Structure, Development and Reform*, Oxford: Oxford University Press.

Calder, K. (1988), *Crisis and Compensation: Public Policy and Political Stability in Japan, 1949–1986*, Princeton: Princeton University Press.

Callick, R. (2010), 'Spat over the yuan will shake global finance', *The Australian* (Brisbane), 22 March, p. 11.

Callick, R. (2011), 'China still has great wall around its economy', *The Australian* (Brisbane), 14 April, p. 24.

Central Election Commission (2008), 'Election Results', Taipei: Central Election Commission, Government of Taiwan, www.cec.gov.tw.

Central Intelligence Agency (CIA) (2002), *The World Factbook*, Washington, DC: Central Intelligence Agency.

Chai, J.C.H. (2011), *An Economic History of Modern China*, Cheltenham, UK: Edward Elgar.

Chai, J.C.H. and K.C. Roy (2006), *Economic Reform in China and India: Development in a Comparative Perspective*, Cheltenham, UK: Edward Elgar.

Chakraborty, S. (1987), *Development Planning: The Indian Experience*, Oxford: Clarendon Press.

Chao, L. and R.H. Myers (1998), *The First Chinese Democracy: Political Life in the Republic of China*, Baltimore: Johns Hopkins University Press.

Chenery, H.B. and A. Strout (1966), 'Foreign assistance and economic development', *American Economic Review*, 56, 679–733.

Cheng, T.J. (1987), *The Politics of Industrial Transformation: The Case of East-Asia NICs*, Berkeley: PhD Dissertation, Department of Political Science, University of California.

Cheng, T.J. (1990), 'Political regimes and development strategies', in G. Gereffi and D.L. Wyman (eds), *Manufacturing Miracles: Paths of Industrialization in Latin America and East Asia*, Princeton: Princeton University Press.

Cheung, A.B.L. (2003), 'Public service reform in Singapore: Reinventing government in a global age', in A.B.L. Cheung and I. Scott (eds), *Governance and Public Sector Reform in Asia: Paradigm Shifts or Business as Usual?*, London: RoutledgeCurzon.

Chibber, A. (1997), 'The state in a changing world', *Finance and Development*, 34 (3), 17–20.

Chu, Y.H. (1999), 'Surviving the East Asian financial storm: The political foundations of Taiwan's economic resilience', in T.J. Pempel (ed.), *The Politics of the Asian Economic Crisis*, Ithaca: Cornell University Press.

Clark, C. (1989), *Taiwan's Development: Implications for Contending Political Economy Paradigms*, Westport, CT: Greenwood.

Clark, C. (1997), 'Taiwan's financial system: Prosperity from countervailing perversities?', in R.D. Bingham and E.W. Hill (eds), *Global Perspectives on Economic Development: Government and Business Finance*, New Brunswick: Center for Urban Policy Research, Rutgers University.

Clark, C. and J. Clark (2002), *The Social and Political Bases of Women's Growing Political Power in Taiwan*, Baltimore: Maryland Series in Contemporary Asia Studies, School of Law, University of Maryland.

Clark, C. and K.C. Roy (1997), *Comparing Development Patterns in Asia*, Boulder, CO: Lynne Rienner.

Clark, C. and A. Tan (2011), *Taiwan's Political Economy: Meeting Challenges, Pursuing Progress*, Boulder, CO: Lynne Rienner.

Coale, A. (1991), 'Excess female mortality and the balance of sexes', *Population and Development Review*, 17, 517–523.

Coase, R. (1974), 'The lighthouse in economics', *Journal of Law and Economics*, 17, 357–376.

Coe, D.T. (2007), 'Globalization and labour market', *OECD Papers*, 7 (11), 1–28.

Cohen, W.M. and D.A. Levinthal (1989), 'Innovation and learning: The two faces of R and D', *Economic Journal*, 107, 569–596.

Colander, D.C. (1984), *Neoclassical Political Economy: The Analysis of Rent-seeking and DUP Activities*, Cambridge, MA: Ballinger.

Collier, P. and A. Hoeffler (1999), *Loot-Seeking and Justice Seeking in Civil War*, Washington, DC: World Bank, Development Research Department.

Committee on the Elimination of Discrimination against Women (CEDAW) (2004), *Consideration of Reports Submitted by State Parties under Article 18 of the Convention of the Elimination of All Forms of Discrimination against Women: Malaysia*, New York: CEDAW.

Common, R. (2003), 'Malaysia: A case of "business as usual"?' in A.B.L. Cheung and I. Scott (eds), *Governance and Public Sector Reform in Asia: Paradigm Shifts or Business as Usual?*, London: RoutledgeCurzon.

Copper, J.F. (1988), *A Quiet Revolution: Political Development in the Republic of China*, Washington, DC: Ethics and Public Policy Center.

Copper, J.F. (2009), *Taiwan: Nation-State or Province?*, 5th ed., Boulder, CO: Westview.

Copper, J.F. (2010), *Taiwan's Democracy on Trial: Political Change During the Chen Shui-bian Era and Beyond*, Lanham, MD: University Press of America.

Council for Economic Planning and Development (CEPD) (2009), *Taiwan Statistical Data Book, 2009*, Taipei: Council for Economic Planning and Development.

Cypher, J.M. and J.L. Dietz (2009), *The Process of Economic Development*, New York: Routledge.

Dawson, J.W. (1998), 'Institutions, investment and growth: New cross country and panel data evidence', *Economic Enquiry*, 36, 603–619.

Dempsey, J. (2011), 'Wen's visit shows concern over euro', *International Herald Tribune*, 25 June, p. 15.

Department of Commerce (2008), *Doing Business in Malaysia: 2009 Country Commercial Guide for U.S. Companies*, online at www.buyusainfo.net/docs/x_411922.pdf

Dev, S.M. (2008), 'India', in A. Choudhury and W. Mahmud (eds), *Handbook on South Asian Economics*, Cheltenham, UK: Edward Elgar.

Dhume, S. (2011), 'Crony socialism stops business from thriving', *The Australian* (Brisbane), 13 July, p. 8.

Dong, X.Y., S.F. Song and X.B. Zhang (2006), *China's Agricultural Development*, Aldershot, UK: Ashgate.

Dore, R.P. (1959), *Land Reform in Japan*, London: Oxford University Press.

Dreze, J. and A. Sen (1989), *Hunger and Public Action*, Oxford: Oxford University Press.

Easterly, W. and R. Levine (1997), 'Africa's growth strategy: Policies and ethnic divisions', *Quarterly Journal of Economics*, 112, 1203–1241.

Echeverri-Gent, J. (1998), 'Weak state, strong reforms: Globalization, partisan competition and the paradoxes of Indian economic reform', Charlottesville: University of Virginia, Transcript.

Economist Intelligence Unit (EIU) (2008a), *Country Profile: China*.

Economist Intelligence Unit (EIU) (2008b), *Country Profile: India*.

Economist Intelligence Unit (EIU) (2009), *Country Profile: China*.

Encarnation, D. (1990), *Dislodging the Multinationals: India's Strategy in Comparative Perspective*, Ithaca: Cornell University Press.

Evans, P.B. (1992), 'The state as a problem and solution: Predation, embedded autonomy and structural change', in S. Haggard and R.R. Kaufman (eds), *The Politics of Economic Adjustment*, Princeton: Princeton University Press.

Evans, P. (1995), *Embedded Autonomy: States and Industrial Transformation*, Princeton: Princeton University Press.

Evans, P.B., D. Rueschemeyer and T. Skocpol (eds) (1985), *Bringing the State Back In*, New York: Cambridge University Press.

Fairclough, G. (2003), 'North Korean puzzle: How far will reforms go?', *Wall Street Journal*, 24 November, p. A-12.

Fan, S.G. and X.B. Zhang (2002), 'Production and productivity growth in Chinese agriculture: New national and regional measures', *Economic Development and Cultural Change*, 50, 819–838.

Faridah, A. (2001), 'Sustainable agricultural system in Malaysia', Bangkok: Paper presented at a regional workshop on integrated plant nutrition systems, September.

Farris, C.S.P. (2000), 'Contradictory implications of socialism and capitalism under "East Asian modernity" in China and Taiwan', in R.J. Lee and C. Clark (eds), *Democracy and the Status of Women in East Asia*, Boulder, CO: Lynne Rienner.

Fei, J.C.H., G. Ranis and S.W.Y. Kuo (1979), *Growth with Equity: The Taiwan Case*, New York: Oxford University Press.

Fields, K.J. (1995), *Enterprise and the State in South Korea and Taiwan*, Ithaca: Cornell University Press.

Fisher, S. and V. Thomas (1990), 'Policies for economic development', *American Journal of Agricultural Economics*, 72, 809–814.

Foster, G.M. (1973), *Traditional Societies and Technological Change*, New York: Harper and Row.

Friedman, D. (1988), *The Misunderstood Miracle: Industrial Development and Political Change in Japan*, Ithaca: Cornell University Press.

Friedman, M. (1962), *Capitalism and Freedom*, Chicago: University of Chicago Press.

Friedman, M. (2005), *The Moral Consequences of Economic Growth*, New York: Alfred A. Knopf.

Fukuda-Parr, S. and A.K. Shiv Kumar (2003), *Readings in Human Development*, New York: Oxford University Press.

Galenson, W. (ed.) (1979), *Economic Growth and Structural Change in Taiwan: The Postwar Experience of the Republic of China*, Ithaca: Cornell University Press.

Gallup, J. and J. Sachs (1998), 'Geography and economic development', in B. Pleskovic and J. Sachs (eds), *World Bank Annual Conference on Economic Development*, Washington, DC: World Bank.

Gampat, R. and C. Weeratunge (2008), 'The rise of China: What it means for the least developed countries in the Asia-Pacific', *Asia-Pacific Trade and Investment Review*, 8, 28.

Gao, X. (1994), 'China's modernization and changes in the social structure of rural women', in C. Gilmartin, G. Harshatter, L. Rofel and T. White (eds), *Engendering China*, Cambridge: Harvard University Press.

Garson, M. (2011), 'Team China eyes the dark continent', *The Australian* (Brisbane), 1 April, p. 8.

Gaylor, O. and D.N. Weil (1999), 'From Malthusian stagnation to modern growth', *American Economic Review*, 89 (2), 150–154.

Gaylor, O. and J. Zeira (1993), 'Income distribution and macroeconomics', *Review of Economic Studies*, 60, 35–52.

Gereffi, G. (1990), 'Paths to industrialization: An overview', in G. Gereffi and D.L. Wyman (eds), *Manufacturing Miracles: Paths of Industrialization in Latin America and East Asia*, Princeton: Princeton University Press.

Gerlach, M.L. (1992), *Alliance Capitalism: The Social Organization of Japanese Business*, Berkeley: University of California Press.

Gerschenkron, A. (1962), *Economic Backwardness in Historical Perspective*, Cambridge: Harvard University Press.

Ghosh, A.K. (2011), 'Informal employment in India', in M. Mohanty (ed.), *India: Social Development Report, 2010*, New Delhi: Oxford University Press.

Ghosh, J. (2004), 'Income inequality in India', online at www.networkideas.org/news/feb2004/news09_income_inequality.htm

Gill, I. and H. Kharas (2007), *East Asian Renaissance: Ideas for Economic Growth*, Washington, DC: World Bank.

Gold, T. (1986), *State and Society in the Taiwan Miracle*, New York: M.E. Sharpe.

Government of China (GOC) National Bureau of Statistics (various years), *China Statistical Year Books*, Beijing: Government of China.

Government of India (GOI) (1957), *Review of India's First Five Year Plan*, New Delhi: Government of India.

GOI (1970 to 1995), *Economic Survey 1970, 1975, 1980, 1985, 1990, 1995*, New Delhi: Government of India.

GOI (2005), *Economic Survey 2004–2005*, New Delhi: Government of India.

GOI (2007), *Economic Survey 2007*, New Delhi: Government of India.

GOI (2008), *Economic Survey 2007–2008*, New Delhi: Oxford University Press.

GOI (2009), *Economic Survey 2008-09*, New Delhi: Oxford University.

GOI (2010), *Economic Survey 2009–10*, New Delhi: Oxford University Press.

Greene, J.M. (2008), *The Origins of the Developmental State in Taiwan: Science Policy and the Quest for Modernization*, Cambridge: Harvard University Press.

Greider, W. (1992), *Who Will Tell the People? The Betrayal of American Democracy*, New York: Simon & Schuster.

Grossman, G.M. and E. Helpman (1991), *Innovation and Growth in the Global Economy*, Cambridge: MIT Press.

Gunnarsson, C. (1993), 'Dirigisme or free-trade regime? A historical and institutional interpretation of the Taiwanese success story', in G. Hansson (ed.), *Trade, Growth and Development*, New York: Routledge.

Gyimah-Boadi, E. (1998), 'The rebirth of African liberalism', *Journal of Democracy*, 9 (2), 18–31.

Hagen, E.E. (1962), *On the Theory of Social Change: How Economic Growth Begins*, Homewood, IL: Dorsey Press.

Haggard, S. (1994), 'From the heavy industry plan to stabilization: Macroeconomic policy, 1976–1980', in S. Haggard (ed.), *Macroeconomic Policy and Adjustment in Korea, 1970–1990*, Cambridge: Harvard University Press.

Haggard, S. and C.I. Moon (1983), 'The South Korean state in the international economy: Liberal, dependent, or mercantile?', in J.G. Ruggie (ed.), *The Antinomies of Interdependence: National Welfare and the International Division of Labor*, New York: Columbia University Press.

Haggard, S. and C.I. Moon (1990), 'Institutions and economic policy: Theory and a Korean case study', *World Politics*, 42, 210–237.

Haggard, S. and S. Web (1994), *Voting for Reform*, Oxford: Oxford University Press.

Hahm, S.D. and L.C. Plein (1997), *After Development: The Transformation of the Korean Presidency and Bureaucracy*, Washington, DC: Georgetown University Press.

Hall, R. and C. Jones (1999), 'Why do some countries produce so much more output per worker than others?', *Quarterly Journal of Economics*, 111, 83–116.

Halsey, A.H., H. Lauder, P. Brown and A.S. Wells (1997), *Education: Culture, Economy and Society*, New York: Oxford University Press.

Hanson, A.H. (1966), *The Process of Planning*, London: Oxford University Press.

Harris, J.R. and M.P. Todaro (1970), 'Migration, unemployment and development: A two sector analysis', *American Economic Review*, 60 (1), 126–142.

Harrison, B. (1994), *Lean and Mean: The Changing Landscape of Corporate Power in the Age of Flexibility*, New York: Basic Books.

Harris-White, B. (2004), 'India's socially regulated economy', *The Indian Journal of Labour Economics*, 47 (1), 49–68.

Hirschman, A.O. (1978), *The Strategy of Economic Development*, New York: Norton.

Ho, S.P.S. (1978), *Economic Development in Taiwan, 1860–1970*, New Haven: Yale University Press.

Hobbes, T. (1651), *Leviathan*, London: Printed for Andrew Crooke.

Hofheinz, R., Jr. and K. Calder (1982), *The Eastasia Edge*, New York: Basic Books.

Hong, S.G. (1992), 'Paths of glory: Semiconductor leapfrogging in Taiwan and South Korea', *Pacific Focus*, 7, 59–88.

Howe, P. (2011), 'China's free trade cheating threatens our jobs', *The Australian* (Brisbane), 17 February, p. 12.

Hsieh, H.C. (1996), 'Taiwan, Republic of China,' in G.C.L. Mak (ed.), *Women, Education, and Development in Asia*, New York: Garland Publishing.

Hu, M.W. and C. Schive (1998), 'The changing competitiveness of Taiwan's manufacturing SMEs', *Small Business Economics*, 11, 315–326.

Hunter, G. (1969), *Modernising Peasant Societies: A Comparative Study of Asia and Africa*, New York: Oxford University Press.

Huntington, G. (2003), 'North Korean puzzle: How far will reforms go?', *Wall Street Journal*, 24 November, p. A-12.

Huntington, S.P. (1968), *Political Order in Changing Societies*, New Haven: Yale University Press.

Huntington, S.P. (1991), *The Third Wave: Democratization in the Late Twentieth Century*, Norman: University of Oklahoma Press.

International Monetary Fund (IMF) (1965 to 1995), *Government Finance Statistics Yearbook*, Washington, DC: IMF.

IMF (2003), *Direction of Trade Statistics Yearbook*, Washington, DC: IMF.

IMF (2008), *International Financial Statistics Yearbook*, Washington, DC: IMF.

IMF (2009a), *Direction of Trade Statistics Yearbook*, Washington, DC: IMF.

IMF (2009b), *International Financial Statistics Yearbook*, Washington, DC: IMF.

IMF (2010), *International Financial Statistics Yearbook*, Washington, DC: IMF.

Islam, R. (2002a), 'Into the looking glass: What the media tells and why – An overview', Washington, DC: World Bank Institute.

Islam, R. (2002b), 'Institutions to Support Markets', *Finance and Development*, 39, 48–51.

Jacobs, A. (2011), 'Farmers in China's south riot over seizure of land', *New York Times*, 24 September, p. A-5.

Jamilah, A. (1996), 'Economic development, industrial trends, and women workers in Malaysia', in K.C. Roy, C.A. Tisdell and H.C. Blomqvist (eds), *Economic Development of Women in the World Community*, Westport, CT: Praeger.

Jaumotte, F. and N. Pain (2005), 'From ideas to development: The determinants of R & D and patenting', *OECD Economics Department Working Paper No. 457*, Paris: Economics Department, Organisation for Economic Co-operation and Development.

Jefferson, G.H. (1999), 'Are China's rural enterprises outperforming state enterprises? Estimating the pure ownership effect', in G.H. Jefferson and I. Sing (eds), *Enterprise Reform in China: Ownership, Transition and Performance*, New York: Oxford University Press.

Johnson, C. (1982), *MITI and the Japanese Miracle: The Growth of Industrial Policy, 1925–1975*, Cambridge: Harvard University Press.

Jomo, K.S., C.Y. Chung, B.C. Folk and I. Ul-Haque (1997), *Southeast Asia's Misunderstood Miracle: Industrial Policy and Economic Development in Thailand, Malaysia and Indonesia*, Boulder, CO: Westview Press.

Jomo, K.S. and E.T. Gomez (1997), 'Rents and development in multiethnic Malaysia', in M. Aoki, H.-K. Kim and M. Okuno-Fujiwara (eds), *The Role of Government in East Asian Economic Development*, Oxford: Clarendon Press.

Jomo, K.S. and E.T. Gomez (2000), 'The Malaysian development dilemma', in M.H. Khan and K.S. Jomo (eds), *Rents, Rent-Seeking and Economic Development: Theory and Evidence in Asia*, Cambridge: Cambridge University Press.

Jones, L. and I. Sakong (1980), *Government, Business, and Entrepreneurship in Economic Development: The Korean Case*, Cambridge: Harvard University Press.

Joseph, R. (1987), *Democracy and Prebandal Politics in Nigeria: The Rise and Fall of the Second Republic*, Cambridge: Cambridge University Press.

Joshi, S. (2006), 'From conventional to new services: Broadened scope of the tertiary sector', *Indian Journal of Labour Economics*, 49, 321–335.

Joshi, S. (2009), 'Who will be the main global IT services hub: India or China?', *Asia Pacific Trade and Investment Review*, 4, 21–49.

Joshi, V. and I. Little (eds) (1994), *India: Macro Economics and Political Economy*, Washington, DC: World Bank.

Jung, C. and C. Clark (2010), 'The impact of the Asian financial crisis on budget politics in South Korea', *Asian Affairs* 37 (1), 27–45.

Junning, L. (2011), 'Greater freedom, not control, boosts China's prospects', *The Australian* (Brisbane), 9–10 July, p. 24.

Kabeer, N. (1998), 'Money cannot buy me love, re-evaluating gender, credit and empowerment in rural Bangladesh', *IDS Discussion Paper, No. 363*, Brighton: University of Sussex, Institute of Development Studies.

Kamenka, E. (1972), *The Ethical Foundation of Marxism*, London: Routledge and Kegan Paul.

Kanapathy, V. (2001), 'Industrial restructuring in Malaysia: Policy shifts and the promotion of new sources of growth', in S. Masuyama, D. Vandenbrink and S.Y. Chia (eds), *Industrial Restructuring in East Asia*, Singapore: Nomura Research Institute and the Institute of Southeast Asian Studies.

Kang, D.C. (2002), *Crony Capitalism: Corruption and Development in South Korea and the Philippines*, New York: Cambridge University Press.

Kang, T.W. (1989), *Is Korea the Next Japan? Understanding the Structure, Strategy, and Tactics of America's Next Competitor*, New York: Free Press.

Karnik, K. (2005), 'Indian ITES-BPO: Vision 2010', *Yojana*, New Delhi, October issue.

Keen, D. (1998), *The Economic Functions of Violence in Civil Wars*, Oxford: Oxford University Press.

Keen, D. (2000), 'War, crime and access to resources', in E.W. Nafziger, F. Stewart and R. Vayrynen (eds), *War, Hunger, and Displacement: The Origins of Humanitarian Emergencies*, Vol. 1, Oxford: Oxford University Press.

Keynes, J.M. (1936), *A General Theory of Employment, Interest and Money*, London: Macmillan.

Khar, A.R. (2004), 'Growth, inequality and poverty in China', *Issues in Employment and Poverty, Discussion Paper No. 15*, Geneva: International Labor Office.

Kim, B.L.P. (1992), *The Two Koreas in Development: A Comparative Study of Principles and Strategies of Capitalist and Communist Third World Development*, New Brunswick, NJ: Transaction Publishers.

Klasen, S. (1994), 'Missing women reconsidered', *World Development*, 22, 1061–1071.

Kohli, A. (2004), *State Directed Development: Political Power and Industrialization in the Global Periphery*, Princeton: Princeton University Press.

Krauss, E.S. and R.J. Pekkanen (2011), *The Rise and Fall of Japan's LDP: Political Party Organizations and Historical Institutions*, Ithaca: Cornell University Press.

Krueger, A. (1974), 'The political economy of the rent seeking society', *American Economic Review*, 64, 291–303.

Krueger, A. (1983), *Trade and Development in Developing Countries*, Chicago: University of Chicago Press.

Krueger, A. (1997), 'Trade policy and economic development: How we learn', *American Economic Review*, 87 (1), 1–22.

Kuo, C.T. (1995), *Global Competitiveness and Industrial Growth in Taiwan and the Philippines*, Pittsburgh: University of Pittsburgh Press.

Kuo, C.T. (1998), 'Private governance in Taiwan', in S. Chan, C. Clark and D. Lam (eds), *Beyond the Developmental State: East Asia's Political Economies Reconsidered*, London: Macmillan.

Kuo, S.W.Y. (1983), *The Taiwan Economy in Transition*, Boulder, CO: Westview.

Kuznets, S. (1955), 'Economic growth and income inequality', *American Economic Review*, 45, 1–28.

Lakshmanasamy, T. and K.C. Roy (2010), 'Human capital and dowry in household bargaining and their implications for women's empowerment', *International Journal of Development Management*, 1 (1), 67–96.

Lal, D. (1983), *The Poverty of Development Economics*, London: Institute of Economic Affairs.

Lal, D. (1988), *The Hindu Equilibrium: Cultural Stability and Economic Stagnation. India C 1500 BC to AD 1980*, Vol. I, Oxford: Clarendon Press.

Lal, D. (1995), 'India and China: Contrast in economic liberalisation?', *World Development*, 23, 1475–1494.

Lam, D.K.K. (1992), *Explaining Economic Development: A Case Study of State Policies Towards the Computer and Electronics Industry in Taiwan (1960–80)*, Ottawa: PhD Dissertation, Carleton University.

Lam, D. and C. Clark (1994), 'Beyond the developmental state: The cultural roots of "guerrilla capitalism" in Taiwan', *Governance*, 7, 412–430.

Lederman, D. and W.F. Maloney (2003), 'Research and development (R & D) and development', *Policy Research Working Paper, No. 3024*, Washington, DC: World Bank.

Lee, T.H. (1971), *Intersectoral Capital Flows in the Economic Development of Taiwan, 1895–1960*, Ithaca: Cornell University Press.

Lee, T.P. and C. Clark (2010), 'The limits of budget reform in Taiwan', in C.E. Menifield (ed.), *Comparative Public Budgeting: A Global Perspective*, Sudbury, MA: Jones and Bartlett, pp. 91–105.

Leng, T.K. (1996), *The Taiwan-China Connection: Democracy and Development Across the Taiwan Straits*, Boulder, CO: Westview.

Lerner, D.C. (1958), *The Passing of Traditional Society: Modernizing the Middle East*, New York: Free Press.

Levi, M. (1988), *Of Law and Revenue*, Berkeley: University of California Press.

Lewis, A. (1954), 'Economic development with unlimited supplies of labor', *Manchester School of Economic and Social Studies*, 22, 139–194.

Lewis, L. (2011), 'Suicide link to Chinese defaults', *The Australian* (Brisbane), p. 12.

Lim, I. and H. Nesadurai (1997), 'Managing the Malaysian industrial economy: The policy and reform process for industrialization', in S. Masuyama, D. Vandenbrink and C.S. Yue (eds), *Industrial Policies in East Asia*, Singapore: Nomura Research Institute and Institute of Southeast Asian Studies.

Lipset, S.M. (1959), 'Some social requisites of democracy: Economic development and political legitimacy', *American Political Science Review*, 53, 69–105.

Little, L.M.D., T. Scitovsky and M. Scott (1970), *Industry and Trade in Some Developing Countries: A Comparative Study*, London: Oxford University Press.

Locke, J. (1690), *Two Treatise of Government*, London: John Churchill and Sam Manship.

Low, L. (1998), *The Political Economy of a City-State: Government-Made Singapore*, Singapore: Oxford University Press.

Luce, E. (2007), *The Spite of the Gods: The Strange Rise of Modern India*, New York: Doubleday.

Lynn, S.R. (2003), *Economic Development*, New York: Pearson.

MacFarquhar, R., T. Cheek and E. Wu (1989), *The Secret Speeches of Chairman Mao*, Cambridge: Harvard University Press.

Mahalanobis, P.C. (1969), 'The Asian drama: An Indian view', *San Khya: The Indian Journal of Statistics*, Series B, 31, 442.

Mahani, Z.A. (2002), *Rewriting the Rules: The Malaysian Crisis Management Model*, Petaling Jaya, Malaysia: Prentice Hall.

Majumdar, R.C., H.C. Raychaudhuri and K. Datta (2009), *An Advanced History of India*, New Delhi: Macmillan.

Mardon, R. and W.K. Paik (1992), 'The state, foreign investment, and sustaining industrial growth in South Korea and Thailand', in C. Clark and S. Chan (eds), *The Evolving Pacific Basin in the Global Political Economy: Domestic and International Linkages*, Boulder, CO: Lynne Rienner.

McCauley, R.N. (2006), 'Understanding monetary policy in Malaysia and Thailand: Objectives, instruments and independence', Basel: Bank of International Settlements (BIS), *BIS Papers*, No. 31.

McClelland, D.C. (1961), *The Achieving Society*, Princeton, NJ: D. Van Nostrand.

Mee, K.E. (1987), *From Dominance to Symbiosis: State Chaebol in the Korean Economy 1960–1985*, Providence, RI: PhD Dissertation, Department of Sociology, Brown University.

Meier, G.M. and J.E. Rauch (2005), *Leading Issues in Economic Development*, New York: Oxford University Press.

Mellor, J.W. (1976), *The New Economics of Growth: A Strategy for India and the Developing World*, Ithaca: Cornell University Press.

Mellor, J. (1998), 'Agriculture on the road to industrialization', in C. Eicher and J. Staatz (eds), *International Agricultural Development*, Baltimore, MD: Johns Hopkins Press.

Mellor, J.W. and B.F. Johnston (1984), 'The world food equation: Interrelations among development, employment and food consumption', *Journal of Economic Literature*, 22, 531–574.

Mill, J. (1947), *Utilitarianism, Liberty and Representative Government*, London: Dent.

Miller, J.W. and J.T. Areddy (2011), 'Trade policies flawed, says WTO', *The Australian* (Brisbane), 22 February, p. 23.

Mood, M.S. (1997), 'The impact and prospects of rural enterprise', in C. Hudson (ed.), *The China Handbook*, Chicago, IL: Fitzroy Dearborn Publishers.

Moon, C.I. (2010), 'South Korea in 2009: From setbacks to reversals', *Asian Survey*, 50 (1), 56–64.

Mukherjee, A.N. and Y. Kuroda (2003), 'Productivity growth in Indian agriculture: Is there evidence of convergence across states?', Agricultural *Economics*, 29 (1), 45–53.

Mukherjee, S. (2009), 'Creation of Bengal', *The Statesman Weekly* (Calcutta), 3 October, p. 10.

Murdoch, S. (2011), 'IMF cautions China on economy', *The Australian* (Brisbane), 22 July, p. 4.

Myers, R.H. (1970), *The Chinese Peasant Economy*, Cambridge: Harvard University Press.

Nafziger, E.W. (2006), *Economic Development*, New York: Cambridge University Press.

Nafziger, E.W. and J. Auvinen (2002), 'Economic development, inequality, war and state violence', *World Development*, 30, 153–163.

Nafziger, E.W. and J. Auvinen (2003), *Economic Development, Inequality and War: Humanitarian Experience in Developing Countries*, Houndmills, UK: Palgrave Macmillan.

Narayan, S. (1962), *Principles of Gandhian Planning*, Allahabad, India: Kitab Mahal.

National Association of Software and Service Companies (NASSCOM) (2005), *NASSCOM McKinsey Report, 2005 – Extending India's Leadership of Global IT and BPO Industries*, New Delhi: NASSCOM.

Naughton, B. (ed.) (1997), *The China Circle: Economics and Electronics in the PRC, Taiwan, and Hong Kong*, Washington, DC: Brookings.

Naughton, B. (2007), *The Chinese Economy: Transitions and Growth*, Cambridge: MIT Press.

Nee, V. (1998), 'Norms and networks in economic and organisational performance', *American Economic Review*, 88, 85–89.

Nehru, J.L. (1954), *Jawaharlal Nehru's Speeches, 1949–53*, Delhi: Government of India.

Nelson, M. and D. Singh (1998), 'Democracy, economic freedom, fiscal policy and growth in LDCs: A fresh look', *Economic Development and Cultural Change*, 46, 677–696.

Nester, W.R. (1991), *Japanese Industrial Targeting: The Neomercantilist Path to Economic Superpower*, New York: St. Martin's.

Noble, G. (1994), 'Japan in 1993: Humpty Dumpty had a great fall', *Asian Survey*, 34, 19–29.

Noble, G.W. (1998), *Collective Action in East Asia: How Ruling Parties Shape Industrial Policy*, Ithaca: Cornell University Press.

North, D. (1981), *Structure and Change in Economic History*, New York: W.W. Norton.

North, D. (1987), 'Institutions, transaction costs and economic growth', *Economic Inquiry*, 25, 24 and 419–424.

North, D. (1990), *Institutions, Institutional Change and Economic Performance*, New York: Cambridge University Press.

Okimoto, D.J. (1989), *Between MITI and the Market: Japanese Industrial Policy for High Technology*, Stanford: Stanford University Press.

Olson, M. (1982), *The Rise and Decline of Nations: Economic Growth, Stagflation and Social Rigidities*, New Haven, CT: Yale University Press.

Oshima, H.T. (1994), 'The impact of technological transformation on historical trends in income distribution of Asia and the West', *Developing Economies*, 23, 237–255.

Ottaway, M. (1995), 'Democratization in collapsed states', in I.W. Zartman (ed.), *Collapsed States: The Disintegration and Restoration of Legitimate Authority*, Boulder, CO: Lynne Rienner.

Panagariya, A. (2007), 'Why India lags behind China and how it can bridge the gap', *World Economy*, 30, 229–248.

Panagariya, A. (2008), *India: The Emerging Giant*, Oxford: Oxford University Press.

Paranjape, H.K. (1964), *Jawaharlal Nehru and the Planning Commission*, New Delhi: Indian Institute of Public Administration.

Perkins, D.W., S. Radelet and D.L. Lindauer (2006), *Economics of Development*, New York: Norton.

Pingle, V. (1999), *Rethinking the Developmental State: India's Industry in Comparative Perspective*, New York: St. Martin's Press.

Pitt, M.M. and S.R. Khandker (1998), 'The impact of group based credit programmes for poor households in Bangladesh: Does the gender of participants matter?', *Journal of Political Economy*, 106, 958–996.

Polanyi, K. (1957), *The Great Transformation*, Boston, MA: Beacon Press.

Prada, P. (2011), 'Brazilian President to confront Beijing on trade', *The Australian* (Brisbane), 12 April, p. 22.

Prebisch, R. (1950), *The Economic Development of Latin America and Its Principal Problems*, Lake Success, NY: United Nations.

Prestowitz, C.I., Jr. (1988), *Trading Places: How We Allowed Japan to Take the Lead*, New York: Basic Books.

Pritchett, L. (1996), 'Measuring outward orientation in LDCs: Can it be done?', *Journal of Development Economics*, 49, 307–355.

Puddy, R. (2011), 'Chinese envoy warns on trade ties', *The Australian* (Brisbane), 7 July, p. 2.

Puri, R. (2009), 'Why Gandhi's silence on Partition?', *The Statesman* (Calcutta), 2 October, p. 7.

Pye, L.W. (1985), *Asian Power and Politics: The Cultural Dimensions of Authority*, Cambridge: Harvard University Press.

Radelet, S. and J. Sachs (1998), 'The East Asian financial crisis: Diagnosis, remedies, prospects', *Brookings Papers on Economic Activity*, 1, 1–98.

Radelet, S., J. Sachs and J.W. Lee (2001), 'The determinants and prospects for economic growth in Asia', *International Economic Journal*, 5 (3), 1–30.

Radhakrishna, R, C. Ravi and B.S. Reddy (2011), 'State of poverty and malnutrition in India', in M. Mohanty (ed.), *India: Social Development Report*, New Delhi: Oxford University Press.

Rakshit, N.B. (2009), 'Nehru and the Partition', *The Statesman* (Calcutta), 28 September, p. 11.

Rasiah, R. (1997), 'Class, ethnicity and economic development in Malaysia', in G. Rodan, K. Hewison and R. Robison (eds), *The Political Economy of South-East Asia: An Introduction*, Melbourne: Oxford University Press.

Rasiah, R. (2006), 'Electronics in Malaysia: Export expansion but slow technical change', in World Bank Staff, *Technology, Adaptation, and Exports: How Some Countries Got It Right*, Herndon, VA: World Bank.

Rauch, J.E. (1993), 'Economic development, urban unemployment and income inequality', *Canadian Journal of Economics*, 26, 901–904, 912–915.

Ray, P. (2011), 'Drop the pretence', *The Statesman* (Calcutta), 4 May, p. 7; Winter issue, pp. 3–22.

Raychaudhuri, T. (1968), 'A re-interpretation of nineteenth century economic history', *Indian Economic and Social History Review*, 5 (2), 84–87.

Reischauer, E.O. (1988), *The Japanese Today: Change and Continuity*, Cambridge: Harvard University Press.

Rigger, S. (1999), *Politics in Taiwan: Voting for Democracy*, London: Routledge.

Rodan, G. (1989), *The Political Economy of Singapore's Industrialization: National, State, and International Capital*, New York: St. Martin's.

Rodrick, D. (2003), 'The primacy of institutions', *Finance and Development*, 40, 31–34.

Romer, P. (1994), 'The origins of endogenous growth', *Journal of Economic Perspectives*, 8, 3–22.

Rosenbluth, F.M. (2011), 'Japan in 2010: Messy politics but healthier democracy', *Asian Survey*, 51 (1), 41–53.

Rosenstein-Rodan, P.N. (1943), 'Problems of industrialization of Eastern and South Eastern Europe', *Economic Journal*, 53, 202–211.

Rosenstein-Rodan, P.N. (1951), 'Notes on the theory of the big push', in S. Ellis (ed.), *Economic Development for Latin America*, London: Macmillan.

Rosenzweig, M.R. and H.P. Binswanger (1993), 'Wealth, weather risk and the composition and profitability of agricultural investments', *Economic Journal*, 103, 56–78.

Roy, K.C. (1986), *Foreign Aid and Indian Development: A Study From the Viewpoint of Peace and Development*, Ahmedabad, India: Gujarat Vidyapith.

Roy, K.C. (1988), *The Sub-Continent in the International Economy 1850–1900*, Hong Kong: International Centre for Asian Studies (ICAS).

Roy, K.C. (1991), 'Public sector performance and managerial efficiency under planner development: India's experience', *Economica Internazionale*, XLIV (2–3), 4–17.

Roy, K.C. (2006), 'Institutional impediments to women's empowerment in rural India', in K.C. Roy and J. Sideras (eds), *Institutions, Globalization and Empowerment*, Cheltenham, UK: Edward Elgar.

Roy, K.C. (2008), 'Institutions and gender empowerment in India', in K.C. Roy, H. Blomqvist and C. Clark (eds), *Institutions and Gender Empowerment in the Global Economy*, Singapore: World Scientific Publishing Company.

Roy, K.C. (2010), 'Managing development is about managing the perception of the state being powerful and developmental', Paper presented at the Seventh IIDS (Australia) International Conference on Development, Brisbane: IIDS Mimeographed.

Roy, K.C. and E. Ali (2011), 'Knowledge accumulation and management in the evolution of economic growth models', *International Journal of Development Management*, 2 (1), 1–20.

Roy, K.C., H. Blomqvist and C. Clark (eds) (2008), *Institutions and Gender Empowerment in the Global Economy*, Singapore: World Scientific Publishing Co.

Roy, K.C. and J.L.H. Chai (1999), 'Economic reforms, public transfers and social safety nets for the poor: A study of India and China', *International Journal of Social Economics*, 26, 222–238.

Roy, K.C. and A.L. Lougheed (1979), 'The Green Revolution in India: Progress and problems', *World Review*, 7 (4), 16–29.

Roy, K.C. and B. Prasad (2007a), 'Good governance for improving development outcomes: Lessons learnt', in K.C. Roy and B. Prasad (eds), *Governance and Development in Developing Countries*, New York: Nova Science.

Roy, K.C. and B. Prasad (2007b), 'Governance and development in developing countries: An overview of issues', in K.C. Roy and B. Prasad (eds), *Governance and Development in Developing Countries*, New York: Nova Science.

Roy, K.C. and A.V. Sidenko (2007a), 'Democracy, governance and growth: Theoretical perspective and Russian experience,' in K.C. Roy and B. Prasad (eds), *Governance and Development in Developing Countries*, New York: Nova Science.

Roy, K.C. and A.V. Sidenko (2007b), 'Institutional failure and the delivery of education in Russia,' in K.C. Roy and B. Prasad (eds), *Governance and Development in Developing Countries*, New York: Nova Science.

Roy, K.C. and J. Sideras (eds) (2006), *Institutions, Globalisation and Empowerment,* Cheltenham, UK: Edward Elgar.

Roy, K.C. and C.A. Tisdell (1998), 'Good governance in sustainable development: The impact of institutions', *International Journal of Social Economics,* 25, 1310–1325.

Roy, K.C., C.A. Tisdell and H. Blomqvist (eds) (1999), *Economic Development and Women in the World Community,* London: Praeger.

Roy, K.C., C.A. Tisdell and R.K. Sen (eds) (1992), *Economic Development and Environment: A Case Study of India,* Calcutta: Oxford University Press.

Roy Chowdhury, J. (2009), 'Trade talks with US hit farm wall', *The Telegraph* (Calcutta), 11 December, p. 9.

Rudolph, L.I. and S.R. Rudolph (1987), *In Pursuit of Lakshmi: The Political Economy of the Indian State,* Chicago: University of Chicago Press.

Sachs, J. and A. Warner (1995), 'Economic reform and the process of global integration', *Brookings Papers on Economic Activity,* 1, 1–118.

Sainsbury, M. (2011a), 'China pours billions into stemming dissent', *The Australian* (Brisbane), 7 March, p. 10.

Sainsbury, M. (2011b), 'Chinese reforms setback decades as the party cracks down', *The Australian* (Brisbane), 8 April, p. 34.

Sainsbury, M. (2011c), 'Foreign investment in China hit by strict new national security regulations', *The Australian* (Brisbane), 14 February, p. 21.

Sainsbury, M. (2011d), 'Mao law keeps China's floating poor jobless', *The Australian* (Brisbane), 11 October, p. 10.

Sainsbury, M. (2011e), 'We will buy iron ore from our own companies', *The Australian* (Brisbane), 26 July, p.6.

Saleh, A.S. and N.O. Ndubisi (2006), SME *Development in Malaysia: Domestic and Global Challenges,* Wollongong, Australia: University of Wollongong Economics Working Paper Series No. 06-03.

Sally, R. (2009), 'Demystifying the hype', *Finance and Development,* 46 (1), 54.

Salvatore, D. (2001), *International Economics,* New York: John Wiley.

Samuels, R.J. (1987), *The Business of the Japanese State: Energy Markets in Comparative and Historical Perspective,* Ithaca: Cornell University Press.

Sandbrook, R. (2002), 'Democratization and economic reform,' in E.W. Nafziger and R. Väyrynen (eds), *The Prevention of Humanitarian Emergencies,* Houndmills, UK: Palgrave Macmillan.

Sandbrook, R. and J. Oelbaum (1997), 'Reforming dysfunctional institutions through democratisation, reflections on Ghana', *Journal of Modern African Studies,* 35, 603–646.

Saul, S.B. (1960), *Studies in British Overseas Trade,* Liverpool: Liverpool University Press.

Schumacher, E.F. (1962), *Roots of Economic Growth,* Varanasi: Gandhian Institute of Studies.

Schumpeter, J. (1961), *The Theory of Economic Development,* Cambridge: Harvard University Press.

Scitovsky, T. (1954), 'Two concepts of external economies', *Journal of Political Economy,* 62, 143–151.

Sen, A. (1992), 'Missing women', *British Medical Journal,* 304, 586–587.

Sen, A.K. (1981), *Poverty and Famines: Essays on Entitlement and Deprivation,* Oxford: Clarendon Press.

Sen, A.K. (1985), *Commodities and Capabilities,* Amsterdam: North Holland.

Sen, A.K. (1999), *Development of Freedom,* New York: Alfred A. Knopf.

Shapiro, H. and L. Taylor (1992). 'The state and the industrial strategy', in C.K. Wilber and K.P. Jameson (eds), *The Political Economy of Development and Under Development*, Singapore: McGraw Hill, pp. 432–464.

Singer, H. (1950), 'The distribution of trade between investing and borrowing countries', *American Economic Review*, 40, 470–485.

Singh, R. (2010), 'Delays and cost overruns in infrastructure projects: An enquiry into extent, causes and remedies', *Working Paper No. 181*, New Delhi: Centre for Development Economics, Department of Economics.

Small and Medium Enterprises Administration, Ministry of Economic Affairs (SMEA) (2008), *2008 White Paper on SMEs in Taiwan*, Taipei: Ministry of Economic Affairs.

Smil, V. (2004), *China's Past, China's Future*, London: RoutledgeCurzon.

Smith, A. (1776; 1976), *An Enquiry into the Nature and Causes of the Wealth of Nations*, Vol. II., Chicago: University of Chicago Press.

Smith, M. (2011), 'Get ready for a rising yuan and waning dollar', *The Australian* (Brisbane), 7 March, p. 14.

Smith, S.C. (1997), *Case Studies in Economic Development*, New York: Addison-Wesley.

Solomon, D. and A. Batson (2010), 'US press China on protection', *The Australian*, Brisbane, p. 22.

Soo, K.M. (1987), *The Making of Korean Society: The Role of the State in the Republic of Korea, 1948–1979*, Providence, RI: PhD Dissertation, Department of Sociology, Brown University.

Spegele, B. (2011), 'Riots erupt over land in China', *The Wall Street Journal*, 24–25 September, p. A-9.

Srinivasan, T.N. (1984), 'Comment [on Bauer]', in G. Meier and D. Seers (eds), *Pioneers in Development*, Oxford: Oxford University Press.

Srinivasan, T.N. (1985), 'Neoclassical political economy, the state and economic development', *Asian Development Review*, 3, 38–58.

Srinivasan, T.N. (2000), *Eight Lectures on India's Economic Reforms*, New Delhi: Oxford University Press.

Stern, N. (1991), 'Public policy and economics of development', *European Economic Review*, 35, 250–257.

Steven, N. and S. Cheong (1973), 'The fable of the bees: An economic investigation', *Journal of Economics and Law*, 16, 11–30.

Stiglitz, J. (2002), 'Transparency in government', Washington, DC: World Bank Institute.

Stiglitz, J. and A. Weiss (1981), 'Credit rationing in markets with imperfect information', *American Economic Review*, 71, 393–410.

Sujaya, C.P. (2011), 'Women, disparities and development', in M. Mohanty (ed.), *India: Social Development Report 2010*, New Delhi: Oxford University Press.

Tan, A.C. (2001), 'Taiwan: Sustained state autonomy and a step back from liberalization', in S. Horowitz and U. Heo (eds), *The Political Economy of International Financial Crises: Interest Groups, Ideologies, and Institutions*, Lanham, MD: Rowman and Littlefield.

Tan, A.C. (2008), 'From state entrepreneurs to political entrepreneurs: Democratization and the politics of financial liberalization in Taiwan', in P. Paolino and J. Meernik (eds), *Democratization in Taiwan: Challenges in Transformation*, Burlington, VT: Ashgate.

Taub, R.P. (1969), *Bureaucrats Under Stress: Administrators and Administration in an Indian State*, Berkeley: University of California Press.

Tawney, R.H. (1932), *Land and Labour in China*, London: George Allen and Unwin.

Teja, R. (1992), 'Crisis, recovery and transformation in India', *Finance and Development*, 29 (4), 31–34.

The Australian (2010), 25 May, p. 10; 27 May, p. 10; 29 May, p. 34; 16 August, p. 10.

The Australian (2011), 11 March, pp. 8–9; 21 June, p. 23.

The Statesman Weekly (Calcutta) (2007), 10 March.

The Statesman Weekly (Calcutta) (2011), 15 January, p. 5; 22 January, p. 2; 26 May, p. 3.

The Telegraph (Calcutta) (2010), 10 December, p. 21.

Thorbecke, E. (1979), 'Agricultural development', in W. Galenson (ed.), *Economic Growth and Structural Change in Taiwan: The Postwar Experience of the Republic of China*, Ithaca: Cornell University Press.

Tien, H.M. (1989), *The Great Transition: Political and Social Change in the Republic of China*, Stanford, CA: Hoover Institution Press.

Tien, H.M. (ed.) (1996), *Taiwan's Electoral Politics and Democratic Transition: Riding the Third Wave*, Armonk, NY: M.E. Sharpe.

Transparency International (2011), *Research Surveys*, Berlin: Transparency International, www.transparency.org/policy_research/surveys_indices/CPI/2010

Tyson, L.D. (1992), *Who's Bashing Whom? Trade Conflict in High Technology Industries*, Washington, DC: Institute for International Economics.

UN (2009), *Asia-Pacific Trade and Investment Report 2009: Trade Led Recovery and Beyond*, Bangkok: UN Economic and Social Commission for Asia and the Pacific (ESCAP).

United Nations Development Program (UNDP) (2006), *Human Development Report, 2006*, New York: UNDP.

UNDP (2008), *Human Development Report, 2007–2008*, New York: UNDP.

UNDP (2009), *Human Development Report, 2009*, New York: UNDP.

UNDP (2010), *Human Development Report, 2010*, New York: UNDP.

van den Berg, H. (2001), *Economic Growth and Development*, New York: McGraw-Hill-Irwin.

Varshney, A. (1999), 'India's economic reforms in comparative perspective', in J.A. Sachs, A. Varshney and N. Bajpai (eds), *India in the Era of Economic Reforms*, New Delhi: Oxford University Press.

Vayrynen, R. (2000), 'Weak states and humanitarian emergencies', in E.W. Nafziger, F. Stewart and R. Vayrynen (eds), *War, Hunger and Displacement: The Origins of Humanitarian Emergencies*, Vol. 1, Oxford: Oxford University Press.

Venkateswara, R.V. (2010), 'Black, bold and beautiful', *Hindu Business Line* (Chennai), 13 August.

Wachman, A. (1994), *Taiwan: National Identity and Democratization*, Armonk, NY: M.E. Sharpe.

Wade, R. (1990), *Governing the Market: Economic Theory and the Role of Government in East Asian Industrialization*, Princeton: Princeton University Press.

Weber, M. (1930), *The Protestant Ethic and the Spirit of Capitalism*, New York: Charles Scribner's Sons.

Weber, M. (1968), *Economy and Society*, New York: Bedminster Press.

Wei, L. (2011), 'Chinese rein in shadow lending', *The Australian* (Brisbane), p. 25.

Wessel, D. (2011), 'Fissures in China's great wall of money', *The Australian* (Brisbane), 17 June, p. 26.

Williamson, J.G. (2011), *Trade and Poverty: When the Third World Fell Behind*, Boston: MIT Press.

Wilson, B.A. and G.N. Kein (2006), 'India and the Global Economy', *Business Economics*, 41 (1), 28–36.

Winters, L.A. (2004), 'Trade liberalization and economic performance: An overview', *Economic Journal*, 14, F4-21.

Womack, J.P., D.T. Jones and D. Roos (1990), *The Machine that Changed the World: The Story of Lean Production*, New York: Macmillan.

Wong, J. (2010), 'From imitator to innovator: The political economy of industrial upgrading in the 21st century', in W.C. Lee (ed.), *Taiwan's Politics in the 21st Century: Changes and Challenges*, London: World Scientific Press.

Woo, J.E. (1991), *Race to the Swift: State and Finance in Korean Industrialization*, New York: Columbia University Press.

Woo, M.Y.K. (1994), 'Chinese women workers: The delicate balance between protection and equality', in G. Gilmartin, C.G. Harshatter, L. Rofel and T. White (eds), *Engendering China*, Cambridge: Cambridge University Press.

World Bank (1980), *World Development Report*, Washington, DC: World Bank.

World Bank (1990), *World Development Report*, New York: Oxford University Press.

World Bank (1993), *The East Asian Miracle: Economic Growth and Public Policy*, Washington, DC: World Bank.

World Bank (1995), *World Development Report*: New York: Oxford University Press.

World Bank (1997), *World Development Report*, New York: Oxford University Press.

World Bank (2000), *World Development Report*, New York: Oxford University Press.

World Bank (2001), *World Development Report*, New York: Oxford University Press.

World Bank (2002), *World Development Report*, New York: Oxford University Press.

World Bank (2003), *World Development Report*, New York: Oxford University Press.

World Bank (2005), *World Development Report*, New York: Oxford University Press.

World Bank (2006), *World Development Report*, New York: Oxford University Press.

World Bank (2007), *World Development Report*, New York: Oxford University Press.

World Bank (2008), *World Development Indicators*, Washington, DC: World Bank.

World Bank (2009a), *Doing Business 2009*, London: Palgrave-MacMillan.

World Bank (2009b), *World Development Indicators*, Washington, DC: World Bank.

World Bank (2010), *World Development Indicators, on-line*, Washington, DC: World Bank, www.data.worldbank.org.

World Bank (2011), *World Development Indicators*, Washington, DC: World Bank.

Wu, H.L. (1988), 'Future for small and medium enterprises?', *Free China Review*, 38 (11), 6–10.

Wu, R.I. and C.C. Huang (2003), 'Entrepreneurship in Taiwan: Turning point to restart', Tokyo: Paper presented at the US-Japan Dialogue on Entrepreneurship in Asia.

Wu, Y.S. (1995), 'Economic reform, cross-straits relations, and the politics of issue linkage', in T.J. Cheng, C. Huang and S.S.G. Wu (eds), *Inherited Rivalry: Conflict Across the Taiwan Straits*, Boulder, CO: Lynne Rienner.

Zakaria, F. (1977), 'The Rise of Illiberal Democracy', *Foreign Affairs*, 76 (6), 22–43.

Zysman, J. (1983), *Governments, Markets, and Growth: Financial Systems and the Politics of Industrial Change*, Ithaca: Cornell University Press.

Index

Japan (*contd*)
  public expenditures on information
    technology, R&D and education
    105
  quality-control techniques 225
  R&D activities, factors influencing
    expenditures on *103*
  relative dependence on developed
    countries for trade *88*
  religious and cultural order 44–5
  share of
    industry and other sectors in GDP
      128
    intra-regional trade in total trade *87*
  simple mean tariff in *93*
  terms of trade indices *92*
  trade facilitation environment in *125*
  zaibatsu (financial houses) in 44
joint ventures 80, 207, 212–13, 218–19,
  232, 255

Karachi Session (1931) 55
keiretsu system, Japan 225, 229, 231, 263
Keynes, J. M. 8, 11–12, 24, 42
Keynesian State, re-emergence of 24–5
knowledge process outsourcing (KPO)
  111
Korean War (1950–53) 47, 54, 68, 196,
  200
Kuznets curve hypothesis, for income
  distribution 151

labour force participation, in Asian
    countries 159–61
  in China 162
  in East Asia 162–3
  features of 162–3
  female participation rates 159
  in India 162
  labour employment and population
    160
labour markets, in India 123–4
labour, skilled 235
laissez-faire economic policies 19, 249,
  262, 264–5, 267, 273
Lam, Danny 117
land reform and income distribution
    policies 42–3
  in China 68–9
  in India 69–71

in Japan 67–8
in Korea 67–8
in Taiwan 67–8
land reform programmes 68–9, 206, 208
land tenancy system, India 69
Land-to-the-Tiller Act (1953), Taiwan
  208
learning-based economies 7
'learning-from-experience' process 121
legitimacy of government
  certificate of 197
  in China and India 197–9
  in East Asia 199–201
lending rates per annum, in China, India
    and East Asia *102*
less developed countries (LDCs) 17
Leviathan (1968) 2
Levi, Margaret 20
Lewis's labour surplus model (1954) 199
Locke, John 2
Locke's Treatise (1690) 197
long-run marginal cost (LMC) 4

macro-economic imbalances 4, 8
Mahalanobis, P. C. 198
Malaysia
  average annual growth rate in income
    per capita *247*
  bumiputera (Malay) enterprises 233–4
  central government's budgetary
    transactions and interest rates
    144
  civil service in 59
  commercial service trade in *112*
  demography and reproductive health,
    trends in *164*
  financial markets, liberalization of 145
  Industrial Master Plan (IMP) of 1986–
    1995 234
  intra-regional trade growth *89*
  Investment Incentives Act (1968) 232
  lending rates per annum in *102*
  monetary policy in 145
  New Economic Policy (NEP) 153,
    201
  public expenditures on information
    technology, R&D and education
    105
  R&D activities, factors influencing
    expenditures on *103*